XVII

THE COTTON MANUFACTURING INDUSTRY OF THE UNITED STATES

LIBRARY OF
EARLY AMERICAN BUSINESS AND INDUSTRY

THE COTTON
MANUFACTURING INDUSTRY
OF THE UNITED STATES

BY

MELVIN THOMAS COPELAND, Ph.D.

ASSISTANT PROFESSOR OF MARKETING IN HARVARD UNIVERSITY

AWARDED THE DAVID A. WELLS PRIZE FOR
THE YEAR 1911–12, AND PUBLISHED FROM
THE INCOME OF THE DAVID A. WELLS FUND

SECOND IMPRESSION

REPRINTS OF ECONOMIC CLASSICS

AUGUSTUS M. KELLEY · PUBLISHERS
NEW YORK · 1966

First Published 1917

Library of Congress Catalogue Card Number

66-23981

PRINTED IN THE UNITED STATES OF AMERICA
by SENTRY PRESS, NEW YORK, N. Y. 10019

TO

MY FATHER AND MOTHER

PREFACE

COTTON manufacturing constitutes at the present time one of the most important industries in the United States, and in volume of output this country ranks second among the nations of the world. The task here undertaken is to set forth the relative position of the American cotton manufacturing industry by means of an international comparison of geographical factors, technical methods, labor conditions, and industrial and commercial organization. To provide a basis for comparisons and conclusions, the history of the industry in America is traced and its present organization analyzed. In the historical section attention is directed particularly to the period since 1860, but in the first chapter the history of the industry prior to the outbreak of the American Civil War is sketched.

The work has necessarily been restricted at several points. The early history is not given more space because, for the purposes of this study, it has seemed advisable to concentrate upon the later period. A history of wages in American cotton mills has not been undertaken because of the vast amount of time that would be required to secure the data on which to base any reliable conclusions. In the second part very little is said concerning the European lace industry, because of its complicated character and the small size of our own lace manufacture. Finally, but slight reference has been made to the social conditions under which the operatives live, and no attempt has been made to compare cost of living in the different countries. The object has been to secure unity, and by no means to imply that the question of laborers' welfare or standard of living is less worthy of investigation.

The data for the analysis of the present situation in America and for the comparison of European and American conditions have been obtained largely by personal investigation and inquiry.

Manufacturers, merchants, and other persons connected with the industry have been consulted, in New England, New York, Philadelphia, and the southern mill towns; in various towns in Lancashire; in Bremen, Berlin, Saxony, The Rhine Province, Bavaria, Württemberg, and Alsace; in Switzerland; and in Paris, the "Nord," the Vosges, and Normandy. Mills have been visited in all these districts. More than two hundred persons have been interviewed personally and information has been obtained from others by correspondence. Statements of fact in the text not otherwise vouched for are usually based on such information. In inquiries of this sort the personal equation must be allowed for, but by checking up the statements of one man with those of others, I feel confident that, although a few errors and misstatements have doubtless crept into the book, they have been reduced to the minimum.

Inasmuch as this monograph was submitted for the Wells Prize competition in November, 1911, and delivered to the publishers in March, 1912, the Tariff Board's *Report on Cotton Manufactures* appeared too late to permit me to utilize its data in this work. My own conclusions concerning comparative costs, however, are substantially the same as those of the Tariff Board.

I began the study of the cotton manufacturing industry while holding the Charles Carroll Everett Fellowship of Bowdoin College, and continued my researches while an Austin Teaching Fellow at Harvard University. Later, to enable me to conduct the investigation of the industry in the European countries, I was granted a Frederick Sheldon Fellowship from the latter institution. Without this aid the task would not have been completed.

To the numerous business and professional men who have assisted in the carrying on of the study grateful acknowledgment is due, particularly to Major H. L. Higginson, Mr. E. A. Whitman, Mr. Sidney Coolidge, Mr. S. S. Dale, and General S. M. Weld of Boston, Mr. H. L. Knoop and Mr. J. R. Barlow of Manchester, England, Mr. C. A. Albrecht of Bremen, and

Dr. Eduard Simon and Professor Schmoller of Berlin. I am deeply indebted to Professor F. W. Taussig for friendly advice and helpful criticism and to Professor Edwin F. Gay for constant encouragement, valuable suggestions, and a kindly oversight over the preparation of the manuscript.

M. T. COPELAND.

CONTENTS

PART I

HISTORY AND PRESENT ORGANIZATION

PART II

THE RELATIVE POSITION OF THE UNITED STATES

PART I

HISTORY AND PRESENT ORGANIZATION

THE COTTON MANUFACTURING INDUSTRY OF THE UNITED STATES

HISTORY AND PRESENT ORGANIZATION

CHAPTER I

GROWTH BEFORE 1860

RAW cotton was imported into New England from the West Indies before the middle of the seventeenth century,[1] and small importations continued during the following hundred and fifty years.[2] This material was spun into yarn and also used for other purposes.[3] But it was not till the last decade of the eighteenth century that the manufacture of cotton was begun on a considerable scale in the United States.

The progress of the industry prior to 1790 had been handicapped by the dearth of labor and capital. It may have been checked somewhat by the colonial policy of the British government. The jealousy with which England guarded the new inventions of cotton manufacturing machinery retarded their introduction into America. Finally the Revolutionary War and the subsequent period of industrial instability also hindered the expansion of the industry. But these last three factors were obstacles of a secondary order in comparison with the fundamental economic conditions in regard to labor and capital.

After several ventures at different places in New England, the first successful cotton mill was started in Rhode Island in 1790. The owners of the mill secured the services of Samuel Slater, a young Englishman who had worked in a cotton mill

---

[1] W. B. Weeden, *Economic and Social History of New England*, vol. i, pp. 163, 170.

[2] *Ibid.*, p. 681.

[3] A. M. Earle, *Home Life in Colonial Days*, p. 206.

in his native land. Seeking a broader opportunity, he came to this country in response to an advertisement of a society for the promotion of industrial growth. He was not able to bring with him any models or plans, owing to the severe restrictions imposed by the British government. Yet he constructed from memory the water-frame and other machines in use in Great Britain. Thus the elementary technical knowledge was supplied and one of the obstacles to the growth of the industry removed.

During the next fifteen years the progress was slow. Several mills were established, but the conditions were not favorable to rapid development. In the first place the competition of the experienced British manufacturer was encountered. Furthermore the inhabitants of the sparsely populated country were engaged in other occupations, chiefly agriculture and foreign trade. Consequently the supply of labor was inadequate. Moreover the capital was invested in shipping and foreign commerce. Another handicap was the difficulty of obtaining the raw material, since it was not till 1793 that the invention of the cotton gin made possible the utilization of the upland cotton of the South.

The period of the second contest with England, however, witnessed a rapid expansion of the cotton manufacturing industry in America. With the Embargo of 1807, the Non-Intercourse Act, and the War of 1812, the supply of cotton goods from Great Britain was almost entirely cut off and the Americans were thrown upon their own resources. The high prices of cotton cloth attracted investors to this form of industrial enterprise, and at the same time the restrictions on foreign trade encouraged the withdrawal of capital from the sea.

Several New England men who had accumulated wealth in foreign commerce now became interested in cotton mills in their own country. Mr. Nathan Appleton, for example, who played a prominent part in the financing of a number of the new mills, had until 1807 been engaged in the import trade.[1] Mr. P. T. Jackson, associated with Mr. Appleton and others in the pro-

[1] *Professional and Industrial History of Suffolk County*, vol. iii, p. 504.

motion of cotton mills, had previously been interested in the
India trade.[1] Mr. Francis C. Lowell was an importing merchant
till 1810, when the international dispute so cut into his business
that he determined to become a cotton manufacturer, crowning
his career in that field by the invention of a power loom.

The statistics for this early period are not very reliable, and
the estimates of various persons differ. Yet they all agree in
showing that the number of spindles increased rapidly after 1807.
The period following that year was the time when cotton spinning was firmly established as a factory industry in the United
States, although it had been founded seventeen years earlier.
The following figures were given by Mr. Woodbury in a report
to Congress.[2]

NUMBER OF SPINDLES IN THE UNITED STATES

1805	4,500	
1807	8,000	
1809	31,000	
1810	87,000	
1815	130,000	
1820	220,000	
1825	800,000	

Although the number of spindles continued to increase after
the close of the war in 1814, the young industry was beset with
difficulties. The American manufacturers were no longer protected from their foreign competitors by the prohibitions of
war, and the British merchants began to ship large quantities
of cotton goods to America. The influx of this pent-up stream
threatened destruction by pushing the exorbitant prices down
to a low level.

From this ruinous competition the American manufacturers
sought relief in two ways. For a time the tariff of 1816 aided
them. Of more importance, however, in warding off the immi-
nent calamity, was their ingenuity in improving their machinery.
All the early mills had been equipped according to the English
plans introduced by Slater, but during the war the manufacturers
began to experiment for themselves. The most important
invention of that period was the power loom in 1814 by Lowell,

[1] *Professional and Industrial History of Suffolk County*, vol. iii, p. 506.
[2] 24th Congress, 1st session, *Executive Document*, No. 146, p. 51.

who constructed the machine independently of any English plans or models. A year later looms of the English type were introduced,[1] and within a few years practically all of the cotton cloth manufactured in the country was woven on power looms, although in Pennsylvania yarn was sold for household use till 1840.[2]

Another factor in the development of the industry was the increasing production of raw cotton in the southern states and the consequent decline in the price of the raw material. While this benefited the foreign manufacturers as well as those in America, it nevertheless stimulated a greater demand for cotton cloth and thus gave all a better chance. This cheaper material partially supplanted wool. Finally, the population of the country was becoming larger and wealthier; hence a larger market was afforded.

The industry progressed steadily from 1830 to 1860, as is indicated by the following table. The statistics for 1831 were collected by a committee appointed at the convention of " The Friends of Domestic Industry "[3] held in that year, and included only the mills in New England and the Middle States. The other figures are mainly from the census reports, and are admittedly inaccurate, though not without significance.

COTTON MANUFACTURES, 1831–1860

	Establishments	Cotton Used (pounds)	Spindles	Value of Product
1831	795	77,800,000	1,200,000	$32,000,000
1840	1,240	113,100,000	2,300,000	46,400,000
1850	1,094	276,100,000	3,600,000	61,700,000
1860	1,091	422,700,000	5,200,000	115,700,000

The greater efficiency of the machinery at the later dates is indicated by the increase in the consumption of raw cotton at a rate more rapid than that of the number of spindles. The

[1] J. L. Bishop, History of American Manufactures, vol. ii, p. 207.
[2] Eighty Years' Progress, vol. ii, p. 284.
[3] A convention of American manufacturers was held in New York, October 26, 1831, with a view to promoting their interests by tariff legislation. The sentiment was strongly protectionist, and its Report, from which these facts were ascertained, was issued in the name of " The Friends of Domestic Industry."

quantity of raw cotton also increased relatively faster than the value of the product, thus reflecting the fall in the price of cloth as a result of cheaper cotton and more economical methods of manufacture. The number of establishments, on the other hand, did not increase after 1840; the mills were becoming larger, and the little ones passing out of existence.

While the industry was progressing in the United States, it did not reach the proportions of the British cotton manufacturing industry. The total number of spindles in Great Britain was estimated at about 21 millions in 1850,[1] and at 30 millions in 1861.[2] The quantity of raw cotton used in England was correspondingly greater than in America. The same factors which had stimulated the introduction of cotton manufacturing in Great Britain in the last half of the eighteenth century, — climate, water-power, coal, inventive genius, and business ability, as well as freedom from social and political restraints, — these forces continued to promote the growth of the industry in later years.

On the continent the development of the industry was retarded by unsettled political conditions and frequent wars, by numerous local customs barriers, and by contentment on the part of entrepreneurs and workmen with antiquated methods. In France there were in 1867 about 6 million spindles,[3] not including doubling spindles; in Germany the number of spindles in 1840 was 658,358,[4] and in 1860 about 2 millions.[5] In both of these countries the industry was still carried on in small plants, and even in the homes.

The first cotton mills in America were in New England and there they increased most rapidly during this period. Some were built in the Middle States, and a few elsewhere, but the conditions were not as favorable in other parts of the country as in New England, where there was abundant water-power and more available capital. The supply of labor to be had was also

[1] L. Levi, *History of British Commerce*, p. 410.
[2] *Ibid.*, p. 410.
[3] H. Lecomte, *Le Coton*, p. 334.
[4] W. Lochmüller, *Die Baumwollindustrie in Deutschland*, p. 21.
[5] A. Oppel, *Die Baumwolle*, p. 656.

relatively greater in that region of rock-ribbed hills and unfertile soil, where the " Yankee " sentiment encouraged thrift and industry on the part of all, including women and children.

The geographical distribution of the industry in 1860 is shown by the Census statistics of that year.

COTTON MANUFACTURES, 1860

Establishments		Cotton Used (pounds)	Spindles	Value of Product
New England .	570	283,700,000	3,800,000	$79,400,000
Middle States	340	87,100,000	1,000,000	26,500,000
South	159	43,900,000	300,000	8,100,000
West	22	7,900,000	40,000	1,600,000

New England with fifty-two per cent of the establishments in 1860 had seventy-five per cent of the spindles, whereas the Middle States with thirty-one per cent of the establishments had only twenty per cent of the spindles. The same ratios held for the number of looms. New England not only had more mills than all the other states combined, but the mills in this section were larger than those elsewhere. The average number of spindles per establishment was 6,700 in New England as compared with 2,900 in the Middle States, and a still smaller number in the other parts of the country. The average New England mill, therefore, was at least twice as large as the average sized mill in the other states.

Within the New England states the industry was centralized in Massachusetts and Rhode Island. These two states had forty-eight per cent of all the spindles in the country in 1860, and Massachusetts alone had thirty per cent. In these states several large centres had grown up, — Providence, Fall River, and Lowell. Manchester in New Hampshire was another. In the Middle States, Philadelphia was the largest cotton manu-facturing city.

Thus, prior to the Civil War the cotton manufacturing in-dustry not only expanded, but showed well-defined tendencies toward concentration and localization. Its internal structure, moreover, was also undergoing change.

The American cotton manufacturers early began to develop

machines especially suited to the prevailing industrial conditions. They were urged on by the dearth of labor to supplant human muscle and eyesight as far as possible with mechanical power and automatic appliances. They found it economical to seek the greatest possible output per operative. On this depended the prosperity of the growing industry. The machinery in all departments was steadily improved so as to accomplish more and better work. Mention has already been made of the invention and adoption of the power loom, one of the first accomplishments. Another invention, of especial significance to the student of the later history of the industry, was that of the ring spindle, about 1830, by Mr. Jenks, a pupil of Slater.[1] It was a modification of the throstle, which had been developed from the water-frame of Arkwright. The modification consisted in the replacing of the double armed flyer of the throstle by a wire, or " traveller," running on a fixed steel ring. At first it was applied only to twisting, but soon came to be used for spinning and even before the Civil War competed on about equal terms with the mule which had been introduced from England.

The use of improved machinery run at high speed and equipped with various automatic stop motions gave a comparatively large output per machine and per unit of labor. One of the most trustworthy accounts of the state of the industry prior to 1860 is that written in 1840 by James Montgomery, who had been engaged in cotton manufacturing in Great Britain before coming to America. He commented on the greater use of stop-motion devices in the American mills,[2] and remarked that " the factories at Lowell produced a greater quantity of yarn and cloth from each spindle and loom (in a given time) than was produced in any other factories, without exception, in the world." [3]

England, in the meantime, was advancing in technical development. The mule, for example, was being increased in length and improved in the working parts. At first the mule contained about 144 spindles, but by 1835 the average length was over 300

---

[1] *Eighty Years' Progress*, vol. ii, p. 286.
[2] J. Montgomery, *Cotton Manufacture*, p. 56.
[3] *Ibid.*, p. 162.

spindles, and by 1860 the latter number had been doubled.[1] The self-acting mule was invented about 1825 and resulted in a reduction of the amount of labor necessary for spinning cotton yarn. The self-actor, however, although improved from time to time, was used only for spinning coarse counts till after 1860.

In weaving, to take another department, the use of the power loom by English manufacturers began before it did in the United States. But the hand loom continued to be employed in Great Britain for weaving cotton cloth after it had been entirely dispensed with in this country. The difficulties with which the transition was made in England are recorded in the Parliamentary reports on the hand-loom weavers and their sufferings. The invention of the Blackburn loom in 1828 sounded the knell of the hand loom, but it was not entirely eliminated till after 1850.

The American manufacturers not only were the first to adopt the power loom exclusively but they secured a relatively greater output per laborer by inducing the weavers to tend more looms. In 1860 the average number of looms per weaver was four in the United States, and two in Great Britain; [2] the higher earnings in the former country being accompanied by greater productivity.

On the Continent new machines and new methods did not find a ready acceptance. Only a fourth of the spindles in operation in France in 1860 were self-acting mules.[3] In the same country the power loom had hardly come into use at that date[4] and did not oust the hand loom till some years later.[5] Likewise in Germany hand mules and hand looms were in general use in 1860.[6] Under such circumstances the French and Germans were not very dangerous competitors, at least on coarse plain goods which could be produced in large quantities.

Cotton manufacturing developed earlier in Great Britain than in the United States and in 1860 there were nearly six times

[1] T. Ellison, *Cotton Trade of Great Britain*, pp. 65–66.
[2] S. Batchelder, *Early Progress of the Cotton Manufacture*, p. 90.
[3] L. Amé, *Les Tarifs de Douanes*, vol. i, p. 312.
[4] *Ibid.*, pp. 312, 395.
[5] *Enquête sur l'Etat de l' Industrie Textile*, vol. ii, p. 12; vol. iv, p. 100.
[6] A. Oppel, *Die Baumwolle*, p. 656.

as many spindles and slightly over three times as many power looms in operation in the former country. Nevertheless the American industry was in a healthy condition and was ahead of the Continental European. The American manufacturers had met the requirements of the conditions incident to a young country with a large area of fertile agricultural land and a consequently high scale of wages. By skillful adjustment of labor and machinery they had established themselves, in the manufacture of the coarser fabrics, on a firm competitive basis. The situation in 1860 was summed up by Mr. Samuel Batchelder, a competent critic, who said: " The advantage of manufacturing in England on account of wages is much less than we have generally supposed. . . . Fine articles, or such as require experience and skill, can undoubtedly be produced cheaper there than here; but it is questionable whether heavy goods such as drilling and sheeting, which make up a very large proportion of the consumption of this country, can be produced cheaper than in the United States." [1]

The substitution of machinery for labor in American cotton mills is roughly indicated by the smaller relative increase in the number of persons employed as compared with the increase in the number of spindles. The latter was over four times as great in 1860 as in 1831, while the former was only twice as large. The following table gives the details of the changes in number of employees. The statistics for 1831 are those collected by " The Friends of Domestic Industry," the others are Census figures.

EMPLOYEES IN COTTON MILLS

	Total	Male	Female	Children
1831	62,177	18,359	33,506	4,691
1840	72,119	......	......	.....
1850	92,286	33,150	59,136	.....
1860	122,028	46,859	75,169	.....

The children were classed in the Census returns only according to sex. Hence it is not possible to ascertain the exact composition of the labor force. As to the prevalence of child labor,

[1] S. Batchelder, *Early Progress of the Cotton Manufacture*, p. 91.

Miss Abbott has concluded that " children formed a very large proportion of the total number of employees." [1]   Since there is no reason to suppose that the girls greatly outnumbered the boys, we may conclude that the number of women employed in cotton mills was considerably in excess of the number of men.

The labor during the first five decades of the nineteenth century was supplied mainly by the native population, that is by descendants of the English settlers.   The sons and daughters of the farmers entered the mills to get a start in life.   But they looked upon it merely as a temporary employment, frugally saving their earnings to help pay for a farm, to enter business, or, in the case of the young women, to assist in furnishing a home. No stigma was attached to work of this sort; on the contrary it was looked upon with favor by a majority of the people.

Inasmuch as the operatives were an independent class, and since they were frequently changing, the managers felt compelled to make the environment as attractive as possible.[2]   It is true that the hours were long, from sunrise to sunset, but there was an absence of abusive treatment and unhealthy conditions. This served especially to protect the children.   Although child labor was practically unregulated before 1860, there seems to have been no brutality,[3] and the children in the American mills were not subjected to those abuses which make the early history of the English cotton factory so dark.[4]   The superior conditions in the American mills were due in part to the fact that there were no pauper apprentices and that the children were usually under the oversight of parents or relatives.   Then, too, perhaps a warning had been taken from the reports of conditions in England.   But the absence of a permanent operative class and the high moral standards of the factory employees had most to do with eliminating abuse.

[1] Edith Abbott, "Study of the Early History of Child Labor in America," *American Journal of Sociology*, vol. xiv, p. 25.

[2] H. H. Robinson, *Loom and Spindle*, p. 71.

[3] Edith Abbott, *op. cit.*, p. 34.

[4] Mr. Persons has concluded that the conditions of child labor in New England mills early in the nineteenth century were " immeasurably above the English level."   C. E. Persons, M. Parton, and M. Moses, *Labor Laws and their Enforcement*, p. 5.

The frequently changing supply of labor exerted an influence in other directions. One of these was technique. It was necessary to adopt machinery which did not require a great amount of skill, since, as Mr. Batchelder phrased it " the greater part of those at work in the mills were only a succession of learners, who left the business as soon as they began to acquire some skill and experience." [1] The automatic devices, the ring spindle, and other inventions not only diminished the quantity of labor required, but made its quality less important. The introduction of immigrant labor took place with less friction than would have been possible had there been a fixed operative class, and the technical improvements were likewise favorable to the utilization of the unskilled foreigner, since it made little difference to the manager whether he employed unskilled Americans or unskilled Irishmen. The exact date when the employment of immigrants in our cotton mills began is uncertain, but it was before 1836, since in that year Miss Martineau wrote: " A large proportion of the labor in the Lowell factories is supplied by women. Much of the rest is furnished by immigrants. I saw English, Irish, and Scotch operatives." [2] The male immigrants were at first employed only for the rough work around the mill, but they gradually assumed positions as machine tenders. Foreign women appeared in the mills somewhat later. Mr. Miles collected statistics for the nationality of the females employed in the Lowell mills in 1847,[3] which show that at that date the greater part of the women were of New England parentage, although a few were from Ireland.

The stream of immigrants, however, which became large in volume after 1845, turned at once toward the cotton mills as the most available point whence to begin the industrial ascent in the new country. The Irish were the first to come in large numbers and they began to take the places of the native employees as the latter dropped out. The transition was made quietly, for the most part, and attracted little comment from contemporary writers.

[1] S. Batchelder, *Early Progress of the Cotton Manufacture*, p. 89.

[2] H. Martineau, *Society in America*, vol. ii, p. 55.

[3] H. A. Miles, *Lowell as it was and as it is*, p. 185.

Neither the machinery nor the labor employed in the United States at this period were favorable to the manufacture of fine or fancy cloths. The greatest demand, moreover, was for plain coarse and medium fabrics, such as could be most economically manufactured in the country. Expensive goods, in the production of which more labor and more skill were required, were obtained from Europe.

The import trade in cotton goods, therefore, was made up largely of the more expensive fabrics and fancy articles. The average annual value of the imports increased from about nine million dollars in the decade 1821–1830 to twenty-six and a half million dollars in the decade 1851–1860, or nearly threefold. The increase in volume of imports was especially great during the last decade of this period, when the average annual value nearly doubled.[1]

IMPORTS OF COTTON MANUFACTURES, 1821–1860[2]
(*Average annual value*)

	Total	Plain Cloth	Colored Cloth	Knit Goods	All Other
1821–1830	$9,200,000	$2,900,000	$5,300,000	$ 500,000	$ 500,000
1831–1840	11,600,000	2,100,000	7,500,000	1,000,000	1,000,000
1841–1850	13,700,000	1,700,000	8,800,000	1,200,000	2,100,000
1851–1860	26,600,000	no data	no data	2,800,000	6,000,000

Owing to an incomplete classification during three years of the last decade, it is not possible to separate the average value of plain cloth from the average value of colored cloth. But the figures for 1860, the year of the largest importation up to that time, reflect what had been taking place during the decade. In 1860 the total value of the cotton manufactures imported was $38,200,000. The value of the plain cloth imported was $1,200,000; of colored cloth, $25,900,000; and of all other cotton goods, $11,100,000; thus those goods classed as " printed, painted, or colored " heavily predominated.

From 1850 to 1860 was the period of greatest prosperity for the cotton industry in this country up to that time, although the duties were low and the importation of cotton goods nearly

[1] All imports increased rapidly during these years.
[2] *U. S. Commerce and Navigation Reports.*

doubled. This points to the conclusion that the general industrial conditions and the prosperity of the country had more to do with the progress of the industry than any stimulating tariff. After the industry was well established it mattered little to the cotton manufacturers whether the tariff was high or low. The act of 1816 probably did serve to assist the infant industry, and later acts may have somewhat encouraged the production of goods of a higher grade.[1] But the latter was also fostered by the technical improvements, the knowledge and experience acquired by the manufacturers, and the increasing demand which resulted from the accumulation of wealth in the country. By 1860, moreover, the protective sentiment was on the wane among American cotton manufacturers, since, as Mr. Webber stated, " the business of cotton manufacture was by that time (1850) so firmly established as to be little affected by changes in legislation in regard to duties on the coarser fabrics required for domestic consumption, to which American machinery had been adapted." [2]

The production of cotton cloth in the United States prior to 1860 was largely for the home market. The export trade had not become extensive.

EXPORTS OF COTTON MANUFACTURES

(Average annual value)

	Total	Plain Cloth	Colored Cloth	All Other
1826–1830	$1,200,000	$920,000	$80,000	$170,000
1831–1840	2,520,000	2,060,000	310,000	150,000
1841–1850	3,960,000	3,180,000	420,000	360,000
1851–1860	7,310,000	3,740,000	1,830,000	1,740,000

Throughout the thirty-five years plain cloth constituted the bulk of the exports, and was disposed of chiefly in Asia. The evident expansion of the export trade from 1850 to 1860 emphasized the prosperity of the industry in spite of low tariff duties and the large importation of cotton goods.

[1] A detailed discussion of the various tariff acts will be found in Taussig, *Tariff History of the United States.*

[2] S. Webber, *History of Cotton Manufacture in the United States*, p. 57.

At just this time, when the rate of progress was great, the war broke out. For five years the industry was disrupted not only by the disarrangement of capital, labor, and markets, but by the impossibility of securing raw material. Thus there is practically a void in the history of the industry during the period of conflict. However, resuscitation was rapid after 1865 and cotton manufacturing progressed along the previous lines of development. The war caused but a slight break in the tendency toward larger scale of production and more efficient organization. It made easier the substitution of immigrants for native laborers, yet did not originate that substitution. After 1865, just as before 1860, the relatively high wages in this country placed a premium upon labor-saving devices, which stimulated invention. Moreover the machinery had to be adapted to the utilization of untrained workers. The war brought in its train the era of high protection. As a result of the tariff or other causes the production of fine and fancy fabrics has been augmented, but the output still consists predominantly of coarse plain cloth for the domestic market. The break caused by the Civil War, therefore, did not divert the development of the American cotton manufacturing industry into new lines.

CHAPTER II

GROWTH SINCE 1860

THE forces which have influenced the growth of the American cotton manufacturing industry during the last fifty years can best be analyzed after the magnitude of that growth has been set forth. Hence we will first consider the general statistics which indicate the volume of expansion. The manufacture of yarn and cloth is the most important branch of the industry, yet the secondary industries of lace, small-wares, and knit-goods manufacturing demand attention. To avoid confusion this statistical chapter is divided into three sections.

Spinning and Weaving

The following table, compiled from Census reports, indicates the growth of the industry in the United States since 1860.

COTTON MANUFACTURES, 1860–1910[1]

	Establishments	Spindles (millions)	Cotton Used (million pounds)	Employees	Value of Product (million dollars)	Exports (million dollars)	Imports (million dollars)
1860....	1,091	5.2	422.7	122,028	115.7	10.9	38.2
1870....	956	7.1	398.3	135,369	177.5	3.8	23.4
1880....	756	10.7	750.3	174,659	192.1	10.0	29.9
1890....	905	14.2	1,118.0	218,876	268.0	10.0	29.9
1900....	973	19.0	1,814.0	297,929	332.8	24.0	41.3
1905....	1,077	23.2	1,873.1	310,458	442.5	49.7	48.9
1910....	1,208	27.4	2,332.2	371,120	616.5	33.4	66.5

These statistics are subject to the criticism which may be directed against all of our Census statistics. Although the methods have tended to become more accurate, they have varied from Census to Census. Some of the statistics given by the Census have been deemed too misleading and insignificant to be included. The amount of capital invested, for example, cannot be ascertained from the Census because of its duplications and ever-

---

[1] The data for 1910 are based on newspaper reports of statements issued by the Director of the Census.

varying definitions.[1]   The above figures for the cotton industry, however, are fairly trustworthy for a general comparison.

The number of establishments has not been affected by changes in the standard, since there were few very small plants in this industry.   They were nearly all well above the dividing line.[2] Similarly with value of product, there has been little duplication in the statistics for this industry since most of the mills manufacture the raw cotton into cloth and the product of one mill does not to a great extent become the raw material for other mills included above.   Prior to 1900 what have since been classed as "cotton small-wares," — braids, trimmings, etc., — were included with cotton goods proper, but they were of such relatively small amount that the error involved is immaterial.

[1] The Census itself condemns the statistics for capital, which by the Congressional Census Act it was required to collect.   " In the inquiry concerning capital, comparisons have no real statistical value prior to the Census of 1890.   The form of inquiry regarding capital, in all Censuses down to and including 1880, was so vague and general in its character that it cannot be assumed that any true proportion exists between the statistics on this subject, as elicited prior to 1890.   At the Census of 1880, the question read: ' Capital (real and personal invested in the business).'   At the Census of 1890, live capital, *i. e.*, cash on hand, bills receivable, unsettled ledger accounts, raw materials, stock in the process of manufacture, finished product on hand, and other sundries, was for the first time included as a separate distinct item of capital."   (12th *U. S. Census*, vol. vii, p. lxi.)   Again it states: "The attempt to measure capital absolutely and accurately has never yet been successful in a Census in the United States or elsewhere," and it quotes approvingly the statement made by General Walker in the 9th Census report: "The Census returns of capital invested in manufactures are entirely untrustworthy and delusive. . . . The results are and must remain wholly worthless." (*Ibid.*, p. xcvii.)   The difficulties in satisfactorily defining capital for Census purposes have been heretofore and will very likely remain insuperable.   The value of the land may be dependent upon its use as a factory site.   The value of rented property may be included, but if so on what basis is it to be capitalized ?   Is machinery to be entered at its original cost, or its present market value ?   Are outside investments, in other manufacturing or financial enterprises, to be included ? Are good will, patents, and trade marks to be capitalized ?   Finally, is credit to be taken into account, as was done in 1890 and 1900, when unpaid accounts due, for instance, were returned as capital?   It is because of the worthlessness of such estimates of capital that they have not been included above.

[2] The line of demarcation in determining what was to be called an "establishment," which the United States Census has followed, has been to exclude from the statistics all plants with an annual product of less than $500.   Moreover no hand trades were canvassed, in 1900 at least, which were not carried on in a shop.   12th *U. S. Census*, vol. vii, p. xxxix.

In pursuance of the tendency for the smaller plants to disappear, which became apparent after 1840, the statistics show a decline in the number of establishments between 1860 and 1880. This process of disappearance or absorption continued in New England after 1880, but was counter-balanced in the summary for the whole country by the increase in the number of establishments in the South.

The number of spindles in operation is the best standard for measuring the size of the cotton manufacturing industry. On this basis cotton manufacturing was four and one-half times as extensive in the United States in 1905 as in 1860. During the same interval the number of spindles in Great Britain increased from thirty [1] millions to forty-eight and one-half millions,[2] an increase greater absolutely, but smaller relatively. Whereas in 1860 Great Britain had six times as many spindles as the United States, in 1905 the number was only twice as great. On the Continent, Germany has shown the greatest expansion in cotton manufacturing, the number of spindles increasing from 2,235,000 in 1861 [3] to 8,435,000 in 1901.[4] Part of this increase was due to the acquisition of Alsace and its cotton mills at the termination of the Franco-Prussian war. In France, the number of spindles was 4,600,000 in 1876 [5] and 6,150,000 in 1903.[6] Italy in 1876 had 715,300 cotton spinning spindles and in 1903, 1,694-000.[7] In Russia there was an increase from 3,000,000 spindles 1878 [8] to 6,555,000 in 1904.[9] Although the expansion has been important in these Continental countries, England and the United States have remained far in the lead. In fact England has acquired more spindles since 1900 than are in operation in any one Continental country.

[1] T. Ellison, *Cotton Trade of Great Britain*, p. 65.
[2] *Commercial and Financial Chronicle.*
[3] H. Lecomte, *Le Coton*, p. 335.
[4] *Enquête sur l' Etat de l'Industrie Textile*, vol. v, p. 458.
[5] H. Lecomte, *op. cit.*, p. 335.
[6] *Enquête, op. cit.*, p. 458.
[7] *Annuario Statistico Italiano*, 1907.
[8] H. Lecomte, *op. cit.*, p. 335.
[9] *Enquête, op. cit.*, p. 458.

In addition to the statistics for the number of spindles, we also have those for looms, but the latter numbers are not as good indices of growth because of the variations in capacity according to the width of the loom and the complexity of design.

The number of looms in American mills was 126,000 in 1860, 451,000 in 1900, and 541,000 in 1905; in British mills 400,000 in 1860 and 680,000 in 1903. The increase was greater both absolutely and relatively in America. Now, while there are twice as many spindles in Great Britain as in the United States, there are only fifty per cent more looms. This is due, in the first place, to sale of yarn for auxiliary trades, such as lace making, and for export from Great Britain; in the second place, to the larger output of yarn per spindle in America; and, finally, to the greater productivity of the English looms, which are generally run at a higher speed than American looms.

The quantity of raw cotton used in American mills was almost four and one-half times as great in 1905 as in 1860. The quantity consumed per spindle was 81.3 lbs., in 1860, and 95.5 lbs. in 1900, but only 80.7 lbs. in 1905. The decline at the last date was caused by unsettled conditions and protracted idleness in some of the northern mill centres during the Census year. And in comparing the present consumption per spindle with that of 1860, it must not be forgotten that more fine yarn is now spun, whereby the average weight per spindle is relatively diminished. It is also to be added that the mills most affected by the disturbances of 1904–05 were those spinning coarser counts.

The average annual consumption of raw cotton in Great Britain in 1856–60 was 947.3 million pounds; in 1905, 1,654.9 million pounds. Whereas England used twice as much cotton as the United States in 1860, the total quantity is now actually less than that taken by the American mills. Twice as many spindles are employed in England for spinning a smaller quantity of cotton than is used in America. This is explained by the larger production of fine yarn in England and the more extensive use of the mule, on which the output per spindle is about two-thirds of that on the ring frame.

On the Continent of Europe the quantity of cotton consumed

averaged 627.4 million pounds per year in 1856–60; and 2,487 million pounds in 1901–05. Not till 1886 did the Continental spinners take a quantity of raw cotton equal to that used in Great Britain, but since that date their " takings " have shown a constantly increasing excess. The greater consumption per spindle on the Continent, as in the United States, arises from a relatively larger number of ring spindles and the predominance of coarse counts.

The number of persons employed in American cotton factories was only three times as great in 1905 as in 1860 although the number of spindles and quantity of raw cotton manufactured had risen in greater ratio. The product per operative was therefore greater at the later date; it averaged 9,412 square yards of cloth in 1860 and 15,134 square yards in 1905. This was brought about by the relative decline in the number of children employed and particularly by the improvements in machinery.

The character of the cotton goods produced in the United States has not been greatly changed since 1860. The cloth is generally of better quality and several mills are now manufacturing fine and fancy fabrics. Yet, to quote from the Census of 1905,[1] " Almost three-fourths of the yardage of all the woven goods reported falls under the classification of coarse or medium counts — print cloths, sheetings and shirtings, drills, ticks, denims and stripes, duck and bagging." Over one-half of the yarn spun in American mills is still coarser than number 20, and five-sixths of the remainder is from number 21 to number 40 in fineness.[2] The bulk of it, evidently, is of coarse and low medium counts.[3] The proportions for the Continental spinning industry are approximately the same, but England would show a higher percentage of fine yarn.

The domestic market has continued to be the chief goal of the American cotton manufacturers and they have supplied the

---

[1] *U. S. Census of Manufactures*, 1905, *Bulletin* No. 74, p. 45.

[2] *Ibid.*, p. 48.

[3] The number (or count) of cotton yarn is the number of hanks, of 840 yards each, required to make one pound in weight. The finer the yarn, therefore, the higher the number. Nos. 1 to 20 are called coarse, nos. 20 to 60 medium, and over no. 60 fine.

greater part of that demand. From a total production valued at more than $616,000,000 in 1910 only $33,400,000 was exported. The imports, including not merely cotton cloth but all fabrics of cotton, — hosiery, embroidery, laces, etc., amounted to $66,500,000. But the imports of cloth were only $9,000,000, or considerably less than two per cent of the value of the cloth manufactured within the country.

The American cotton manufacturing industry, therefore, has expanded during the last fifty years at a pace fast enough to keep up with a rapidly increasing population. This expansion of cloth manufacturing has been supplemented by a similar development of the production of other fabrics made of cotton.

Lace and Small-Wares

Although the statistics for the lace and lace-curtain manufacture are included by the Census under woven goods, the growth of this subsidiary branch of the industry is worthy of separate consideration. Like the other supplementary branches it has developed recently, and has its own peculiarities. The manufacture of lace curtains was begun in the United States in 1885,[1] and 642,061 square yards of lace and lace curtains were reported at the Census of 1890. The value of this product was $354,987. In 1900 the Census reported 9 establishments with 183 machines, employing 2,383 persons, and producing 37,825,000 square yards, valued at $3,585,000. By 1905 the number of lace machines had increased to 417; the number of establishments to 13; the number of employees to 4,502; and the product to 53,451,000 square yards, valued at $7,203,000. In spite of the increased production, however, more lace is imported than is made in this country. In 1900 the value of the imports of lace and embroideries was $19,200,000; in 1905, $25,900,000.

The miscellaneous products of cotton, not included in the preceding categories, are grouped by the Census as " small-wares." " At the Census of 1900 for the first time a separate classification was made of the establishments producing cotton small-wares, including cotton embroideries, edgings, boot and

---

[1] *Report of the Secretary of Internal Affairs*, Pennsylvania, 1899, p. 56.

shoe lacings, corset lacings, lamp and stove wicks, tapes, webbings, and trimmings." [1] At that date there were 82 establishments of this class, employing 4,932 persons and having an aggregate product valued at $6,394,164. In 1905 the number of establishments had decreased to 77, but the number of employees had risen to 5,416, and the value of the product to $8,016,186. [2] These industries are too heterogeneous to permit of further analysis.

Knit Goods

The second half of the nineteenth century has witnessed the emergence of knit-goods manufacturing from the household stage into a factory industry. Before 1850 hosiery was chiefly the product of the knitting needle, and many a frugal American housewife spent her odd moments in making stockings for her family. Some were thus made at home for sale and some manufactured in small mills. That system of production has since yielded to the factory, with several far-reaching effects. Knitted undergarments have superseded the flannels worn a generation ago, and cotton underwear and cotton stockings are far more common than before this industrial change took place. With the development of the knit-goods industry relatively more cotton and less woolen yarn has been manufactured in this form.

A confusion of statistics and other data places serious obstacles in the path of the investigator who wishes to trace the history of a single branch of the knit-goods industry. The same methods and machines serve for knitting woolen, cotton, and silk yarns. Many knitting mills use more than one sort of yarn. And some products contain a mixture of two fibres.

The Census reports for knit-goods manufacturing have become more elaborate with the general development of such statistical inquiries and with the progress of this particular industry. But for purposes of comparison it is possible to give only the statistics which include all knit goods.

[1] 12th *U. S. Census*, vol. ix, p. 70.

[2] In 1910 the number of employees was 7,698 and the value of the product $13,174,111.

KNIT GOODS [1]

	Establishments	Machines	Employees	Value of Product
1860	197	no data	9,100	$7,300,000
1870	248	5,625	14,800	18,400,000
1880	359	12,659	28,900	29,200,000
1890	796	36,327	59,600	67,200,000
1900	921	69,047	83,400	95,500,000
1905	1,079	88,374	103,700	136,600,000
1910	1,374	no data	129,300	200,100,000

The number of establishments was about seven times as great in 1910 as in 1860, the number of employees over fourteen times as great, and the product nearly thirty times as high in value. All this has taken place in fifty years! The advance has been especially rapid since 1880.

The relative importance of the different branches of the industry is shown by a table of classified products.

KNIT GOODS

(*In thousands*)

		1905	1900	1890	1880
HOSIERY					
Woolen					
Half Hose	doz. prs.	1,310	940	1,361	288
Value		$3,402	$1,739	$2,893	not stated
Hose	doz. prs.	1,084	1,177	2,243	1,216
Value		$2,205	$2,268	$4,723	not stated
Merino					
Half Hose	doz. prs.	1,611	958	376	627
Value		$2,215	$1,385	$605	not stated
Hose	doz. prs.	746	437	433	2,653
Value		$1,182	$660	$791	not stated
Cotton					
Half Hose	doz. prs.	15,223	11,352	5,342	
Value		$11,822	$7,907	$3,937	
Hose	doz. prs.	24,170	15,028	7,387	
Value		$22,765	$13,276	$6,214	
UNDERWEAR					
Shirts and Drawers					
Woolen	doz.	485	1,085	1,089	
Value		$3,648	$4,981	$8,882	
Merino	doz.	2,114	2,675	2,526	
Value		$13,032	$13,294	$15,056	
Cotton	doz.	17,108	12,058	3,247	
Value		$39,659	$26,883	$9,024	

[1] Data for 1910 obtained from preliminary statement published in newspapers.

KNIT GOODS — Underwear (*continued*).

Combination Suits	1905	1900	1890	1880
Woolen............doz.	68	10		
Value..................	$965	$202		
Merino ....doz.	105	140		
Value..................	$1,200	$1,133		
Cotton ....doz.	1,260	824		
Value..................	$4,479	$2,240		

In addition to these articles there was a small production of silk knit goods, sweaters, shawls, and minor specialties.

The elaboration of the classification at each succeeding Census emphasizes the increasing diversification of product. From a simple statement of the total production of hosiery and underwear as given in 1860, the new divisions and sub-divisions have been introduced until at the Census of 1900 twenty-four classes of cotton and woolen hosiery and underwear were separately enumerated. In 1860, 1,906,000 dozen pairs of hose and half-hose were manufactured in our factories, as compared with the combined output of 62,825,000 dozen pairs in 1910. In 1870 the product was reported as 2,917,000 dozen pairs of woolen and mixed hose and half hose, and 2,600,000 dozen pairs made of cotton. In 1880 the woolen and mixed hosiery were separated (see table) but cotton hose and half-hose were still enumerated together, their total being 2,491,000 dozen pairs. In 1890, however, they too were fully classified.

The first classification of underwear also appeared in the Census of 1890, the totals at the previous Census dates having been 550,000 dozen shirts and drawers of all descriptions in 1860; 1,132,000 dozen in 1870; and 2,671,000 dozen in 1880. Combination suits are such a recent innovation that no mention of them was made till 1900.

The manufacture of cotton knit goods has advanced at a faster rate than any of the other branches of the knitting industry. The rapid increase in the output of cotton hosiery after 1880 and of cotton underwear after 1890 was due to the technical inventions introduced at those dates. Woolen knit goods, on the contrary, have declined in volume of output and their place has been only partially filled by goods of mixed cotton and wool, called " merino."

The success of cotton knit goods and their substitution for woolen articles has resulted from the lower prices at which they are sold. Raw cotton is cheaper than raw wool, and in the United States the normal difference is enhanced by the high import duty on the latter. The cost of spinning is also greater for wool than for cotton, and the price of the yarn thereby augmented. Finally, cotton yarn lends itself with greater readiness to manipulation by rapidly moving machinery; hence the cost of knitting is less. In consequence of these advantages the cotton fabrics can be sold more cheaply, and are favored by the demand where climatic conditions are not too rigorous.

This preliminary survey prepares the way for the detailed discussion of the several aspects of the growth of the entire cotton manufacturing industry. The first of the subjects to which attention is directed is geographical distribution.

CHAPTER III

THE cotton manufacturing industry has not expanded at the same rate since 1860 in all parts of the United States. Although New England continues to be the largest centre, its predominance has been lessened. The Middle Atlantic states are also relatively less important in this branch of manufacturing. The cotton mills of the West, moreover, are still a negligible quantity. But in the southern states there has been a great change. It is to the South, therefore, that especial attention will be directed in the following discussion of the growth of the industry in the separate sections and the localization within each.

New England

The number of establishments [1] has steadily declined in New England, from 570 in 1860 to 308 in 1905, but the number of spindles has increased from 3,859,000 in 1860 to 13,911,000 in 1905. The latter figure indicates the flourishing condition of the industry in this section. Till 1880 the cotton manufacturing supremacy of New England was not threatened. But when mills began to spring up in the South like mushrooms, grave fears were entertained for the future of the industry in the section where it had first taken root. These fears have now almost entirely disappeared, since by readjustment and economy the New England manufacturers have given evidence of being able to keep their foothold.

Within New England the mills are still scattered, but certain localities have grown faster than others. The industry was first established in southern New England, and today a larger number of spindles are concentrated within thirty miles of Providence than are to be found in a similar area anywhere

---

[1] This does not include knitting mills.

else in the United States.[1]   Fall River is the largest centre with New Bedford, only twenty miles distant, not far behind.   Other large centres in New England are Lowell, Lawrence, Manchester, Pawtucket, and Taunton.

Statistics of the number of spindles per city are not given, but a statement of the value of the cotton goods manufactured in these New England cities conveys some idea of the local con-

VALUE OF PRODUCT

	1890	1900	1905
Fall River	$24,925,000	$29,286,000	$32,538,000
New Bedford	8,185,000	16,748,000	22,412,000
Lowell	19,789,000	17,046,000	19,384,000
Manchester	10,957,000	11,723,000	14,366,000
Pawtucket	3,955,000	5,635,000	10,099,000
Lawrence	6,047,000	8,151,000	5,745,000
Taunton	2,748,000	4,593,000	6,141,000
New England	181,112,000	191,690,000	224,072,000

centration.   The low figure for Lawrence in 1905 was not normal and that city may be given a higher rank when the statistics for 1910 are published.

The reasons for the more rapid growth of the industry in these places are the advantages which accrue from centralization in general, and the natural advantages possessed by the different localities in particular.   In the early growth of the cotton manufacturing industry in New England the factor which determined the location of the mills was water-power.   Fall River, Lowell, Lawrence, Manchester, Nashua, Saco, Lewiston, and other cities grew up because of the water-power which was available at those points.   Although water-power is still a very important factor in the continued prosperity of several of these cities, during the last half-century steam has become more important in supplying power for cotton mills.[2]

[1] *U. S. Census of Manufactures*, 1905, vol. 1, p. ccxxxviii.

[2] In 1870 water furnished 99,073 horse power and steam 46,967 horse power for cotton mills; in 1905, the former supplied 251,884 horse power, the latter, 702,023 horse power; and in addition 77,936 horse power were obtained from other sources, chiefly electricity.   *U. S. Census of Manufactures*, 1905, *Bulletin* No. 74, p. 62.

The system of canals which was constructed at Lowell has been of great value to that city and shows the foresight of those who planned for its future growth, since by means of these canals the water flows through the heart of the city and is used over and over again as it passes from one mill to another. In Lawrence and Manchester canals were also constructed, from which a considerable part of the power for driving the machinery in the mills is still derived. In 1900, according to the Census,[1] water furnished 49 per cent of the power for cotton mills in Lowell, 36 per cent in Lawrence, and 50 per cent in Manchester. However, since all the water-power privileges in these centres have been appropriated, few new mills have been built there, and the growth which has taken place has been merely the enlargement of the older plants.

The more rapid growth of the industry in southern New England cannot be ascribed to water-power. Fall River and New Bedford do not rely upon that to a great extent. Nor is the reason to be found in labor conditions, since the more northern cities possessed as large and as skilled a supply of labor as Fall River and New Bedford, when the latter cities began to forge ahead. Nor is the location of machine and repair shops the reason, since Lowell is well provided for in that respect.

One reason, as Mr. Sidney Coolidge has pointed out, is the advantage which the tide-water cities gain in transportation rates. This saving, however, is not in the rates on raw cotton, since for that portion (about 40 per cent) which is shipped to the North by rail, a blanket rate is given for all New England and the railroads meet the water rates. Neither does the advantage arise in the freight on the cloth, since practically the same rate is paid from all sections of New England to New York or the West. The tide-water mills, however, are able to obtain their coal at lower rates, inasmuch as the charges from Boston to points north are relatively high. The cost of discharging coal is about the same in Fall River and New Bedford as in Boston, and in the former cities it can be sent directly to the mills without further transportation. Thus, as the use

[1] 12th *U. S. Census*, vol. vii, p. cxciv.

of steam power has become more and more common, cheaper coal has favored the cities of southern New England.

Climatic conditions have been another reason for the more rapid increase in the number of spindles in that district. New Bedford, of all the cities in New England, has progressed most rapidly in cotton manufacturing during the last thirty years. The Wamsutta Mills were built in 1845, but only a few similar establishments followed till after 1880. At the present time, however, there are more than 2,100,000 spindles in the city. In that particular locality the temperature is less variable and the atmosphere more humid than in the neighboring regions. The climate has been particularly adapted to the manufacture of fine yarn and cloth. Although the natural advantage of humidity has been partially equalized elsewhere by artificial humidifiers, the greater stability of the temperature retains its potency. These are the chief bases for New Bedford's progress, but an important supplement was the wealth which had been accumulated in the whale fisheries by New Bedford residents, and which became available for building cotton mills when the whaling industry declined. The largest mill interests in New Bedford at the present time are in the hands of families which had acquired fortunes in whale fishing. This transfer of capital to cotton manufacturing stimulated the industry and its evidences of prosperity attracted investments from other sources.

While new mills continue to be built and additions to old mills are made from time to time in all parts of New England, economies in transportation and favorable climatic conditions will very likely cause an even greater predominance of the southern section of that district. The relative position of New England as a whole, however, can best be indicated after considering the progress of the industry in the Middle States and the South.

Middle Atlantic States

Since the Civil War the number of establishments in the Middle Atlantic states has diminished from 340 to 204. But until 1900 the number of spindles increased slightly. From 1900 to 1905 there was a slight falling off. The number of spindles reported in 1860 was 1,042,000; in 1900, 1,647,000; and in 1905, 1,548,000. Thus since 1860 the industry has been practically stationary in this section.

Cotton factories are located in Pennsylvania, New York, and Maryland, and a few are found in the other states of this group. But Philadelphia is the only point at which there is concentration. In the Philadelphia district small weaving establishments are particularly numerous; three-fourths of the mills in the United States which weave but do not spin are located in Pennsylvania, chiefly in Philadelphia, and the average number of looms per mill is only 101.[1] Textile manufacturing is a long established industry in that city and immigrant labor was probably employed there sooner than in New England. The immigrants, however, who entered the textile industries of Philadelphia, were more or less experienced in textile manufacturing and therefore could be employed in the production of more fancy fabrics. Thus we can account, at least in part, for the existence of these mills and the character of their product. The labor supply has been the chief asset, supplemented by machine-shops and market facilities. The textile industries of Philadelphia, moreover, are urban enterprises dependent on urban conditions and in that respect are more or less analogous to the clothing industries of New York.

The Middle Atlantic states are pre-eminent in the knit-goods industry. Establishments were reported in thirty-five states in 1905, but three-fifths of the total number were in the Middle Atlantic states, chiefly New York and Pennsylvania. Here are also the largest knitting factories, as a rule, although there are several large mills of this sort in Massachusetts, which ranks third among the states of the Union in knitting.

In both New York and Pennsylvania there is a localization of the knitting industry, — around Cohoes in the Mohawk Valley, and at Philadelphia. Each of these localities was a pioneer in its own field, and the advantages accruing therefrom have been a strong attraction. At Cohoes power was first

[1] *U. S. Census of Manufactures*, 1905, *Bulletin* No. 74, p. 57.

successfully applied to knitting frames,[1] and from that nucleus a large underwear manufacture has grown up. Philadelphia has been the principal seat of the hosiery industry in the United States ever since the Germans settled in Germantown.[2] The success of the knitting industry in these districts has, like a magnet, attracted new enterprises of the same character.[3]

Southern States

The number of establishments[4] in the southern states in 1860 was 165; in 1900, 550, of much larger size. This statement brings us face to face with one of the most important industrial developments since the Civil War. The growth of cotton manufacturing in the South has caused an extensive change in the social and economic conditions of certain sections of those states. It has increased competition in one of the long established industries of the North, and thereby affected the whole United States. As a factor in enlarging the export trade of the country in cotton goods, it has had an effect upon the world's trade.

This growth is significant of a change in southern ideals. It signifies a change from a social system in which work was held to be degrading, to one in which great interest is taken in industrial enterprise. It marks the decline of an industrial system based upon slave labor, and the rise of one in which the black man has almost no place. The spirit of contempt for northern industrial methods has been superseded by an intense rivalry with those very methods. From the ashes and ruins left by the war a " new South " has emerged. Between the cessation of hostilities and the beginning of this development, a period of fifteen years, the South was slowly recovering from the losses which it had suffered. During this period of convalescence a new generation was growing up, less hampered

[1] 12th *U. S. Census*, vol. vii, p. xcviii.
[2] Part of Philadelphia.
[3] Knitting mills have also been located in numerous hard-coal mining towns of Pennsylvania where they could employ the women and children of the miners' families.
[4] Not including knitting mills.

than the fathers by old ideals and prejudices, and capable of directing the recent rapid growth.

This rise of cotton manufacturing in the South has been due not so much to newly realized advantages or newly discovered resources, as to a change in the attitude of the people themselves and the release from the system under which all of their savings had to be invested in slaves. That it was not a newly discovered opportunity there is good evidence. In 1833 and again in 1845, Mr. William Gregg appealed to the people of South Carolina to establish cotton mills. James Montgomery, writing in 1840, prophesied the growth of the industry in the South, but considered it unlikely that the South would ever surpass the North.[1] Col. J. B. Palmer, in a report on cotton manufacturing read before the Immigration Convention at Charleston, South Carolina, in 1870, called attention to those advantages which have been enumerated so frequently during the last thirty years, even mentioning the possibility of furnishing work for the poorer white people. Thus the advantages were recognized long before they were utilized.

The reasons for the delay in exploiting these resources are to be sought in the economic and social conditions which prevailed in the South before the Civil War. The South preserved the characteristics of a frontier agricultural community in which many goods were made in the household. In this respect the South resembled the West. All the available capital and labor were employed in agriculture. The demand for capital, moreover, was augmented by the amounts required to purchase slaves. And at that time there was in no section of the country a considerable surplus of capital seeking investment; local supplies were used for local purposes. In the next place, a supply of adaptable labor was not available for manufacturing in such a community. The negro slave was too ignorant, too clumsy, too unreliable to be employed advantageously in a mill equipped with intricate, expensive, and delicately adjusted machinery. Again, the slave system hindered the employment of free laborers in a dependent

[1] J. Montgomery, *Cotton Manufacture*, p. 194.

position. The entrepreneur ability of the South, lastly, was drawn into the management of plantations, and little interest was taken in manufacturing. After the War, however, conditions changed, and a new attitude was a significant feature of the Cotton Exposition at Atlanta in 1881, a convention which gave impetus to the movement for the erection of cotton mills.[1]

The cotton manufacturing industry has grown up in the South within the last thirty years, or since 1880. From 1900 to 1905 the rate of increase was more rapid than ever before, but at the present time a more conservative tendency is apparent. The growth is shown by a comparison of the number of spindles in the South and in the North at five year intervals since 1880.

SPINDLES [2]

(*Millions*)

	1880	1885	1890	1895	1900	1905	1910	Increase 30 years
North	10.1	12.2	12.6	13.7	14.5	15.3	17.4	7.3
South	.5	1.1	1.7	2.4	4.5	8.8	11.2	10.7
Total	10.6	13.3	14.3	16.1	19.0	24.1	28.6	18.0

In 1880 there were twenty times as many spindles in the North, but in 1910 the Northern spindleage was only fifty per cent greater, the increase during the thirty years having been about seven million spindles in the North and over ten millions in the South. The increase in the number of spindles in the South was approximately sixty per cent of the total increase in the United States in that period. Of this increase in the South, over one-half took place after 1900. Various reasons why this rate of growth is not likely to continue will be given later.

Cotton mills have not been built in all parts of the South, as the following table shows.

[1] 12th *U. S. Census, Bulletin* No. 215, p. 12.
[2] Compiled from *Commercial and Financial Chronicle.*

SOUTHERN MILLS [1]

	Establishments		Spindles		Looms	
	1880	1910	1880	1910	1880	1910
South Carolina	14	145	82,000	4,019,000	1,700	88,427
North Carolina	49	292	92,000	3,174,000	1,800	50,979
Georgia	40	139	199,000	1,939,000	4,500	35,069
Alabama	16	61	49,000	947,000	900	15,853
Tennessee	16	29	36,000	293,000	800	4,391
Virginia	8	14	44,000	329,000	1,300	8,694
Mississippi	8	19	19,000	177,000	600	3,586
Texas	2	16	3,000	112,000	100	2,331
All Other	11	16	37,000	241,000	600	2,942
Total	164	731	561,000	11,231,000	12,300	212,272

The most extensive construction of mills has been in three states, — North Carolina, South Carolina, and Georgia. Alabama has also had an important share in the progress, although not to the same extent as its eastern neighbors. In the number of establishments North Carolina has led from the start, but South Carolina has surpassed both North Carolina and Georgia in the number of spindles and looms. The average size of the mills, therefore, is larger in South Carolina, and has increased more rapidly than in the other states. In 1880 the average number of spindles per establishment was 1,900 in North Carolina, 5,000 in Georgia, and 5,900 in South Carolina. But in 1905 the average per establishment was 9,360, 12,500, and 24,600 respectively. During the same period the number of looms per establishment increased from 36 to 176 in North Carolina, from 112 to 235 in Georgia, and from 126 to 520 in South Carolina. Yet in comparison with northern mills, these variations are not important, for a typical New England mill has from 50,000 to 100,000 spindles. There are, to be sure, several large mills in the South but small concerns are far more numerous.

The states with the larger spindleage spin the finer yarn. In 1910 the average number of yarn for the entire southern section was 20.[2] In Texas it was number 15, whereas in Alabama it was 18, in North Carolina 19, in Tennessee and Georgia 20, and in South Carolina 24. This is another proof that South

---

[1] *Commercial and Financial Chronicle.*   [2] *Ibid.*, vol. xci, p. 623.

Carolina has reached a more advanced stage than its neighbors; it not only has its business concentrated in larger establishments but spins finer counts.

The advantages usually specified as the reasons for the progress of cotton manufacturing in the South are: — (1) proximity to the source of supply of raw cotton, whereby the spinner is enabled (a) to save in freight rates on raw material, and (b) to take advantage of favorable market conditions, (2) water-power, (3) lower taxation, and (4) cheap labor. To what extent has each of these alleged advantages affected the development ? How far are they still operative ? And in what degree are they offset by disadvantages ?

(1a) A saving in freight on raw materials is doubtless realized by some mills, but this economy is not so great as would at first sight appear. Where the mills have become so numerous that the local supply is insufficient to satisfy their demands, the price paid to the local merchants for cotton grown in the immediate neighborhood is equal to the cost of the cotton in other states plus the freight charges. In North Carolina about one-fourth of the cotton used in the mills is brought from other states, particularly Mississippi, and the price of all the cotton is determined by the Mississippi price plus the freight charge from Mississippi to Charlotte or to whatever city or town it may be delivered. And the freight rate from Mississippi to Charlotte, for example, is nearly as high as the rate from southern shipping points to New England.

In parts of South Carolina the same conditions obtain, but there is more saving on freight for the mills in that state than in North Carolina. The mills in Georgia and Alabama, as well as certain sections of South Carolina, can frequently procure their supply of cotton from the immediate vicinity at prices no higher than those at which it is sold to be shipped to the North or to Europe, thus eliminating freight charges. Long staple cotton, from which the higher counts of yarn are spun, is not grown near the manufacturing region. Therefore the southern mills purchasing such cotton have to pay freight charges about equal to those incurred by New England mills.

The mills which obtain their cotton locally gain as much from saving in tare as in saving on freight rates. In such cases the cotton is not compressed but delivered to the mills in the large, loosely packed ginnery bales. Not only is there no compress charge, but the manufacturer does not have to buy the several pounds of old bagging which are almost always placed in the covering at the compress, supposedly to cover holes, but more frequently to find a resting place between them.

One mill, in Rome, Georgia, even eliminates baling by receiving the cotton directly from the field and ginning it at the mill. This method, however, is not practicable for most mills, since they must select the grade of cotton for which their machinery is adjusted, and not take the general mixture which would be offered to them by the farmers. Several grades are found in the cotton from a single farm, and it is one of the functions of the merchant to classify this and sort it into lots of uniform grade. Some of the mills in the heart of the eastern cotton growing area warehouse the farmer's cotton after it has been ginned, use it when needed, and pay for it not at a price fixed when delivered, but at the current price whenever the farmer wishes to call for his money. That portion which is too high in quality as well as that of too inferior a grade must be disposed of to a cotton merchant. Obviously the risk involved is not inconsiderable and hardly consistent with economical management.

Economy in freight on raw cotton, therefore, is realized only by the mills in the more southern part of the cotton manufacturing district, and probably a majority of the southern spinners pay nearly as much as the New England spinners for their raw material. Furthermore, the cloth is generally shipped to the North. There are practically no bleaching, dyeing, or printing works in the South, as the water is not suitable. Hence if the cloth is to be finished it must go to the North, usually New England. And if it is to be exported in the gray it is generally shipped through New York, sometimes through Seattle. Since the market is in the northern states, it matters little, so far as freight charges are involved, whether the cotton is shipped before or after manufacturing. Until the South is able to obtain pure water for finishing and becomes commercially independent of New York by establishing its own export market, the saving of freight on raw cotton will be counterbalanced by the freight on the cloth. When that goal is reached, if at all, the growth of the industry may have forced all the manufacturers to obtain at least part of their cotton from distant states and thus nullify what slight advantage now accrues from proximity to the cotton fields. Although by appealing to the imagination this advantage has given some stimulus, it seems very doubtful if there has been sufficient economy to bring about the building of many mills, or if in the future it will have much effect on the growth of cotton manufacturing in the South.

(1b) The proximity of the southern manufacturer to the source of supply of raw cotton does not enable him to gain any advantage in purchasing. The New York price rules and that quotation depends upon the state of the world's cotton market. There is not sufficient divergence in any locality to place local manufacturers in a superior position. In the second place, the majority of the southern manufacturing companies have not as much ready money as the New England mills. It is available cash rather than geographical location, which determines who will be able to buy cotton when the price falls.

(2) The saving in cost of power is a more difficult point to decide upon. A number of mills are located on streams where they can use water-power, and their charges for this element in the cost of manufacturing are small. But the spot where water-power can be secured may be remote from the railway and may involve other sacrifices. Moreover, less than one-fourth of the power for southern cotton mills is furnished by water.[1] For those using steam the cost of coal varies, being cheap in Tennessee where there are local mines and dearer in other states according to the distance it must be transported. While cheap

---

[1] In 1905, water furnished 22%, electricity 7.2%, and steam 67.4% of the power for southern cotton mills; and water 28%, electricity 4%, and steam 66.6% for New England mills. — *U. S. Census of Manufactures*, 1905, *Bulletin* No. 74, p. 62.

power has encouraged the inception of some of these cotton manufacturing enterprises, it has not been general enough to be considered the paramount factor in the whole movement.

(3) Southern municipalities have frequently exempted the mills from taxation for a period of years as an inducement to location within their borders, and the rates are generally lower than in the North. But the southern mill owners, in contrast with those of New England, have had to provide sanitary improvements, and to subsidize schools, churches, and other public institutions in their villages.

To offset whatever gains may have accrued to the southern manufacturers from the minor advantages already mentioned, the dispersion of the mills must be reckoned with. The factories are scattered throughout the Piedmont district, from Greensboro in the north to Atlanta in the south, and also here and there in the lowlands. Charlotte, North Carolina, is the commercial centre for a large part of this district, but there is no considerable localization. The cotton industry, however, like many others, is naturally gregarious, and thrives best where the labor market is fairly steady and where repair shops are close at hand. This source of economy is realized in New England but not in the South. Yet this inconvenience will probably disappear along with other advantages and disadvantages, as the industry emerges from the period of transition.

(4) Although these advantages have aided mill building in the South, the corner-stone of the structure has been the supply of cheap and tractable labor. When the industrial revival began, the enthusiasm spread in every direction. The newspapers gave the movement hearty support. Leading men sanctioned and encouraged it. Farmers who had made money in cotton growing invested their savings in mill shares. And, not least, there was available a supply of adaptable laborers, who also took an interest in what was going on. The old lethargy was shaken off and all joined in the common cause.

The operatives are of the class called " poor whites." They have come from the hills and farms of the Piedmont district, and are descendants of the Scotch and Scotch-Irish who in earlier generations had pushed down into this section. The ante-bellum plantation system held them back in this infertile region, since they could not keep up in the race with the large plantation owners, and labor as wage-earners was impossible for them under that social and industrial system. Thus forced back into the hills, they remained a crude and undeveloped people, not degraded but unprogressive.[1]

The supply of labor for the southern cotton mills has been obtained from two classes, the mountaineers and the tenant farmers. The former, known as "Tackies" in North Carolina and as "Crackers" in Georgia, had eked out a meagre livelihood from their small patches of barren soil and the fruits of their rifles. Their food was simple and not abundant, their clothing scanty, and their home a small cabin with dirt floor and devoid of all except the crudest furniture. But in spite of their "hand-to-mouth" existence in squalid conditions, they retained a proud and independent spirit, with no trace of servility. Although lacking ingenuity, foresight, and ambition, they were, however, adaptable to factory life.

The tenant farmers, the class which has provided the larger proportion of the mill workers,[2] had lived more comfortably though not accustomed to many of the luxuries of life. The returns to be obtained from growing a few bales of cotton were not large, and occasional crop failures combined with a general improvidence to keep them more or less deeply in debt. The depression which began in 1893 and the prevailing low prices of cotton probably induced or compelled some to enter the mills and swell the exodus from the farm. But this drain upon the agricultural class has, perhaps, had some effect in raising the remuneration to be secured from tilling the soil. The rapid building of cotton mills throughout the world has, at the same time, increased the demand for cotton, and the price is now from two to three times as high as it was fifteen years ago. The result is that the pendulum has begun its backward swing and the people are to some extent returning to the farms.

[1] H. Thompson, *From Cotton Field to Cotton Mill*, p. 113.
[2] A. Kohn, *The Cotton Mills of South Carolina*, p. 26.

The change from agriculture to manufacturing has, on the whole, been beneficial to the workers, although their standard of living changes slowly. They receive larger money incomes than before, but many do not exercise a wise choice in the disposal of their earnings. They spend a great deal on food, but the cooking is bad.[1] They select food-stuffs like those on which they were formerly accustomed to live, only in larger quantities, and have learned little of the culinary art. This tends to impair their health. They pay scant attention to literature and entertainment, but dress extravagantly.[2] These people are not thrifty. In all the mill towns the story is the same. A few save money to buy a house and occasionally there are small bank accounts, but the vast majority are improvident. They relinquished a certain amount of their former freedom when they submitted to factory discipline, but they have maintained an independent spirit which not infrequently leads them to follow the impulse of the moment and absent themselves from the mill whenever they have earned enough to provide for the time being. Mr. Kohn states:[3] " Every cotton mill in South Carolina recognizes that to have a full complement of labor in the mill each morning, it is practically necessary to carry a surplusage of twenty to twenty-five per cent of spare ' help.' " Prolonged contact with the industrial world, however, may be expected to eradicate this restlessness, and acquaintance with higher standards to instil more of the spirit of frugality.

The dwellings have not always been furnished with proper sanitary conveniences but they have been better than the previous habitations in the mountains or on the farms. The mill owners have generally provided cottages for their employees, and have encouraged tidiness inside and out. A family is sometimes discharged if it persists in living in filth. Small gardens of flowers frequently adorn the yards in front of the cottages, the employers as well as the employees enjoying the

---

[1] H. Thompson, *From Cotton Field to Cotton Mill*, p. 145; also Mass. Bureau of Statistics of Labor, *Report*, 1905.

[2] H. Thompson, *op. cit.*, p. 143.

[3] A. Kohn, *The Cotton Mills of South Carolina*, p. 61.

cheerful appearance. The employers in many cases have also exercised a careful supervision over the morals of the workers,[1] to prevent the creeping in of vices such as might be expected to appear among people not accustomed to town life.

Within the factories the conditions of labor have not been altogether praiseworthy. The hours of labor have been long. Until 1906 sixty-six hours per week was the lowest legal minimum in any southern state, and during the preceding years seventy-five hours per week was not uncommon. The different states have now imposed limitations which are gradually approaching those in New England. It is curious how a man's arguments change when his pocket-book is affected. Before the Civil War, the southerners defended slavery on the ground that that climate would not permit a white man to engage in manual labor. Now they justify the long hours of employment in the cotton mills with a statement that climatic conditions are more favorable to prolonged exertion than in the North.

The southern mills until recently were often operated at night, sometimes, it is said, keeping the machinery in motion twenty-three hours out of every twenty-four. This was an advantage in that it used the machines to the utmost before they were supplanted by an improved type. It was also an advantage in the interest account. But there were several drawbacks to night work, aside from the cost of lighting the mill. Less was accomplished; the product was less satisfactory; and the wages were higher for night work. It was also difficult to keep the children awake, — a disadvantage, which, unfortunately, was not so serious from a money-making point of view as from that of society. The practice of night work, though not yet extinct, has diminished and the employment of young children at night has been restricted.

The greatest evil attendant upon the industrial progress of the South has been the employment of children in the mills. 4,097 children were reported by the Census of 1880, and 27,571 in 1905. In addition to those included in these statistics, there were an indefinite number whose names did not appear on the

[1] H. Thompson, *From Cotton Field to Cotton Mill*, pp. 165, 180.

pay-rolls, but who were permitted to come in and "help" their parents or older brothers and sisters. The manager calmed his conscience by declaring that he did not hire them. This indirect employment of young children has not been forbidden by law as in the North.[1]

The proportion of cotton mill employees who are under the age of sixteen is much higher in the South than in the northern states. The absolute number has been so augmented that there has been but a slight relative decline, in contrast to the tendency shown in the North.

COTTON MILLS

(Percentage of employees under age of 16) [2]

	1905	1900	1890	1880
New England	6.0	6.7	6.9	14.1
Middle Atlantic States	8.7	12.4	12.6	21.4
South	22.9	25.0	24.2	25.1
Total United States	12.9	13.4	10.7	16.4

The relative decline from 1900 to 1905 will probably continue since more and more severe age restrictions are being imposed by the state governments, and especially because the conviction is gaining ground amongst employers themselves that the employment of young children is not profitable. This sentiment was frequently expressed to me by the manufacturers with whom I talked, and Mr. Cherington, who corresponded with numerous southern employers on this subject,[3] obtained similar evidence. Perhaps the laws which have been enacted are due in part to this change of attitude on the part of the mill owners.

The employers have not been altogether at fault in employing children. The parents themselves have frequently insisted that employment should be given to the whole family, and a

---

[1] Mr. Young found one instance exactly analogous in Rhode Island, — T. M. Young, *American Cotton Industry*, p. 24.

[2] *U. S. Census of Manufactures*, 1905, *Bulletin* No. 74, p. 39.

[3] Mr. P. T. Cherington kindly permitted me to read an unpublished manuscript in which these statements were set forth.

manager in need of operatives would hesitate to reject the whole family merely because some of the children were young. But the whole family has not always worked, to judge by the statements of Mr. Thompson.[1] He pictures a large number of idle fathers, " tin-bucket toters " he calls them, who are supported by their children. These worthy personages lounge around the village loafing places and discourse upon the capabilities of their children, much as farmers gather at a country store to argue upon the relative merits of their cattle. This abuse does not prevail to the same extent today as in former years. That it should have arisen was not unnatural. The older men could not easily adapt themselves to tending machines and fell into the habit of depending on the women and children for support. They were poor and uneducated when they came to the mills, and they did not realize that it was more unhealthy for the women and children to work in a factory than to labor in the field.

These social conditions have been discussed not only because of their bearing upon the success of the cotton manufacturing industry in this section, but also on account of the wide attention that they have attracted.[2] While the evils have been numerous, it is an injustice to criticise too harshly. It must be remembered that long hours and child labor were once common in New England, and the latter evil has not yet been eradicated from the mills and factories in various northern states. The southern mill operatives are, as a rule, better off than before they entered the mills. And their dwellings and modes of living do not compare unfavorably with those in the tenement districts of New England mill towns. The mills are generally well lighted, well ventilated, and some are artificially cooled in summer.

---

[1] H. Thompson, *From Cotton Field to Cotton Mill*, p. 115; also E. G. Murphy, *The Present South*, p. 106; and *Report of the Industrial Commission*, vol. vii, pp. 545, 566.

[2] The magazine articles on this subject have been numerous. The following may be mentioned as presenting the subject from different points of view: — A. J. McKelway, *Annals of American Academy*, vol. xxvii, and *Outlook*, vol. lxxxv; M. A. Bacon, *Atlantic Monthly*, vol. xcix; A. W. Page, *World's Work*, vol. xiv; H. Robbins, *Gunton's Magazine*, vol. xxiii; D. A. Willey, *Chatauquan*, vol. xxviii.

The conditions in the South are not praiseworthy; yet in the North they are often nearly as bad. The pictures of southern child operatives in the popular magazines give an unfair impression. Let a photograph be taken of a dozen children emerging from a northern print-cloth mill, glass works, or silk factory, and how much more prepossessing an appearance would they present?

The school system has been inadequate and the regulations in regard to attendance lax, yet the children have received more education than if they had remained in the mountains or on the farms. While recognizing the abuses that still exist and appreciating the opportunities for betterment, my own impression is that the conditions in many southern mills, not all, are not inferior to those in northern mill centres. The outlook for the future is brightened by a wide-spread spirit of progress. The employers are by no means heartless. They are generally quite the reverse and take an active interest in uplifting their employees. The operatives themselves are slowly adopting higher standards, and improving their condition. Whether they are to use the cotton mill as a stepping-stone, or whether, because of ignorance and lack of thrift, they are to become a permanent operative class, remains to be seen.[1]

These people, with limited wants and accustomed to inexpensive living, were employed at wages lower than were paid in New England. No statistics are available which can safely be used for an exact comparison of labor cost, but it has been sufficiently below that of the northern mills to stimulate a rapid increase in the number of spindles in the South.

The following table illustrates the difference in earnings in the two sections. It gives the computed full time earnings

[1] The conditions in the United States are gradually approaching the European standard, so that it is becoming more difficult for the mill operatives and other workmen of that class to raise themselves to a higher level. Yet the absence of social restrictions and firmly fixed customs as well as the promise of further industrial expansion in this country seem to afford sufficient opportunity for these people to emerge from their position as factory employees. To the author, the progress of the operatives appears to depend chiefly on their own efforts. The falling off in the proportion of women employed (see p. 114) may be an indication that they are not to become a permanent factory class.

for an average week, as shown by the investigations of the Department of Commerce and Labor in 1907–08.

(COMPUTED) FULL TIME WEEKLY EARNINGS

(*Of males and females over 16 years of age.   1907–08.*) [1]

| | 44 New England Mills | | 151 Southern Mills | |
	Males	Females	Males	Females
Doffers	$6.77	$6.07	$5.08	$4.70
Ring Spinners	6.77	7.36	5.96	5.71
Speeder Tenders	9.64	8.88	8.21	7.09
Spoolers	..	6.77	6.08	5.71
Weavers	9.93	8.99	8.53	7.21

Although these figures are inadequate, since they do not cover all departments nor take into consideration the quality of the product or the output per operative, they roughly indicate the comparative cost in the two sections.   The piece-rates, as well as earnings, have been lower in the South.

The lower wages, nevertheless, have been partially counterbalanced by the lack of skill and the fickleness of the workers. They had to be taught how to manage the machines, and while they have learned readily they are even now inferior artisans to those New England operatives who have worked in cotton mills for a longer time.   The efficiency of the southern operatives has also been impaired by their inconstant attendance.

Although the wages and probably the labor cost have been lower in the South, at present they have risen almost to the level of New England.   The growth of the industry has taken away the advantage which was its chief asset.   The stratum of cheap labor has been exhausted and in the boom of 1905–07 employers bid against each other so that wages were raised nearly onefourth.   The competition for laborers was so keen that the mills frequently offered free transportation as an extra inducement to attract operatives from other localities.   The *Manufacturers' Record*, a standard authority for the southern industrial world, printed, in nearly every issue during the period of 1905–07, statements that " with very few exceptions all the cotton mills in

---

[1] U. S. Commissioner of Labor, *Report on Condition of Woman and Child Wage-Earners in the United States*, vol. i, p. 328.

the South were short of their full complement of operatives," and that " for the time being the South had built more mills than it had labor to operate." [1] Corroborative evidence is given by the employers themselves.

The attempts of southern mill owners to attract foreign immigrants are likewise indicative of the exhaustion of the local supply of labor. In South Carolina a special committee was appointed by the state government [2] to promote immigration. The instigators and supporters were the manufacturers. They were successful in inducing a few hundred foreigners to enter the state, but not in keeping them there.[3] The immigrants found that they could earn more elsewhere. The undertakings, therefore, have borne little fruit, and under present conditions the prospects are not encouraging. The restrictions imposed in the mill villages are irksome to the European who is accustomed to his beer, and there is likelihood of friction with the American laborers. And the higher wages of the North and association with their kinsmen are more attractive to the immigrants than any temptations which have yet been offered in the South.

But why not employ the negro in the cotton mill ? Before the Civil War the use of slaves in the factories was occasionally suggested, and since 1880 the negro has frequently been mentioned as a labor asset of the southern mills. Although no competent business man has yet ventured to make a real test and the failures of previous attempts cannot be ascribed entirely to the inefficiency of the laborers, there are good grounds for doubting the possibilities of employing negroes in the southern cotton mills.

There is little likelihood that the negro will become the mill operative of the future. In the first place, the average negro is not temperamentally adapted to monotonous, mechanical work. His mental development does not seem to fit him for

[1] See, for example, *Manufacturers' Record*, Aug. 10, 1905, p. 87, and Oct. 19, 1905, p. 340.

[2] H. Thompson, *From Cotton Field to Cotton Mill*, p. 61; Mass. Bureau of Statistics of Labor, *Report*, 1905, p. 45.

[3] A. Kohn, *Cotton Mills of South Carolina*, p. 197.

understanding the complex machines. Neither does it fit him for applying himself with assiduity for the required length of time. He can apply himself to one thing only, and to that not too constantly. Oftentimes he will work no longer than is necessary to provide his meagre livelihood. The result is that the negro cannot be depended upon, whereas the very essence of successful factory operation is that each workman should attend constantly and carefully to his own work. This is just what the negro would be least likely to do. Hence he would require more supervising than his labor would be worth.

The mill, moreover, would have to be operated entirely by negroes with white men as overseers. While white men and black men would work together in harmony, provided the room were well ventilated, public opinion in the South, for the present at least and for a long time to come, would not tolerate the employment of negroes within the same room in which white women were at work. Negroes now perform some of the rough outside work, and in numerous mills are tending the pickers. But there they are by themselves. They can also be put to work in the halls and stairways as sweepers and scrubbers, but were they to be placed at one of the machines in the card room or spinning room, the white laborers would leave immediately. It is either a white person's job or a negro's job; it cannot be the work of both. The negro women have not the deftness of white women and could not, therefore, economically take their place. The same is true of the children. Hence the dilemma, — all black is not satisfactory to the manager, and part black and part white is practically impossible. Were the prospects for success bright, the solution of the race problem would, perhaps, be nearer at hand; but unfortunately there is little evidence to encourage such optimism. Instead there is the possibility of a complication of southern racial conditions by immigration of foreigners.

We may conclude, therefore, that so far as labor is concerned, the advantage which the southern manufacturers have enjoyed has been nearly neutralized by the expansion of the industry. As the industry has become greater its competition has tended to be less severely felt. Yet this does not mean that progress is not to continue. On the basis of the present supply of labor existing mills are provided for, and the natural increase in population will furnish workmen for additional spindles. But wages will henceforth be more nearly equal to those in the North and the costs of production in the two sections less divergent.

The southern mills built during the last fifteen years have ordinarily been equipped with machinery of the latest type. This enhanced the advantage arising from low wages. The southerners at first purchased second-hand machines which had been discarded in the North, but they learned that it was more economical, when capital could be obtained, to buy the newest machines. Consequently ring spindles with the latest improvements were purchased, a large number of Northrop looms installed, and other most modern improvements adopted.

The management of southern mills has generally been inferior to that of the northern factories. It has been less systematic and less economical. The superintendence has been less careful and the cost keeping less accurate. The managers have been for the most part trained in southern mills, and the overseers are commonly southern born and have gained their experience in the mills of that section. In the early years a few of the overseers and managers were northern men who had been sent to erect machinery in the South, but not many such are to be found at the present time. Besides their laxity in management the southern manufacturers have not taken care to keep up the quality of their product with the foresight that is characteristic in New England. Southern goods bring a slightly lower price than northern cloths, not only because of inferior workmanship, but also because they are less trustworthy. Since the southern manufacturer is more likely to use poorer cotton or economize in some other way rather than incur a temporary loss, the reputation of his cloth suffers. There are numerous exceptions, however, and the general tendency is toward better management and maintenance of quality.

The capital for building the earlier mills was obtained in

the South itself. They were small establishments and represented the savings of local business men and farmers.[1] Frequently the mill building was short-sighted, local pride and the
infectious spirit of the moment blinding the promoters to the
inadvisability of investment in the manner pursued. Such
mills have frequently failed and passed through numerous
reorganizations. The speculative mania introduced an element
of unsteadiness, but this, as in other industries, was an incident
of early growth and on the whole contributed to the establishment of the new business in the South.

Once the profitableness of cotton manufacturing in this
section had been proven, capital flowed in from the North, in
part from bona-fide investors and in part from other sources.
Of the latter, the machinery manufacturers were heavy con-
tributors. They took shares in the company's stock in payment
for machinery, just as the English machinery firms have done
during the recent period of rapid erection of mills in Lancashire.
The machinery companies, in both countries, unloaded the
stock at their earliest opportunity.

Stock in southern mill companies has also been taken by
business firms which have held the stock but with the object
not so much of securing interest on the investment as of obtaining remunerative privileges. These firms were New York
commission houses which purchased stock on condition that they
be granted the agency for the product. These financiers,
however, more commonly helped to supply ready money by
making advances on the goods with a lien on the cotton as
security, instead of accepting shares of stock. The selling
agents have not always treated the mills fairly, and the higher
commissions which they have received have been a burden
to the southern manufacturers.

Several mills have been built on southern soil by New England
companies, with a view to profitable investment and because
of apprehension that the industry was to shift away from the
North. While some of these ventures have paid, others have
been unsuccessful financially because of the choice of an un-

[1] H. Thompson, *From Cotton Field to Cotton Mill*, p. 64.

favorable location and have handicapped the parent company. No new southern branches have been established for several years, and one hears no suggestion that any are contemplated. On the contrary, one of the Lowell manufacturing companies which has a southern mill that is supposed to have yielded good returns chose to enlarge its northern plant in 1909, thus indicating that the prospects were better in Lowell than in the southern states.

The product of the southern mills has been mainly coarse yarn and cloths, as is shown by the greater consumption of cotton per spindle. In 1907 the southern mills averaged 127 pounds, and in 1909, 122.8 pounds of cotton per spindle. The northern mills averaged 76 pounds per spindle in both of those years.[1] After making due allowance for inaccuracies in the estimates and other modifying circumstances, it is evident that the average product is considerably heavier in the South. These goods have been in good demand for export, and several mills manufacture entirely for the foreign market. The less skilled labor of the South is better adapted to manufacturing this class of goods.

A division of the field has been predicted on the basis of the conditions which have prevailed up to the present time, the North to manufacture fine goods and the South coarse goods. Although a plausible view, judging from the past, it is by no means certain that this will be the ultimate outcome. On the one hand the production of coarse goods has shown no sign of diminishing in the North, and on the other hand several fine goods mills have been erected in the South. Furthermore there may grow up in the South a permanent class of operatives who will develop especial skill in the manipulation of cotton while the inundation of foreign immigrants continues in New England. The one prediction is as good as the other.

To summarize the present situation: — the advantages accruing to the Southern manufacturers from proximity to the cotton fields, good water-power, light taxes, long hours, and new machinery are counterbalanced in the North by more

[1] Computed from statistics given in *U. S. Statistical Abstract*, 1910, p. 710.

abundant capital and credit facilities, greater public conveniences, more experienced managers and better disciplined workmen, concentration instead of dispersion, superior climate, and nearness to markets and finishing works. The chief asset of the southern manufacturers has been the supply of cheap labor, but this source is nearly exhausted. Hence a rise in wages has taken place, and it is to be expected that by the competition of employers they will be forced up to the New England level. Few more native whites are to be secured; the negroes are unavailable; and immigrants cannot be attracted by low earnings.

With higher wages and longer experience will come an improvement in social conditions. We may expect shorter hours, less night work, and a mitigation of the evil of child labor. The employees will gradually become accustomed to town life and learn to use their incomes more wisely. Unfortunately thriftiness does not appear to make much headway among these people. The industry and the conditions surrounding it are still in a stage of transition. England had a worse experience early in the nineteenth century, and effective legislative regulations did not at once follow upon the establishment of the industry in New England. They all approach the same level, and the indications are that the South will take less time than its predecessors.

The competition from southern manufacturers was severely felt in New England, especially during the depression from 1893–97. With the return of business prosperity, however, there was a good market for the products of all the mills. And by the time of the next slump, conditions had readjusted themselves so that the depression was as serious in the South as in the North. Not only had the relative disadvantages of the North been counteracted by the changes which had taken place in the South, but the New England manufacturers had been forced by the competition to strengthen their own position. This they accomplished by economizing in selling costs, and especially by improving their organization. They introduced better systems of cost keeping and of factory management, and they cut down labor cost by new machines and higher speeds. The struggle was beneficial to the older mills, as well as to the new mills which began to undertake the manufacture of fine goods. That the fear of southern conquest has now almost entirely disappeared is attested by numerous fresh undertakings in New England. Of undoubted benefit to the southern people by furnishing a more productive employment for a large number of persons and by instilling a greater spirit of enterprise, the development of cotton manufacturing in the South has also indirectly benefited the New England manufacturers, and therefore has been a gain to the whole country.

CHAPTER IV

TECHNICAL DEVELOPMENT

Yarn and Cloth Manufacturing [1]

IN the last half of the eighteenth century the technique of cotton spinning and weaving was revolutionized by the great English inventors. But their inventions, remarkable as they were, were only the beginnings of improvements which have continued to the present time. What have the American manufacturers contributed to this development ? How far have their contributions been the result of conditions peculiar to this country ? On the answer to these questions depend to some extent our conclusions as to the stability of the basis on which our cotton manufacturing industry stands. In the United States a high wage-level has always encouraged economy in labor. If a manufacturing industry was to succeed in this country, the introduction of labor-saving machinery was essential. Moreover, during the last fifty years the most available supply of labor has been that furnished by the foreign immigrants. Those machines which required little skill, and the management of which could be easily learned, made possible the utilization of labor of that class. Let us see, then, how the American cotton manufacturers have met the industrial conditions with which they were confronted.

For convenience and greater clearness I will discuss the subject under five heads, — (1) preparatory processes; opening, carding, combing, drawing; (2) spinning; (3) spooling, warping, sizing; (4) weaving; (5) converting and finishing. But by way of preface it may be well to give an outline of these various processes in the manufacture of cotton goods.

The first process is opening and picking. After the cotton from a number of bales has been mixed and loosened up in the

[1] This chapter is reproduced, with some modifications, from my article in the *Quarterly Journal of Economics*, vol. xxiv, pp. 109–159.

bale-breaker, it passes to the opener where it is further loosened up. Then it goes to the pickers, where the fibres are separated and the dirt shaken out. From the finisher picker the cotton issues in the form of a lap ready for the card. The card removes whatever dirt remains, at the same time straightening out the fibres. As the rope of cotton, called " sliver," about the size of a man's thumb, comes from the card, it is mechanically coiled in a can. If the cotton is to be used for spinning fine yarn or hosiery yarn, it is next combed. But for ordinary purposes the cans of sliver are taken directly to the drawing-frame, where several ends, usually six, are drawn into one by means of two sets of rollers revolving at different rates of speed. All the processes up to this point are designed partly to clean the cotton, but more especially to secure greater evenness in length and weight. While they are adjusted somewhat differently, according to the grade of work desired, the object is the same throughout, a continual re-doubling and drawing.

The fly-frames next receive the cotton, and here the twisting of the sliver begins. There are always three sets, and in some mills four sets, of these fly-frames, — the slubber, intermediate, jack, and roving frames. These machines, though called by various names in different mills or in different sections, are the same in principle. Each succeeding frame draws out the cotton into a finer thread and puts in slightly more twist. From the last of the fly-frames the cotton passes on to the spinning machine, either a mule or a ring-frame.

The weft yarn is ready for the loom as soon as spun. But the warp yarn, that which is to form the threads lengthwise of the cloth, must be spooled, warped, and sized. On the spooler the yarn from several bobbins is wound on spools, for convenience in warping. A number of these spools are placed on a large frame called a creel, whence the yarn is re-wound on the beam of the warper. This beam, a small roller, varies in length with the number of ends which are to be wound upon it. The number of ends, in turn, varies according to the width of cloth to be made. The beam when filled, is carried to the slasher, where the yarn is sized, *i. e.*, run through a solution of starch, China clay, tallow, flour, and other ingredients, varying according to the particular formula of each mill. After this treatment the ends of the sized warp yarn are drawn into the harnesses of the loom, on which the cloth is woven. For converting and finishing the cloth there are numerous methods, and consequently a variety of machines, including those for dyeing, bleaching, and printing, also loop-cutters, shearers, brushes, calendars, as well as machines used in inspecting, folding, and packing.

Such are the main processes through which the cotton passes from the time it leaves the bale till it is ready to be shipped to the jobber or retailer. In all of these processes improvement has been made during the last fifty years, the period to which our attention is particularly directed.

I. Preparatory Processes

Opening, Carding, Combing, Drawing

The machines of this group loosen the matted cotton of the bale, remove the impurities and shorter fibres, straighten and lay parallel the fibres retained, and draw them out into a finer and finer thread of even weight. The object is uniformity in length of staple and in weight of lap and sliver.

In the machinery used for the initial processes the chief changes have been in the direction of perfecting machines already employed in 1860. The bale-breaker has come into more general use, so that, in the United States at least, hand labor is no longer used for loosening up the cotton after the bale has been opened. The heavy laps of cotton are thrown from the bale directly into the bale-breaker. The method of carrying the cotton from this machine to the next still varies widely in different mills. In a few mills the cotton is delivered automatically into bins, and thence fed by hand into the opener[1] or the automatic feeder. But the use of machines for feeding the cotton directly to the automatic feeder is becoming more general. For this purpose blowers are used to transport

---

[1] In England the opener is called a hopper-feeder.

the cotton from the room in which the bales are opened to the room in which the openers are located. The blower consists of a large pipe through which the cotton is forced by fans. At the present time, as a result of improvements, cotton in some plants is blown a thousand feet by this means. The economies of this method of transportation are two. In the first place, the bale-breaker can be put in a separate building, whereby the danger of fire is lessened, no cotton being stored in the mill proper. In the second place, cotton from several bale-breakers can be fed into the same pipe and a better mixture obtained.

For delivering the cotton directly to the automatic feeder or the opener several machines have been devised. Of these the Morton Automatic Distributor is probably the most economical. This machine, a recent American invention, consists of a steel trough extending over the feeders. Into this trough the cotton is delivered from the blower. The bottom of the trough is a travelling apron, and on the side over the hoppers of the feeders are gates. When a hopper is nearly empty, the gate in the trough above opens automatically, permitting the cotton to run out till the hopper is refilled. Then the gate closes automatically and the cotton in the distributor passes on till it comes to the next open gate. This machine saves floor space, since no bins are required and no cotton is piled on the floor behind the openers. It also saves labor, since after the cotton is fed into the bale-breaker it does not have to be handled again till it has come from the breaker-picker.

The cotton is fed automatically from the opener to the first or breaker-picker. If the openers and pickers are in the same room, a combination machine is commonly used. Otherwise the cotton is carried from the opener to the picker by a blower or a trunk. The methods depend upon the arrangement of the plant and the judgment of the superintendent, but the principles are the same. After the cotton comes from the breaker-picker, it is passed as a rule through an intermediate and a finisher-picker, though in some mills the intermediate picker is omitted. These machines, both openers and pickers, have

been greatly improved since 1860, especially by English manufacturers. The most prominent contribution was Lord's feed-
regulator (1862), which automatically adjusted the feeding
of the picker so as to secure even laps.

While the openers and pickers in use in England and the
United States are very similar and are run at practically the
same speeds, there are several significant contrasts. In the
first place, there are still a few English mills in which the cotton
from the bales is loosened up by hand without the employment
of a bale-breaker. But this primitive method is rare. In the
next place, within the last ten years at least three similar devices
have been put into use in England for automatically transferring the cotton from the bale-breaker to the opener. Unlike
the Morton Automatic Distributor, these appliances connect
a single bale-breaker with one hopper-feeder, and the two
machines are located in the same room. The latter arrangement
does not cause as great inconvenience as it would in America,
since the English mills rarely have a separate warehouse but
store their cotton in one of the rooms in the mill proper. Where
these feeders are in use, means are provided for automatically
stopping the bale-breaker when the hopper of the opener is
full of cotton. The saving in cost of attendance is said to be
fifty per cent.[1]

The proportion of English mills equipped with the automatic
feeder was estimated in 1910 by one of the machinery manufacturers to be sixty per cent, the other forty per cent having
the cotton from the bale-breaker delivered into bins. The latter
practice continues because of its advantage for certain grades
of work. It permits of a better blending where different kinds
of cotton are mixed, and by permitting the fibre to lie loosely
in the bin for a time the moisture becomes more nearly equal
throughout the whole mass. This method is also advantageous where it is not possible to keep the breaker running
constantly on the same mixture for the same machines, *i. e.*,
where one bale-breaker serves for several openers not operated
on a single grade. These conditions are found in the mills

[1] A. F. Barker, *Textiles*, p. 328.

spinning high grade yarn. As the cotton passes on its way through the pickers, sometimes called scutchers or lappers, there is no essential difference in the method of treating it in the two countries, except that one or two additional machines are frequently interposed in England.

For transporting the laps from the picker room to the card room the newer English mills are equipped with a device not yet introduced in America, so far as I know, — a mono-rail track along which pass trucks bearing the laps in a vertical position. It requires no extra room, and its use is far less laborious than carrying the lap on the shoulder. It is a minor detail, but none the less interesting, as it shows the attention given to small matters.

The English have taken the lead in improving the card. They have, in fact, brought about a revolution in carding since our Civil War, by the introduction of the revolving-flat card. The stationary-flat card had been improved in the 'fifties by Wellman, an American, who introduced a device for automatically stripping the flats.[1] In those American mills which had not previously adopted it, this type of card came into general use immediately after the war. But about the same time the English manufacturers were developing the revolving-flat card. On this card the flats are arranged to move in a sort of endless chain, part of them at work and part exposed to be cleaned. It is built entirely of steel, whereas the frame of the Wellman card was wooden. The steel construction makes possible more accurate adjustment; the card can now be set to one-thousandths of an inch, and adjusted minutely to the grade of work desired. It also can be more easily cleaned, more easily and more accurately ground, and less floor space is required. But of especial interest to us is the fact that the output both per machine and per operative is greater.

The principle of this revolving-flat card is said to have been known since 1834, but it was not taken up till 1857.[2] The first revolving-flat cards were then introduced in England,

[1] R. Cowley, *History of Lowell*, p. 145.
[2] 12th *U. S. Census*, vol. ix, p. 43.

and after the "cotton famine" gradually replaced the old roller-and-clearer cards. Even before 1867 some revolving-flat cards were imported into the United States,[1] and in 1883 a card of this type was first made in this country. Yet it was not till after 1885 that the rapid replacement of the stationary-flat cards began.[2] By the present time, however, the few remnants of the old style cards in our mills are being thrown out.

The improvement of carding machinery by the English manufacturers is significant of the attention which they have always given to the introductory processes, — the same attention which resulted in the improvements in opening and picking machinery. This characteristic was shown early in the nineteenth century, for Montgomery, in 1840, commented on the better carding in English mills.[3] And very recently Mr. Whittam noted a similar difference.[4] The greater waste in carding in American mills is explained by the extra labor cost of preventing this waste and also by the desire of the American manufacturers to get rid of a larger percentage of the short fibre than is removed in England. The American manufacturers economize in labor rather than in raw cotton, and in order to obtain the maximum output per operative push their machinery harder, thus impairing the quality of the work, perhaps, and causing more waste. In the main, however, there is no great difference in the machines or in the speed at which they are run, in the two countries. The improvements have been made in England, but they have been adopted in the United States. And the saving has probably been greater for the American manufacturer, inasmuch as the reduction of the labor cost of carding, if relatively the same, must have been greater absolutely in our mills. Further,

[1] New England Cotton Manufacturers' Association, *Transactions*, no. 3 (1867), p. 21.

[2] A German modification of the revolving-flat card has attained success in its own country but is practically unknown elsewhere. During the last two decades the Alsatian Machine Manufacturing Company has been perfecting a card on which the flats move in a direction opposite to that of English designed machines. Its chief virtue is asserted to be a better cleaning of the fibre.

[3] J. Montgomery, *Cotton Manufacture*, p. 32.

[4] W. Whittam, Jr., *Report on England's Cotton Industry*, p. 19.

these cards require little skill on the part of the operative except for the few grinders necessary, and consequently the immigrant can be used for this work. The revolving-flat card, therefore, is adapted to the conditions in both the United States and England.

The cotton combing machine was invented in France by Heilmann in 1845.[1] Later it was improved in England. Its use in American mills has been very limited until recent years. This limitation was due to the fact that the comber, which separates the long fibres and combs out the short ones so that the staple can be spun to greater fineness or with looser twist, is employed only in the manufacture of fine yarns or hosiery yarns. Since the recent development of the production of these yarns with the rise of the knit-goods industry and the increase in the output of fine cloth, more combers have been installed. Up to 1897 all combers in American mills were imported.[2] In that year, however, an American cotton machinery firm introduced a new and improved comber. About the same time similar improvements were made in England and in Germany,[3] showing that other cotton manufacturing countries were feeling the need of reducing the cost of producing combed yarn. The principle of all of these new combers was that of the Heilmann, the differences being in details. In the American comber (to take this for illustration) the speed was increased from 85 or 90 nips per minute to 130 and 135 nips per minute, the number of heads per machine from six to eight, and the width of the lap from 8¾ inches to 12 inches. Yet the quality of the work was not impaired. The effect of these improvements has been to cut in two the labor cost of combing,[4] doubling the output per operative. The saving on the English or Nasmith comber,[5] and on the German combers, the Montfort and Alsatian, has

---

[1] J. Zipser, *Textile Raw Materials and their Conversion into Yarn*, p. 169.

[2] National Association of Cotton Manufacturers, *Transactions*, no. 82, p. 340.

[3] New England Cotton Manufacturers' Association, *Transactions*, no. 69, pp. 342–346; no. 78, pp. 183–194; no. 82, p. 342.

[4] *Ibid.*, no. 82, p. 344.

[5] The improvements embodied in the Nasmith comber, manufactured by Hetherington, were particularly important in making it possible to comb cotton of shorter fibre.

been nearly as great. In fact, many American manufacturers prefer the foreign-made combers and use them in their mills. This preference may be due in part to prejudice, but very likely to more careful construction of the foreign machines, whereby the higher initial cost resulting from the import duty is counterbalanced. The economy in labor is about the same in either case, and, as in carding, the saving has been absolutely greater for the American manufacturer.

Combers are not in general use in this country, however, since the use of the comber necessitates several additional handlings. Not only must the cotton be combed, but the sliver from the card must first be transformed into a lap on the sliver lapper to prepare it for the comber, and usually is also put through a ribbon lapper to secure greater evenness. Each of these processes enables greater doubling and drawing, whereby the uniformity is improved, but the extra labor involved causes a considerable increase in the labor cost. This is an important reason for the greater cost of manufacturing fine yarns and knitting yarns. None the less, the improvements in the comber have promoted the manufacture of fine goods and of knit goods in the United States.

Since 1860 no change has been made in the drawing-frame except to improve its construction. The railway-head, which collects the slivers from several drawing-heads and draws them into a single sliver, has, however, been abandoned by most American manufacturers. Some mills now employ only a single process of drawing. And where two sets of drawing-frames and a railway-head were formerly used, the American manufacturers have adopted the English practice of using three sets of drawing-frames,[1] since the machinery is simpler and more easily regulated. Not only has the construction of the drawing-frame been made more accurate, but its efficiency has also been increased by improvements in the stop-motions which were in use before 1860.[2] Now the machine stops if

[1] New England Cotton Manufacturers' Association, *Transactions*, no. 71, p. 259.

[2] The first stop-motions for the drawing-frame were invented at Saco, Maine, in 1832, by Samuel Batchelder. (S. Batchelder, *Early Progress of the Cotton Manufacture*, p. 8÷.)

the back sliver breaks, if the front sliver breaks, or when the can is full. The electric stop-motion, which has come into general use, is the most important of the innovations. The result has been to enable the operative to tend more machines, thus reducing the labor cost, and to turn out product of better quality.

The progenitor of the fly-frame was the speeder, invented by Danforth, an American, in 1820.[1] Other types of speeder followed. One of these speeders, widely used in American mills in 1840, twisted the roving by means of running it through belts passing in opposite directions.[2] The English manufacturers, however, radically improved the speeder [3] and eventually evolved the present type of fly-frame. By 1860 speeders had been largely superseded in American mills by fly-frames such as are used today, except that the modern machines are longer and work more accurately.

The lengthening of the frame has made it possible for the operative to tend more spindles. But of more importance, — in fact the thing which has made feasible the greater length of the frame, — has been the perfecting of the machine. Roller bearings have been introduced, and the construction improved throughout. Since 1875, electricity has been applied to the stop-motions of the fly-frames, producing economies similar to those accruing from its use on the stop-motions of the card and drawing-frame.[4] For the perfecting of these fly-frames the cotton manufacturing world is largely indebted to the English manufacturers. It is true that some improvements have been made in this country, as for example that recently introduced by a Boston firm, whereby the arm of the flyer is changed so as to increase the output per spindle. But in the main the changes have originated in England, and many English-made fly-frames are to be found in American mills. As between the two countries, the machines are similar and run at about the same speeds. The improvements have, however, been of especial advantage to the American manufacturer since

---

[1] S. Batchelder, *op. cit.*, p. 72.
[2] J. Montgomery, *Cotton Manufacture*, p. 61.
[3] *Ibid.*, p. 60.
[4] Centennial Exhibition, 1876, *Reports and Awards*, vol. iii, Group 8, p. 19.

the labor cost has been greatly lessened by increasing the output per machine and per operative.

From this survey of the processes introductory to spinning, it appears that there are few differences in the machinery used in England and in the United States, and that manufacturers in the latter country have on the whole followed in the steps of their foreign competitors, even to the extent of using many English-made machines in all these processes except opening and picking. The readiness with which these inventions have been adopted in America shows how well they were adapted to the conditions in both countries. Their introduction has brought fully as great savings to the manufacturers in the United States by the reduction in the labor cost. The cumulative effect on the quality of the work has also been important. As the elementary processes have been improved, it has become possible to obtain better results in the succeeding stages of manufacture. The cotton is better prepared for the next machine and hence its work is facilitated.

Since the changes have been at least equally important to the American manufacturers, the question may well be raised as to how it happens that the English have taken the initiative in perfecting these machines. The explanation must be that the English have felt the greater pressure at these points. The necessity of economizing in raw cotton may have had some influence; there is less waste on the improved machines. But the chief cause has been the development of fine spinning in England. As other countries have established cotton mills which have competed in the coarse and medium grades of goods, the English manufacturers have engaged in the manufacture of finer and finer grades. In order to spin fine yarns it is necessary to exercise great care in the preparation of the cotton. This has attracted attention to the machinery for those processes. In the United States the manufacture of fine goods has begun to develop only recently. Consequently the American manufacturers have been content to adopt the improvements introduced by their English rivals, and in the manufacture of coarse goods they have received as much if not greater benefit.

II. Spinning

By spinning, the fibres of cotton are firmly twisted together to form yarn. In the preceding processes only enough twist is put in to make the fibres hold together while being doubled and drawn. At this stage the cotton is made into a firm, compact thread.

If the American manufacturers [1] have shown little initiative in improving the machines for the preparatory processes, the story for all the later processes is quite different. Here they have introduced new types of machines which to a certain extent are peculiar to this country. This characteristic is manifested to as great an extent in spinning machinery as in any.

There are two types of spinning machines, the mule and the ring-frame. The former is of English parentage and descent. The latter is an American product. As the machines are different in principle it may be well to give a brief description of each.[2]

First as to the mule. The bobbins of roving as they come from the roving frame are placed in rows on top of the machine. Then the ends of cotton are drawn through sets of rollers, geared so as to revolve at different rates of speed and thus draw out the sliver. From the rollers the thread of cotton passes to the spindles, which are mounted on a carriage. This carriage runs on an iron track, and as the rollers revolve the carriage backs away at a speed great enough to draw out the threads still more. The carriage withdraws to a distance of about sixty-three inches, and during this outward movement the spindles revolve, thus spinning the yarn. As the carriage returns the yarn is wound on the spindle to form the cone-

---

[1] By "American manufacturers" are meant both the cotton manufacturers proper and the machine manufacturers. In many instances the machine manufacturers introduce improvements or invent new machines. But these are not a success till they have been accepted by the mills. Not infrequently some person connected with the mill originates an important improvement. Hence the term is used in a general sense. It should also be added that the term "manufacturer" is applied indifferently to spinners and weavers in America, although used in England to designate the latter.

[2] A good brief description, but more in detail than that given here, can be found in J. Zipser, *Textile Raw Materials*, pp. 184–200. Similar descriptions are to be found in other technical books.

shaped cop, the process of building being regulated by the faller wire, a device which moves up and down to guide the yarn. In the meantime the rollers have been inactive, since they revolve only during the outward journey of the carriage.

The mule was invented in England in the eighteenth century. At first it was operated by hand, but about 1825 the self-actor was introduced. The greatest alteration in the mule since that date has been the increase in length, from 144 spindles to 500 in 1856 and 1,000 to 1,300 at the present time.[1] Other minor changes have also been made, — for example the adoption of the self-centring principle for the spindle in 1885,[2] and more recently the construction of an all-steel carriage. The mule has from the first been a very complex machine; few in any industry are more complex.

The ring-frame is less complicated. It consists of sets of rollers, similar to those in the mule, for drawing out the roving. But the spindles are directly underneath, and around each spindle is a steel ring. There are at least one hundred and twelve spindles per machine, and all the rings in each machine are fixed in a single frame. On each ring is a little wire, called a traveller, through which the thread passes to the bobbin on the spindle. As the spindle revolves this traveller is drawn around the ring, receiving its impetus from the yarn. Thus it revolves a little more slowly than the bobbin, and thereby the twist is put into the yarn. At the same time the yarn is wound on the bobbin, and in order to secure uniformity in winding the frame of rings moves up and down slowly. The ring-frame was invented by an American in 1831, but it did not at once replace the mule. In fact, in 1860 the number of mule spindles and the number of ring spindles in use in the United States were still about equal.

After the close of the Civil War, the American manufacturers directed their ingenuity to the betterment of spinning machinery, with the result that in the early 'seventies several improvements were made in the ring spindle. In these improvements

[1] A. F. Barker, *Textiles*, p. 328.   [2] 11th *U. S. Census*, vol. vii, p. 170.

Sawyer and Rabbeth were foremost, although other inventors soon added their contributions.[1] Several of the inventions were combined and the whole construction of the machine perfected. The spindle was reduced in weight, made self-acting, and its point of support changed to an elevated bolster. By these alterations the power cost was reduced, the speed increased, and the quality of the work improved. The limit of production on the ring spindle is the speed of rotation. Before these improvements were introduced the average speed was 5,500 turns per minute, although higher speeds were attained even before 1860.[2] By 1875 the average speed had been raised to 7,500 revolutions, and soon after it was further increased to 10,000 revolutions per minute. At the present time, while the average speed is still 10,000 revolutions, on fine yarns it sometimes is as high as 12,000 or 13,000 revolutions.[3] The speed is now limited by the rapidity with which the operative can make good piecings, and by the tendency of the traveller to fly off if the spindle revolves at a speed much over 10,000 turns per minute. These higher speeds require no more power than was employed to drive the old spindle at the lower speed. The work is better and the output per spindle greater. The length of the frame has been increased and the spinner can care for more spindles. As a result the output per spinner has been at least doubled.

There are essential differences, not only in principle, but also in operation, between the ring-frame and the mule. On the same grade of yarn the speeds of the ring spindle and of the mule spindle are about equal. But the product is one-third greater

[1] For an account of the development of the ring spindle see the address by W. F. Draper on "The History of Spindles," New England Cotton Manufacturers' Association, *Transactions*, no. 50, pp. 13–46. A good summary is also given by G. O. Draper, *Textile Texts*, 2d ed., pp. 141–154.

[2] Baird stated, in 1851, that the ring spindle "may be driven at a speed of 9,000 revolutions per minute, with perfect security, when making coarse yarn, and when operating upon the finer numbers 10,000 revolutions per minute is not an extraordinary speed to be attained." (Baird, *American Cotton Spinner*, p. 155.) Other accounts do not seem fully to justify this statement, and it is probable that the average speed then was considerably less.

[3] *Textile World Record*, vol. xxii, p. 81.

on the former,[1] since it spins continuously, whereas the latter spins intermittently. Mule yarn, however, is superior, since it is evener by reason of not being wound upon the cop at the same time that it is spun. As the thread leaves the rollers it is not of exactly the same diameter, and the twist from the revolution of the spindles is taken up to a greater extent by the thin places. But as the carriage is moving faster than the thread comes from the rollers, there is a strain on the yarn and the portions in which there is the least twist are drawn out, thus reducing the yarn to an even diameter. On the ring-frame, however, the spinning is coincident with the winding on the bobbin, hence inequalities are not neutralized. Moreover, the yarn spun on the ring spindle is subject to greater strain, from continually dragging around the traveller. The constant strain of the traveller of the ring-frame tends to make the yarn harder, and the amount of twist can be less easily regulated than on the mule. The harder ring-spun yarn is better adapted for the warp than for the weft, and was at first used only for warp yarn. But improvements making possible the spinning of softer yarn have resulted in the spinning of filling also on the ring-frame, although even now some manufacturers, particularly the English, maintain that they produce cloth with a superior " clothy " feeling by using mule-spun yarn. Other manufacturers declare that they can produce equally good cloth with ring-spun yarn.

However that may be, it seems probable that other factors have more to do in determining which method of spinning shall be used than the feeling of the product. Since mule yarn is not twisted as hard and its diameter is greater for the same count, it will absorb more sizing and presents a greater surface for the size to adhere to. Hence it is preferred for warp yarn in the manufacture of certain grades of coarse goods. Furthermore the mule has a decided advantage in the spinning of fine numbers since the greater strain on the ring-frame militates

[1] Nasmith (*Recent Cotton Mill Construction*, p. 152) estimates the output per spindle per week on 32's warp yarn to be 46 hanks (1.4375 pounds) with the ring-frame and 32 hanks (1 pound) with the mule.

against its use beyond a certain point. It is to be said, however, that the improvements in the ring-frame have lessened the strain and made it suitable for spinning finer and finer numbers,[1] so that in this country it is now employed to spin the warp yarn even in those mills which still use mule-spun weft.

There are still other differences. On the ring-frame wooden bobbins must be used,[2] while on the mule the yarn is wound on a little paper tube or on the bare spindle. The mule does not require doffing, *i. e.*, the removal of the yarn from the spindles, as frequently as the ring-frame, since the cops hold more yarn. This enables a saving of time in doffing the mule. Furthermore if the yarn is to be shipped out of the mill, the freight charge on the wooden bobbins is to be reckoned with. One writer estimates that while the cost of carrying paper cops is ten per cent of the freight charge on the yarn, the relative freight expense for the wooden bobbins is two hundred per cent.[3] It costs more to carry the bobbins than to carry the yarn which they contain. Moreover the bobbins must be returned. This is an extra expense; and there is the possibility of their complete loss, especially if the yarn is exported to another country. To be sure, much of the warp yarn is shipped in the form of spools, skeins, beams, or cones, but the filling is shipped on bobbins or as cops.

The difference in complexity is also important. The simpler ring-frame is less liable to break-down and consequent loss of time. It is more easily repaired in case of accident. The greater complexity of the mule necessitates more care on the part of the operative, and the more frequent breaks in the yarn require greater attention and more skill in piecing. As a result men are always employed as mule spinners. The danger which a woman's skirts would entail is another factor hindering the employment of women in this occupation. On the ring-frame,

---

[1] Several American mills are spinning 120's, and even finer yarn on the ring-frame. The ring has one advantage here in that the speed is greater than on the coarser counts.

[2] In England and Germany paper tubes are used instead of wooden bobbins in some ring spinning mills, but the bobbins yield better results.

[3] J. Lister, *Cotton Manufacture*, p. 51.

on the contrary, the necessary knowledge can be acquired in
a short time. Little skill is required and the spinners are usually
women or children. For social reasons it may be preferable
to have men rather than women and children employed in the
cotton mills. But from the manufacturer's point of view it
is often desirable to employ women and children.

The ring-frame also has an advantage in that it takes up less
floor space and gives greater facility for lubrication. But
the most important differences between the ring and the mule —
to sum up — are those in complexity, in the use of bobbins
and cops, and in the yarn itself. It is by reference to these
that we can explain why it is that the ring has been adopted
to a relatively greater extent in the United States than in England.

As already stated, the ring spindle is an American invention.
It has been perfected by Americans,[1] and is most widely employed
by the American manufacturers. The attention which it has
received is shown by the number of patents taken out on ring
spindles in the United States, — no less than three hundred
and seventy-three between 1870 and 1903.[2] As a result of the
improvements the ring-frame has largely superseded the mule
in this country, except for the spinning of fine yarns and hosiery
yarns. In 1870 the number of ring spindles was but slightly
greater than the number of mule spindles. Since that date,
however, almost the entire increase has been in the number
of ring spindles. This is shown by the Census returns which
give separately the numbers of ring spindles and of mule spindles
for each Census year except 1880.

SPINDLES IN UNITED STATES

(*In millions*)

	1870	1890	1900	1905
Ring	3.7	8.8	13.4	17.9
Mule	3.4	5.4	5.6	5.2
Total	7.1	14.2	19.0	23.1

[1] English machine manufacturers have made occasional improvements in the
ring-frame, but they have been overshadowed by the American contributions.

[2] G. O. Draper, *Textile Texts*, 2d ed., p. 142.

Thus in 1905 there were more than three times as many ring spindles as mule spindles in operation in the United States. At the present time numerous mills are discarding worn out mules and replacing them with ring-frames. Hence the proportion of mules, in spite of the increase in the quantity of fine spinning, is becoming constantly less.

In Great Britain, on the contrary, the mule predominates. It is in that country that the mule has been developed to its present high standard of efficiency. Although the ring-frame was introduced into England during the 'seventies [1] and its use gradually extended, it has never been as extensively adopted by the British manufacturers. At the present time the number of mule spindles is five times as great as the number of ring spindles. In 1909, according to the returns to the International Federation of Master Cotton Spinners' and Manufacturers' Associations, there were 39,800,000 of the former and 7,900,000 of the latter in England. Instead of warmly receiving the ring-frame the English manufacturers bent their energies to the perfection of the mule. In 1860 the self-actor was used in the manufacture of only the coarsest yarns,[2] the hand-mules still being used for all other work. Gradually, however, the self-actor has superseded the hand-mule for all but the highest counts, so that today the hand-mule is used in England for spinning only the very finest yarns.

The reasons why the ring-frame predominates in America and the mule in England are to be found in the differing conditions of the two countries. It is not over-conservatism, nor preference for spinning by the more scientific method, which has induced the British spinner to cling to the mule while the American spinner has been introducing the ring-frame. Rather it is because the mule fits the needs of the British spinner better, while the ring-frame is peculiarly adapted to the conditions in this country.

In the first place, the English mills spin much more fine yarn than do the American mills. As the mule is used for finer yarns,

---

[1] J. Nasmith, *Recent Cotton Mill Construction*, p. 10.
[2] S. J. Chapman, *Lancashire Cotton Industry*, p. 70.

this partially accounts for the greater number of mules in England. Again, in spinning the lower counts more short-staple cotton is used in England than in this country. The English purchase more short staple, and they re-work more of the waste from the card and comber, thus economizing in raw material. This shorter staple would not stand the strain of the ring-frame as well since the ends would break more frequently. In the third place, the British manufacturers size the yarn more heavily for certain grades of cloth. In the United States there is no heavy sizing, and no coarse mule warp yarn is demanded for this purpose. Finally, we have an important factor in the separation of spinning and weaving in England, and their combination in this country. In England spinning and weaving are more generally carried on in separate mills. Relatively few establishments both spin and weave. Hence for the English spinner the use of the ring-frame would increase expense, in shipping weft yarn at least,[1] because of the freight charges on the bobbins. In the United States the yarn is usually spun and woven in the same mill. If woven in the mill where it is spun, it can be handled as conveniently on bobbins as on cops. This helps to explain why the use of the ring spindle has been restricted in England. So far as this country is concerned, however, the combination of spinning with weaving is as much a result as a cause of the preference for the ring spindle.

There are other factors, however, which make ring spinning adapted to cotton manufacturing in the United States. These are connected with the labor situation. The output per operative is greater upon the ring spindle than upon the mule spindle. In this country, where the scale of wages is higher, the manufacturers must seek to economize in labor, to reduce the labor cost. Even more important than the greater output per operative on the ring-frame, is the fact that less skilled labor is necessary. Thus the labor cost is further reduced. In Great Britain a class of skilled cotton mill operatives, almost a hereditary

[1] Ring warp yarn is frequently beamed at the spinning mill, and delivered to the weaver in that form. The practice is increasing, in spite of the handicap that the weaver incurs by not being able to supervise the warping.

class, provides an adequate supply of skilled mule spinners. In America, on the contrary, the cotton manufacturers have always had to adapt themselves to a class of shifting and unskilled workmen.

During the first half of the century, when the ring-frame was being introduced and when the operatives were native born, the labor force in the cotton mills was constantly changing. The employees looked upon the cotton mills as a convenient place whence to get a start in life. Once having obtained that start, they left for other employments, so that no skilled class was developed. Since the Civil War the foreign immigrants have invaded the cotton mills of New England. Some of these immigrants have come from Great Britain, and have been possessed of sufficient skill to become mule spinners. But not all of them became mule spinners. Many of them took up weaving or slasher-tending. Hence the English immigrants could not supply the entire demand for spinners, or even a considerable part of it. The ring-frame, unlike the mule, required little experience or skill. Consequently the wives and children of the French Canadian, the Irishman, the Pole, and the other foreigners that we find in the mill today, could be employed as ring spinners. Here, as in many other American industries, the possibility of employing the unskilled immigrants and the adaptation of machinery to that end has been an important factor in promoting the success of manufacturing.

The situation has been substantially the same in the South. The southern manufacturers also have had no supply of skilled labor to draw upon, and the ring-frame has been of equal importance to the rise of the industry in that section, by making possible the employment of unskilled native help.

It has been frequently stated, and is even now asserted by some employers themselves, that the troublesomeness of the mule spinners' union has led to the replacement of the mule by the ring-frame. It may have had something to do with it. But at present mules are being replaced in mills where there is not a mule spinners' union no less rapidly than in the Fall River mills where the mule spinners' union is considered to be the chief

disturbing factor. The fundamental reasons for the throwing
out of the mules from the American mills are those just stated;
the lower labor cost of spinning on the ring-frame, the greater
output per operative, and the possibility of employing " cheap
labor " for this work. In Great Britain the supply of skilled
labor, the separation of spinning and weaving, and the special
qualities of the product have perpetuated the use of the mule.

III. Spooling, Warping, Sizing

By these processes the warp yarn is prepared for the loom.
It is wound from the bobbins or cops of the spinning machine
on spools, thence to the beam of the warper. From this beam
the yarn is unwound, passed through the slasher, and then
rewound on another beam on which it is carried to the loom.

Most of the improvements in the spooler have originated in
this country and have been adapted to the needs of our manufacturers. The most important of these improvements has been
the introduction of the wire bobbin-holder, invented by Wade
in the 'seventies.[1] This holder has since been modified somewhat,
but only in detail. Its advantage consists in the possibility of
running the spooler at a higher rate of speed, and at the same
time lessening the wear and tear on the bobbins. Means have
also been provided for taking care of the empty bobbins. The
first device for this purpose, the chute, delivers the bobbins into
boxes by the side of the machine.[2] Recently the travelling belt
has been introduced, whereby the bobbins are collected into
boxes at the end of the spooler. By these appliances time is
saved and there is less loss of bobbins. The labor cost of spooling
has always been relatively high; hence the significance of these
improvements in cutting it down. They show how the American
manufacturers have sought to relieve the pressure.

Not only have the Americans made these improvements in
the spooler, but the English have been slow in adopting them.
The wire bobbin-holder is not at all common in England. It is
not adapted for spooling, or, as the English term it, winding the

[1] Centennial Exhibition, 1876, *Reports and Awards*, vol. iii, Group 8, p. 20.
[2] G. O. Draper, *Textile Texts*, 2d ed., pp. 184–185.

yarn from mule cops, but even in winding from ring bobbins many English mills still use the old style frames on which the bobbin is placed on a pin. The speed is not only lower on these machines, but more labor is involved in replacing empty bobbins with full ones. The ring bobbin, it may be remarked, has an advantage over the mule cop, in that the wire bobbin-holder can be utilized and there is none of the skewering necessary for cops. The American manufacturers by the use of the ring-frame, therefore, have profited not only in spinning, but in this process as well.

Another machine which has brought about a saving in the labor of spooling is the Barber Knotter. This little machine, invented by an American in 1900,[1] is a small affair, worn on the hand of the girl who tends the spooler. When a thread breaks, the two ends are put together in the machine, and by pressure of the thumb the ends are tied and the loose pieces cut off. The knotter saves at least ten per cent in the time of spooling. Moreover its economies do not stop there, since it ties the ends better than they are tied by hand. Consequently in warping the yarn of its tying, there are fewer breaks, and less time is lost in piecing. In weaving, its effects are no less apparent, since bad knots are very likely to cause imperfections in the cloth. The percentage of " seconds " in weaving is cut down by its use. Last but not least, the knotter not only reduces the labor cost by saving time, but also makes possible the employment of less skilled labor by doing the work which required most skill on the part of the operative.

The spooler may be on the point of disappearing from gray goods mills, since within three years a new creel has been invented by Messrs. Fessmann and Hammerle of Augsburg, Germany, which makes it possible to beam the yarn directly from the cops or bobbins. The chief object of spooling is to secure continuous threads of sufficient length for the operation of the warper. The latter would have to stop too frequently if single bobbins or cops were used. To obviate this difficulty, the new machine is devised

[1] New England Cotton Manufacturers' Association, *Transactions*, no. 72, p. 212.

with three cop-holders for each thread from any one of which the yarn can be unwound with equal facility. Thus by placing a cop on each holder and fastening the inside end of the first to the outside end of the second and uniting the second and third in the same way, a continuous thread of three cop lengths is available for each warper end. As the cop-holders become empty they are replenished without stopping the machine. From two to six girls, armed with Barber Knotters, are employed to keep the creel full. The warper is equipped with a regulator which prevents irregularity in strain and speed. The greatest economy is the elimination of the labor and power required for spooling, and the saving of the floor space previously occupied by the spoolers. There is also less waste of yarn and greater productivity per warper. The speed of the warper is higher since the strain is reduced, and no time is lost in creeling. The American manufacturers have not yet had opportunity to test this new machine, but if it has no more drawbacks than are at present apparent, it will probably find favor in this country.

The present type of beam warper was invented in England and was in use both in that country and in America before 1860. But it has been greatly improved during the last fifty years, especially by American manufacturers. The improvements have consisted in the general perfection of the construction, and in the application of superior speed regulators and stop-motions better than those invented in this country early in the century.[1] The result has been an increase in speed and in output per machine. At the same time the number of machines per warper-tender has become larger. At present one woman almost invariably tends four machines, whereas thirty or forty years ago there was one tender for every warper. In England the manufacturers have been less progressive in bringing their warpers up to date, and generally there is but one machine per operative. On the Continent hand machines have been employed for warping till comparatively recent years.[2]

---

[1] J. Montgomery, *Cotton Manufacture*, p. 86.

[2] G. Beaumont, *L'Industrie Cotonnière en Normandie*, p. 17; also R. Martin, " Die wirtschaftliche Aufschwung der Baumwoll-spinnerei im Koenigreiche Sachsen," *Jahrbuch für Gesetzgebung*, 1893, pp. 686–689.

The chain warper, which is used for the yarn dyed or bleached before being woven, has also been improved. The improvements have especially aided those manufacturers producing certain kinds of colored goods, such as stripes and ginghams. But the most important inventions in connection with this process have been those which aim to prevent snarls and breaks in the dye-house and in re-warping and quilling. This object has been attained by winding around the chain from end to end a thread which holds the yarn together.[1] After the yarn has been bleached or dyed this protecting thread must be unwound; and for this purpose a special machine, Straw's Patent, has been devised. These innovations, the product of American ingenuity, are of recent origin and reflect the greater attention which this class of work is receiving from the American manufacturers. The dyed warp yarn is re-beamed after the protecting thread has been unwound. The machinery for re-beaming is a spot yet untouched by the inventor, and the work is still laborious. But the introduction of the long-chain quiller for preparing the dyed weft yarn for the shuttle has reduced the labor cost of that operation. This long-chain quiller is another recent American invention. It requires but one operative, a woman or girl, who with the aid of this machine, does the work for which eight or nine men were formerly employed. Yet in spite of the reduction in the labor cost of preparing dyed yarn for the loom during the last ten years, the extra labor involved therein is still one of the chief reasons for the greater cost of manufacturing goods in which dyed yarn is used.

Since 1860 the old dressing process for sizing the warp yarn has been superseded by the slasher.[2] The slasher consists primarily of a large cylinder with its under surface immersed in the sizing solution. Around this the yarn passes, then over other cylinders where it is dried before being wound upon another beam for the loom. The slasher was invented in England and adopted there before 1860, but was not imported

---

[1] G. O. Draper, *Textile Texts*, 2d ed., p. 212.

[2] The Yorkshire dressing process is still employed in England for preparing small quantities of colored warp yarn.

into the United States till 1866.[1] In regard to the economies
which resulted from its introduction, Mr. Atkinson in his report
for the Census of 1880,[2] stated that " in the use of the slasher
one man and a boy working in a thoroughly well ventilated room,
at a moderate degree of heat, took the place of seven or eight
men who had previously been employed in the same work in a
room which was of necessity kept at over 100° F., the atmosphere
saturated with sour starch."   Another statement of the saving
accomplished by the slasher was given by Mr. Tyron in an address
before the New England Cotton Manufacturers' Association
in 1894.[3] He said " one dresser formerly would only supply
warp for 100 looms on ordinary sheeting at a labor cost of from
$18 to $24 per week; at present one slasher will supply warp
for from 500 to 700 looms on the same class of goods at a cost of
from $9 to $12 per week."   In addition to this economy in labor
the quality of the product has been improved, since the yarn is
more evenly sized. The American manufacturers at first
hesitated to adopt this machine, but were not long in recognizing
its advantages and as early as 1875 it had come into general use.

In the United States about the same quantity of size is admin-
istered to yarn in all the mills, in contrast to the wide variation
in England. In American mills the amount of size which is
added to the yarn is usually about six per cent of the weight of
the yarn, enough to make the yarn weave well. But in Great
Britain the amount of size varies from less than fifteen per cent
(pure sizing) to over two hundred per cent (very heavy sizing).[4]
Thus some English cloth called cotton really contains as much,
or even more, of other material. When the yarn is sized more
than fifteen per cent the object is not so much to improve its
weaving quality as to substitute for cotton a cheaper material.
The practice of heavy sizing in England progressed by gradual
steps. The stress of competition first encouraged adulteration.[5]
Later the Russian War cut off the supplies of the regular sizing

[1] New England Cotton Manufacturers' Association, *Transactions*, no. 64, p. 208.
[2] 10th *U. S. Census*, vol. ii, p. 13.
[3] New England Cotton Manufacturers' Association, *Transactions*, no. 64, p. 199.
[4] *U. S. Daily Consular Reports*, March 22, 1907, no. 2824, p. 5.
[5] British *Parliamentary Papers*, 1833 (690), vol. vi, p. 326.

materials, and thus increased their price. As a result China clay came to be substituted.[1] Again, during the American Civil War, when the supply of raw cotton was curtailed, the English manufacturers used still more of the "Lancashire cotton," [2] and thus the practice of weighting cotton cloth spread. It was continued even after the supply of raw cotton resumed normal proportions, for the adulterated grades of cloth could be manufactured very cheaply. Because of their cheapness they have made a market for themselves, especially in Asia. The British manufacturers have frequently been accused of cheating their customers, of selling their goods under false pretenses. These accusations may have been true at an earlier date, but at the present time the customers are well aware of the character of the cloth which they are purchasing, and are satisfied with their bargain. The fact is that the goods are better adapted to their purses. At the same time their wearing qualities are not seriously impaired. The native purchaser does not wish to wash his clothes. He would not wash them even if half their weight would not be lost in the operation. He simply wears them till they wear out. By catering to this class of customers the English manufacturers have enlarged their markets. Just as they have reached out in the one direction to cater to the class desiring to buy very fine fabrics, so have they reached out at the other extreme to the class of purchasers who can afford to buy only the cheapest goods.

The American manufacturer has been urged constantly to adopt this method of heavy sizing to expand his foreign trade. Why has he failed to accept this advice? In the first place, as already pointed out, the yarn spun on the ring-frame is not so well adapted to taking a heavy size. Hence the method of spinning more economical for the American manufacturer is not so well suited to this purpose as is that of the English manufacturer. Furthermore, for heavy sizing more supervision is necessary. It is to the advantage of the American manufacturer to economize in labor for spinning and sizing rather than in raw

---

[1] British *Parliamentary Papers*, 1872 (c. 221), p. 2.
[2] *Ibid.*, p. 2; also R. Marsden, *Cotton Weaving*, p. 325.

cotton. All these reasons, however, are less important now than they have been in the past. New appliances facilitate the spinning of more loosely twisted yarn on the ring-frame, and if the heavy sizing were done on a sufficiently large scale the American manufacturer could probably turn out this class of goods as cheaply as is done in England. But the American manufacturer has not yet been compelled to turn regularly to foreign markets for the disposal of large quantities of cloth. To carry on the trade in heavily sized goods profitably a large market would be necessary, since the cost of frequently changing the slasher from heavy sizing to pure sizing, and vice versa, would be prohibitive. The machine can be run far more economically on a single grade of work. Consequently so long as a rapidly expanding domestic market continues to absorb the bulk of the cloth manufactured in American cotton mills, so long will the American manufacturer neglect other markets where the competition is keener. Inasmuch as there is no outlet for heavily sized goods in the domestic market, he cannot advantageously run part of his machinery on that grade of work. It is not because the American manufacturer is more honest that he has failed to develop a trade in heavily sized goods. It is because he has found other lines more profitable.

Let us return, after this digression, to our history of the technical development in the remaining departments, — the weaving and finishing processes.

IV. WEAVING

To make the cloth the threads are interwoven according to the pattern desired. The threads lengthwise of the cloth, called the warp, are sub-divided into two or more sets, which are alternately raised and dropped to allow the shuttle to pass under and over them. The yarn crosswise of the cloth, called weft or filling, is carried by the shuttle, and if only one color of weft is used a single shuttle is sufficient. But for certain fancy goods and especially for ginghams, in which there are several colors of weft, a drop-box loom is used, the shuttles being placed one on top of the other so that they can be brought into place at the proper time by the up and down motion of the box.

After the warp has been sized, the ends must be drawn through the harness of the loom. The harness consists of a frame of heddles, — cords or wires with eyelets in the centres, through each of which a warp thread is drawn. The number of harnesses per loom varies from two upward according to the complexity of the pattern to be woven.[1] Although several unsuccessful attempts[2] had been made to devise a machine for drawing in the warp, until very recently the ends were still laboriously drawn in by hand. But during the last ten years two machines have been invented in this country which are supplanting the girls formerly employed for drawing in.

The first of these machines is a warp tier, the Barber Warp-Tying Machine. It was offered to the trade for the first time in 1904. To quote from one of the men engaged in introducing it, " the broad principle of the machine is to tie the ends of the last of an old warp to the corresponding ends of a new warp." [3] When one warp is nearly used up, the ends are cut so as to leave a short piece of each thread in the harness. Then, when it is desired to weave another piece of cloth of the same pattern, the harness, with these ends still in it, is brought to the tying machine, which ties together, one by one, the ends of the old warp and those of the new. The principle of the machine is the same as that of the spooler knotter previously described. It ties about two hundred and fifty knots per minute, and does the work of twenty girls. Drawing in by hand had always been a relatively heavy expense to the manufacturer; by the use of this machine the labor cost is cut down two-thirds.[4] The disadvantage in its use is the necessity of keeping many harnesses on hand, one for each of the different patterns. For every variation in the number of ends or in the number of harnesses per pattern, a different set of harnesses must be kept in readiness. Moreover the machine cannot distinguish colors. Hence it can be used only on plain work. But those mills which make only three or four styles of plain cloth are not hindered by these disadvantages.

[1] The most complex patterns are woven on Jacquard looms, on which each warp thread is independently controlled.

[2] National Association of Cotton Manufacturers, *Transactions* no. 81, p. 286.

[3] *Ibid.*, no. 78, p. 226.　　　　　[4] *Ibid.*, p. 227.

The second of these inventions actually draws the ends through the heddles.[1] There is no accumulation of harnesses as under the other system, but the drawing-in machine does not turn out as much work as the tying machine and wears out the heddles more rapidly. Yet it does effect a marked saving over hand labor, since one man operating a drawing-in machine will draw in about six times as many warps per day as a girl can draw in by hand on the same grade of goods. This machine is not limited to simple patterns. By means of a Jaquard arrangement, it can be used for six harness work. But, like the tying machine, the drawing-in machine cannot detect differences in color. Hence it, too, can be used only for plain work. Girls are still employed for drawing in the warps where there are threads of different colors. And even on plain work the machines have not entirely superseded the girls, owing to the conservatism of some managers. These machines are the result of the burden which the American manufacturers have felt because of the relatively high labor cost of drawing in the warps by hand, and the difficulties of obtaining labor for this work. The growth of the industry in this country had intensified the latter difficulty.

The introduction of the warp-tying machine and the drawing-in machine has not only cut down the labor cost to the manufacturer, but has also made possible the mechanical performance of work which was a severe strain upon the mill workers. Drawing in requires very close application on the part of the operative, who has to sit in the same position for several hours, and watch unremittingly every movement which she makes. The release from this exhausting work will be of benefit to the health of the operatives.

While the danger of mistakes prevents the use of these machines for drawing warps in which there are various colored threads, the bulk of the goods manufactured in this country are plain. Hence the machines are adapted to the needs of the majority of our cotton mills. As a result of their introduction one of the

[1] Described in National Association of Cotton Manufacturers, *Transactions*, no. 81, pp. 286 ff.

remaining hand processes in the manufacture of cotton cloth is at the present time passing out of existence.

For weaving, the power loom had entirely superseded the hand loom in American cotton mills long before 1860, and since that date has also shared in the general technical progress. The loom invented by Lowell in 1814 was a cam loom,[1] the English type, introduced by Gilmore a year later, a crank loom.[2] The latter method of driving gradually gained a predominancy.[3] An early American invention of importance was Draper's self-acting temple (1816). The Cartwright loom (1786) had been provided with temples for stretching the cloth to its full width as fast as it was woven, but the Draper temple was an important innovation. Self-acting temples were not adopted in England till long after they were in general use in America.[4] In 1860, however, English and American plain looms were on a nearly equal footing.

The dobby, for controlling a larger number of harnesses than can be used on a plain loom, was invented in England, although it is said to be an adaptation of the chain motion devised by William Crompton of Worcester, Massachusetts, in 1837. George Crompton brought the dobby to America in 1878, and then proceeded to improve it. Similarly the drop-box loom which had been invented by Robert Kay and adapted to power in England in 1845,[5] was improved after its introduction into the United States. These looms received attention earlier in England since the production of fancy fabrics was much larger in that country.

In consequence of the numerous improvements of the loom the speed was increased and the amount of necessary attention reduced. In 1879 one weaver of cotton cloth could tend five or six looms running at a speed of 130 to 140 picks per minute, whereas in 1832 in producing the same fabric one weaver tended

---

[1] Samuel Webber, *Manual of Power*, p. 31.

[2] *Ibid.*, p. 35.

[3] *Ibid.*, p. 31.

[4] J. Montgomery, *Cotton Manufacture*, p. 102; S. Batchelder, *Early Progress of Cotton Manufacture*, p. 87.

[5] *Encyclopedia Brittanica*, 11th ed., vol. xxviii, p. 446.

two or three looms which ran at 70 picks per minute.[1]   Between 1860 and 1880 the improvements in the plain loom caused an increase of twenty per cent in the output per machine.[2]   After 1880 the changes were not so much in the direction of higher speeds as in more perfect work and especially the reduction of the amount of oversight required, which enabled the manufacturer to give more looms to each weaver.   The Census report of 1880 stated[3] that a weaver with six looms would produce about 1,500 yards of cloth per week.   That average would hold true today, as representing the output per loom, but instead of four or six looms[4] a weaver now has eight, ten, or even a larger number.

The improvement in the quality of the product of the loom and the diminution of the amount of necessary attention have been facilitated by the application of better stop-motions,[5] — devices which stop the loom automatically when a warp thread breaks, or when the shuttle is out of place.   Those warp stops which had been introduced prior to the Civil War were adapted only to looms weaving coarse cloth.   With the increase in the manufacture of fine and medium goods it became desirable to apply warp stop-motions to the looms on those grades, and as a result of the successful use of finer and thinner wire in their manufacture,[6] they are now found in every up-to-date mill on all grades of work.   These stop-motions have received their greatest improvements and exploitation in this country.   As a result of the use of the stop-motion and an increase in the length of the shuttle (1905) the piece rate for weaving was reduced thirty-three and one-half per cent in Fall River.[7]

The most significant feature in the development of looms has been the introduction of the automatic loom.   Of several types of automatic loom, one stands out preëminently, the Northrop

---

[1] National Association of Wool Manufacturers, *Bulletin*, vol. ix, p. 40.

[2] 10th *U. S. Census*, vol. ii, p. 52.

[3] *Ibid.*, p. 52.

[4] In 1860 there were practically no weavers tending more than four looms.

[5] New England Cotton Manufacturers' Association, *Transactions*, no. 68, p. 319.

[6] *Ibid.*, p. 319.

[7] Mass. Bureau of Statistics of Labor, *Bulletin* No. 36, p. 63.

loom. This loom was put upon the market in 1894 by the Draper Company, a perfected machine. It was the outcome of the efforts of five inventors devoted to this task for several years with the definite object of producing a practicable automatic loom. The fundamental principle of the machine was originated by Northrop, whose name it bears, but at least equal credit is due the Draper Company, because of the foresight and ability of their managers and experimenters through whose efforts success was ultimately achieved. The new features embodied in it are, in the words of one of the inventors, " a bobbin changing device, a filling hopper from which bobbins or cops are automatically transferred to the loom shuttle, a peculiar shuttle which can be threaded automatically by the motion of the loom, devices that act to stop the loom if the shuttle is not in position, and a warp stop-motion to prevent the making of poor cloth." [1] The most important of these innovations is the weft changing device. The shuttle is not changed when it has exhausted the thread on a bobbin, but the empty bobbin is automatically thrown out, and a full bobbin just as automatically put in its place. This change is made so quickly that the speed of the loom is not retarded. The amount of time which was formerly spent in the stoppage of the loom on account of exhausted shuttles is thus saved. On the common loom the shuttle has to be changed every eight minutes or oftener.[2] The Northrop loom stops only when a warp thread breaks or the shuttle is out of position, thus saving perhaps one hundred stops a day.[3] The use of one shuttle eliminates a large amount of labor in setting the pick, *i. e.*, adjusting the mechanism which drives the shuttle. And the saving in the wear and tear of the machinery from frequent stoppage is not inconsiderable. In order to bring these results to perfection, a reliable warp stop was necessary, and it is in the designing of the Northrop loom that particular attention was bestowed upon

[1] New England Cotton Manufacturers' Association, *Transactions*, no. 59, p. 91.

[2] 12th *U. S. Census*, vol. ix, p. 44.

[3] In 1895, W. F. Draper estimated the saving in the number of stops per day to be 200; see New England Cotton Manufacturers' Association, *Transactions*, no. 59, p. 93.

the subject. This stimulated an interest which resulted in the application of a similar device to plain looms.

Another point, and one on which enough emphasis has not been laid, is the automatic threading device, a boon to the weaver who formerly had to thread the shuttle from five hundred to one thousand times a day,[1] sucking in the filling each time. In doing this he inhaled more or less cotton lint, to say nothing of sizing materials, dust, and dye-stuff. No wonder that weavers had been spoken of as a consumptive class! The automatic threading device has stimulated other manufacturers to devise means for mechanically threading the shuttle on plain looms.[2] Yet in many mills the shuttles are still threaded in the old way.

Since its first introduction the Northrop loom has been improved in various details so as to enable it to weave fabrics more nearly perfect and to adapt it to a wider range of work. At the outset it was necessary to use ring-spun filling, but by means of skewers mule cops can now be transferred to the shuttle as easily as bobbins. And it is no longer confined to the manufacture of coarse, plain goods. Several manufacturers are now successfully weaving fine cloth on Northrop looms, and other manufacturers are producing fabrics of more and more complicated patterns.[3]

The chief advantage of the Northrop loom consists in a saving of labor. It has reduced the labor cost of weaving one-half, a fact which is particularly significant since the labor cost of weaving previously constituted one-half of the entire labor cost of manufacturing cotton cloth. This saving has resulted from the increased number of looms per weaver. One weaver now tends from fourteen to thirty Northrop looms,[4] where before he tended six to eight common looms. At the same time less skill is required on the part of the operative. Notwithstanding this

[1] New England Cotton Manufacturers' Association, *Transactions*, no. 59, p. 93.

[2] *Ibid.*, no. 68, p. 325. This subject is receiving careful attention from the English weavers' union, with the expectation that self-threading shuttles may be universally adopted in that country. In 1911, the Massachusetts legislature enacted a law requiring the use of mechanically threading shuttles in all cotton factories in that state.

[3] G. O. Draper, *Textile Texts*, 2d ed., p. 252.

[4] In one Southern mill one weaver was tending 34 Northrop looms in 1909.

increased output of the weaver, there has been no lack of work for this class of mill operatives. Rather has the change relieved a strain felt by the manufacturers, who often found it difficult to obtain enough weavers. With the rapid expansion of the industry during the last fifteen years the difficulties of obtaining skilled weavers would have been much greater had it not been for the introduction of this loom. Yet the Northrop loom has not been adopted in all mills which are making goods that could be woven on it. Since the initial cost is heavy, many manufacturers have not deemed it profitable to scrap their plain looms. But it has been installed in most of the new mills, especially in the South. As the plain looms in the older mills wear out, they will, without doubt, be replaced by automatics.[1]

The Northrop and other automatic looms of analogous type were at the outset suitable for weaving only plain cloth and fabrics with stripes or figures formed by manipulation of the warp threads. It was a more serious problem to devise a means for automatically supplying weft to a drop-box loom, which uses filling of several colors.[2] A drop-box loom, it may be repeated, has two or more shuttle boxes, according to the number of colors of weft yarn. The boxes are placed vertically, one above the other, and their movement is made to conform to the details of the pattern which is being woven. The best known cloths woven upon drop-box looms are checks and ginghams. Some of these fabrics have very narrow weft stripes; hence the failure to change shuttles at exactly the proper moment, the passage of an empty shuttle, or the insertion of a thread of the wrong color, would produce a noticeable and serious fault. These stringent requirements for accuracy and the multiplicity of shuttle boxes were obstacles in the path of an automatic drop-box loom. Nevertheless the difficulties have been overcome.

In 1895, immediately after the appearance of the Northrop loom, Crompton and Knowles, loom manufacturers of Wor-

[1] The number of Northrop looms installed in American cotton mills up to January 1, 1911, was approximately 200,000, and several thousand had also been placed in European factories.

[2] This subject was discussed at slightly greater length by the author in the *Quarterly Journal of Economics*, vol. xxv, pp. 746–750.

cester, Massachusetts, began to experiment with automatic gingham looms. The first patent was taken out by Charles Crompton and Horace Wyman, and in 1905 a few such machines were placed in operation. During the following five years continual refinement and alteration materially improved this loom, which was adapted to the use of " filling of different colors inserted at pre-determined intervals, and equipped with the necessary detector and safety devices to admit of weaving practically perfect goods." [1]

The first examples of these automatic drop-box looms were equipped with circular revolving magazines from which the bobbins were supplied to the shuttles, and in which the bobbins were arranged in such an order that the machines always took yarn of the proper color. That form of magazine has been discarded, however, in favor of a vertical stationary magazine provided with a separate section for each color of weft yarn. Similarly, the original electrical detector has been largely superseded by a mechanical detector which feels the amount of thread on the bobbin at each passage of the shuttle. When a bobbin is nearly depleted another of the same color is automatically selected from the magazine. Yet it cannot always be introduced immediately into the shuttle, since the pattern may demand a shuttle from another box for the next pick. Consequently the selected bobbin is held in suspense until the shuttle for which it is intended again comes into action. The parts work in unison so that a fresh bobbin cannot be placed in the wrong shuttle. Several of the patents of the Northrop loom were utilized and great credit is due to that pioneer work. Nevertheless, the surmounting of the difficulties peculiar to an automatic drop-box loom is an achievement of the first order.

The automatic gingham loom runs at least as fast as the ordinary loom employed for similar work, namely 165 picks per minute, and occasionally exceeds that speed by five picks per minute. Therefore there is no loss in that direction. Moreover the automatic loom is more constantly in operation, inasmuch as it does not stop each time a bobbin is empty. Thus there is

---

[1] Quoted from circular published by the company.

a closer approach to its highest potential productivity. Of even more importance, particularly to American manufacturers, is the reduction in the amount of attendance required. In this country a weaver customarily tends six ordinary drop-box looms, but with the automatic loom the number is at least doubled and may be as high as sixteen per weaver. Although a recent innovation, one manufacturer has already installed two thousand of these looms and several others have ventured to try them.

With the introduction of the Crompton and Knowles loom one may prophesy that eventually all types of cotton looms will be provided with automatic weft-changing devices. The history of the power loom in the nineteenth century is being repeated by the automatic loom in the twentieth century.

In England the plain looms have undergone as great improvements during the last fifty years as have the plain looms in the United States. In the latter country, however, the under-pick loom is universally employed, whereas the English manufacturers use a different type, — the over-pick, loose-reed loom, invented by Dickinson of Blackburn, in 1828.[1]

The two types of looms are different in that the picking sticks, which propel the shuttle at each end of the loom, are for the over-pick fastened horizontally above the loom sley and shuttle boxes and for the under-pick are fixed to each end of the sley, passing through a slot in the lower part of the shuttle box.[2] The over-pick loom can be driven at a speed 20 to 40 picks faster per minute, or about fifteen to twenty per cent quicker than the under-pick. But the over-pick loom requires more careful attention to guard against the collection on the picker of dirt, which would fall upon the cloth and cause oil stains; and the higher speed more rapidly exhausts the yarn in the shuttle.

The English manufacturers prefer the over-pick loom since it can be run at a higher rate of speed, and a greater output per

---

[1] R. Marsden, *Cotton Weaving*, p. 88. This over-pick loom, sometimes called the Blackburn loom, was not altered for about twenty-five years and has since been changed only in minor details. The invention of this loom was especially influential in driving out the hand loom.

[2] H. B. Heylin, *Cotton Weaver's Handbook*, p. 110.

loom obtained.   But the number of looms per weaver in English mills is about one-half of that in American mills.   Consequently, although the speed of the looms is greater, the output per weaver is less in England.   The adherence of the English manufacturers to the over-pick loom is due in the main to the difference in labor conditions.   They have a larger supply of skilled weavers, and a somewhat lower wage scale.   Hence it is to their advantage to increase the output per machine even if the output per operative is less.   Moreover, owing to the strength of the labor unions in the English cotton industry, a weaver is paid at the same rate per cut without reference to the number of looms which he tends.   In American mills, on the contrary, a weaver is paid less per cut when he tends more looms.   Though the rate per cut is less, his total earnings are greater, because he " gets off " a greater number of cuts.   At the same time, the lower rate per cut effects a considerable saving to the manufacturer in the labor cost of weaving.   The American manufacturers have not adopted the over-pick loom because it requires more attention from the operative.   They have clung to the loom which gives the greatest output per weaver.

The hand loom remained in use on the Continent long after it had disappeared from American and English cotton mills.[1] In the United States the hand loom was not used in cotton mills after 1830, nor in England to any extent after 1860.[2]   But in France, as late as 1885 cotton cloth was being woven on more than 33,000 hand looms,[3] which was more than one-third of the total number of looms in the country at that time.   In Germany the use of the hand loom persisted even longer.   In 1861 only nine per cent of the looms in Germany were power looms,[4] and in 1908 Rieger's list showed about 3,000 hand looms in German cotton mills.[5]   About 4,500 of the looms in Switzerland at

[1] E. Helm, " An International Survey of the Cotton Industry," *Quarterly Journal of Economics*, vol. xvii, p. 422.

[2] W. J. Ashley, *British Industries*, p. 69.

[3] H. Lecomte, *Le Coton*, p. 368.

[4] A. Oppel, *Die Baumwolle*, p. 654.

[5] W. Rieger, *Verzeichnis der im Deutschen Reiche auf Baumwolle laufenden Spindeln und Webstühle*, ed. 1909.

the present time are hand looms.[1]   In Italy in 1903, 13,807
of the 78,700 looms employed for weaving cotton cloth were
hand looms[2] and the number is still large.[3]   The antiquated
type of machine has persisted longer in these countries because
of the difference in labor conditions.   With a large supply of
more or less skilled labor willing to work for low wages, there
has not been the same incentive for the introduction of labor
saving machinery.   The lack of this incentive, the conservatism of the managers and of the workmen, and the greater cost
of the more expensive power loom, have retarded the extinction
of the hand loom.   The Continental manufacturers have econo-
mised in capital; the English manufacturers, and to a greater
extent the American, in labor.

A similar hesitancy has been shown by the European manufacturers in accepting the Northrop loom.   Although in England
this loom has secured a firm foothold, it has not been accepted
there nearly so readily as in the United States.   Its inventor,
an Englishman by birth,[4] attempted to induce English machine
manufacturers to take up his idea.   Failing in that, he came
to the United States, the " inventor's Paradise," [5] where his
suggestions were welcomed and developed.   For the same
reasons that its introduction has been slower, its use will probably be more limited in England than in the United States.
In the first place, the mule cop is not so well adapted to the
hopper of the Northrop loom as is the bobbin of the ring-frame.
Although this difficulty has been partly removed by skewering the
cops, that operation takes time.   Again, the loom has been
adapted but gradually to the weaving of fine goods, and even
now many of the fine goods manufactured in England could
not be woven advantageously on the Northrop loom.   Thus
there is a considerable field in England which it cannot reach,
a field which is not only absolutely, but relatively larger than
in the United States.   In spite of the advance in the production

[1] S. L. Besso, *Cotton Manufacturing in Switzerland and Italy*, p. 4.
[2] *Annuario Statistico Italiano*, 1907, p. 452.
[3] S. L. Besso, *op. cit.*, pp. 165 ff.
[4] T. M. Young, *American Cotton Industry*, p. 22.
[5] *Ibid.*, p. 136.

of finer cotton cloth in this country, the bulk of our output is still the coarse and medium grades of plain goods. Another retarding factor has been the risk and expense of introducing the new device.[1] In the United States, even, many manufacturers have delayed the installation of Northrop looms until their common looms should be worn out. Similarly in England the cotton manufacturers have been unwilling to scrap their machinery and put in these expensive looms so long as their old looms are still serviceable. The orders, moreover, are smaller in England, and the number of looms running upon a single pattern is generally less than in an American factory. Changes are more frequent in the mills of the former country and, what is more important, it is often impossible to avoid employing a Northrop loom weaver upon fabrics of several designs. When that is done the weaver cannot undertake the supervision of so large a number of machines. Finally, the attitude of the workmen has not favored the introduction of the automatic loom. While there has been no open opposition, the weavers do not look with favor upon the automatic loom and have not carefully sought to secure its best results. The employers have apprehended difficulty in inducing weavers to accept lower piece rates, and only with lower piece rates would the Northrop loom be a profitable investment. The English manufacturers, moreover, do not feel so great pressure to introduce labor saving machinery. Even were the loom to be generally adopted by them, the absolute saving would be less than in this country.

As in England, so in the other cotton manufacturing countries of Europe, the Northrop loom has been introduced but slowly. In France a few mills have experimented with it, but the number

---

[1] The high price of the loom has had a very deterrent influence on prospective purchasers. The loom aroused the interest of the European manufacturers, but its expensiveness has led them to search for a cheaper substitute. The scope of their experiments is indicated by the fact that I saw no less than eight types of automatic looms, all of domestic manufacture, in European cotton mills during the year 1910–11. This probably does not exhaust the list, since several of the looms were in operation only in the factories where they were invented, and it is reasonable to suppose that other experiments were being carried on more or less secretly in mills not visited.

of the new looms per weaver has been only from eight to ten,[1] about one-half as many as in the United States. Similar experiments in other countries do not succeed in bringing the average output per weaver up to that in the United States. Once more the lack of economy in labor in European cotton mills shows itself. The Northrop loom is not only the product of American enterprise, but it is peculiarly adapted to the industrial conditions prevailing in this country. Nevertheless, the widespread interest in automatic looms manifested by European manufacturers suggests that the plain loom will eventually be superseded, even in the more conservative countries.

In all of the processes in the manufacture of cotton cloth, the question of humidity is important. The machinery and the cotton passing through the machinery generate a certain amount of electricity which, by causing the cotton to curl up, affects the smoothness with which the work runs. Cotton manufacturing is therefore facilitated by a humid atmosphere which reduces the amount of electricity generated. Localities with an unusually moist climate formerly possessed a great advantage over the districts less favored in this respect, but during the last half of the nineteenth century American cotton manufacturers have devised means for artificially humidifying the atmosphere in their mills and are now able to regulate the moisture with a fair degree of accuracy. Not many American mills are without such an equipment, although a few still adhere to the old fashioned practice of injecting raw steam directly into the rooms. In Lancashire, as every one who has experienced its climate knows, the natural humidity is great and the mills less frequently find artificial humidification necessary. Yet there the practice of " steaming," especially where heavily-sized cloth was to be woven, became so serious that to protect the health of the operatives the Cotton Cloth Factories Act was passed. This prescribes the quantity of air per head and the maximum humidity. In the United States, unfortunately, no such protection is afforded.

A new device is being introduced in America at the present

---

[1] *Enquête sur l'Etat de l'Industrie Textile*, vol. iv, p. 77.

time which may make air moisteners unnecessary. This device attacks the problem from a different quarter by seeking to neutralize the static electricity in the machine and the cotton, through the generation of a counteracting current of electricity. The very simplicity of its principle makes it seem almost strange that no one has applied it before. If it proves a success, as it bids fair to, the necessity of humidification will be done away with, and thereby the health of the operatives benefited and the manager relieved of the trouble of regulating the degree of humidity.

V. CONVERTING AND FINISHING

There is great variety in the machines for converting and finishing cotton cloth, since, after it has been woven, it may be bleached, printed, dyed, or mercerized, and then put through numerous other machines to finish it, before being shipped. Each of these machines and processes has a history of its own. A brief summary will suffice to show the general tendencies of the development.

The methods of bleaching have undergone few changes during the last fifty years, or even during the last century. With more accurate knowledge of the chemicals employed it has become possible for the bleachers to adjust their methods more scientifically to the different grades of work. The machinery in general, and the boiling kiers in particular, have been improved, so that a greater quantity of work can be turned out per machine with less labor.[1] Better facilities for drying have also been an important factor in lessening the amount of time necessary for the process.[2] The methods and machinery for bleaching are much the same in Europe and America, although there is, perhaps, more machinery in American bleacheries, and the cloth is run through at a somewhat greater speed. Because of this difference in speed a greater quantity of cloth is bleached with a given amount of labor.

As in bleaching, so in printing, no new types of machines have been introduced during the last half-century. Cylinder

[1] New England Cotton Manufacturers' Association, *Transactions*, no. 77, p. 170.
[2] See *infra*, p. 97.

printing was first used in England in the last quarter of the eighteenth century, and in the United States in 1810.[1] The machine was gradually elaborated so that more and more rollers could be used, and patterns embodying a larger number of colors printed. About 1876, an Englishman (Gadd) invented the double-faced machine which printed eight colors simultaneously on both sides of the cloth.[2] But the greatest change has come about in the coloring materials, as a result of the discovery and application of the coal-tar colors.[3] A young Englishman, Perkin, discovered the first of these in 1856, and in 1858 Hofmann, a German, discovered aniline red. Since then many more have been found. In the development of this auxiliary industry the Germans have been preëminent and consequently have developed a large export trade in these products. While some synthetic dye-stuffs are now manufactured in this country, the greater part used in our mills is still imported from Germany. The introduction of these dyes has brought about a revolution by reducing the labor cost and widening the range of colors. All cotton manufacturing countries, however, have benefited to the same degree from these inventions.

Concurrently with this change in coloring materials has come an improvement in the designs of American prints. But the one has been rather a means than a cause of the other. The improvement in design has been the result of the general development of the cotton manufacturing industry, and particularly of the rise of cotton manufacturing in the South. The competition of the southern mills has forced the New England manufacturers to produce goods of a higher grade. But even yet there is little originality in American designs; they are largely copied from Paris. Moreover, the American manufacturers use fewer designs, and turn out a much greater quantity of cloth of any one design, than do the European manufacturers. This

[1] 8th *U. S. Census,* " Manufactures," p. 18.

[2] *L'Industrie de Mulhouse,* p. 368.

[3] A good description of these discoveries is given by A. Sansone, *Recent Progress in Dyeing and Calico Printing,* vol. i; also *Cyclopedia of Textile Work,* vol. vi, pp. 149–235; and A. H. Allen, *Commercial Organic Analysis,* vol. iii, pp. 100–104.

is because of the economies of large scale production.   It costs
less per yard to print large quantities of a single design.   There
is an additional saving in that, where fewer designs are printed,
it is not necessary to keep so many copper rollers in stock.[1]

The invention of the artificial dye-stuffs obviously has been
an important factor in the progress not only of printing
but of dyeing, a progress which has been especially rapid since
the discovery of " Congo red " by Böttiger in 1884.[2]   This was
the first of the so called " direct cotton dyes," and it has been
followed by many others.   As in printing, the cost of dye-stuffs
has been reduced and the results improved.   This has led to
an increase in raw-stock dyeing.[3]   For ginghams and other
goods in which yarns of different color are used, the dyeing of
the raw stock eliminates the expense of preparing the yarn for
dyeing, and of re-warping or quilling it after it has been dyed.[4]
But there are some disadvantages which, partially at least,
offset this saving.   It is true that one difficulty has been overcome.   Formerly the dyed cotton did not spin well, but this
has been remedied by the introduction of single-dip dyes.   Yet
there is still the loss of dye-stuff which colors the cotton that
goes to waste; a loss, to be sure, which becomes less as the
price of the dye-stuffs falls.   The chief difficulty is that raw-
stock dyeing necessitates the addition of a dyeing equipment
to the manufacturing plant.   The yarn can be sent away to a
special dye-house to be dyed; the raw cotton cannot.   Hence,
while many of the gingham mills and some other mills dye
their raw stock, there is still a great deal of yarn dyeing.
Finally, new machines, Straw's Patent and the chain quiller,
have reduced the cost of re-warping and quilling the dyed yarn.

Piece dyeing, too, has shared in the general progress.   As
in bleaching and printing, large lots are dyed at once in an

[1] S. H. Higgins, *Dyeing in Germany and America*, p. 49.

[2] *Cyclopedia of Textile Work*, vol. vi, p. 149.

[3] New England Cotton Manufacturers' Association, *Transactions*, no. 70,
p. 318.

[4] Recently a new method of cop dyeing, by means of which the yarn is dyed
without being re-wound, has attained success in England.   But ring yarn (on
bobbins) obviously cannot be treated in that way.

American dye-house,[1] since it does not pay to put through small quantities. The necessity of economy in labor has forced the American to carry on the work of dyeing, like other work, on a large scale.

A recent development of importance in the converting of cotton cloth has been the introduction of mercerization. This process " consists in treating cotton, in the condition of yarn or of woven goods, to the action of caustic soda dissolved in water, and treating it subsequently with pure water and with dilute sulphuric acid for the purpose of washing out or chemically extracting the soda that remains in the yarn or fabric. The process effectuates both a chemical and a physical change in the constitution of the fibre."[2] The results of this mercerization are an increase in the strength of the material, greater affinity of the goods for certain dyes and mordants, and a silk-like appearance. But the yarn is less elastic. Moreover it has been successfully applied only to Egyptian and Sea Island cotton. The process is simple, but great care must be exercised in its application. It was invented by John Mercer, an Englishman, in 1844 or 1846, and first put into practice in England. But only since the improvements of the last twenty years has it developed to any extent either in England or in other countries. At present, cotton manufacturers are gradually taking it up both in the United States and in Europe. The methods are the same in the different countries.

In connection with converting machinery, mention should be made of the progress since 1860 in the machinery for drying the cloth.[3] Drying cylinders were first used for colored cloth, but with the increase in the amount of cloth to be dried cylinders came to be used also for white goods which had formerly been dried in sheds. Recently the cell drier has been introduced into a number of plants for all grades of work.[4] This machine, in which the large cylinders are replaced by small copper boxes filled with high pressure steam, about fifty of them being enclosed

[1] S. H. Higgins, *Dyeing in Germany and America*, p. 78.
[2] 12th *U. S. Census*, vol. ix, pp. 52–53.
[3] New England Cotton Manufacturers' Association, *Transactions*, no. 63, p. 237.
[4] S. H. Higgins, *Dyeing in Germany and America*, pp. 54–55.

in one big box, was invented by an American, and is adapted
to the conditions peculiar to this country. The cloth can be
run through at a high rate of speed, and the machine is consequently used to advantage only where large quantities of cloth
are to be dried at once.

There has been a similar development of other machines for
finishing cotton cloth. We now find improved machines of
American origin for sewing together the ends of the pieces of
cloth. The shearing machines are much larger, more complete,
with more cleaning appliances, and have rolling attachments.
And they are run at a higher speed. Stretching machines have
been greatly improved. Calendering machinery is more efficient,
and runs faster. In singeing practically the same methods are
employed as fifty years ago.[1] But the inspecting is now done
more carefully, with the aid of mechanical devices. And finally,
the cloth is now mechanically measured and folded. Some of
these machines are used in finishing all kinds of goods. Others
are used only for a single kind, as for example, the loop-cutter
that cuts the loose warp-threads on the back of warp-spot
goods,[2] which previously had to be cut by hand before shearing.

The same types of finishing machines are, in general, used in
both English and American mills. Great improvements in
finishing machines have been made in this country during the
last fifty years, especially those patented by Curtis and Marble,
of Worcester, large manufacturers of brushing, shearing, and
cleaning machinery for cotton cloth. But imported machinery
is also employed. The machines are run at a somewhat faster
speed, however, in American mills. Thus, as in almost every
instance where the type of machine is the same in England and
in the United States, the manufacturers push their machines
harder in this country.

[1] Yarn singeing, or gassing, has received more attention in England because
of the greater demand for gassed yarn for lace manufacture and like purposes.
The result is that yarn gassing machines have been improved. The Joseph Stubbs
Co. have played an important part in this progress, and Asa Lees & Co. have
recently placed a new machine upon the market.

[2] Warp-spot goods are those in which small spots or figures are made by weaving
in a group of warp threads only at intervals.

To sum up: the effect of all the improvements in cotton manufacturing machinery during the last fifty years has been cumulative as regards both quantity and quality. An improvement in one machine has not only facilitated its work, but at the same time prepared its product better, so that the next machine could in turn be operated more rapidly and more efficiently. In these improvements the American cotton manufacturers have played an important part. We cannot say that their contributions have been greater than those of their English rivals. But in these two countries have been made nearly all the important inventions in cotton machinery since 1860.

Of the occasional inventions in other countries, most have originated in Mülhausen, — the Heilman comber, the new Alsatian comber, and the peculiar card and new automatic loom of the Alsatian Machine Manufacturing Company. The Germans have also made a very important contribution by developing the synthetic dye-stuffs. Yet it should not be forgotten that the entire western world is tributary to Paris for original designs to be used in weaving and printing as well as in the lace and embroidery industries. Perhaps this continual manifestation of French artistic skill should not be classed with mechanical inventions. As regards the latter, the contributions made in Continental countries have been conspicuous because so infrequent.

The English inventions have been, perhaps, more in the direction of quality, while the American inventions have been along the line of quantity. It is true that the Americans have not sacrificed quality, and at times have actually sought it, but their object has been primarily to secure quantity. The American manufacturer must needs economize in labor, and accordingly he has developed machines to that end. He has adopted machines suited to the peculiar conditions with which he was face to face, especially those which would cut down the labor cost. He has adapted them to the production of large quantities of standardized patterns. And, further, he has developed machines which permit the utilization of the most available supply of labor, the unskilled immigrant. It is to this development and adaptation, far more than to any protective tariff, that the progress of cotton manufacturing in the United States during the last half-century has been due. For that reason the American cotton manufacturing industry stands on a firm foundation at the present time. On a similar adaptation its continued prosperity must depend in the future.

CHAPTER V

TECHNICAL DEVELOPMENT (CONTINUED)

Knitting

THE history of machine knitting commences in 1589 with the invention of the stocking frame by William Lee, an Englishman. One hundred and seventy years later (1758) the first noteworthy alteration in that machine was made by Strutt, who adapted it to ribbed work. After another uneventful period in its history this frame was driven for the first time by power at Cohoes, New York, in 1832.[1] Power frames of this type came into use in England about ten years later[2] and predominated there till after 1860.[3]

The second half of the nineteenth century, however, has witnessed a complete revolution of knitting technique and a change from the household and putting out systems to the factory method of production. Two general types of knitting machine, flat-bed and circular, have been evolved, and elaborate finishing machinery has been invented. Contributions of more or less value have been made by inventors so numerous that it is impossible to disentangle rival claims. All that is attempted here is to indicate the general lines of development and the characteristics of the leading systems.

The problems to which inventors of knitting machinery turned their attention were the increase in output and the shaping of the fabric. In 1834 an American introduced into England a machine of novel design, which made ten to twelve hose at once,[4] although each had to be fashioned separately.

---

[1] 8th *U. S. Census*, "Manufactures," p. xliii. (Nothing had come of patents for a power frame taken out by New York and Massachusetts men in 1813 and the following years.)

[2] *Ibid.*, p. xliii.

[3] Wm. Felkin, *History of Machine-Wrought Hosiery and Lace*, p. 489.

[4] Wm. Felkin, *op. cit.*, p. 543.

101

These frames were expensive and few were installed.   Yet by 1845 stocking frames making two or more legs simultaneously had become common in England.[1]   In 1836 machines were in use in France, on which two, three, or four stockings were knit at one time.[2]   Thus a large production was being secured.   Meanwhile Barton, in 1838, had devised a means for shifting stitches on the needles and shaping the fabric.[3]   The epoch-making invention of flat-web machinery, however, was the Cotton machine.

The Cotton knitting frame, so called from its inventor, was brought out in England in 1864, the first patent having been taken out in 1851.   Since that date it has been improved from time to time but is still extensively used and remains essentially the same in principle.   The bed of the frame is flat, and the product is a flat web, which can be shaped as desired.   " Fashioning, narrowing, and widening the knitted web is done on these machines by transferring the loops from several of the edge needles in use onto a separate instrument, moving them one or two needle spaces in or out, and then replacing them upon the needles."[4]   All this is done mechanically.   Garments made in this way are called " full-fashioned."   To finish them, they must be sewed or seamed.   For underwear a strip is knitted twice the desired length of the garment, then folded, and the sides seamed.   For stockings the shaped legs are knit on one machine, then transferred to a second which knits the heels and to a third which knits the feet.   If there is a ribbed top, that is made on still another machine.   In making the foot there are two methods, the English by which the foot is seamed on the sides, and the French, the more common, by which it is seamed along the middle of the sole, thus making a continuous seam from the top of the leg to the toe.

These machines are automatic in that one controlling mechanism regulates the shaping of the garment.   This mechanism is

---

[1] Wm. Felkin, *op. cit.*, p. 489.
[2] A. Mortier, *Le Tricot et l'Industrie de la Bonneterie*, p. 42.
[3] Wm. Felkin, *op. cit.*, p. 489.
[4] *Cyclopedia of Textile Work*, vol. v, p. 263.

adjustable, so that the machine can be adapted to knitting many patterns. At first each frame consisted of four or six beds, but the size has been augmented, till now on the largest machines twenty-four stockings may be made at one time.

The history of circular frames covers a century, but it was not till after 1850 that substantial success was achieved. The object of these machines was to produce a tubular web. In 1769 Samuel Wise, an Englishman, experimented with a circular knitting frame,[1] and in 1816 Brunel patented a circular frame.[2] They were not put into use at that time, however. A circular frame, supposed to be of French origin, was introduced into America about 1835,[3] while another was invented in France in 1844, and a third in 1853.[4] These endeavors show the direction in which invention was moving.

About 1844 the Brunel machine of 1816 was taken up by Paget, an English firm of hosiery manufacturers, and after modification gained a wide acceptance.[5] Fifteen years later the same firm added a narrowing device and adapted it to power. The quality of the product was excellent, but the speed was slow. Equipped with supplementary improvements, Paget machines still have a limited use amongst Continental manufacturers. Another Englishman, Moses Mellor, took up the circular machine in 1849 and made important innovations at that and later dates.[6] The French manufacturers also made independent contributions. From these sources the machines in use at the present time for knitting tubular webs for cut hose, and particularly for underwear, were developed. The American manufacturers have taken part in the progress [7] and have succeeded in making machines which give a much larger output than those of purely European origin.

---

[1] A. Mortier, *op. cit.*, p. 43.

[2] Wm. Felkin, *op. cit.*, p. 490.

[3] 8th *U. S. Census*, " Manufactures," p. xliii.

[4] Models of these machines are to be seen in the " Musée d'Arts et Metiers" at Paris.

[5] Wm. Felkin, *op. cit.*, p. 490.

[6] *Ibid.*, p. 511.

[7] W. G. Gist, for instance, increased the number of feeders from one to eight in 1858. Wm. Felkin, *op. cit.*, p. 507.

It is in stocking machinery than the Americans have made the greatest advances. Pepper in 1851,[1] Aiken in 1855,[2] Raymond in 1860[3] and Lamb in 1867, patented circular knitting machines. The Aiken and Lamb machines were most widely used, and a few of the latter type are employed in Europe at the present day. On these machines, as well as on the English Griswold frame, the mechanism for shaping the stocking was controlled by hand, even when the machine was run by power. Nevertheless they were the fastest producers brought out up to that time.

In 1867 came the first of a series of inventions by J. L. Branson and his son, E. R. Branson, of Philadelphia. Their efforts culminated in 1889 in the production of a completely automatic seamless knitting machine, which made circular and self-reciprocating motions, carried half of the needles out of action before commencing the heel and toe, narrowed and widened in heel and toe by throwing needles into and out of action, and automatically inserted an extra or splicing yarn to reinforce the heel and toe. Other types of automatic seamless knitting machines, varying more or less in detail, appeared about the same time, or soon after 1890, and during the last twenty years these have been constantly improved and supplemented.

In regard to these automatic seamless machines the *Cyclopedia of Textile Work* states that " full-automatics may run continuously on women's goods, passing from stocking to stocking without assistance from the operator. In making half-hose or socks the machines are automatic to a like degree, except that they must be stopped at the end of each article, so that another cylinder may be introduced with the rib top on the needles." [4] The number of wales remains the same throughout the garment produced on this machine, but the ankle for hose is made smaller by drawing shorter stitches. For half-hose there is no alteration in tension. Very recently a device has been invented for auto-

---

[1] 11th *U. S. Census*, vol. vi, p. 65.
[2] 8th *U. S. Census*, " Manufactures," p. xliii.
[3] Wm. Felkin, *op. cit.*, p. 543.
[4] *Cyclopedia of Textile Work*, vol. v, p. 188.

matically lessening the number of stitches at the ankle, in that way eliminating the inelasticity caused by shortening the loops. Another recent invention is an arrangement whereby the rib top and the plain web for seamless half-hose can be knit upon the same machine without changing cylinders. The commercial success of these two innovations would give additional advantage to the seamless machine.

The progress of the seamless machine has also been promoted by several subsidiary inventions. The latch needle, invented about 1856, was the first of these. The eye of this needle is closed by a little latch, instead of being pressed together like the spring-beard needle. A hole detector was another invention of vital importance. That appliance stops the cylinder whenever a hole appears in the web and thus prevents bad work and possibly injury to the machine.

The two types of knitting machine, the flat-bed and the circular, are quite different in their operation. The circular machines used in knitting underwear produce a web of uniform diameter. On these machines either spring or latch needles may be used, but the speed is higher on the circular machine than on the Cotton frame, and inasmuch as one operative tends about as many of the former as there are heads on one of the latter, the output per laborer is greater with the circular frame. Moreover if the body of the shirt is not cut to the exact shape of the human form but remains seamless, the expense of making up is less for the circular goods, and in any case it will be no greater than for the full-fashioned. On the other hand, the full-fashioned underwear is more elastic and of rather better quality.

The differences between the full-fashioned machines and the seamless machines [1] employed for knitting stockings are equally significant. Latch needles are almost always used on this class of seamless machines, whereas the Cotton frame has spring needles. The latch needles can be run at a higher speed, but

---

[1] Formerly large quantities of cut hose were made from the uniform tubular web, but that method has been practically abandoned, since the product was inferior to the full-fashioned goods and those shaped on the new circular frames.

the product is less elastic. The automatic action of the seamless frame enables one operative to tend several heads, just as on the Cotton machine several stocking blanks are knit at once on each machine, — a point of similarity. But the greater speed of the seamless machine results in greater product per operative, and the operative, who is usually a girl or woman instead of a man as on the Cotton frame, need not be possessed of as great skill and experience. Less labor of a cheaper grade is required to turn out the seamless stockings.

The transferring of the stocking from the legger to the heeler, and then to the footer, as is necessary for the full-fashioned goods, takes time and labor; the seamless machine runs on continuously. Again, the full-fashioned stocking requires more making up, since the leg and foot must be seamed, whereas the only seaming on the seamless hose is the closing of the short hole across the toe where the stockings are cut apart. More boarding and pressing are necessary to give the seamless goods their proper shape, but this is a comparatively slight expense and does not go far toward counterbalancing the higher labor cost of full-fashioned goods.

Although the seamless stockings cost less to manufacture, it is possible that they are not of as high quality. They are less elastic than the full-fashioned stockings, not only because of the use of latch needles instead of spring needles, but also on account of the method of narrowing the leg (for hose) by shortening the loops. Yet the less elastic texture of the seamless stocking is offset, partially at least, by the disadvantage of the seam underneath or along the sides of the foot of the full-fashioned stocking. The seamless machine, finally, is better adapted to coarse work than fine work, and to plain work than fancy work; but its field is constantly being extended and the quality of the product improved.

The majority of the knitting machines employed in the knit-goods industry in the United States are of the circular latch-needle type. The total number of knitting machines of all kinds as given by the Census in 1870 was 5,625; 1880, 12,659; 1890, 36,327; 1900, 69,047; and in 1905, 88,374. Previous to 1900 the Census did not separate the different types, but the following table shows the predominance of the circular latch-needle machine in 1900 and 1905.

NUMBER OF KNITTING MACHINES IN THE UNITED STATES [1]

Flat

	1900	1905
Spring needle	4,257	3,666
Latch needle	4,818	6,840
Total	9,075	10,506

Circular

	1900	1905
Spring needle	9,920	9,898
Latch needle	44,183	61,472
Total	54,103	71,370
Hand [2]	5,809	6,498

These statistics include machines at work upon wool and silk as well as those upon cotton, but the volume of the cotton knit-goods products is by far the largest.[3] Another qualification of these figures, though by no means invalidating them, is their incompleteness. " It should be understood that the actual number of knitting machines is larger than that stated, inasmuch as the important machines only are counted. For whereas but one machine is required, ordinarily, for knitting hose, several machines are needed to produce a single article of some classes of underwear. The number stated is, therefore, in the case of underwear, the number of body machines; and those which are used to knit sleeves, wrists, ankles, and other parts of the garments are not counted." [4]

The predominance of the circular latch-needle machine, the seamless automatic, in this country is due to its larger productivity and greater simplicity of operation. It has enabled the American manufacturers to reduce the cost of knitting and in that way has stimulated the growth of a large factory industry.

[1] *U. S. Census of Manufactures*, 1905, *Bulletin* No. 74, p. 75.
[2] These hand frames were employed for knitting specialties, such as mittens.
[3] *U. S. Census of Manufactures*, 1905, *Bulletin* No. 74, p. 77.
[4] *Ibid.*, p. 75.

The English manufacturers have kept a much larger proportion of the Cotton machines in operation, particularly for the manufacture of stockings. Many circular spring-needle machines are employed in England for knitting underwear but the number of seamless stocking frames is relatively small.[1] Several hundred hand frames, also, are still operated in the Nottingham district in the manufacture of high grade cotton and lisle stockings. The stockings knit on the hand frame are even more elastic than the full-fashioned goods. Although the cost of manufacturing is about twice as great for the hand-made goods as for the full-fashioned, and for the latter about twice as high as for the seamless, the demand for hand-made goods induces the manufacturers to keep up the production. In the United States the difference in cost is so great as to prevent the use of the hand frame for any purpose except the manufacture of specialties such as mittens, and the employment of the Cotton machine is restricted for the same reason.

In Germany many types of knitting machines are employed, from the hand frame to the circular automatic. The number of hand machines is not small, and other machines of a laborious sort, such as the Paget, are used. American knitting machines are relatively scarce in that country. For manufacturing underwear the circular frame is most common, and in hosiery factories the Cotton frame predominates. The Chemnitz manufacturers, in fact, have been the most progressive in improving the Cotton machine during the last thirty years.

As might be judged from what has just been said, the American manufacturers produce large quantities of relatively few patterns, the Germans smaller lots of diverse structure. Both adapt their methods to labor conditions.

All knit goods require some making up, and for this purpose special machines have been introduced. The tops of seamless hose are hemmed on a sewing machine, and the toe is seamed on a looper. A single machine suffices for seaming the full-fashioned stockings. Hence the task of finishing stockings is quite simple, far simpler than the making up of underwear.

---

[1] Part of those which have been installed are of American manufacture.

The processes in the finishing of underwear are numerous, and vary according to the kind of knitting machine employed. For a shirt made on a Cotton frame the strip (twice the length of the body) is folded over and the sides sewed together, spaces being left unstitched for the insertion of the sleeves which are made on a separate machine. But the tubular web from the circular machine, if it is to be shaped to fit the body, must be cut. This is usually done by hand, although the largest and best equipped mills employ a cutting machine driven by electricity or other power. After the bodies are cut they are seamed in the same way as the full-fashioned web.

From this point on the processes are the same for full-fashioned and cut or uncut goods, the garment travelling rapidly from hand to hand. Almost every operation is performed with the aid of machinery, in many cases of specialized design. Loopers loop on the cuffs to the sleeves and the rib tails to the bottoms of the shirts. The sleeves are sewed up and joined to the bodies. The neck flaps are cut and sewed down, the fronts marked and cut for button stays and button hole facings, the facings stitched on and the flaps covered. The button holes are spaced and made, and a button sewing machine sews on the buttons and trims off the threads. Finally inspectors and menders examine the garments, after which they are pressed, sorted, and marked according to sizes, and packed. In nearly all of these operations the machines are run by girls, whose nimble fingers acquire great dexterity.

In the development of machines for making up knit goods the American manufacturers have taken a prominent part. To be sure some machines, as for example the looper, have been introduced from England, but the American contributions have been more numerous and more important. As a consequence of this leadership a large number of American-made machines are now in use in Europe. Among the American inventions should be mentioned " the special stitching and covering machines of the Union Special Machine Company and the Willcox & Gibbs Sewing Machine Company, the button sewing and button hole machines of the Singer Sewing Machine

Company, and the edging machine of the Merrow Machine Company." [1] One of these machines stands out preëminently, the Overlock sewing machine invented by Messrs. Borton and Willcox, and placed upon the market in the United States in 1890. [2] Since its introduction here it has also been widely adopted abroad for finishing knit goods. It trims, seams, and over-edges the fabric in one operation, and runs at a high rate of speed, over 3,000 stitches per minute. This is but one of a number of important inventions which have been made during the last thirty years, particularly since 1890. The statement in the Census report of 1890 that, " for many products of machine-knit goods, a large proportion of the work must be done by hand, connected with the finishing of the goods," [3] would not hold true today.

This series of inventions, which accompanied the development of knitting machines, was not a mere coincidence. With the improvements in the knitting machines and the increasing scale of production and standardization of product, the need of labor saving devices for finishing the goods was more and more felt. As a result the perfection of the knitting machine was closely followed by the introduction of these supplementary machines, which in turn aided in the development of the factory system and large scale production. They manifest to a high degree that fundamental characteristic of the factory system, the minute sub-division of labor. Furthermore they have not only substituted machinery for hand labor, but the operative can learn to perform the work on a machine much more quickly than she can learn to do it by hand; hence less skilled labor may be employed, as is indicated by the predominance of immigrant girls in our knitting mills.

Thus during the last fifty years the knit-goods industry has been revolutionized, and in this transformation the American manufacturers have introduced machines which were adapted

---

[1] R. W. Scott, *Evolution of the Knit Goods Industry*, p. 4.

[2] A description and history of the machine is given in the *Textile Manufacturers' Journal*, October 31, 1908, p. 11.

[3] 11th *U. S. Census*, vol. vi, p. 66.

to their own peculiar needs. On this basis they have established a large and expanding industry. It has been pointed out that the improvements in technique progressed gradually until they culminated about 1890 in the fully automatic seamless knitting machine and the specialized machines for finishing the goods. Coinciding as it did with this culmination, the highly protective tariff of 1890 has received too great credit for the rapid growth of the industry during the last twenty years. The increase in tariff duties during the period of the Civil War very likely stimulated the growth of the industry for which the foundations had already been laid; but to emphasize too strongly the effects of the McKinley Tariff or of its successors is to overlook the part which has been played by American inventive genius.

CHAPTER VI

LABOR

Employees

WHILE the output per machine and per laborer has been augmented during the last five decades by means of technical improvements in cotton manufacturing, the labor force itself has assumed new characteristics. The sex and age composition is not the same at the present time as in 1860, and in New England the foreign element, which had appeared in the 'forties and 'fifties, has become predominant. In the cotton industry, moreover, as well as in other industries, labor unions have been organized, and strikes and lockouts have occurred.

The numbers of men, women, and children employed in cotton mills, as shown by the Census, have increased, but the proportion in each group has not remained constant.

AVERAGE NUMBER OF EMPLOYEES IN AMERICAN COTTON MILLS [1]

	Men	Women	Children	Total
1870	42,790	69,637	22,942	135,369
1880	59,685	84,539	28,320	172,544
1890	88,837	106,607	23,432	218,876
1900	134,354	123,709	39,866	297,929
1905	145,718	124,711	40,029	310,458
1910	190,531	141,728	38,861	371,120

In compiling these tables all males over sixteen years of age were classed as men, all females over sixteen as women, and all persons under sixteen as children. The data were collected from the manufacturers and doubtless contain many inaccuracies, of which it is not possible to determine the extent. The statistics for the later years are the more accurate, as the Census improved its methods and the manufacturers became more accustomed to furnishing such information.

[1] *U. S. Census of Manufactures*, 1905, *Bulletin* No. 74, p. 39.

For purposes of comparison the relative numbers in each class are also to be considered; hence a table of percentages is presented.

PERCENTAGE OF THE AVERAGE NUMBER OF EMPLOYEES

	Men	Women	Children
1870	31.5	51.4	17.1
1880	34.6	49.0	16.4
1890	40.6	48.7	10.7
1900	45.1	41.5	13.4
1905	46.9	40.2	12.9
1910	51.3	38.2	10.5

The first table shows that the number of men has increased absolutely; the second indicates a relative advance for that class. This tendency to employ a larger proportion of men has been apparent since 1870. Although the absolute number of women shows an increase, the percentage has steadily declined. There has not been an actual replacement of women by men, inasmuch as the number of women has not diminished, but with the expansion of the industry men have obtained a larger share of the work in departments where women are employed.

The proportion of children has fluctuated but is now lower than at any time since the close of the Civil War. The reaction which appeared after 1890 was the result of conditions in the southern states. In New England the number of children employed actually declined, falling from 17,704 in 1880 to 9,385 in 1905.[1] They constituted 14.1 per cent in 1880 and only 6 per cent of the total in 1905. In the South the tendency was the reverse; the number was 4,097 in 1880 and 27,571 in 1905. The greatest increase in that section was manifested between 1890 and 1900, from 8,815 to 24,438. But even in the southern states there has been a slight relative decline, from 25.1 per cent in 1880 to 22.9 per cent in 1905. However, as there has been little restriction on the employment of children in the South, and no adequate factory inspection, these figures may consider-

[1] The detailed statistics for the different sections in 1910 have not yet been published.

ably underestimate the facts.   In those states children have been employed to do work performed by women in northern mills; in 1905 only 31.6 per cent of the employees in southern mills were women in contrast to 45 per cent in New England.   The proportions of men at the same date were nearly equal in both sections, 45.5 per cent in the South and 49 per cent in New England.   Thus a certain proportion of light work in a cotton mill, wherever located, falls to the share of women and children.

Considering the men on the one hand, and women and children on the other, the former class of cotton mill employees has increased at the faster rate.   This has been occasioned in part by the larger available supply of men.   In the South, where the men have increased from 28.4 per cent of the total number of employees in 1880 to 45.5 per cent in 1905, the boys and young men who entered the mills twenty or thirty years ago have remained and have been recruited, whereas at the outset the older men were not easily adaptable to the needs of the factory system.   In New England the increased supply of adult male labor has come from the stream of immigrants, a source whence the cotton manufacturers could draw large numbers of men willing to work for comparatively low wages.

Secondly, and even more fundamentally, the demands imposed by technical changes have called for more male labor.   The machinery has become heavier and is run at a higher speed, thus requiring greater muscular exertion and causing a more intense nervous strain on the operatives.   The departments especially affected have been roving and weaving.   The fly-frames are longer, with the result that men have been advantageously employed to tend them.   A male weaver, similarly, can take care of more plain looms than a woman, and for the Northrop loom, in particular, male weavers are preferred. Although the men earn more than the women, the piece rates paid the former are the same or lower.

The restrictions upon the employment of women and children have become more stringent, but the noticeable increase in the proportion of men among the employees in southern mills, where there have been almost no restrictions until recently, indicates that factory legislation has been a secondary cause. In fact it may be that it became easier to pass the laws when the employers began to perceive that they would not be seriously handicapped by such enactments.

The various states have not imposed uniform restrictions on age or hours of labor, nor have they the same provisions for inspection.[1] In Massachusetts no child under fourteen may be employed in cotton mills, and the enforcement of the law by the factory inspectors has kept the proportion of children to the total number of employees lower in Massachusetts than in any of the other large cotton manufacturing states. Nevertheless the conditions in several Massachusetts mills are said to be wretched. Rhode Island, also, has had fourteen years as the minimum age for employment since 1906, but there, according to Mr. Towles, who has made a special study of labor conditions in that state, " the child labor law is not rigidly enforced " though the violations are not flagrant.[2] Maine, similarly, has since 1907 required that all children should be fourteen years of age before entering the mills, but, in the past at least, has been rather lax in enforcing its labor laws.[3] New Hampshire permits children twelve years old to be employed when schools are not in session, but with that exception prohibits the employment of all under fourteen and also those under sixteen who are not able to read and write English. Likewise in Connecticut and Pennsylvania fourteen years is the minimum age limit.

In the South restriction upon child labor is of very recent origin. The four important cotton manufacturing states in that section have, within the last six or seven years, adopted twelve years as the minimum age at which children may be

[1] U. S. Commissioner of Labor, 22d *Annual Report*, 1907, Labor Laws of the United States.

[2] J. K. Towles, *Factory Legislation of Rhode Island*, p. 56.

[3] The recent investigation of the conditions of woman and child labor by the Department of Commerce and Labor indicated an extensive violation of the Maine law restricting the employment of children in cotton mills. Rhode Island also showed numerous infringements of the age limit. U. S. Commissioner of Labor, *Report on Condition of Woman and Child Wage-Earners in the U. S.*, vol. i, pp. 150 ff.

employed, with particular qualifications and modifications in each state. The additional provision in North Carolina is that no child from twelve to thirteen years of age may be employed in a factory except in an apprenticeship capacity, and then only after having attended school for four of the preceding twelve months. Alabama requires that children from twelve to sixteen years of age shall attend school eight weeks out of the year, and for the enforcement of its laws has created the office of "Inspector of Jails, Alms-Houses, and Cotton Mills." In South Carolina any child may be employed during the months of June, July, and August, providing he or she can read and write and has attended school for four months during the preceding year. In that state, however, the twelve year limit does not apply to orphans and children of widowed mothers or disabled fathers. Georgia makes the same exception for orphans and so forth, but requires that child operatives under fourteen shall be able to read and write.

In none of the southern states is the system of inspection as efficient as in Massachusetts and some of the other northern states, and ordinarily the evidence of age required is merely a signed statement from the parents or guardian. The evils are slowly being mitigated, yet the laws are flagrantly violated, particularly in North and South Carolina.[1]

The hours of labor, similarly, are more restricted in the northern states. No child under eighteen years of age nor any woman may be employed in Massachusetts for more than fifty-four hours per week, and night work for these classes is also forbidden. New Hampshire protects the same classes from night work, but permits them to work fifty-eight hours per week. In Maine, Rhode Island, and Connecticut the hours for persons under sixteen and for women are limited to fifty-eight per week, and night work is prohibited. In Pennsylvania no child under eighteen and no woman may be employed in a cotton mill more than sixty hours per week or twelve per day, and night work for all under sixteen is illegal.

[1] U. S. Commissioner of Labor, *op. cit.*, pp. 171 ff.

Of the southern states in which cotton is manufactured Alabama has the most stringent regulations of hours of labor and night work. In that state children from twelve to fourteen are to be employed not more than sixty hours per week; those under sixteen are not to work at night; and those from sixteen to eighteen are not to be employed more than eight hours per night. South Carolina limits the hours for all cotton mill employees to ten per day and sixty per week, and since 1903 has not allowed children under twelve to work at night. North Carolina prohibits children under eighteen from working more than sixty-six hours per week, and those under fourteen from working at night. Georgia, also, has a sixty-six hour law, and forbids nocturnal employment of those under fourteen. These restrictions by the southern states are but a beginning, and very likely before this appears in print will have been extended.

In all parts of the country, when reformers have sought to introduce restrictions on the employment of children, they have met with opposition from the laborers themselves. The foreigners in New England have wished to procure places for their young children, and in the South the manufacturers have had to meet the demands that work be given to all the members of the families. The ignorance of many parents has been an obstacle to the complete restriction of the employment of young children. The fathers and mothers fail to see that this infringement of their liberty is ultimately to benefit their children.

The manufacturers are gradually discovering that they gain little by employing young children. In many Massachusetts mills one sees relatively few children at the present time. They are likely to be conspicuously absent in a fine cloth mill, whereas they are most in evidence in a print cloth mill or other factory manufacturing coarse fabrics. In order to secure the best results where particular attention is given to quality, the managers have found child labor undesirable. The higher the grade of work, the fewer the children. This is true in the South as well as the North.

The most important change which has taken place on the side of labor in the New England mills has been the influx of foreigners. The change commenced about ten years before the Civil War, when the Irish began to supplant the native workmen. During the war many of the laborers were called to arms, and most of the remainder thrown out of work. When the mills resumed full-time operations, the native employees did not return. The majority of the cotton mill operatives were foreigners or of foreign parentage, the Irish at first predominating. At the same time a considerable number of English added themselves to the labor force of the New England mills. During the 'seventies the French Canadians made their appearance, and for two decades many of them crossed the border from Quebec. As soon as that current ceased, a stream of Poles, Portuguese, Greeks, and other south Europeans headed its way toward the cotton mills of New England. Thus there was a constantly augmented supply of cheap, unskilled labor, which the manufacturers devised means of utilizing.

The Census has attempted since 1870 to record the nationalities of employees, and the statistics indicate the prevalence of the foreign element.

NATIONALITY OF COTTON MILL EMPLOYEES

Born in	1870	1880	1890	1900 [1]	Percentages 1870	1880	1890	1900
United States	71,547	94,010	90,494	110,220	64.1	55.4	52.6	44.7
British America	7,683	36,385	40,690	62,591	6.9	21.4	23.7	25.5
Ireland	18,713	19,732	16,396	28,573	16.8	11.6	9.5	11.6
Great Britain	11,805	16,237	17,131	19,269	10.6	9.6	9.9	7.8
Germany	1,214	1,988	3,763	6,063	1.1	1.2	2.2	2.5
All other	644	1,419	3,587	19,675	0.5	0.8	2.1	7.9
Total (occupation statistics)	111,606	169,771	172,061	246,391	100	100	100	100
Manufacturers' returns, total	135,369	174,659	218,876	297,929				

The second line of totals states the figures given by the manufacturers for the average number of persons employed, whereas

---

[1] The figures for 1900 are for the place of birth of parents, the others for place of birth of the operatives themselves.

the detailed statistics are from the Census volume on *Occupations*. It is evident from comparison that the occupation statistics, which were collected from the employees themselves, were inaccurate and far from complete. A large number were returned under " Textile Mills not otherwise specified." But inasmuch as that indefinite group showed about the same percentages, the proportions indicated in the table above are not far wrong. The value of all comparisons, however, is lessened by the greater inaccuracy of the returns for 1890 and 1900.[1] Beside this difficulty there is yet another disturbing discrepancy. In 1900 the figures are for parentage, not for nationality.[2] Hence they cannot be compared with those for earlier years. Probably the classification according to the place of birth of parents is a better index to the prevalence of the foreign element than the classification according to the place of birth of the employees themselves, but for the purposes of comparison consistency is the first requirement. With these qualifications in mind, let us consider the composition of this cosmopolitan personnel at the various dates.

In 1870 the Irish predominated among the foreign born employees in our cotton mills, and the number has remained about the same although the proportion has declined. The number of English and Scotch, likewise, has not manifested much change; the outflow and inflow have balanced. The Irish and particularly the British operatives, however, have moved upward in the scale of employment within the mills. Nearly all of the English are mule spinners, weavers, slasher tenders, or overseers. The comparatively small French Canadian element of 1870 expanded rapidly during the next ten years, and since 1880

[1] The greater inaccuracy has been a result largely of the increase in the number of non-English-speaking foreigners since 1880. In the New England States and Pennsylvania, where the foreign element predominates, the proportion of workmen returned as employed in " textile mills not otherwise specified " was much greater than in the South. And the indefinite returns were greater for foreign born than for native born, with the exception of Pennsylvania where the returns were indefinite for three-fourths of both native and foreign born. 12th *U. S. Census,* " Occupations."

[2] The Census of 1890 also classed the operatives according to birthplace of mothers, but those figures are not comparable with any of the others.

has far out-numbered any of the other foreign nationalities.[1] When the French Canadians first arrived, they were regarded with hostility since they were not easily assimilated and frequently made but a brief sojourn before returning to Quebec with their savings.   However, the majority of those who came have ultimately settled in New England and become a permanent factor in the labor supply of the cotton mills.   Since 1890 the immigration of French Canadians has declined, and new-comers of that nationality are not numerous at the present time. The return movement has also practically ceased.   The French Canadian population grows rapidly, nevertheless, since they are a very prolific race, and their large families provide many operatives.

The French Canadians are not without their peculiar characteristics.   They intermarry with other nationalities less frequently than almost any other race which has been brought under the same influences.   They are devoutly religious and their religion has been the chief bond which has held them together in the New England cities and prevented a fusion with other nationalities.   They are considered very desirable "help" by the employers, inasmuch as they are generally docile and do not make trouble.   They do not object to long hours nor disapprove of their children's working in the mills.   Moreover, they generally look with disfavor upon strikes which interrupt their labor and lighten the pay envelope.   This attitude toward strikes was one reason which caused the other operatives to dislike them, especially at first when they were not so numerous.   These French Canadians are employed in work of all degrees of skill, — in the preparatory processes, in ring spinning, and in weaving. Some who have been in the mills longest have assumed responsible positions.

The unskilled labor has, during the last two decades, fallen more and more into the hands of newly-arrived Europeans, — a conglomeration of Poles, Portuguese, Greeks, Syrians, Italians,

[1] In the table the English Canadians are included under the same heading as the French, for the sake of securing comparability, but their number has been so small as to be practically negligible, 3,113 out of 62,591 in 1900.

and others. They have taken up the heavier and more disagreeable work, for which little experience is necessary, and
which is the more poorly paid. In the picker room, the card
room, and to some extent in the ring-spinning room, they have
made their appearance. For illustration, in a Lowell mill a few
years ago foreigners of this class were distributed as follows: [1]

	Total Employees	Poles	Portuguese	Greeks	Other
Picker Room	33	10	...	11	12
Card	101	38	...	41	22
Carding and Picking	137	75	...	...	62
Roving hands	118	43	...	...	75
Spinning	564	30	...	167	367
Dressing	174	..	...	...	174
Weaving	625	99	85	...	441

In this instance the slasher room was the only department into
which these unskilled workmen had not entered. In all of the
others they had found some tasks suited to their untrained
hands, although not to the same proportion in each. For these
racial conglomerations the notices in each mill have to be printed
in three or four languages.

Each nationality is sprinkled over the New England cotton
manufacturing district, but more densely at certain points.
The Irish and the French Canadians are fairly evenly distributed. The English are more numerous in southern New England
owing to the superior opportunities for them in the fine goods
mills. The Portuguese may have hit upon New Bedford, the
cotton manufacturing city in which they are found in largest
numbers, because of their previous connection with the whaling
industry. The Greeks have been attracted to Lowell, and
the Syrians to Lawrence.

At the present time there are very few foreigners in the mills
of the southern states, and the large number of native born in
that section accounts for a majority of the native born in the
table given above. In an average New England mill, in contrast,
there is a conspicuous scarcity of " Yankees."

[1] Mass. Bureau of Statistics of Labor, *Bulletin* No. 41, p. 199.

A majority of the knitting mill operatives have also been drawn from the immigrant population. The Irish, Germans, and French Canadians are the most numerous. The numbers of foreign born in 1880 and 1890, and of foreign parentage in 1900 were as follows: —

KNITTING MILL OPERATIVES

	1880 Birthplace	1890 Birthplace	1900 Parentage	1880	1890 Percentages	1900
Native	9,774	22,882	21,381	80.1	77.3	45.4
Irish	610	1,236	7,460	5.0	4.2	15.8
German	387	1,213	6,046	3.2	4.1	12.9
Canadian	428	1,793	4,707	3.5	6.1	10.0
British	871	1,569	2,767	7.1	5.3	5.8
Polish	...	.....	801	0.0	0.0	1.8
Other	124	862	3,958	1.1	3.0	8.3
Total	12,194	29,555	47,120	100	100	100

The native employees are distributed in the southern and western states, whereas the foreigners are to be found chiefly in the larger mills of the northeastern section of the country. The employment of a larger proportion of foreigners since 1880 reflects the adoption of the new types of machinery.

The immigrants have been a very potent factor in the progress of the cotton manufacturing industry, just as in many other industries which have enjoyed a rapid growth since 1860. The same characteristic is to be observed in the mining industry, the tin-plate industry, the meat-packing industry, and others. The immigrants have furnished a supply of unskilled workmen for the manufacturers, who have not feared the " pauper labor " of Europe when it came to our own shores. They have expanded their business on the basis of this very labor all the while that they have been demanding protection for the " American laborer." These foreigners were the workmen that the manufacturers must have had in mind when they were advocating protection. They claim to protect the standard of living of this class, many of whom had been in the country but a short time. To be sure it is highly desirable that the standard of living of this class be maintained, and fully as desirable that it be raised. Nevertheless, the importation of laborers seems to be a greater menace to those already in the country than the importation of products made abroad. The discussion of the tariff, however, is best reserved till later.

Labor Unions

The presence of so many foreigners in our cotton mills has hindered the formation of labor unions in this trade. Although local textile unions have existed in the past, it is only within the last few years that there has been a national association. A history of labor unions in the American cotton industry, therefore, would be an account of the local unions that have appeared from time to time. To unravel that tale is a task that could not be undertaken at this point, and I shall give merely a few of the more pregnant facts.

The mule spinners' unions have always been the strongest among those in the cotton industry. The Mule Spinners' Union of Fall River was organized in 1858, and from that date until 1889 experienced a rather precarious life. At times strong, at other periods it temporarily passed out of existence after a particularly unsuccessful strike. However the mule spinners kept alive the union spirit amongst the cotton mill employees, and gained for themselves the reputation of being the most troublesome class of employees. The strength of their union resulted partly from the absence of women in their occupation, but more particularly because of the high degree of skill required. Other workmen could not easily be substituted for mule spinners. Moreover these workmen have, on the average, been superior to the other operatives in intelligence, and therefore keener for advancement. They better appreciated the advantages of combining to promote their own interests.

A national organization was formed in 1889, the National Cotton Mule Spinners' Association of America, and since that date practically all of the mule spinners in the country have become members. Yet the union has gained little in power. The number of mule spindles has remained nearly stationary and the manufacturers are no longer dependent upon the mule spinners in order to keep their mills in operation. Formerly, when mule-spun yarn was required, even if only for the weft, a strike of the mule spinners could force the closing of an entire plant. But the extension of the use of the ring-frame has relieved the manufacturers, since for its operation easily replaced labor could be employed. The combination of the ring-frame and the immigrant has weakened the mule spinners' organization.

The loom fixers and slasher tenders have also made loyal union members. Like the mule spinners they are possessed of more than ordinary skill and new workmen cannot readily be trained to take their places. However, they are not numerous, a circumstance which facilitates the settlement of disputes. They are not the ones whom the manufacturers would seek to oppress, nor are they likely to make exorbitant demands upon their employers. Although these workmen have a strong strategical position, they seldom have undertaken to dictate in the interests of the great mass of their fellow employees.

In the late 'eighties and during the 'nineties other unions were formed in Fall River, and some are still alive. In other cotton manufacturing centres, also, unions have been organized from time to time, but nowhere have they been strong enough to secure many permanent concessions from their employers.

The organization of the United Textile Workers of America was effected in 1901, to include all the textile operatives in the country. In January, 1909, it had a membership of 154 local unions. The experience of this association well illustrates the obstacles to a thorough-going organization of American cotton mill operatives. Some unions have joined and then dropped out. Others have been formed, entered the association, and then expired. Great difficulty has been experienced in persuading the local unions to levy assessments large enough to give the association a suitable working fund. Jealousies among the union leaders have resulted in dissension and frequently in desertion. The strength which this national organization possesses is largely the result of the efficiency of the officers who have been at its head.

Throughout the history of cotton mill unions, leadership has been of primary importance. Among the local unions which have come, and in many instances gone, since 1875, each union has usually been weak or powerful, according to whether or not it had a good leader. A union has been in a way a combination of the followers of a certain man. A leader with good organizing ability could form a union which would follow his advice on all matters. Occasionally, it is to be regretted, the leader has used his influence to further personal ends, to the detriment of the interests of those whom he represented.

A strong union spirit, therefore, has not been manifest among the cotton mill employees, except in rare instances. The great mass of operatives have not yet come to appreciate the benefits accruing from united action at all times. When anything has occurred to cause wide-spread dissatisfaction, they have joined in a strike whether or not affiliated with the unions, and in troublous times unions in certain localities have secured large additions to their membership. But as soon as the dispute was settled, the union was deserted, and a period of disorganization followed. One element of weakness has been the employment of so many women and children in the cotton mills. The women join in the strikes about as readily as the men, but they are seldom constant supporters of the union cause. Women, however, are employed in the cotton factories of England, where there are vigorous labor unions. Hence their presence is not the chief obstacle.

It is, above all, the continual inflow of foreigners which has sapped the strength of the union movement in the New England factories. The congregation of so many languages and dialects in a single industry, to say nothing of a single mill, has embarrassed communication and the formation of mutual agreements. Racial antagonism, also, has not been absent. Moreover the immigrant seeking employment has cared little where or how he secured it, and has had no scruples against taking the place of strikers. He has also desired continuous employment, so that anything which cut into his income has been obnoxious to him. Inasmuch as there have been no strong affiliations of workmen throughout the cotton manufacturing district, there has been nothing to hinder the gradual migration of workmen from place to place at the time of a strike.

Strikers' places were filled by outsiders in Fall River as early as 1850, when a six months' strike was broken by the introduction of workmen from other places.[1]   Again, in 1867 new operatives were substituted for Lawrence strikers.[2]   In regard to a strike at the Waltham Bleachery in 1874, it was said that " the manufacturers were not unwilling to make a complete change of help," and after the settlement less than one-third of the former employees were taken back.[3]   French Canadian " knobsticks " were brought to Fall River in 1879 to take the place of strikers.[4] These instances indicate the part that the immigrant has played in supplying the manufacturers with fresh workmen when occasion required.   The readiness with which new operatives could be secured enabled the employers to withstand the demands made upon them by their employees.   But the operatives who were replaced generally had little difficulty in obtaining new positions.   Soon after a strike commenced, the operatives would drift away to other cities, and if the dispute were not settled immediately the number who migrated was usually not inconsiderable.

The statistics given in the *Twenty-first Annual Report* of the United States Commissioner of Labor emphasize the ill-success of strikes in the American cotton manufacturing industry. During the period from 1881 to 1905 there were 665 strikes and lockouts in that industry, affecting 832 establishments.   In 153 of these establishments the workmen were victorious, and in 97 partially successful, whereas they failed in 580 establishments.   Thus in only 30 per cent of the establishments affected did they gain even part of their demands, and obtained all that they sought in only 18.4 per cent of the establishments.   A comparison of these percentages with those for the disputes in all industries shows that the cotton mill employees have been particularly unsuccessful.   In the total for all industries during the same period the strikes in 47.9 per cent of the establishments were entirely successful, and completely failed in only 36.8 per cent.

---

[1] Mass. Bureau of Statistics of Labor, *Report*, 1880, p. 8.
[2] *Ibid.*, p. 23.   [3] *Ibid.*, p. 35.   [4] *Ibid.*, pp. 55–56.

The period since 1880, moreover, has not differed in this respect from the preceding years. We have no statistics prior to 1880, but the Massachusetts Bureau of the Statistics of Labor collected and published in its report for 1880 the records, so far as obtainable, of all the strikes in Massachusetts for many preceding years. These records show that the strikes of any magnitude in the cotton industry failed with a single exception, and in that instance success was but temporary, inasmuch as the manufacturers withdrew the concessions as soon as trade conditions furnished them with a pretext. This successful strike was in Fall River in 1875. Later in the same year another strike to prevent the employers from rescinding their earlier action ended in failure, and the strikers not only accepted the reduction in wages after having been out for nine weeks, but signed an agreement that they would not join a union and that " only one out of every eight operatives could give notice to leave work at the same time." A temporary victory thus ended in bitter defeat. This was the only occasion of even temporary success shown by the records. The workers' demands were acceded to occasionally after disputes of short duration, when the manufacturers were especially desirous of averting trouble. But on the whole the operatives have seldom been able to secure concessions.

The lack of union spirit amongst the foreign element has not been evidenced to the same degree by all nationalities. The English are usually the strongest union men, and the greater frequency of strikes in Fall River has been attributed, probably with justice, to the larger number of English employed there. Accustomed to unions in the " mother country," and more intelligent than many of the other immigrants, they have been ready to join hands in their common cause. The French Canadians, on the contrary, have never caught that spirit. When they were coming to New England in largest numbers, in the 'seventies and 'eighties, they were called " knobsticks," a term of reproach because of their willingness to take positions vacated by strikers. Energetic and frugal, they ordinarily accepted without complaint the terms offered by the employers.

The Portuguese, Poles, Greeks, and other recent acquisitions have taken much the same attitude as the French Canadians. The Greeks, to be sure, are reputed to be rather troublesome, but not because of their loyalty to union principles.

The southern mill operatives have also failed to manifest much union sentiment, and labor organizations are of very recent origin in that section. The people themselves have been strongly individualistic, and the scattered mill villages and the somewhat paternalistic attitude of the employers have not fostered the movement. Harmony between employees and employers, although often exaggerated, has prevailed. Continued association, however, is likely to bear fruits in the form of combinations among the operatives, and a nucleus has appeared within the last three or four years. The mill owners are organized and concerted action on their part will compel the laborers to adopt protective measures.

The employers, both northern and southern, have been able to maintain the upper hand in the past, so that the operatives were allowed to say little about the terms of employment, and in New England the union movement is likely to lack virility so long as new workers can be so easily procured. To be sure, a manufacturer seldom cares to change the personnel of his factory and to train new workmen. He prefers to keep those who are familiar with his methods. But the readiness of the work people to change their place of abode has served to protect them to only a slight degree. This brings us to the subject of wages.

Wages

In the first place, what do we mean by wages? To define wages as the income received by laborers is not sufficient for our purposes, since it does not clearly indicate the relations that must be borne in mind. The wages question can be approached from two points of view, that of the employee or that of the employer. For the former, money wages are to be considered in connection with the prices that have to be paid for the goods which he purchases. If a laborer receives fifty per cent higher money wages now than twenty years ago, he is better off only in so far as he can buy more commodities at the present time. For the manufacturer, on the other hand, the money wages which he pays to his employees are significant only when the productivity of the laborers and the price of the product are taken into consideration. He may pay higher weekly wages and at the same time find the relative expense for labor less because of technical improvements or a rise in the price at which he sells. A mere statement of the changes in the money wages, therefore, has in itself little significance. Moreover an average wage for all cotton mill employees, such as that given in the Census, is based upon the earnings of laborers of many grades of skill, and if the number of laborers in any grade has become proportionately less during a given period, or if the wages of all have not undergone the same fluctuations, a comparison of general averages is misleading. It is worse than useless.

In this study it is the manufacturer's point of view which is taken, or the relation of wages to cost of production.[1] To trace the history of changes in the proportional cost for labor, however, is a task which, unfortunately, cannot be undertaken with any great pretense at accuracy. Owing to alterations in the composition of the labor force, in technique, in methods of payment and accounting, and the diversity of different qualities of product, the problem is beset with many difficulties.

Earnings do not serve as an index to changes in labor cost, for reasons indicated above. A majority of the laborers employed in a cotton mill are paid piece rates. These are not the same in all mills turning out the same grade of cloth, and there is even less correspondence in mills manufacturing different grades, the rates being somewhat higher, as a rule, the finer or more fancy the fabric. In the United States there are no standard wage lists similar to those in the English cotton manufacturing districts, so that we have not that assistance, however formidable the interpretation might appear. The technical improvements in cotton mill machinery during the last five decades have been accompanied by the fixing of new piece rates, usually at lower

---

[1] This does not imply that the relation of income to cost of living is not equally important.

levels, but all departments and all grades have not been affected alike.

Cost keeping methods are not the same as those of 1860, even in individual concerns, and are not at all uniform. While some companies may have made but slight changes, others have adopted far more accurate systems for ascertaining the expenditure per yard for each item in the cost. Granting that variations of this sort would not invalidate all comparisons, there is still the practical difficulty of obtaining the data. Few cotton manufacturers are willing to state just what percentage of their expenses is for labor or what proportion of the cost per yard goes to wages.[1]

The most definite information obtainable is for the weaving piece rate in Fall River, and that shows little advance during

RATE PAID PER CUT FOR WEAVING REGULAR PRINT CLOTH
IN FALL RIVER [2]

1884	Feb.	4......18.50 cents	1899	Feb.	27......18. cents
1885	Jan.	19......16.50	1899	Dec.	11......19.80
1886	March	1......18.15	1902	March	17......21.78
1888	Feb.	13......19.	1903	Nov.	23......19.80
1892	July	11......19.60	1904	July	25......17.32
1892	Dec.	5......21.	1905	Oct.	30......18.61
1893	Sept.	11......18.	1906	July	2......19.80
1894	Aug.	20......16.	1906	Nov.	26......21.78
1895	April	22......18.	1907	May	27......23.96
1898	Jan.	1......16.	1908	May	25......19.66

the last twenty-five years. The rate per cut (45 yards) paid for weaving regular print cloth is the basis on which the sliding scale of wages has been adjusted and is used as an index for all

---

[1] It is regretted that it has not been possible to present at least a summary of the course of wages in this industry. There was not time, however, for the collection of the data. Satisfactory results could be obtained only after a long search through the U. S. Census, the State censuses (particularly the Massachusetts Census of 1885), the Aldrich Report on Prices and Wages, the reports of the state labor bureaus, the information collected privately by such investigators as Young and Uttley, and finally the records of the manufacturing corporations themselves. Moreover the figures must not only be unearthed, but they must be compiled and the numerous discrepancies accounted for. As just stated, lack of time forbade the assumption of such a task.

[2] Mass. Bureau of Statistics of Labor, Bulletin No. 51, p. 33.

wages in Fall River. Except for the high rate of 1907, during the period of great activity that preceded the crash, these piece wages have remained at practically the same level.[1]

This evidence from Fall River that piece wages have increased but slightly since 1884, is supported by data furnished privately by a large mill in another part of New England, manufacturing a different grade of goods. These figures show the reductions and increases in wages by this concern since 1881. The fluctuations have corresponded to those in Fall River and probably to those in New England generally. In this mill the wages were below the level of 1881 from 1885 till 1907, when, on June 3, they became one-half of one per cent higher and on December 31, five per cent higher than in 1881. But they dropped during the ensuing depression to five per cent below that standard.

These are only general indices, however, and do not show how each department has been affected. As new machines have been introduced, the piece rates have generally fallen, as for instance the weaving rate on Northrop looms. This has meant a lower labor cost for the manufacturer. Increases in earnings have occurred only when the reductions in piece rates have not balanced the increase in the output per workman. Technical improvements have enabled one operative to tend more machines or to secure a larger output from a single machine, but lower piece rates have checked the advance of earnings. In general the immigrants have tended to keep wages at nearly a constant level.

The only system of collective bargaining for fixing wages in the American cotton manufacturing industry is the sliding scale agreement in Fall River.[2] This arrangement was introduced in 1905, after a protracted strike which had caused severe losses to both parties. According to the first plan,[3] which

---

[1] The prices of cloth underwent similar fluctuations. In 1884 the average price for regular print cloth in New York was 3.36 cents per yard; in 1892, 3.39 cents; in 1889, 2.06 cents; in 1907, 4.62 cents; and in 1908, 3.50 cents.

[2] J. T. Lincoln, "The Fall River Sliding Scale," *Quarterly Journal of Economics*, vol. xxiii, pp. 450–469.

[3] Mass. Bureau of Statistics of Labor, *Bulletin* No. 51, p. 27.

originated with Governor Douglass who was called upon to settle the dispute, eighteen cents per cut was made the basis when there was a margin of $72\frac{1}{2}$ cents between the cost of eight pounds of middling upland cotton (New York quotation) and the average selling price of 45 yards of 28-inch 64×64 print cloth and 33.11 yards of $38\frac{1}{2}$-inch print cloth. The employers agreed to pay, at the end of every four weeks, to those who had been in their employ two weeks or more, one per cent additional on their earnings for every cent that the margin exceeded $72\frac{1}{2}$ cents. The plan did not prove satisfactory, however, and on July 2, 1906, it was abolished.[1]

A new agreement was entered into May 3, 1907,[2] between the Manufacturers' Association and the Textile Council in which the five unions were joined. By this scheme the wages were to be regulated by the same margin as before. But instead of the percentage arrangement, certain definite rates were fixed for a graduated scale of margins, with a maximum of 23.96 cents per cut for a margin of 115 and a minimum of 18 cents for a margin of $72\frac{1}{2}$ cents. Wages were not to exceed the maximum nor fall below the minimum even if the margin became greater or less than the limits set. The agreement of 1905 had had the same minimum, but no maximum. Revisions of wages were to be made only every six months, instead of every month, thus giving greater stability. Another provision stipulated the length of notice to be given if either party desired to change the contract.

This agreement was amended in August, 1907,[3] so that a change in the rate took place with a drop or rise of two and one-half points in the margin instead of for five or ten points, and on August 27, 1907, the Weavers' Union and the Manufacturers' Association agreed upon $47\frac{1}{2}$ yards as the standard cut.[4] The operatives became dissatisfied with the terms, however, and on February 16, 1910, gave notice of their withdrawal from the agreement.

[1] Mass. Bureau of Statistics of Labor, *Bulletin* No. 51, p. 29.
[2] *Ibid.*, p. 32.
[3] *Ibid.*, No. 60, p. 268.
[4] *Ibid.*, No. 52, p. 102.

The scale, it will be noticed, was based upon the print cloth margin only, but a change was made in the wage paid each operative in just the same proportion that weavers' wages were altered. The wages of all the employees were subjected to these regulations, although only a small percentage were members of the unions which were a party to the contract. Over twenty-five thousand employees were affected by the agreement. To avert possible dissatisfaction the employers waived their rights to a reduction of wages at the three settlement dates following the panic of 1907. The motives of the manufacturers in declining to follow the letter of the agreement were two-fold: in the first place they took an interest in the general welfare of their employees, and in the second place they were in a position where they could continue the old rates in force in spite of the depression. They wished to placate the laborers and promote a feeling of good-will in order to discourage strikes in the future. Objections were urged against certain features of this scheme,[1] but it was a step in the direction of industrial peace.

[1] The chief objections were that there was no insurance to the workmen against partial closure of the mills (short time) which operated to the same effect as a cut in wages, and that it was possible for a slump in the market to cause an excessive reduction in a single year.

CHAPTER VII

TEXTILE SCHOOLS

THE need of special facilities for technical education in various branches of industry has been recognized in all the countries where the factory system has assumed an important rôle. The apprenticeship system sufficed for the training of young men in the arts of production so long as that production was carried on in the home, the shop, or even in a small sized factory. But with the steadily increasing size of the industrial establishment, the more minute division of labor, the use of more complex machinery and the quickened pace of work, the factory became even more unsatisfactory as a school in which to train men for the higher positions, and the average unskilled workman no longer had much chance to pull himself up to a higher level. On the other hand, the very increase in the scale of operations and the keenness of the competition placed a premium upon the competent overseer and superintendent, and where it was desired to improve the quality of the product a greater demand for skilled workmen arose.

Technical education may be given in schools which offer instruction in a variety of subjects that are connected more or less closely with several industries, or it may be given in a trade school which undertakes to teach the principles and practice to be met with in only a single industry or a single group of industries. Textile schools, obviously, belong to the second group. These textile schools may serve either one or both of two objects. The course may be planned with a view to turning out overseers, superintendents, and experts in certain departments, such as chemists or designers, or its chief purpose may be to enable the laborers to become better workmen. From the industrial point of view both objects are highly desirable, while from the social point of view the second, by assisting the laborer to help himself, is especially commendable.

The United States lagged behind the European countries in introducing textile education, a sluggishness due in part at least to the fact that our mills were manufacturing coarse and medium goods of simple design. The first textile schools in the United States gave instruction only in designing. These were the Lowell School for Practical Design established in Boston in 1872, and the Rhode Island School of Design founded in Providence in 1878.[1] The first school to provide instruction in other branches of textile work was established at Philadelphia in 1884.

The Philadelphia Textile School offers a three year course, including instruction in all the various processes connected with the manufacture of cotton, wool, and silk. Classes are held during the day and in the evening, but, on the whole, more attention is given to the day classes. In 1905 there were 86 day pupils and 168 evening pupils enrolled in the school.[2] A majority of the students take the general course, which aims at starting them on the road for the higher positions in textile manufacturing. The graduates also find a field open to them in merchandizing, and occasionally as experts for insurance companies. The night classes are not unimportant in this school, yet it does not reach many of the common workmen in the mills. It specializes in the education of men to fill the places at the top.

The New England cotton manufacturers were stimulated by the pressure of the competition from the mills in the South to seek some way of safeguarding their position and turned to textile education as one means of relief. They hoped that this would foster the development of the manufacture of the finer grades of cotton goods in New England. Their efforts resulted in the passage of a law in Massachusetts in 1895 authorizing the establishment of a textile school in any city in the state which had at least 450,000 spindles, and granting state aid to the amount of $25,000 on condition that the municipality raised an equal amount. There were four cities with the requisite number of spindles, — Lowell, Fall River, New Bedford,

---

[1] U. S. Department of Labor, *Bulletin* No. 54, p. 1379.
[2] Mass. Bureau of Statistics of Labor, *Bulletin* No. 43, p. 337.

and Lawrence, and the first three have availed themselves of the opportunity.[1]

The movement took tangible form with the establishment of the Lowell Textile School in 1896. For the day students five regular courses are offered, each of three years' length, on the completion of any one of which a diploma is granted. These courses are (1) Cotton Manufacturing, (2) Wool Manufacturing, (3) Textile Designing, (4) Chemistry and Dyeing, and (5) Textile Engineering. Evening classes provide instruction in the same subjects, and a certificate is given to those who satisfactorily complete a course. When a sufficient number of certificates have been obtained, they may be exchanged for a diploma. Students are admitted to the evening classes on presentation of a certificate of graduation from a grammar school or a school of higher standing, or upon passing an examination in English and arithmetic. For entrance to the day classes a high school diploma, or its equivalent, is necessary.

The school aims at instilling the principles of textile manufacturing, and the relatively high standard of requirements for entrance show that the primary object is to instruct the more intelligent workmen and those who can fill places of responsibility. The number of day students in 1905 was 141, of evening students 588.[2] Four years later the former had increased to 173 and the latter had fallen to 505.[3] The larger number of evening students shows that it is serving local needs as well as the needs of the textile world at large. The classification of day students by courses reveals the fact that on January 1, 1909, sixty-four per cent were specializing in designing, chemistry and dyeing, or textile engineering. Seventy-two per cent of the evening students were pursuing subjects that would fall within the same field. The remainder were enrolled in the special courses for one or the other of the separate textile industries.

The New Bedford Textile School was opened in October, 1899, and is devoted principally to instruction in the manufacture of

[1] Lawrence was so near to Lowell that it helped to support that school instead of establishing another of the same sort.

[2] Mass. Bureau of Statistics of Labor, *Bulletin* No. 43, p. 323.

[3] *Mass. Documents*, 1908–09, *House*, no. 263, pp. 5, 6.

cotton. It offers a three year course in cotton manufacturing, a one year course in cotton carding and spinning, a similar course in cotton weaving, a two year course in designing, a course of the same duration in chemistry and dyeing, a complete three year course in knitting, and one year courses in seamless hosiery and in latch-needle underwear knitting. The various branches of the above subjects are taught in the evening classes.

The evening classes are the most important feature of the New Bedford school's work. The number of day students was 29 in 1905 and 40 in 1909, whereas the evening students numbered 363 in 1905 and 509 in 1909. For admission to the evening classes there are practically no requirements, and instruction is provided in certain elementary subjects for those whose primary education has been defective. In one weaving class, moreover, the instruction is given entirely in French. A majority of the evening students are young men from twenty to thirty years of age, although one evening student in 1909 was sixty years old. They are the more ambitious of the ordinary workmen, possessed of a relatively small amount of skill. The training of that class of operatives is particularly desirable in New Bedford where skilled laborers are needed for carrying on the manufacture of fine cloth.

The Fall River Textile School, founded in 1900, has pursued a policy similar to that of the school in New Bedford. It had, in 1905, 11 day pupils and 419 evening pupils; in 1909, 38 of the former and 701 of the latter. The subjects taught embrace the various branches of cotton manufacturing, with a general course for the day students and evening classes in special subjects to assist the operatives from the mills.

The Industrial School opened at Lawrence in 1907 is of a somewhat different character. It undertakes to provide for the working men a practical education in the textile and metal trades. There are no entrance requirements, no fees, and classes are held only in the evening.[1] Thus this school tries to reach the lowest grade of laborers, especially the immigrants, who are, to a certain extent, kept out of the textile schools by

[1] *Textile World Record*, vol. xxxvi, p. 231.

their ignorance of the English language. The service which it may in this way perform is no less valuable than that unquestionably performed by the more advanced institutions.

The example set by Massachusetts probably had some influence in inducing southern institutions to introduce textile education. In addition to this spur, the very growth of cotton manufacturing in that section, accompanied by a deeper appreciation of the need of skilled men, acted as a stimulus. Textile departments have been opened at five southern colleges,[1] — Clemson College, South Carolina, in 1898, the North Carolina College of Agriculture and Mechanical Arts, and the Georgia School of Technology in 1899, the Mississippi Agricultural and Mechanical College in 1901, and the Agricultural and Mechanical College of Texas in 1905. The number of students in the textile courses at Clemson College in 1905 was twenty, at the Mississippi College sixteen,[2] and at the others a correspondingly small number. As these institutions are not located in cotton manufacturing centres and have no evening classes, their purpose is to train experts and men for managerial positions.

Instruction in subjects connected with textile manufacturing is also given by several correspondence schools. The number of persons pursuing this course cannot be ascertained, but it is not negligible. This means of education is utilized by what may be called the middle class of operatives, those who cannot afford the time or expense of attending a regular textile school and yet who have had sufficient training to enable them to profit from this sort of study.

Labor unions are not always in favor of trade education, fearing that it will so increase competition as to cause a fall in wages. In New Bedford there was some opposition from this source at the outset, but the unions soon became indifferent[3] and later took a more or less positive interest. In the same way at Lowell, while there was no outright opposition, it was several years before the unions became really sympathetic. At the

---

[1] U. S. Commissioner of Labor, 17th *Annual Report*, 1902, p. 133; also Mass. Bureau of Statistics of Labor, *Bulletin* No. 43, pp. 338–345.

[2] Mass. Bureau of Statistics of Labor, *Bulletin* No. 43, p. 345.

[3] U. S. Commissioner of Labor, 17th *Annual Report*, 1902, p. 148.

present time, in both of these cities as well as in Fall River, the unions are supporting the schools, their changed attitude being due, perhaps, to the non-realization of any evil effects upon their earnings, but more likely to the fact that a large number of the laborers find it worth while to attend the schools.

The employers, as well as the laborers, have a direct interest in these schools. The New England textile schools owe their origin largely to the efforts of manufacturers, and in spite of the fact that some managers of New England mills are only lukewarm and a few others consider that the time spent in the textile schools could be used to better advantage in a mill, the manufacturers are, in the main, enthusiastic supporters. In the South there seems to be less interest taken in the schools by the employers.

Chemists and certain other experts must have a scientific training, and in general the American employers find the graduates of textile schools satisfactorily equipped in these branches, so that there is a fairly good demand for the services of such specialists. With designing it is somewhat different. A great deal has been heard about the need for the American cotton manufacturers to develop original designs, but the demand continues to be chiefly for men who can copy European designs, not for those with originality. Although there has been little to encourage the schools to put forth more effort in this direction, they do continue to urge men to take up that line of work.

The concensus of opinion in America seems to be, both on the side of the administrators of the schools and of the manufacturers, that the experiments have not yet had time to show their effects, that their fruit has not yet ripened. It is quite probable, however, that in the future the textile schools will be of vital importance in aiding to bring about technical improvements, in educating the rank and file of the workmen, and in helping to provide men capable of managing a department of a cotton mill, or of superintending a whole mill. The last function has assumed more and more significance with the growth of the industry and the development of its organization.

CHAPTER VIII

SCALE OF PRODUCTION AND SPECIALIZATION

THE history of the expansion of the American cotton manufacturing industry under the influence of various factors has thus far been traced. The analysis of its organization should next be considered, since improvements in organization have resulted in savings which have probably been greater than those arising from the advance in technique. There are two distinct divisions of the subject, the industrial organization and the commercial organization. The former includes size of plant, specialization, and combinations. The opening chapter is devoted to the first two topics under the subject of industrial organization.

Large Scale Production

For many years cotton yarn and cloth have been produced in the United States only under the factory system. The essential characteristic of this system, as contrasted with the domestic or "putting out" system, is a better organization of the unit of production under the direct supervision of the manufacturer, — better adjustment, better discipline, better regulation. Consequently, whatever changes aim at improving the organization of manufacturing methods and management under such direct oversight are to be considered as extensions of the factory system. Hence within this category falls the increase in the scale of production since that has for its primary object either a better utilization of natural resources and advantages, a greater subdivision of labor, a nicer adjustment of machinery and processes, or economies in management.

During the period which has elapsed since the Civil War the size of American cotton mills has increased, although the average size differs between different sections of the country and also between kinds of work. In New England the average number of spindles per establishment in 1860, according to the Census of that year, was 6,700; in Massachusetts 7,700. These statistics, though admittedly inaccurate, indicate the size of the mills in the chief cotton manufacturing centre immediately before the outbreak of the Civil War. In 1870, to show the scale of production at the time when the rate of expansion was becoming accelerated, the average number of spindles per establishment in New England was 10,823; in Massachusetts 13,715. At each of these dates there were few cotton mills in other parts of the country, and they were smaller than the New England mills. Hence we can conclude that the representative mill in 1870 had not over twenty thousand spindles.

At the present time a representative New England mill has from fifty to one hundred thousand spindles. This is shown by statements of manufacturers, by the textile directories, and finally by the Census statistics of 1905. According to the Census the average number of spindles per spinning and weaving mill in New England in 1905 was 55,000.[1] As a rule the advantages of large scale production are fully obtained by a plant of fifty to seventy-five thousand spindles, and one to two thousand looms.

There are various reasons for this increase in the size of the plants. In the first place, it enables economy in management. A large concern can afford to employ a more efficient superintendent and more efficient assistants to direct the work in the different departments, since the larger the plant the less the overhead expense in proportion to product. In the second place, with the advance in technique, machinery has become more expensive; and there are some labor saving machines which can be employed economically only when the industry is on a large scale, as for example the machines for tying or drawing in the warps. In securing the proper adjustment and balancing of the different departments the large plant has an advantage. Again, many of the larger establishments have their own repair shops, and the burden of the cost of

---

[1] *U. S. Census of Manufactures*, 1905, *Bulletin* No. 74, p. 55.

equipping and maintaining such a shop is relatively less for a large plant. There is also a saving in power, since it can be supplied more economically for one large plant than for several small ones. In some New England cities, control of water-power rights has led the older corporations to make additions to their plants; they have exploited their monopoly privileges. Finally there is doubtless some economy in buying supplies and in selling the goods, especially when a mill owns valuable trade marks.

There are a number of plants much larger than the average, however, which as a class present certain peculiar characteristics. The Amoskeag Mills in Manchester, New Hampshire, have 650,000 spindles; the Fall River Iron Works, 466,800; the Wamsutta Mills in New Bedford, 222,500; the Pacific Mills in Lawrence, 179,600; and several more operate over 100,000 spindles. These great plants are really combinations of several mills, since each is divided into separate departments in which both spinning and weaving are carried on. All the spindles are not grouped in one building and all the looms in another, but each department is a more or less complete cotton mill in itself. The Wamsutta plant comprises nine mills, and the Fall River Iron Works seven. This decentralization would probably not have taken place if the division of labor among the operatives were not carried to the extreme in a mill of about fifty thousand spindles, so that little is to be gained in that respect by further concentration of the processes. A saving results from this splitting up, as each mill can be specialized and the yarn prepared and more easily delivered to the looms. Better adjustment is secured, while at the same time each department is large enough to make it profitable to employ a capable supervisor to direct it.

In view of this division within the plant, the question may fairly be raised as to what advantages accrue from combining the mills into one plant. The benefits of large scale production, to be sure, make themselves felt here. The burden of overhead expense is lightened, some advantage in capital and credit obtained, and economy in machinery, power, and repairs secured. But after a certain point is reached, the saving through reduplication becomes relatively less and less. The chief reason for such combination lies in the fact that nearly all of these exceptionally large concerns bleach, print, or dye their own products. This can be done more economically in the larger plant, since the finishing must be on a fairly large scale in order to make it pay to equip and maintain the works and employ efficient overseers.

In the South the mills are smaller than in New England. Taking as the unit the spinning and weaving mill, as we did for New England, the average number of spindles per establishment in 1905 was 27,300 in South Carolina, 15,700 in Georgia, and only 11,500 in North Carolina. Thus the representative mill in South Carolina is only half as large as that in New England, and in North Carolina only slightly over one-fifth as large. To be sure, there are a few big mills in the South, — in South Carolina the Olympia Mills with 100,300 spindles, the Union-Buffalo Company's plant at Union with 94,000 spindles, and the Anderson Mills with 70,000 spindles; in Georgia, the Massachusetts Mills in Georgia with 90,000 spindles, and the Eagle and Phoenix Mills with 70,000 spindles; and in Alabama the Merrimack Mills with 92,500 spindles. But these big mills are exceptional and stand out strongly in contrast with the numerous small establishments distributed all over the Piedmont district. Many of the small concerns have less than 10,000 spindles, frequently only three or four thousand.

The small sized mills have come into existence and have continued to live by reason of certain local advantages. Water-power was available at numerous points, and a little mill was sometimes started to utilize a local water-fall. Local pride induced investors, such as farmers or merchants, to put their savings into a mill, though small, in their own neighborhood rather than in a more remote centre. The most influential factor, however, was labor. Frequently a mill was established in an out of the way place so as to employ workmen who were not willing to move but would work for low wages near their homes. And wherever the small factories were situated, in large towns or country villages, it was the lower wage level which made it possible for them to compete successfully with the larger mills in the North.

The little mills in the South, when they have not failed, have gradually increased in size though the average is still far below that in New England. They have found themselves handicapped in various ways. Some have suffered from unfavorable location, others from other disadvantages, and all from the sacrifice of the technical and administrative advantages to be gained by centralization and large scale production. The management of such mills has generally been inefficient or disproportionately expensive. They have either been unable to employ efficient superintendents, or else have employed men who could manage a large plant and therefore command a salary out of proportion to the work which they were called upon to do. A superintendent of the former class has been known to stop his whole mill while he figured out how he could remedy a slight defect in the gearing.

The mills which produce specialties such as braids and tape, wherever located, are smaller than the cloth mills. The establishments in the vicinity of Philadelphia, which manufacture lace, lace curtains, and upholstery goods, are likewise relatively smaller. The market for these classes of goods is narrower, and the product less standardized.

While the knitting industry has manifested the same tendency toward large scale production, its progress in that direction has been independent of the development of cloth manufacturing. It was not until after 1860 that there was a factory production of knit goods of any magnitude in the United States, and only during the 'eighties that the manufacture of cotton knit goods assumed first importance. With the improvements in technique, the factory system developed, and at the same time the knitting of cotton yarn became more important than the knitting of woolen yarn. In 1890 the statement was made in the Census report that the knitting industry was still half domestic. But the inventions which were just then being introduced soon brought the manufacture of cotton knit goods under the factory system.[1] The automatic knitting machines could be used to best advantage in the production of large quantities of standardized goods, and the specialized finishing machines necessitated subdivision of labor.

The introduction of the factory system into the knitting industry has been followed by an increase in the size of the plants. We have no satisfactory index to show this growth, since there is a difference in the machines used and the number of processes included. The large mills usually spin their own yarn while the smaller establishments buy their supplies. Moreover in the Census, cotton, woolen, and silk knit goods are unavoidably grouped together in such a way that it is not possible to present statistics relative to the size of the establishments in any one branch. But an examination of a textile directory shows that the largest establishments in the knit-goods industry are those producing cotton knit goods, particularly those manufacturing hosiery and underwear staples. The majority of the smaller establishments manufacture gloves, mittens, and various other articles for which the demand is more limited. The Census of 1900 states that " the great variety of goods made facilitates a tendency shown by this industry to maintain itself in comparatively small mills which purchase their yarns and require but small capital." The large mills which manufacture staples have an advantage in better management, and especially in greater division of labor, nevertheless the small mills are able to maintain themselves during the period of transition. It would not be advisable for them to attempt to spin their own yarn as long as they are not able to consume it in large quantities. Although small establishments still exist, their number will probably diminish with the concentration of the industry and the sharper definition of the lines along which it is to develop in the future.

Specialization

As the industrial units for the manufacture of cotton have become larger in size, as the volume of product has increased,

---

[1] The domestic system, it should be stated, has not entirely died out, since the products of a few small mills are still put out to be finished.

this product has become more and more diversified. Hand in hand with diversification has gone specialization. Localities, because of natural or acquired advantages, are more or less identified with the production of a certain class or classes of goods. The plants also have been more or less specialized, and even within individual plants there is not infrequently a further specialization.

The distinction which naturally first attracts attention is that between the products of northern and southern mills. To show the character of the output for these sections the statistics of the Census for 1900 and 1905 are available, but the classification for earlier years unfortunately does not permit of detailed comparison.

PRODUCTS

(*Million sq. yds.*)

	United States		New England		South	
	1900	1905	1900	1905	1900	1905
Print cloth, (not finer than No. 28 warp)	1,056.3	812.3	847.9	575.3	111.1	159.8
Print cloth (finer than No. 28 warp)	525.3	1,006.0	383.2	556.2	139.2	446.0
Sheetings and Shirtings	1,212.4	1,172.3	481.3	373.1	644.6	737.0
Twills and Sateens	235.9	366.1	198.8	277.9	15.6	79.1
Fancy Woven Fabrics	237.8	306.3	188.1	215.2	11.5	49.8
Ginghams	278.4	302.3	111.5	163.2	151.9	130.8
Duck, sail	11.8	9.6	.5	.7	2.7	6.5
Duck, other	117.5	113.0	31.0	22.4	66.8	74.9
Drills	237.2	194.7	48.2	30.0	188.8	164.3
Ticks, Denims, and Stripes	171.8	256.4	108.4	109.1	50.4	138.6
Cottonades	26.3	25.4	5.6	2.7	12.4	14.5
Napped fabrics	268.9	330.8	218.6	243.5	40.6	86.1
Corduroy, Cotton Velvet, and Plush	7.9	16.0	3.7	7.6	....	1.7

These statistics show that New England predominates in the manufacture of print cloth, twills and sateens, fancy woven fabrics, napped fabrics, and corduroy, cotton velvet, and plush; the South in sheetings and shirtings, duck, drills, and cottonades; while in ginghams and ticks, denims, and stripes, the two sections are about equal. The apparent decline in the manufacture of coarse print cloth in New England in 1905 was due to the protracted strike in Fall River in 1904 which greatly cut down the total output. It is to be noted that the bulk of the goods in both sections are still of coarse or medium grade. Although the New England mills are producing more and more fine goods, they continue to turn out large quantities of the coarse grades, and the South has made only a small beginning in the manufacture of the finer fabrics.

Various factors have caused the increase in the production of fine and fancy goods in New England. In the first place, the advance of the industry in the South stimulated the New England manufacturers about 1890 to seek new fields.[1] In the manufacture of the higher grades they had an advantage in a larger supply of skilled labor, since there were some operatives in New England who had been in the mills long enough to have become more or less skilled, and in addition a considerable number of English, Scotch, and German immigrants were available, who had acquired a knowledge of these branches in Europe. The supply of capable overseers was a most important item in this labor force. At the same time, the demand for finer goods was expanding, a demand arising from the material prosperity of the country. The technical improvements introduced since 1860, also, were becoming adapted more and more to fine spinning and weaving and the finishing of fancies. And with the growth of the trade new inventions especially adapted to its needs have been introduced, partially a result of the expansion and at the same time an added impetus.

Another factor has been the protective tariff. The manufacturers would doubtless give this as the chief reason and cite it as a justification of the "infant industries" argument. Yet it may well be asked why the infant did not commence to grow sooner. Since the days of the Civil War the tariff on fine and fancy goods has certainly been high enough to stimulate the growth of almost any branch, if that were all that were needed. But it was not till after the competition of the southern mills became ominous, and the production of cotton cloth had become

[1] Chamber of Commerce of the State of New York, 33d *Annual Report*, p. 82. The movement became more general at this time, although there had previously been changes by the more far-sighted managers.

so great that at last our mills could supply the coarse goods demanded by a rapidly growing population, that the manufacturers began to take advantage of the protection offered by the high tariff. Secure in their possession of the domestic market which expanded as fast as new mills were built, the stimulus of competition from within was necessary to induce the mill owners to turn to hitherto unexploited fields. The high profits which the fine goods mills have made testify to the wisdom of their undertakings.

The distinctions between the products of the local centres can be but roughly drawn. In Lowell and Lawrence, drills, sheetings, and shirtings are still manufactured, but of possibly greater importance is the output of such goods as fancy prints, corduroys, velveteens, and other seasonal fabrics. This characteristic is due primarily to the inclusion of printing and dyeing departments in the original equipment of the older mills in those cities. As the competition in the more common grades became keener, these mills undertook the printing of more fancy patterns and the output of other specialties. In Manchester, New Hampshire, the bulk of the cotton goods manufactured are ginghams, and in several other cities in this district there are mills which manufacture fabrics of similar character. Such products are seasonal goods, not staples.

The cloth manufactured in the southern section of New England eludes classification. Fall River has long been a centre for the weaving of print cloths, a print works having been established there in 1825.[1] This print works, however, as well as those later erected in Fall River, was not connected with a weaving mill. The growth of Fall River was particularly rapid after 1865, at the time when calico was popular. Hence most of the mills built at that time wove print cloth, and at the present day Fall River dominates the print cloth market. These goods are mainly standardized staples and are not converted by the manufacturer. The separation of converting (in this case printing) and of manufacturing checked a development similar to that which has come about in the Lowell and Lawrence dis-

---

[1] H. H. Earl, *History of Fall River*, p. 23.

trict. With a change in fashion, however, the market for calico ceased to expand at the same rate as that for other cotton goods. As a result the building of print cloth mills ceased about fifteen years ago in Fall River, and practically all of the new mills have been equipped for the manufacture of fine white goods, as in New Bedford.

The expansion of cotton manufacturing in New Bedford during the last twenty years has been rapid, and fine white goods have been predominantly the characteristic product of the new factories. The time at which this development became accelerated in New Bedford was not one in which the prospects for the production of coarse goods were favorable in New England. Competition from the South was most severe. But there was an increasing demand for cloth of higher quality, and the favorable climate of New Bedford has been an important factor in enabling her fine goods manufacturers to meet this demand, since humidity and freedom from rapid fluctuations in temperature are essential in the spinning and weaving of fine yarns.

No local specialization can be distinguished in the South, owing in part to the recent establishment of the industry in that section, and in part to its not being strongly localized. The Middle Atlantic States more closely resemble New England. Philadelphia is not only the centre of the hosiery and lace manufacturing industry, but also of the production of cotton upholstery goods. As previously stated, the Mohawk Valley in New York is the leading district for the manufacture of underwear. The knit goods produced in Massachusetts, it may be added, are both hosiery and underwear, and in the southern and western states primarily hosiery.

As between different establishments there has always been more or less specialization of product, each confining itself, as a rule, to the manufacture of one general class of goods, although there is frequently considerable variety within this class. Prior to the Civil War the bulk of the goods made in this country were coarse, and each mill produced but a few grades. Since the manufacture of goods of higher quality began, several of the older mills have changed their whole plant to the production of some single class of high grade fabrics. Some, as for example the Amoskeag, have become gingham mills. Others have specialized on fancy prints, corduroys, or fine sheetings and shirtings. And the newer mills in southern New England, as already stated, have been equipped for the manufacture of fine white goods. In the South there are only a few mills which produce anything but coarse cloth. The small size of most of the southern mills prevents much internal diversification of product, while the larger mills produce mainly export goods of three or four styles.

The large northern concerns with a diversified output are composed of a series of units. The plants are divided into separate mills, Mill Number 1, Mill Number 2, and so on, each of which is confined to a single grade of work. In each of these departments yarn is spun and woven and all the processes carefully adjusted to the kind of cloth to be produced. To be sure, the cloth from all the mills is finished by a single department, if the concern finishes its own product, but in the manufacture of the cloth there is more or less specialization even in those plants which at first seem exceptions to the general tendency.

Although there are some mills which do no weaving but spin yarn for sale to supply knitting mills and weaving mills which are temporarily unable to meet their own needs, most of the mills in the United States both spin and weave. This practice of combining weaving and spinning arose early in the last century. The power looms introduced by the mills which had previously woven their yarn on hand looms or disposed of it for household weaving while the industry was still in its infancy, fostered the extension of the combination as the industry grew. In the early days it would have been difficult for weaving mills to obtain a regular supply of yarn since the factories were scattered and the means of communication crude. Accordingly, after the introduction of the power loom, each mill undertook from the first to carry on all the processes of manufacturing cotton cloth, and as the industry expanded the practice continued, partly from custom and partly because the mills remained scattered over a relatively wide area.

The technical development, furthermore, was such as to discourage separation, and has been the determining factor since the great improvements in means of communication which would have made possible the disposal of yarn by the spinner and its purchase by the weaver. The development of ring spinning, which is especially adapted to the industrial conditions in the country, makes it desirable to weave the yarn where it is spun, because of the heavy expense of transporting the wooden bobbins.

The extent to which spinning and weaving are combined is shown by the following table from the Census of 1905.

COTTON MILLS IN UNITED STATES, 1905 [1]

	Spinning and Weaving Mills	Spinning Mills	Weaving Mills
Establishments	590	295	169
Spindles	19,171,542	3,984,071	.....
Looms	522,301	.....	18,609

While only fifty-five per cent of the establishments in the United States in 1905 carried on both spinning and weaving, these mills contained eighty-three per cent of the total number of spindles and ninety-seven per cent of the total number of looms. The greater number of the mills devoted to weaving solely are small establishments in Pennsylvania producing fancy goods. The majority of the mills which are engaged in spinning only are located in the South. These southern spinning mills, especially numerous in North Carolina, are for the most part small establishments of five thousand spindles or less. The reasons for their existence have already been explained in describing the conditions peculiar to the industrial development of that section. That they should be engaged in spinning rather than in weaving is obviously due to their location near the supply of raw material. The spinner could save more on freight than the weaver, if his capital were not sufficient to warrant the undertaking of both processes.

Cotton cloth is seldom converted at the mill where it is woven. Several of the older mills have continued to operate the bleaching

---

[1] *U. S. Census of Manufactures*, 1905, *Bulletin* No. 74, p. 55.

plants, print works, or dye-houses which were installed early in their history. Gingham mills, also, usually have facilities for dyeing, since they use large quantities of dyed yarn. But by far the greater part of the cloth converting is done in independent establishments, a proportion which has become greater and greater with the increase in the number of large bleacheries, print works, and dyeing establishments dependent upon job work. These converting establishments, with a few exceptions, do not purchase the goods but convert them for the manufacturer, or more frequently for the merchant-converter.

There are two reasons why the converting of cotton goods has become more highly specialized during the last fifty years. First, it is more economical to do the work on a large scale, since it requires skill and experience, and the output of many mills can be converted much more cheaply by a single large establishment.[1] Secondly, the demand for a greater variety of finishes and designs has resulted in the rise of the merchant-converter and the specialization of the converting business.

The extent to which this specialization has gone is shown by the Census report of 1905.[2] In that year over four-fifths of the cloth printed, three-fourths of the cloth bleached, nine-tenths of the cloth dyed, and practically all of the cloth mercerized was operated upon in independent establishments. On the other hand the greater part of the raw stock dyeing, and yarn dyeing and bleaching was done by the mills themselves. The converting plants are located in New England and the Middle States, this branch of the cotton industry still being in an experimental stage in the South where the water is not suitable for bleaching and dyeing without filtering, and where there is a dearth of men capable of directing the work. Moreover, as most of the southern goods are shipped north to be sold, it is as economical to convert them near that market.

---

[1] There is an exception to this. Mills making heavy cloth, such as quilts and crash, often bleach their own goods and will probably do so to a greater extent in the future, since in this grade of work little skill is required and freight charges are an important item.

[2] *U. S. Census of Manufactures*, 1905, *Bulletin* No. 74, p. 205.

The manufacture of knit goods is another specialized branch. Some of the large knitting mills spin their own yarn, but a majority rely upon spinning mills for their supply. Some mills knit both hosiery and underwear, whereas others, especially the smaller ones, confine themselves to one branch.

Standardization of product is more characteristic of American cotton mills than specialization. Long ago the coarse and medium plain goods were standardized so that the manufacturer seldom changed his machines from one kind to another. Similarly at the present time he produces large quantities of each sort for which he accepts orders. These are the goods which are manufactured for stock when trade is temporarily dull. Likewise many designs of fine white cloth are standardized. They, too, are staples. The patterns of other white and striped goods are frequently changed,. but no small orders are accepted. In the manufacture of fancy prints, also, new designs are offered each season, but in this case the changes affect only the printing department inasmuch as the distinguishing feature is not weave but the pattern printed upon them. Yet each of these designs is for the time being standardized, since, as in the case of stripes and other fancy weaves, no mill will take an order for less than two thousand yards of a single pattern, and in many mills the minimum order acceptable is from six to ten thousand yards. The labor cost of preparing the pattern and setting up the machinery, both for fancy woven designs and for prints, is so high that small orders are not profitable for the American manufacturer.

CHAPTER IX

ASSOCIATIONS AND COMBINATIONS

THE cotton manufacturing industry of the United States is frequently pointed out as an instance of a large industry in which the so-called " trust movement " has not, to any extent, made itself apparent. When we speak of the " trust movement," we usually have in mind the combination of a large proportion of the firms engaged in any industry, under a unified management. The large " trusts," however, which attract so much attention, are only the more prominent manifestations of a deep-rooted and far-extending movement which is going on throughout the business world today.

Just as on the one hand the factory system and large scale production represent the development of a higher organization of manufacturing, so on the other hand, as Professor Gay suggests, the movement for combination is primarily one for more effective organization of the market. The formation of trade associations, amalgamation, and integration are manifestations of the attempt to economize in buying and selling. As the various units engaged in the manufacture of any article or class of articles have become grouped in certain localities, have specialized their business, and especially as they have become larger in size and the market has become broader, the need for united action has made itself more and more felt. At the same time these changes have made it easier for the manufacturers to act together in preventing ruinous competition.

With this incentive to combination the motive for production on a larger scale, or aggregation, is closely connected and at times even confused. In the case of the United States Steel Corporation, the American Sugar Refining Company, and the so-called " Beef Trust," for example, the two elements are intimately joined together. In the cotton manufacturing industry, as we shall see, a similar interweaving exists in the case of the large trade associations and of the few amalgamations which have taken place. On the whole, however, the fact that under present conditions of manufacturing and of the organization of the market a plant of one hundred thousand spindles, at the most, secures practically all of the advantages of large scale production has tended to encourage united action in ways less conspicuous than those followed by the great " trusts."

In the analysis of combinations in the cotton manufacturing industry four classes are to be distinguished, — loose trade associations, local associations, amalgamations of several plants, and finally integration.

Associations

There are two large associations of cotton manufacturers, which aim primarily at the improvement of the methods of manufacture. The older of these is the National Association of Cotton Manufacturers, which had its origin in the Hampden County (Mass.) Cotton Spinners' Association, established in 1854. This became the New England Cotton Manufacturers' Association in 1865, and the National Association of Cotton Manufacturers in 1906. The benefits which resulted from the establishment of the parent association aroused wider and wider interest among cotton manufacturers and led to its expansion. The membership, which now numbers nearly one thousand, is individual, but includes representatives of almost all of the cotton manufacturing companies in New England and of many companies in other parts of the country. Two meetings are held each year, at which papers are presented on topics connected with the various phases of the industry. The discussion upon these papers furnishes opportunity for an exchange of ideas, thus bringing to the attention of the manufacturers new methods and recent improvements, and giving them the benefit of the experience of others. The papers and discussions are published, and in that way made available for all of the members. It is impossible to measure the influence which this association has had upon the development of the industry during the last fifty years, but it must have been by no means small.

The second large association is the American Cotton Manufacturers' Association which was founded in 1903. This is an association primarily of southern cotton manufacturers, its purposes and methods being similar to those of the older organization.[1] The knit-goods manufacturers, likewise, in 1905 established the National Association of Hosiery Manufacturers.

These associations are what might be termed educational. Their purpose is to keep their members informed of the progress which is taking place in the manufacturing of cotton goods, and of the ways in which further improvement can be brought about on either the technical or the administrative side.

The local associations have a different purpose. In this class are the Fall River, New Bedford, and Lowell associations of local manufacturers. They aim to secure better coöperation among the managers of the mills in their respective localities, and especially to deal with labor troubles. They have enabled united action in preventing strikes and in settling labor disputes. The Fall River association reached the highest point by becoming a party to the sliding scale agreement, according to which the wages of the operatives were fixed. To be sure, such an agreement was possible only when both employers and employees were organized, and the fairly strong labor unions in the Fall River cotton mills brought this about. In other localities the local associations have succeeded in holding out against such a recognition of the operatives' unions, and the weak organization or non-organization of the laborers has enabled the manufacturers to do more nearly as they pleased. These local associations do not include every concern in their respective localities, as there are always one or two manufacturers who prefer to act independently. For example, Mr. M. C. D. Borden, president of the Fall River Iron Works, the largest cotton manufacturing plant in Fall River was not a member of the local association, and did not coöperate with it. However, these associations are strong enough to exercise great influence

---

[1] In the agitations among the cotton manufacturers in 1909–10 to secure curtailment because of the high price of cotton, this association took the lead in the South.

in the regulation of local questions. They deal with other matters besides labor disputes, but the ability to present a solid front to the laborers is their primary purpose.

The next class of associations have a somewhat different object. They undertake to adjust output when the market is out of balance, and also to follow labor legislation and oppose the enactment of new restrictions. In the South there are several such associations, — the Southern Hard Yarn Spinners' Association, the Southern Soft Yarn Spinners' Association, the North Carolina Cotton Manufacturers' Association, the South Carolina Cotton Manufacturers' Association, and the Georgia Industrial Association. The first two of these attempt to secure coöperation in curtailment of output when the market seems to demand it. The others seek to obtain uniform enforcement of the labor laws, and to regulate the conditions of labor. They have of themselves initiated some reforms, but have also successfully opposed the passage of other more stringent laws.

An older and larger association of this type is the Arkwright Club, which was organized in Boston in 1880. The preamble to its constitution states that " its purpose is to cultivate social intercourse among managers of corporations or private establishments manufacturing textile fabrics or machinery, or of allied industries, and to promote good understanding and united action upon affairs of general interest to these industries." [1] At first the membership was limited to one hundred, but later this restriction was abandoned. The club is a purely voluntary association of individuals, and no means are provided for enforcing recommendations. The members of the club are the treasurers of many of the larger New England cotton mills, and at first included chiefly those with their offices in Boston.

The club meets monthly for a lunch or dinner, and at these meetings trade conditions are talked over and recommendations as to regulation of output made. Until recently at least, more than fifteen or sixteen members have seldom been present at one of the meetings, and those who attended have not been bound to accept the decisions of the majority. Frequently a

---

[1] *By-Laws of the Arkwright Club*, published in 1884.

committee has been appointed to communicate with all of the members to obtain their views upon a given situation, and to attempt to induce them to act together, for instance in restricting output. While the organization is thus loose and without mandatory power, it has brought the mill treasurers together and through social pressure has been able to secure more or less general observance of its recommendations. It has also followed labor legislation, and opposed further restrictions upon the age and sex of the laborers, and upon the hours of labor.

The club, while continuing to carry out these objects, greatly widened the scope of its activities in 1906 by establishing a transportation agency. This was a marked step toward greater coöperation among New England cotton manufacturers, who had, on the whole, acted very independently hitherto. With the new undertaking, the membership was also increased [1] and now the club includes all the important cotton mills in New England, except those in Connecticut which are engaged chiefly in the manufacture of specialties, the thread mills, the mills owned by the Knights of Providence, those owned by the Goddards, and the Fall River Iron Works. In January, 1909, the number of affiliated cotton manufacturing firms was one hundred and fourteen.

This transportation agency, the New England Cotton Freight Claim Bureau, is a subordinate organization under the control of the Arkwright Club. It was created by the members of the club in conjunction with various cotton brokers and buyers in Boston, Fall River, New Bedford, and Providence, the brokers and buyers giving financial assistance. The objects in the creation of this bureau were to concentrate the tracing of cotton shipments, to secure the settlement of claims, which had previously been done by individual mills, brokers, and buyers, and to obtain a better and more complete delivery of cotton shipments. It has also enabled the mills to act together in the matter of freight rates, especially on coal, and to deal concertedly with other problems which arise from time to time. An experienced railroad man has been employed to direct the work, and

---

[1] Previously few of the Fall River and New Bedford mills had been affiliated.

the efforts of the agency have already met with success. Several favorable adjustments have been made with the railroads. The stealing of cotton at points of transhipment has been investigated, and the questions of switching charges and changes in classification have been taken up. Through this single agency these matters can evidently be handled to far greater advantage and with much less cost to the mills.

Its efforts have not ended there, however. It has secured a reduction of twenty per cent in " marine insurance " rates, that is in rates of transit insurance, the term " marine insurance " being applied to insurance on the cotton in transit whether it is shipped by water or by rail. Moreover, an arrangement with the insurance companies is now pending, whereby these companies will annually report their net losses, that is the losses over and above what they recover from the railroads, in that way furnishing a basis for the adjustment of the rates of insurance. Again, steps have been taken toward the buying of certain supplies and the selling of waste through the one agency. This new branch of the activities of the Arkwright Club has already effected important economies for the mills, and a further expansion may be expected. The manifestation of the spirit of coöperation is significant as it shows how some of the benefits of combination can be secured without actual amalgamation.

The community of interest among New England cotton manufacturers is an important factor to be considered in connection with the development of associations for regulating output and securing uniformity of policy. The stock of the New England cotton mills is in many cases closely held. In a few instances the stock of one company is all in the hands of a single family, but more frequently a large proportion of the stock is owned by the members of a few families. A number of these families hold stock in several mills, and a net-work of such inter-relations extends over the greater part of the New England cotton manufacturing district. At one point one set of interests comes in contact with another set, at the next point with still another, and the weaving in and out of these controlling interests makes it much easier to secure a uniform policy.

This community of interest is shown by the connections of prominent men with different mills. For example, one man may be president of one or two mills, treasurer of another, and director of several more; or he may be president of more and not treasurer of any; or he may be treasurer of two or even three mills. These men are usually connected by birth or marriage with several other men in similar positions. This community of interest must have had some influence in encouraging united action in times of emergency. In the South several groups are being formed, but as yet there has not been an interweaving of interests in the southern cotton mills as great as that among the cotton mill owners in New England.

Although the mutual fire insurance companies are alliances for a special purpose distinct from that of the other associations and combinations, they nevertheless should be mentioned in this connection. There are now nineteen companies for the mutual insurance of textile factories against loss by fire, the first having been organized in 1835. It has proved to be more economical for the mills to group together in a mutual company than to place their insurance with outside companies. The policy holders pay premiums which are estimated approximately to cover the losses without yielding a large surplus. No capital stock is issued. Each member is liable to assessment to five times the amount of his premium, but in practice such assessments are never necessary. All these companies have joined in the support of an Inspection and Adjustment Department, each company sharing the expense in proportion to its outstanding risk. Inspectors are employed to ascertain the condition and protection equipment of each factory insured and to study every fire that occurs so as to try to prevent another from arising through a similar cause. The result of the organization of these companies and their progressive methods has been to reduce the cost of insurance from 40 cents per $100 fifty years ago to about 8 cents per $100 at the present time.[1]

[1] J. R. MacColl, " Factory Mutual Insurance in America," *Report of the 6th International Congress of Master Cotton Spinners' and Manufacturers' Associations* (Milan, 1909), pp. 159–160.

Amalgamations

Another form of combination, next in order after the loose associations which seek to promote the general interests of their members, is the amalgamation of competing establishments. There are, in general, two purposes for which amalgamation may be brought about. The first is economy in manufacture or distribution, and is, therefore, analogous to increasing the scale of production. The other aims at securing a monopolistic control whereby prices may be fixed. The success of amalgamation for the former purpose depends upon the economies to be gained from a further increase in the size of the units, for the latter upon the possibility of securing control of supplies of raw material, or of methods and machinery, whereby it may restrict the rise of competitors.

Local amalgamations, as for instance the absorption of neighboring concerns by the Amoskeag Company of Manchester, have occasionally been formed. And in the South there have recently been two large combinations, apparently for the purpose of securing economies in selling. One of these, the Parker group, was said in 1911 to have merged nine mills, operating 357,952 spindles. The other group, controlled by the Cannon interests, comprises twelve mills in North Carolina, with 288,500 spindles and 3,734 looms. Aside from these mergers, there have been four prominent examples of amalgamation in the cotton manufacturing industry in the United States, — the Consolidated Cotton Duck Company, the New England Cotton Yarn Company, the United States Finishing Company, and the American Thread Company.

The Consolidated Cotton Duck Company had its origin [1] in the formation of the Mount Vernon-Woodberry Cotton Duck Company of Baltimore in 1899. This was a combination of seven firms, owning fourteen mills. The company was capitalized at $9,500,000, and was authorized to issue five per cent first mortgage bonds to the amount of $8,000,000, and five per cent income bonds to the amount of $6,000,000. All the stock

---

[1] *Commercial and Financial Chronicle*, vol. lxix, p. 129.

was issued and also $13,000,000 of the bonds, the remainder being reserved for the acquisition of new properties. In 1901 the United States Cotton Duck Corporation was organized to take over the control of the Mount Vernon-Woodberry Company and to absorb the Stark Mills in New Hampshire and two mills in Georgia.[1] The object of this absorption was to eliminate serious competition in sail duck. At this time the Stark Mills were increasing their output of duck, although even then it constituted but one-third of their total product. The Baltimore combination especially felt the competition from this source and accordingly made an offer to the shareholders of the Stark company to buy their stock at fifty per cent more than its par value. The offer was accepted, and the new United States Cotton Duck Corporation assumed control. At the same time two southern mills were purchased. These southern mills continued to be engaged in the production of duck, but the Stark Mills were not changed over to the manufacture of duck entirely; in fact the quantity of duck turned out at that plant rather tended to diminish in favor of other goods. The strain of the competition, however, was removed.

The combination, in the next place, closed some of its plants. In 1902 the small mill in Hartford, Connecticut, was shut down,[2] and in 1903 three small mills in Maryland were closed and the machinery transferred to the larger Maryland mills.[3]

During the first five years of its existence the Mount Vernon Company paid good dividends, but in 1905 a reorganization became necessary.[4] Up to this time the Mount Vernon-Woodberry Cotton Duck Company, although controlled by the United States Cotton Duck Corporation, had maintained a separate corporate existence. The latter company owned $9,031,000 of the $9,500,000 common stock of the former, and in addition owned the Stark Mills and the two southern mills. There were outstanding at this time the following securities, — the Mount Vernon-Woodberry Company's common stock, $9,500,000; its

---

[1] *Commercial and Financial Chronicle*, vol. lxxii, p. 992.
[2] *Ibid.*, vol. lxxv, p. 295.
[3] *Ibid.*, vol. lxxvi, p. 1038.
[4] *Ibid.*, vol. lxxx, p. 1916.

first mortgage bonds, $8,420,000; and its income bonds, $6,000,-000; the United States Company's preferred stock, $2,750,000, and its common stock, $10,000,000. This made a total of $36,670,000. According to the plans of reorganization this total capitalization was to be reduced to $21,420,000. For each $1000 of the Mount Vernon-Woodberry Company's income bonds the holders were to receive $500 preferred stock and $166⅔ common stock in the new company. For each $1000 of the preferred stock of the United States Corporation the holders were to receive $1000 preferred and 727\frac{3}{11}$ common stock in the new company. And for each $1000 of common stock in the United States company the holders were to receive $400 common stock. Thus the holders of the income bonds of the Mount Vernon-Woodberry Company received new securities to two-thirds of the par value of the old securities. The common stock of that company was practically all owned by one of the consolidating companies; hence no provision for its exchange was made. The holders of the preferred stock of the United States Corporation received new securities of a par value seventy-three per cent greater, in fact a bonus of seventy-three per cent in the common stock of the new company. But the common stock of the United States Corporation was exchanged for new stock of only forty per cent of its par value. Thus the new company, the Consolidated Cotton Duck Company as it was called, had a capitalization of $13,000,000, including $6,000,000 six per cent cumulative preferred stock and $7,000,000 common stock. It had no bonded debt of its own, but had assumed responsibility for the $8,420,000 first mortgage bonds of the Mount Vernon-Woodberry Company.

The reasons for the adjustment of the scale of exchange are not apparent, nor do they especially concern us here. The important point for us is that it was necessary to squeeze some of the water out of the stock of the original companies. The objects of the reorganization were stated by the officials in charge to be a more conservative capitalization, less taxation, and more unified management whereby the work could be distributed to better advantage. This reduction of capitalization is significant as showing that the combination did not bring as great advantages as had been anticipated; no great saving had resulted.   Later, in order that it might control the marketing of its product, the Consolidated Cotton Duck Company purchased the entire capital stock of the J. Spencer Turner Company of New York,[1] one of the largest dealers in cotton duck.

A second reorganization was deemed necessary in 1910. The object was set forth by the directors in the following words. " Recognizing that increased selling arrangements are essential to the best results in the disposal of our products, we are making arrangements whereby the admirable selling organization of the Boston Yarn Company will, in conjunction with the J. Spencer Turner Company, handle the product of our mills and the Turner Company will handle, in conjunction with the Boston Yarn Company, the sales products controlled by the latter."[2]   To this end the International Cotton Mills Corporation was incorporated in New York in July, 1910,[3] with $20,000,000 authorized capital stock, consisting of $10,000,000 seven per cent cumulative preferred and $10,000,000 common stock.   The properties comprised those of the Consolidated Cotton Duck Company, the three mills controlled by the Boston Yarn Company, one other mill in Massachusetts, and two in Canada.   This gave the new corporation the control of twenty-two mills and two selling houses, manufacturing and distributing about 3,000 varieties of cotton fabrics.

The reason for this new move was the hope of securing better financial results.   The Consolidated Cotton Duck Company had not been able to pay dividends on its common stock and for the four years ending in 1909 had averaged only four and three-quarters per cent on its preferred stock, while in 1909–10 a deficit was incurred.[4]   Moderately successful in the period of brisk business, it could not withstand the tribulations of depression.

---

[1] *Commercial and Financial Chronicle*, vol. lxxxii, p. 336.
[2] *Ibid.*, vol. xc, p. 844.
[3] *Ibid.*, vol. xci, p. 279.   [4] *Ibid.*, vol. xc, p. 845

What was the significance of the formation of this combination ? In the first place, it was an important factor only in the sail duck trade. The Census of 1900, speaking of the early combination, said that it produced " a considerable part of the sail duck made in the country." [1] In the *Commercial and Financial Chronicle* it was stated [2] at the time the first combination was formed that its plants produced ninety per cent of all the cotton duck manufactured in the United States. But that statement could have referred to sail duck only, as can be ascertained from the Census returns. In 1900 all the plants owned by the combination were located in Maryland, and that state produced 8,510,148 yards of sail duck in that year, or seventy-two per cent of the total of 11,750,151 yards manufactured in the whole country. But sail duck was only one-tenth of the total production of cotton duck in the United States, the total quantity of other duck being 117,583,925 yards. Hence the combination controlled but a small proportion of the duck trade. Moreover, it was subject to potential competition from the other mills which could change over to the manufacture of sail duck if the combination attempted to raise prices. The strength of the combination lay chiefly in its control over popular brands of sail duck.

The absorption of the two selling companies is significant of a change in purpose. At first the combination evidently sought to control a certain branch of the duck trade. It desired monopoly power and hoped to obtain this in part by what amounted to an increase in the scale of production. Competition, however, could not be eliminated and substantial economies in production were not forthcoming. As a result, economies in selling became the aim. But up to the present time there has been no great saving from that source. One must conclude that the costs of combination, the speculative element, and overcapitalization have exerted a detrimental influence on the success of the undertaking. At all events, the combination is by no means an exceptionally important factor in the

---

[1] *12th U. S. Census*, vol. ix, p. 31.
[2] *Commercial and Financial Chronicle*, vol. lxix, p. 129.

cotton manufacturing industry of the United States. Perhaps
the greatest significance of its history is the object lesson to
would-be promoters of combinations in this line of industry.

The New England Cotton Yarn Company was incorporated
in 1899 under the laws of New Jersey.[1] It was a consolidation
of nine plants, four in New Bedford, three in Fall River and two
in Taunton, operating at that time 588,400 spindles. The company was authorized to issue $6,500,000 five per cent bonds and
$11,500,000 stock, — $6,500,000 seven per cent cumulative preferred and $5,000,000 common. The estimated cost of replace-
ment of the plants was $10,700,000, and additional assets
amounted to $2,300,000, making a total of $13,000,000. Thus
the par value of the bonds and preferred stock combined was
just equal to the estimated value of the plants and other assets.
The common stock represented water. Of the amounts authorized, $5,577,000 bonds, $5,000,000 preferred stock, and all the
common stock were issued.

In 1903 a reorganization of the company was made, since the
venture had proved financially disappointing and it seemed
advisable to reduce the capitalization. According to the plan
of reorganization[2] the bonded debt was not disturbed. But
the $5,000,000 of seven per cent cumulative preferred stock
was reduced to $2,000,000 six per cent non-cumulative pre-
ferred, and the $5,000,000 common stock to $3,900,000. At
the same time the company was re-incorporated under the
laws of Massachusetts.

After the reorganization the combination made several changes
in its property. In 1903 the small plant of the North Dighton
Company was stripped and the machinery removed to the
other mills.[3] In 1905 the Canoe River Mills at Taunton were
purchased,[4] and the property of the Lambeth Rope Company
acquired.[5] In 1907 a box factory at Rochester, New Hampshire, was purchased in order to avoid difficulty in securing a

[1] *Commercial and Financial Chronicle*, vol. lxix, p. 28.
[2] *Ibid.*, vol. lxxvii, p. 40.
[3] *Ibid.*, vol. lxxiii, p. 443.
[4] *Ibid.*, vol. lxxxi, p. 1608.
[5] *Ibid.*, p. 617.

supply of boxes.[1] Other property was bought, new mills constructed, and earnings invested in improvements, thus rendering the properties more valuable than at the time of consolidation.

Whatever success the New England Cotton Yarn Company achieved was due to efficient management. When the company was first organized, the following statement was given out. " All the officers of the new company are of the opinion that large reductions will be made in the cost of production when all the mills are operated as one concern." [2] But as the necessity for reorganization showed, the savings were less than anticipated, and it was only after a more conservative policy was adopted that the business became profitable. The success which was attained was the result of good administration, not of monopoly. The company produced yarn for sale to hosiery mills and to weaving mills which were temporarily unable to supply their own needs. There were other yarn mills, however, particularly in the South, and also several spinning and weaving mills which sold more or less yarn. Hence this company had little control over the price of yarn. Like the duck combination, the New England Cotton Yarn Company was forced to re-organize, to squeeze some of the water out of its stock. Similarly it was not able to secure a monopolistic advantage, and only by returning to a sound business basis, by reducing the amount of outstanding securities, and by turning earnings into improvements of the plants and the acquisition of supplementary concerns could it succeed.

Although the New England Cotton Yarn Company is still in existence, it gave up its individuality in 1910 by becoming part of a still larger combination. In that year the property of the company was leased to the Union Mills of New York, a group of knitting mills, for ninety-nine years at a fixed rental of six per cent on the preferred and seven and one-half per cent on the common stock. The lessees also agreed to pay annually $57,810 to be applied to the redemption of outstanding mortgage bonds, and to set aside annually $231,240 for the maintenance of

[1] *Commercial and Financial Chronicle*, vol. lxxxv, p. 1338.
[2] *Ibid.*, vol. lxix, p. 81.

the property of the yarn company or further redemption of its bonds. The Union Mills also received the right to consolidate its properties with those of the yarn company. Hence the New England Cotton Yarn Company has now become part of an integrated knitting combination.

The third amalgamation in the cotton manufacturing industry of the United States, the United States Finishing Company, was also formed in 1899. This was a consolidation of the Norwich Bleaching, Dyeing, and Printing Company at Norwich, Connecticut, the Dunnell Manufacturing Company at Pawtucket, and the Reid and Barry Company at Passaic, New Jersey.[1] Later acquisitions have been as follows: in 1901 the plant of the Sterling Dyeing and Finishing Company at Sterling, Connecticut, in 1903 the plant of the Silver Spring Bleaching and Dyeing Company at Providence, in 1907 control of the Apponaug Print Works at Apponaug, Rhode Island, and in 1909 the Queen Dyeing Company of Providence.[2] At this last date the combination, which employed over 3,000 workmen, was capitalized at $6,000,000, half preferred and half common stock. Its accumulated surplus was $2,240,993, thus showing that it had been financially successful.

The company finishes other kinds of cloth as well as that made of cotton; hence its total output does not represent exclusively cotton goods. In fact it does not finish one-quarter of the total quantity of cotton goods produced in the United States. The combined output of the Sayles Bleachery, the Fall River Bleachery, and the Lowell Bleachery equals that of the bleaching departments of the United States Finishing Company. The American Printing Company of Fall River equals it in quantity of cloth printed. And there are other finishing plants in the country besides these. Hence the United States Finishing Company has no monopoly. Its plants are smaller than those of the other companies mentioned. Its specialty is the finishing of fine goods on commission. This combination can be placed in the same class as the duck company

---

[1] *Commercial and Financial Chronicle*, vol. lxxxi, p. 1435.
[2] *Ibid.*, vol. lxxxviii, p. 1377.

and the yarn company. It is essentially strong in a single class of work, but has no power to fix monopolistic prices.

The American Thread Company, like the three other combinations described, produces a specialty. It affects only a single small branch of the cotton manufacturing industry. Unlike the others, however, it controls a large percentage of the total output, and, furthermore, has international connections. The company was organized in 1898 to take over the operation of fourteen plants engaged in the manufacture of spool cotton.[1] Its object, as stated before the Industrial Commission, was " to unite the business of the manufacture of spool, crochet, knitting, mending, and other cottons, including the allied businesses of cotton spinning, doubling, twisting, dyeing, bleaching, polishing, and spool making." The consolidating firms were the most important in the industry, including such well known establishments as the Willimantic, Kerr, Hadley, Merrick, and Clark Mills. Since its formation several of the small plants have been closed and the manufacture concentrated in the larger mills. The company was authorized to issue $6,000,000 in bonds, $6,000,000 in five per cent preferred stock, and $6,000,000 in common stock. All the bonds and $4,890,475 of the preferred stock, fully paid up, were issued, and $4,200,000 of the common stock on which seventy per cent was paid in.[2]

The company was organized by a representative of the English Sewing Cotton Company,[3] and all the common stock is held by that company.[4] Moreover all the voting power is vested in the common stock holders,[5] so that the English company has absolute control. In 1901 it was stated that the company controlled one-third of the total cotton thread production in the United States.[6] But the Coats company controlled another third, and the Coats company is closely allied with the English Sewing Cotton Company through holdings of stock. Hence

---

[1] Industrial Commission, *Report*, vol. xiii, p. 343.
[2] *Commercial and Financial Chronicle*, vol. lxxxv, p. 525.
[3] Industrial Commission, *Report*, vol. xiii, p. 348.
[4] *Commercial and Financial Chronicle*, vol. lxxix, p. 153.
[5] Industrial Commission, *Report*, vol. xiii, p. 348.
[6] *Ibid.*, p. 343.

these two companies together control two-thirds of the output and dominate the cotton thread market in the United States, just as in England.

The American Thread Company has paid good dividends. In the year ending in 1900 the dividend on the common stock was ten per cent, 1901 ten per cent, 1902 none, 1903 four per cent, 1904 sixteen per cent, 1905 eight per cent, 1906 fourteen per cent, 1909 four per cent, 1910 fifteen per cent. The rate of dividends for 1906–07 and 1907–08 was not published, but inasmuch as the year ending in 1907 was a very prosperous one for all branches of the cotton industry, it can be surmised that the thread company paid high dividends in that year, perhaps too high to announce publicly. These dividends, it should be remembered, were in addition to the five per cent on the preferred stock, and were paid on stock of which only seventy per cent of the par value had been paid in. This combination has at least not been a financial failure, and it is possible that some monopoly profit is included in the fairly high dividends, which, during the nine years for which we have information, averaged nine per cent on the par value of the common stock, and twelve and nine-tenths per cent on the amount paid in on that stock.

The amalgamations have resulted in gain in so far as they have improved their methods of production or of distribution. As has already been indicated, the limits to a profitable increase in the scale of production are relatively inelastic,[1] but some economies in marketing have doubtless resulted. The formation of the amalgamations here discussed has been facilitated by the small number of units to be included and the comparatively small amount of capital involved, but, with the possible exception of the thread company, they were not able to gain much of a monopolistic advantage.

In the history of the cotton manufacturing industry, taken as a whole, amalgamation has as yet played a small part. The relatively slight advantages to be gained from further increase in the scale of production would be more than offset by the difficulties attending any attempt at wholesale amalgamation.

[1] See *ante*, p. 141.

These difficulties lie in the immense amount of capital involved, the number of mills distributed over a wide area, and the probable unwillingness of the large stockholders in many of the most successful concerns to take part. Nor would it be an easy matter to maintain a monopoly, since the supply of raw material could hardly be controlled, and processes could not be kept secret with the present mobility of labor. Potential competition, both at home and abroad, would restrict any attempt at monopolistic manipulation of prices. The Arkwright Club and some of the lesser associations, as well as community of interest, are securing adjustment to supplies of raw material, while some economies in selling are being obtained by integration.

Integration

There is yet another type of combination in the cotton manufacturing industry, namely integration. As it is of very recent development, it is impossible to determine definitely the extent to which it has proceeded, or to forecast the extent to which it will proceed. Even in the existing amalgamations, involving primarily the combining of coördinate, competing units, there has often been more or less integration, or the combining of supplementary branches, as, for example, the purchase of the box factory by the New England Cotton Yarn Company. But in addition to these instances, we find a distinct tendency toward integration. It appears in various stages of progress, and is complete in few cases. It consists in the bringing together of several establishments, perhaps producing the same grade of goods, perhaps producing different grades, under a single management, with a single selling agency, and with its own finishing plant. Its object is not so much the elimination of competition, as the securing of economies through the control of supplementary branches and particularly in buying and selling.

Its most significant feature, possibly, is the position which the agency for marketing the goods assumes. In some cases the selling house is the leader in promoting the combination, in others an old selling house has been absorbed, and in still others a new selling agency established.

In the first class, where the selling house has been the leader, we include the groups of mills controlled by several of the large selling houses of Boston and New York. An example of this is the recent formation of a syndicate by Deering, Milliken & Co., commission agents, for the purchase of the Garner Print Works in the state of New York, these works to be used for converting cloth produced in southern mills controlled by the selling house. Similarly, other large selling houses control many of the mills for which they act as agents. They do not always control a converting plant, but that is unnecessary in the case of mills which finish their own cloth, and which constitute a large proportion of the concerns employing selling agents.

The best illustration of the absorption of a selling house by the mills is the purchase of the Turner Company by the Consolidated Cotton Duck Company, to which reference has already been made. There are probably other instances, which have not been made public, where control of the selling house was secured as soon as the mills were strong enough financially.

The establishment of a private selling agency is well illustrated by the concern of B. B. & R. Knight of Providence. This company has four mills in Massachusetts, and thirteen mills, a print works, and a bleachery in Rhode Island. The head office is in Providence and has combined with it a selling department. The company controls more than 500,000 spindles and 12,000 looms. The greater part of the product is sheetings, especially fine sheetings, but shirtings, twills, and other fabrics are also manufactured in smaller quantities. The Fall River Iron Works and the American Printing company are largely owned by Mr. M. C. D. Borden, and within a year the selling of the product has been taken over by M. C. D. Borden & Sons, of New York. A similar example is furnished by the Sayles interests, which control the Lorraine Manufacturing Company and a bleachery and dye-works, and have their own selling office in New York. The Cannon Mills Company, also, has established an office in New York where it sells the product of its North Carolina mills.

This movement of integration has assumed more importance within the last five years. The causes are, in general, those which have stimulated combination in all parts of the industrial world, and in particular the necessity for perfecting the merchandizing organization, the desire of the selling house to justify its existence, and the narrowing of the margin between the cost of raw material and the selling price of the cloth. The fundamental cause, the one into which practically all of the others can be resolved, is keen competition arising from the increase in the size of the establishments and the growth of the cotton manufacturing industry in the South.

The narrowing of the margin between the cost of raw materials and the selling price of the product reflects the stress of the competition. Throughout the ten year period from 1896 to 1906 the margin, although fluctuating more or less, as the accompanying chart shows, was constantly below the lowest level hitherto reached. The method used in this chart for ascertaining the margin is that adopted in Fall River as the basis for fixing the sliding wage scale. It is the difference between the cost of eight pounds of middling cotton and the average selling price of forty-five yards of 28-inch, 64 x 64 print cloth and of thirty-three and eleven one-hundredths yards of $38\frac{1}{2}$-inch, 64 x 64 print cloth.[1] While open to the criticism that may be directed against any average or index, it nevertheless seems to bear out the statement frequently made by manufacturers that the margin has been unusually low during the last ten years. Its upward leap in the year 1907 was due to the great boom preceding the panic. Although the data submitted cover only the period since 1881, one may safely say, in view of the reduction of the costs of production during that time, that previously the margin was never as low. This has stimulated the introduction of economies in manufacturing and in management, and has started this movement to economize in selling, either by direct sales or through closer relation of the selling agency to the manufacturing branch.

[1] Tables of prices are given in the appendix.

The expansion of this form of combination is limited by the extent to which goods are sold through selling agents. As will be pointed out in a later chapter, the practice of selling direct is fully as common as the employment of a selling house, and the latter is not especially favored by the trade in general. It seems probable, therefore, that a large proportion of the industry will not be included, for the present at least, in any of these integrated groups.

The possible ramifications of the movement for integration, however, are suggested by the formation of the United Dry Goods Company.[1] This is a holding company, organized May 21, 1909. At its head is Mr. John Claflin, President of the H. B. Claflin Company, one of the largest dry goods jobbing houses in the country. The United Dry Goods Company acquired from the Associated Merchants Company, an older Claflin combination dating from 1901, the control of the following stores, — H. B. Claflin Co. (wholesale); James McCreery & Co., New York (two stores); O'Neil-Adams Co., New York; Stewart & Co., Baltimore; J. N. Adams & Co., Buffalo; and four-fifths of the common stock of C. G. Gunther's Sons, New York (furs). In addition, from Mr. Claflin it purchased outright Hahne & Co., Newark; Powers Mercantile Co., Minneapolis; William Hengerer Co., Buffalo; and the Stewart Dry Goods Company of Louisville. Mr. Claflin is also said to control stores in Cleveland, Pittsburgh, Cincinnati, Spokane, Seattle, Butte, Denver, Augusta, and other cities.[2] In 1910 a controlling interest in the long established firm of Lord & Taylor (New York) was purchased. The company has been conservatively capitalized, and has been assisted in its financial dealings by J. P. Morgan & Co. of New York.

The H. B. Claflin Company is the link which connects this chain of retail stores with the cotton manufacturing industry. And it controls the Defender Manufacturing Company of New York, which manufactures sheets, pillow cases, muslin underwear, and other products. This may be the beginning of a

[1] *Commercial and Financial Chronicle*, vol. lxxxviii, p. 1377.
[2] *Ibid.*, vol. lxxxvii, p. 547.

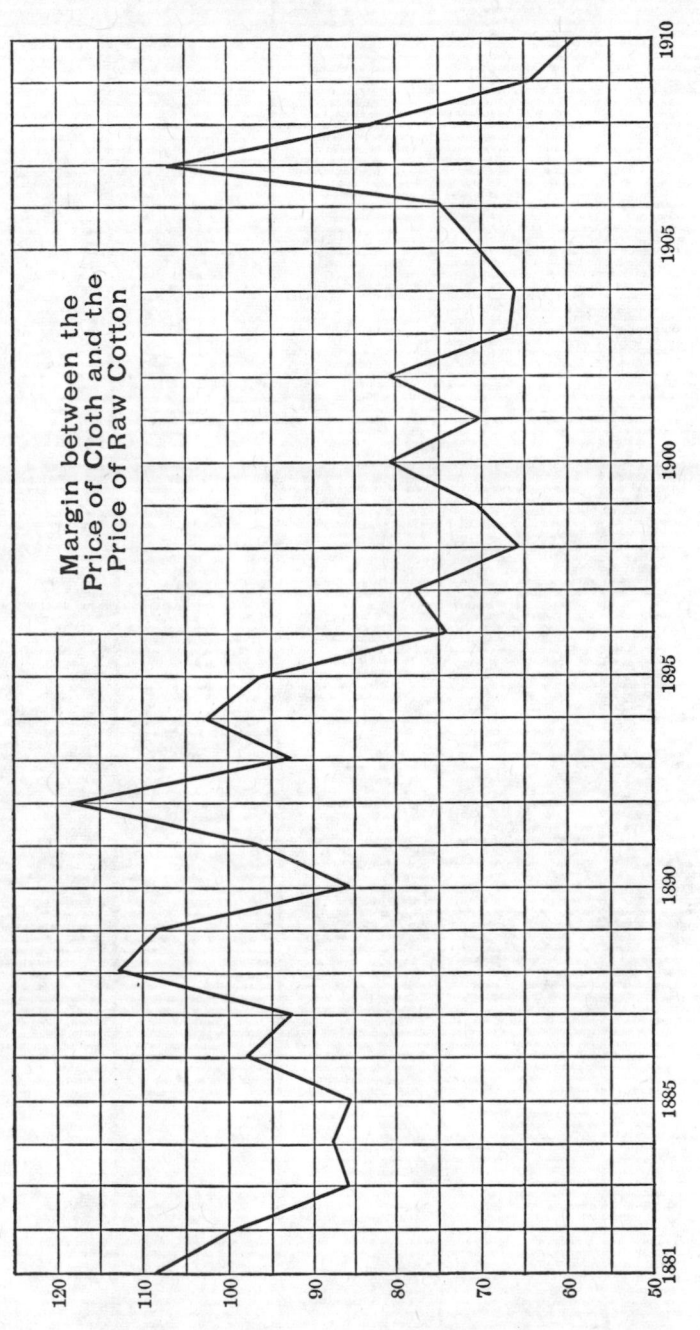

Margin between the
Price of Cloth and the
Price of Raw Cotton

complete combination for the manufacturing and marketing of cotton goods on a great scale, but, on the other hand, it may represent merely an effort to ward off difficulties such as numerous jobbing houses have recently been experiencing. The very magnitude of such schemes makes it unsafe to speculate as to their possible extension.

The recent purchase of cotton mills by Marshall Field & Co., the big Chicago house, is another application of the principle of integration, the retail house in this instance invading the manufacturing field. The mills thus acquired in 1910 include several cotton factories and a finishing plant, all located at Spray, North Carolina. Previously the same company had established a lace factory.

The need for greater coöperation between the manufacturing and the mercantile branches has been the chief stimulus to integration in the American cotton industry. It has manifested itself in diverse directions since it first appeared, and no one can anticipate where it will end. It has an advantage in that each mill generally retains its separate corporate existence and is permitted a large amount of individual action, while at the same time it is subject to a central authority. The success of the whole is not endangered by the weakness of a single part. There is no new incorporation, and no issue of watered stock. The control through holdings of stock in the constituent companies has made possible the pursuance of a more consistent policy. Amalgamation, as we have seen, has played a comparatively unimportant part, because of the inelastic limits to the advantageous increase in the scale of production, the difficulties in the way of carrying through an amalgamation at all comprehensive, and the obstacles to the securing of a monopoly. Loose associations and, especially, the Arkwright Club are probably the most important, since they are obtaining adjustments to supplies of raw material, dealing with freight rates, and providing means for common action in other matters.

CHAPTER X

THE commercial organization, to which we next turn our attention, has various aspects. The first section, which is taken up in this chapter, is concerned with the purchase of the raw materials, the second with the sale of the product, the third with the export trade, and the last with the import trade.

Practically all of the cotton mills in the United States are in the hands of incorporated companies, with the ordinary forms of corporate organization. But, as a rule, the president of a cotton manufacturing company merely presides at the meetings of the directors without taking an active part in the management of the mill. The active member of the board of directors, the man who is the highest authority, is the treasurer. The treasurer assumes the responsibility for the management of the business. All the officials in the mill are responsible to him, directly or indirectly, and to him the stockholders look for their dividends. If the mill is not financially successful, the blame falls on the treasurer. This official leaves to his agent or superintendent the practical management of the mill itself, the inside work as it is called, while he attends to the outside work, the buying of supplies and the selling of the goods.

The duties assumed by the treasurer of a cotton mill are not identical in all centres or in all establishments. They depend upon whether or not he is treasurer of more than one mill, and whether the goods are sold direct or through selling agents. This variation can best be shown by a comparison of the practices in different localities. In Fall River and New Bedford the treasurer usually has his office at the mill. He buys the supplies, and in a majority of the mills sells the goods himself, that is he receives the orders from the customers and fixes the terms of sale. Few men are treasurers of more than one mill each in that section of New England.

The treasurers of cotton mills located in other parts of New England usually have their offices in Boston. They purchase most of the supplies for their mills, but the product is, in a majority of cases, sold through a selling house, so that the treasurer merely exercises an oversight and collects the bills. Frequently one man is treasurer of two or even three " Boston " mills. In other instances, where the mills are controlled by a selling house, a member of that firm acts as treasurer, part of his duties of direction being cared for by a special department in the merchandizing establishment. In the South the president may be the active head of a cotton manufacturing company and employ a low salaried man to attend to the routine work of a treasurer; he may even perform the duties of treasurer in addition to his own if the mill is small. With these exceptions the distribution of the responsibility in southern corporations resembles the northern practice. There are southern mills the treasurers of which are members of northern selling firms, and others where the treasurers each direct several mills. But the management of many southern mills is directed by a treasurer who has no official connection with any other mill, just as in New England.

If the treasurer has his office at the mill and is in constant touch with it, the official who has charge of the inside work is usually called a superintendent. That official becomes an agent, however, if the treasurer's office is located in another city. Yet this distinction is not a fine one and has little value inasmuch as exceptions are numerous, and in either case the duties of the man in charge of the practical operation of the factory are much the same. Although the degree of responsibility varies, greater responsibility is placed on the agent if the treasurer does not have his office at the mill. The duties of the superintendent are to manage the actual working of the mill. The subordinates report to him, and the treasurer expects him to account for any falling off in the quality or the quantity of the product. If several mills are combined in one plant the superintendent is aided by one or more assistant superintendents.

Both the treasurer and the agent or superintendent are institutions practically as old as the American cotton manufacturing industry, and the elimination of neither is to be expected. However, the duties of the treasurer may undergo a change. At the present time the treasurers of some mills seem to be coming into closer contact with the actual operation of their plants and thus assuming part of the duties hitherto left to the agents. On the other hand, several selling houses, which control the mills that they represent, have established special departments to direct the management of the various plants, while members of the firms are made the nominal treasurers of the mills. In this way expenses are reduced. Yet the larger concerns manufacturing on an extensive scale can give full employment to both a treasurer and an agent and the volume of production can bear the overhead expense. With this statement of the distribution of responsibilities in mind we can proceed to our analysis of the commercial organization.

Two classes of supplies are purchased for a cotton mill. The first includes machinery, repair goods, and other materials bought in small quantities. The second is the raw cotton, by far the more important of the two.

The purchases of repair goods and incidentals, such as sizing materials, oil, and ring travellers, are usually made by the agent or superintendent. When a large order for new machinery is given, the treasurer transacts the business, but such purchases are made only at infrequent intervals. For receiving and disposing of the current supplies of this sort a separate supply department has been established in the larger and more progressive mills. In it is kept a record of all supplies received and given out, thereby ascertaining the requisitions from the separate departments so as to prevent continued abnormal use of materials in any one department. The management may limit the amount of supplies to be issued to one overseer within a certain time. If no such limit is set, an excessive demand on the supply department is investigated. Economy is thus fostered among the overseers and the determination of the distribution of the expense burden facilitated.

The purchase of the raw cotton constitutes one of the most important duties of the treasurer. The market in which he buys is highly organized. Because of its magnitude and the importance of the interests affected, this market will be described in detail.

The cotton crop of the United States averaged 1,749,400,000 pounds per year from 1856 to 1860 and 6,157,200,000 pounds per year in 1906–10. The quantity taken by the American mills was 414,800,000 pounds, or 23.7 per cent of the total, during the former period, and 2,277,600,000 pounds, or 37 per cent, during the last quinquennium. Hence in spite of the continual increase in the size of the crop, a larger and larger proportion has been retained in this country. The development of the American cotton manufacturing industry, therefore, has rendered the domestic market relatively more important.

Separating the numerous grades of cotton broadly into the two classes of long staple and short staple, the latter predominates quantitatively whereas the former is of superior quality since it can be employed for spinning finer yarns. In addition to their purchases of Sea Island cotton and the long staple fibre from the Mississippi Valley, the American spinners also import some of the high grade Egyptian cotton. Three-fourths of the long staple cotton consumed in the United States is manufactured in New England where a majority of the fine goods mills are located.

Our short staple or upland cotton supplies the greater part of the demand, however, not only in this country but abroad. It varies in length and strength of fibre, in color and in freedom from dirt, and possesses characteristics peculiar to the locality in which it is grown. With the machinery and methods in vogue a century ago "cotton was cotton," but, as a result of refinements in technique and diversification of product, nowadays the spinner must give careful attention to the exact quality of the cotton which he purchases.

The northern mills, to discuss the manufacturing regions separately, buy their cotton through cotton merchants. These merchants have offices in the large northern cities and agents in the important mill centres.   A few of them also have branches in Europe.   They obtain the cotton through buyers located in the cotton growing section and at the shipping points in the South.   The sale to the mill treasurer is consummated on the basis of samples made up by taking several handfuls of cotton from each bale, the samples being submitted for inspection.   If the cotton on delivery proves to be of a lower grade than the sample, the merchant makes restitution to the purchaser.   The spinner, to safeguard his interests, generally employs an expert to test all cotton received at the mill, since the protection against the loss that would result from the substitution of an inferior grade offsets the extra expense.   A contract, calling for delivery either of the total quantity at one specified date or by monthly instalments, may be entered into at any time during the year, but the greatest activity in the purchasing of raw cotton is in the months from October to January.   At that period the New England mills provide for future needs, purchasing supplementary supplies in steadily diminishing amounts during the ensuing months.   The new crop begins to come upon the market in September, and the bulk of it is picked during the next four months, thus becoming available for delivery to the mills.   The manufacturers of the highest grades ordinarily buy at an early date a larger proportion of their total supply than those using ordinary staple.   The former wish to exercise a wider choice in their selection and also to make sure of an adequate quantity. The demand for long staple cotton is frequently so great that the manufacturer who delays is unable to obtain the quality which he desires, or can secure it only at a very high price.

The spinner of common grades gauges his purchases according to the course of the market; he buys early or late according to his judgment of the favorableness of price quotations.   However, he usually obtains a large quantity during the harvesting season. The following averages, computed from Shepperson's *Cotton Facts*, indicate the takings by northern mills.

(For the years ending August 31)

	1881–1884 Thousand Bales	Percentage	1908–1910 Thousand Bales	Percentage
September	72	4.3	102	4.4
October	211	12.6	284	12.3
November	310	18.6	422	18.3
December	291	17.4	325	14.1
January	199	11.9	287	12.4
February	134	8.	219	9.5
March	126	7.6	160	7.
April	102	6.1	136	5.9
May	82	4.9	124	5.3
June, July, August	144	8.6	250	10.8
Total	1671	100	2309	100

The amount taken during the season is slightly lower at the present time than thirty years ago. Yet at both dates about one-half of their year's supply was taken by the northern mills before January first, and over sixty per cent before February first.

Prior to 1860 it was likewise customary for the New England spinners to purchase their stock of raw material early,[1] and in 1872 it was stated in the report of the Boston Board of Trade [2] that " in most years four-fifths of the cotton supply was bought for the mills in the first five months after the crop began to come in, and usually one-half was taken by January first, or within the first three months of crop movement." The practices of 1872 and 1910, therefore, show a fairly close correspondence.

The cotton is shipped as soon as purchased and warehoused at the mills, which are provided with commodious storage rooms. The merchant does not have a warehouse of his own, and public warehouses in the northern cities are seldom utilized for storing cotton. Payment for the cotton is made ordinarily within three days after its receipt at the mill. Thus the northern manufacturers bear the burden of carrying a large quantity of raw cotton from the time that it is harvested till it is manufactured.

[1] Boston Board of Trade, 5th *Annual Report*, 1859, p. 166.
[2] *Ibid.*, 18th *Annual Report*, 1872, p. 138.

The mills found it advantageous in the first half of the nineteenth century to buy their cotton early in order to make sure of their supply and also to have a basis for price quotations. With the cotton in their own warehouse they could quote prices for cloth with less risk of loss. The development of organized speculation, with its steadying effect on prices and opportunity for hedging, has made this factor less potent at the present time. Another reason was that the credit conditions encouraged the mills to carry the cotton. During the period of the cultivation by slaves the southern planters had to realize upon the cotton as soon as it was marketable. Capital was relatively more available in the North, and interest rates lower; hence the manufacturers could better afford to bear the burden directly. There is not the same difference now, yet the financial strength of the mills is of sufficient superiority to induce a continuation of the former practice. However, prosperity is rendering the southern planters more and more independent, and the erection of warehouses in the South is a step toward enabling the farmers to hold their cotton and obtain higher prices later in the year.

The extension of railroad facilities and the lowering of railroad freight rates has caused a change in the proportion of raw cotton shipped by water. In 1857–58 ninety-nine per cent of the cotton was shipped coastwise;[1] in 1887–88 seventy per cent; in 1897–98 sixty per cent; and at the present time about fifty-five per cent.

In the South there is wider variation in the practice of the manufacturers in buying their cotton. The few mills in that section which use long staple cotton purchase their supply early for reasons the same as those which influence the fine goods manufacturers in the North. But with the great majority of the southern mills, which manufacture coarse cloth, the practice depends upon the location, size, and financial strength of the individual mills. In North Carolina, around Charlotte, about fifty per cent of the year's supply of cotton is bought during the picking season. This percentage is slightly lower than in New England since the mills have not as much quick capital. More-

---

[1] *Monthly Summary of Commerce and Finance*, March, 1900, p. 2567.

over they have a certain reserve in the hands of the neighboring farmers, even if the total supply of the state does have to be augmented by cotton from Mississippi. A few of the small mills in this section buy their cotton only as they have orders for yarn or cloth.

The quantity bought early in the South Carolina district around Greenville, Spartanburg, and Anderson, is large. The mills obtain a considerable part of their supply from the immediate neighborhood, and buy it before the farmers sell it to outsiders to be shipped away, thereby saving the freight. The proportion bought early, however, is less than it was twenty years ago, since the farmers hold it longer now. The local supply in Georgia is still larger relatively, but the mills also buy early since they can better afford to carry the cotton than can the farmers.

While it is thus common for the southern mills to carry cotton for which they have not immediate requirements, the proportion bought during the season is probably less than in New England. The southern manufacturers do not obtain the cotton entirely from merchants, but frequently deal directly with the farmers, in a few instances sending out their own buyers through the district in which cotton suited to their needs is grown.

The manufacturers, especially those in the North, are giving more and more attention to the selection of their raw cotton. During the last twenty years the spinners have become more insistent on the terms of the agreement, and on the actual fulfilment of these terms by the merchant. The grade of the cotton and the length of staple are more carefully selected. For example the merchant is asked to specify the grade and staple which he will deliver, and such fine distinctions are made as those between " average middling " and " middling "; between " middling to good middling " and " middling and good middling." To take the second of these examples, where the distinction is between " to " and " and," if the agreement was " middling to good middling," the merchant might deliver ninety per cent middling and ten per cent good middling; but if it was for " middling and good middling " he would have to deliver approximately

half of each.   The manufacturer wishes to know which proportion he is to receive.   The same attention is given to length of
staple.

This more careful selection of the raw material shows that
more attention is being given to the demands of customers, and
especially that the machinery is more nicely adjusted.   It is
significant of more careful management and greater specialization.
With the increase in the spinning of fine counts and in the manufacture of fine goods, it has become necessary for the manufacturer to discriminate in the quality of cotton which he buys, and
in the manufacture of coarser yarn and cloth the machinery
adjusted for a certain grade of cotton cannot be operated advantageously on a lower grade, while a higher grade adds a needless
expense.   The spinner must also be careful in his selection of the
raw cotton because of the preference of the operatives to work
continuously upon the same grade.   If an attempt is made
repeatedly to substitute an inferior grade, it is difficult to retain
the better class of operatives.

Prior to the Civil War the methods were similar, but not so
clearly defined, and in the speculative period immediately following the war more of the raw cotton was bought through
the New York Cotton Exchange.   But the rather simple organization of the raw cotton market, the relation between the
manufacturers and the merchants, has undergone few changes
during the last thirty years.

Since the cotton is bought by spinners through cotton merchants who obtain it directly from the South, the question may
well be raised as to what function the New York Cotton Exchange
now performs.   There are thirteen exchanges, big and little,
in the southern states, which are more or less closely connected
with the actual movement of the crop.   But that is not a function of the New York Exchange, since little cotton is sold there
for actual delivery, even to New England spinners.   How then
is its existence to be justified ?   Or how far can its existence be
justified ?

In regard to the sales of spot cotton in New York the Commissioner of Corporations makes the following statement in his

recent *Report on Cotton Exchanges.*[1] "Years ago New York was a broad spot cotton market [2] where large quantities of the various grades were received and resold to spinners. In recent years, however, the great bulk of the cotton consumed by spinners has been shipped directly to them from the cotton belt instead of being sent first to cotton merchants in New York. Whereas in the early 'seventies the spot business at New York amounted to roughly 500,000 bales yearly, or, say, fifteen per cent of the crop, in recent years it has rarely amounted to 200,000 bales, or to two per cent of an average crop." Thus there has been a great decline both absolutely and relatively, as is shown by the following table.

SPOT SALES IN NEW YORK [3]

	Number of Bales—Annual Average	Per cent of Crop
1870–71 to 1879– 80	434,865	9.9
1880–81 to 1889– 90	221,719	3.4
1890–91 to 1899–1900	159,467	1.9
1900–01 to 1906– 07	145,873	1.3

Not only has the volume of spot sales diminished as indicated by the average for ten year periods, but the decline began in the early 'seventies. In 1870–71 the spot sales amounted to 733,905 bales, in 1879–80 to 319,573. Hence they have been steadily declining from the beginning of the period covered by the table. The exports of raw cotton from New York, moreover, are less than one-tenth of the total from the country.

The New York Cotton Exchange, which came into existence in 1870 and was incorporated in 1871, was established to aid the marketing of the southern cotton crop during the period of uncertainty and speculation which followed the close of the war. It had not existed prior to the war, and, so far as the selling of spot cotton is concerned, its usefulness has steadily waned with the re-establishment of the simpler method of marketing.

[1] U. S. Commissioner of Corporations, *Report on Cotton Exchanges*, part I, pp. 22, 23.

[2] In the 'fifties, New York was a spot market of importance. — J. S. Homans, *Cyclopedia of Commerce*, vol. 1, p. 452.

[3] U. S. Commissioner of Corporations, *Report on Cotton Exchanges*, part I, p. 249.

The situation of New York does not make it a natural spot cotton market. It is not the most convenient export point nor is it sufficiently near the mills for it to be used as a storing place for cotton. Of the cotton which is sent to the North by the water-rail route only a part enters New York, while for the all-rail route the railroads quote through rates to the northern mill centres lower than the combined rate to New York and from New York to those mill centres. Therefore transhipment at New York would add an extra expense.

Again, with the increasing prosperity of southern planters and southern cotton dealers, they have accumulated wealth which has made them less dependent upon the New York bankers for financial assistance in marketing the crop. At the close of the war the impoverished condition of the South forced its planters and cotton dealers to seek outside aid. They then turned to New York, the financial centre of the country. But they are not subject to the same need at the present time.

Finally, there is the reason usually given by spinners for their not using the New York market for actual purchases of cotton; the form of the contract of the New York Exchange makes it undesirable for them to buy there. This applies especially to the purchases of cotton for future delivery, but is none the less significant. That the spinners cannot use " contract " cotton is easily understood when we consider the terms of the contract governing the delivery of cotton on the New York Cotton Exchange.[1] The contract is based on middling cotton, but the seller may at his option include in his delivery cotton of several grades, between " fair " and " good ordinary," that is between the highest and lowest of the eighteen grades recognized by the rules of the exchange. Consequently the buyer may receive all high grade cotton, all low grade cotton, or a mixture of the two. And if he forces delivery, he usually does receive a general mixture with a predominance of the low grades. The spinner, as already stated, purchases from the merchant cotton of a certain specified grade since he can use

---

[1] The *Report on Cotton Exchanges,* referred to above, is devoted chiefly to a discussion of this contract.

only fairly even-running lots. If he bought cotton on the New York Exchange with the expectation of using it in his mill, he would find upon receiving it that only a part was adapted to his needs. To be sure the payment is adjusted to the grade of cotton delivered, according to a scale of " ons " and " offs " arranged with reference to the price of middling cotton. But that does not help the spinner to obtain immediately just what he wants and to dispose of the portion that he does not desire. Moreover the spinner is uncertain not only as to what grade of cotton he will receive, but also as to when it will be delivered. The seller may deliver at any time during the month fixed by the contract, upon giving three days' notice.

It is not necessary for our purposes to go further into the intricate methods of grading and fixing of differences on the New York Cotton Exchange. It is evident that the New England cotton manufacturer does not and could not economically employ that exchange for buying cotton. If the regulations of the Exchange were altered so as to favor the buyer as much as the seller, and if the lower grades, which constitute one of the sources of difficulty, were eliminated, the employment of the Exchange for the actual purchase of cotton might, perhaps, be augmented. However, the present more simple method of purchase, and the financial strength of the New England mills renders it improbable.

The justification of the existence of the New York Cotton Exchange is not to be found, then, in connection with the actual marketing of the great bulk of our cotton crop. It is not a " traders' market," but a " speculative exchange." The New York " futures market," that is, the speculation or dealing in futures on the New York Cotton Exchange, affords the cotton merchant and the manufacturer an opportunity to insure against loss. This is done by " hedging." The term " hedge " was well defined by Mr. Marsh, a member of the Exchange, in an address before the National Association of Cotton Manufacturers. " A hedge," he said, " is the purchase or sale of contracts for one hundred or more bales of cotton for future delivery, made not for the purpose of receiving or delivering the actual cotton, but as an insurance against fluctuations in the market that might unfavorably affect other ventures in which the buyer or seller of the ' hedge ' is actually engaged." [1] Such contracts are not fulfilled by delivery of cotton, but by the payment of the difference between the price called for in the contract and the price of spot cotton on the day when the contract matures.   If the price of spot cotton is lower than the price agreed upon in the contract, the buyer pays the difference to the seller.   If delivery were forced, the seller could obtain cotton to fill the contract at the spot price, whereas the man who received the cotton could not get more than the spot price for it.   Hence the buyer pays the seller the difference and no cotton changes hands.   Had the price risen, the seller would have paid the buyer the difference.   Not only professional speculators, but also cotton dealers and manufacturers become parties to these contracts.

A cotton merchant sells cotton for future delivery without having already secured any cotton, fixing his price according to the quotations current in New York.   He will obtain the cotton from the South, but to protect himself he buys " futures " on the New York Exchange.   If he has to pay more for the cotton which he delivers than the price agreed upon, he will make good his loss on that transaction by selling his " futures " contract, or, if he waits till it matures, by the difference which he receives from the buyer of the " futures."   Ordinarily he liquidates his New York contract as soon as he has secured the cotton to fill the order.   These transactions, of course, presume a corresponding fluctuation in the price of spot cotton and quotations on the futures market.[2]

The manufacturer, also, may hedge, by either buying or selling futures, according to circumstances.   If he has accepted orders for goods for the manufacture of which he does not have cotton on hand, he may buy futures to the amount of cotton that he will need.   The contract price of the goods is based upon the

[1] National Association of Cotton Manufacturers, *Transactions*, no. 83, p. 285.

[2] The rules now in vogue on the New York Exchange do not seem adequately to insure this correspondence, and it is against this weakness that the criticism of the Commissioner of Corporations is directed.

price at which he expects to buy his cotton if he does not already
have it in his warehouse. Should he be compelled to pay more
for the cotton than he anticipated, he will on the other hand
make a profit from the sale of the future contract when it matures.
If he secures the cotton at a lower price, he will in turn be prevented from getting any advantage therefrom as he will lose on
his futures. But he is insured against loss on the combined
transactions.

In the second place, the manufacturer may sell futures to
protect himself on cotton which he has already bought, but for
the use of which he has not made contracts. If the price of
cotton advances, he will lose on the futures contract, but gain on
the sale of the cloth which tends to follow the fluctuations of
raw cotton in price.[1] If the price of cotton falls, he will gain on
the futures contract, but receive less for his cloth. Similarly he
may sell futures to protect himself on goods for which he has
orders but for which the price is not fixed, such goods occasionally
being ordered to be paid for at the current market price at time
of delivery.

Both these forms of hedging by the manufacturer, that is both
buying and selling futures, are said to be practised at present
by New England cotton mills, but as to the development, extent,
and present methods of hedging, there is little consistency in the
answers received in reply to inquiries on the subject. All seem
agreed that the practice is becoming more common, especially
during the last seven years or since the period of fluctuation
attendant upon the short crop and the Sully manipulations of
1904. The reason for its recent growth is the narrowing of the
margin on which the cotton manufacturing business is carried
on.[2]

It is more common, however, for the cotton dealer than for
the cotton manufacturer to hedge. In the first place, the manufacturer does not, under ordinary conditions, hedge the cotton
which he has in his warehouse, but relies upon his judgment in

---

[1] This form of hedging is rendered rather unreliable, however, by the effect of
other factors which sometimes prevent the price of cloth from readily responding
to changes in the price of cotton. See table and chart in appendix.

[2] See *ante*, p. 173.

gauging the probable course of the market to buy when the price is at a level sufficiently low to enable him to manufacture cloth at a profit. He knows what the cotton has cost him and can, to a considerable extent, fix his prices accordingly. Moreover the relative inelasticity of the price of cloth makes somewhat unreliable a hedge based upon an assumed correspondence in fluctuations in the prices of cotton and cloth. In the second place, if the manufacturer does not have enough cotton on hand when an order is tendered, he communicates with a cotton dealer and, providing the price quoted is low enough, makes a contract for the future delivery of the necessary quantity, thereby eliminating all risk to himself. The dealer, while fixing the price according to market quotations, usually has to make the contract before actually obtaining the cotton, and consequently hedges. Yet even this practice seems to have developed largely since 1893, for in that year a man thoroughly acquainted with conditions in the New England cotton industry stated to the Senate Committee, which was then investigating the New York Cotton Exchange,[1] that at that time the sale of cotton for future delivery was a comparatively new development in cotton manufacturing. Hence the merchants previously had less need for protecting themselves.

The practice of hedging by the manufacturers seems to have developed somewhat earlier in the South than in New England, but at present it is doubtful if it is relatively any greater in the former section. There has been more of an element of speculation in the hedging by the southern cotton manufacturers. This is emphasized by certain events during the last few years. One mill lost $3,000,000 at a single stroke, through speculation in futures by its president. Another mill lost $69,000 in the same way. The president of a third mill invoiced goods to his selling agents, drew seventy-five per cent on the value of the goods amounting to $155,000 and then did not make the goods but used the money to speculate in cotton contracts. Fortunately he did not lose on his dealings. In each of these cases the president acted without the knowledge and consent of the directors,

[1] Senate Committee on Cotton Growers, *Report*, vol. i, p. 441.

sometimes, it is alleged, on the basis of " heads I win, tails you lose," so far as the mill was concerned. Such abuses led to the passage of a law in South Carolina in 1909 prohibiting the use of the credit of any corporation by its individual officers. New England, to be sure, has not been immune from these speculative transactions, for one mill in that section lost $1,500,000 in that way eight or nine years ago, and is just resuming dividend payments. These are exceptional instances, however, and the greater part of the hedging in the South as well as in the North is legitimate, both sections using the New York Exchange almost exclusively for this purpose.

The New York Cotton Exchange, therefore, while it is no longer regularly the scene of large transactions in actual cotton, does assist the merchants and manufacturers by providing a means of insurance through its dealings in futures. Provided it is properly regulated, its patrons can divest themselves of risk of loss, if they will forego the chance of unusual gain by transferring to the professional speculators the responsibility of forecasting market conditions. It also serves as a price barometer. The prices quoted on the Exchange for spot cotton and for cotton for future delivery determine to a large extent the prices at which the farmers in the South will sell and the prices at which cotton will be offered by the merchants, thus forming the basis for dealings in cotton in all parts of the country. Of course the Exchange does not determine arbitrarily the prices which are quoted, but rather displays the resultant of all the forces acting on the price of cotton throughout the western world, from Memphis, Galveston, New Orleans, and Savannah to Boston, Havre, Bremen, and Liverpool. It represents the working out of the equilibrium.

The New York Exchange is unique in that it is, perhaps, more essentially speculative than any other exchange, either stock or produce, in the world, in that so small a percentage of its contracts are fulfilled by actual delivery. Yet this may enhance its value by relieving it of local influences, such as those which cause New Orleans to be a " bull market," or Liverpool a " bearish market." Nevertheless, under its present rules it is subject to manipulations which detract from its value as a price indicator. With every recurring " corner " a public agitation for the legal prohibition of dealings in futures appears.   Such a measure, however, would merely transfer the speculation to Liverpool, since some opportunity for hedging must be utilized by the merchants. Instead of state or federal regulation, it is to be hoped that the members of the Exchange will, of their own accord, revise the rules either along the lines suggested by the Commissioner of Corporations or in some other way that will minimize abuses.

CHAPTER XI

THE CLOTH MARKET

The manufactured goods are produced in large quantities by the manufacturers and eventually parcelled out in small pieces over the counters of the retail stores. This process covers a period of time of greater or less duration, so that credit has to be provided. The present chapter attempts to trace the history of this market, to analyze the present methods of distributing the product, and to discuss the credit and financial relations of the middlemen who effect the distribution.

History of the Market Organization

The history of the organization of the cotton cloth market is the story of a gradual evolution, influenced by changing conditions, such as the growth of the industry, the economic progress of the country, and the building up of the credit structure. Some of the earlier methods served their purpose for a time and were then abandoned. New forms have been introduced from time to time and have become clearly defined parts of what is now a complex system. The records, however, are in many places obscure. Though technical inventions have been chronicled with more or less accuracy by patent records and contemporary accounts, methods of doing business have received attention, in many instances, only when they have assumed large proportions. Yet from the economic standpoint the methods of marketing are of equal if not of greater importance.

With the introduction of cotton manufacturing various devices were experimented with for placing the product on the market. The first mills were only for spinning. Their yarn was sold for the manufacture of homespuns, and a " portion of it was woven on hand looms, either belonging to the firm or to private parties working for the firm on contract." [1] This con-

[1] W. R. Bagnall, *Textile Industries of the United States*, vol. i, p. 253; also p. 275.

tinued from 1788 till 1814 and even 1820. The concern with
which Samuel Slater was identified was the first in the United
States to put successfully into operation machinery for power
spinning. Slater was the manager of the mill; the capital was
supplied by Almy & Brown. In this arrangement we find the
genesis of the selling house, an institution which has been peculiarly prominent in the American dry goods trade.

Almy & Brown had an office in their store in Providence,
whence they directed the distribution of the yarn spun in their
mills and of the cloth woven for them in the country districts.
The mill of which Slater was in charge was the first, but his
partners soon promoted other mills in the same neighborhood
and sold the product.[1] They had agents in various cities to
whom they consigned goods, and they also solicited orders by
post through advertisements in the newspapers of the different
cities.[2] During the first decade of the nineteenth century
Philadelphia was the largest central market, but after 1815 it
had to share that distinction with Boston. After 1850 both
were in a measure superseded by New York. In Philadelphia
there were dealers who sought permanent agencies for the products of the New England mills, as is shown in a letter by Slater,
published in his memoirs.[3] In that letter Slater discussed
arrangements with an agent to whom should regularly be consigned the former's share of the goods manufactured in the mill
with which he was connected.

The first cotton mill in Fall River was erected in 1811, and
it gave out the cotton to be picked and cleaned by hand in the
homes and the yarn to be woven,[4] just as was done at the Slater
mill. This concern also sold part of its yarn in Philadelphia
through commission houses[5] which had no immediate financial
connection with the mill. The Troy Company, another of the
Fall River pioneers, opened its own stores in New England
cities, in Hallowell, Maine, for example, in 1819, and in the same

[1] W. R. Bagnall, *Textile Industries of the United States*, p. 163.
[2] *Ibid.*, pp. 163, 164, 254.
[3] G. S. White, *Memoir of Samuel Slater*, pp. 214–215.
[4] H. H. Earl, *History of Fall River*, p. 9.
[5] *Ibid.*, p. 18.

year " the company's agent was authorized to make a shipment of cotton and other goods to the State of Georgia, for the purpose of purchasing cotton and other kinds of southern produce on account of the company." This, however, was but a temporary expedient, and did not conform to the later practices which were even then in embryo.

Commission houses were evidently employed by the earliest cotton cloth manufacturers in the United States. The goods were consigned to them to be sold for a specified commission. This practice continued for the first quarter of the last century as appears from occasional advertisements inserted in the contemporary newspapers by firms which requested consignments of domestic goods to be sold on commission. There had begun, however, a different form of commission house, the selling house or selling agent. The selling house ordinarily sold, as it does today, the total output of the mills which it represented, giving more or less financial assistance to the manufacturer or the purchaser, and receiving therefor a commission. While Almy & Brown were a firm of merchants selling cotton goods for the mills, they could hardly be styled selling agents in the sense in which that term has come to be used in the trade, since they were really owners of the cloth. But their financial connection with the mills is significant, as a prototype of a later custom. The first real selling house of which we have record is that which undertook the marketing of the first cloth woven in this country upon the power loom. How the selling house made its appearance and the function which it performed has been told by Mr. Appleton, the man who was most intimately connected with the venture.

When the Waltham company began to weave cloth there was but a single dealer in Boston who handled domestic goods, and new arrangements had to be made. The first cloth woven by the company was a heavy sheeting, and the probable market for the goods could not be forecasted. " At that time it was supposed that no quantity of cottons could be sold without being bleached," Mr. Appleton states, " and the idea was to imitate the yard wide goods of India with which this country was then largely supplied. Mr. Lowell informed me that he would be satisfied with twenty-five cents the yard for the goods, although the nominal price was higher. I soon found a purchaser in Mr. Forsaith, an auctioneer, who sold them at auction at once, at something over thirty cents. We continued to sell them at auction with little variation of the price. This circumstance led to B. C. Ward & Co. becoming permanently the selling agents." [1] Mr. Appleton was financially interested in the Waltham mill, and he was also a partner in the Ward Company, which had been formed to deal in imported goods. Thus the first selling house obtained its agency because of the financial connection of one of its members with the manufacturing company; on the other hand, its services were necessary, since the manufacturer could not attend to the selling of the cloth which he made.

The commission charged by the selling house was at first one per cent,[2] and later increased to one and one-quarter per cent [3] when the agents undertook the preparation of the patterns and employed experienced designers.

Other selling houses were established in Boston as soon as the growth of the industry warranted it. A. & A. Lawrence entered into the sale of domestic cottons and woolens after their import business was cut into by the tariff of 1816, and in 1830 they became interested in mills in Lowell.[4] After 1837 they gave their attention entirely to the sale of the products of the mills which they represented.[5] In this instance, as in the case of the Ward Company, the selling house owned stock in the mills. In 1825 W. & S. Lawrence, who had previously carried on an import trade in dry goods, likewise became interested in domestic concerns.[6] The selling houses, therefore, had a direct part in

---

[1] N. Appleton, *Introduction of the Power Loom*, pp. 11, 12.

[2] *Ibid.*, p. 12.

[3] *Ibid.*, p. 27.

[4] N. Appleton, *Memoir of Abbott Lawrence*, p. 7. The firm of A. & A. Lawrence was dissolved at a later date; the present firm of Lawrence & Co. was built up by A. A. Lawrence. Wm. Lawrence, *Life of Amos Lawrence*, p. 269.

[5] H. A. Hill, *Memoir of Abbott Lawrence*, p. 23.

[6] F. Hunt, *Lives of American Merchants*, vol. ii, p. 372.

providing capital for manufacturing cotton goods, and this capital had been accumulated in foreign trade. The transfer of the interests of these merchants, indicating what was going on elsewhere, throws light upon the tariff struggles of those days, since it helps us to understand why New England changed its attitude toward protection between 1824 and 1832.

The selling house was of assistance to the manufacturer in placing the goods on the market, but the credit which it provided was no less important. The manufacturing enterprises at first involved risks which caused banks to hesitate in granting credit to the new concerns. The selling house, on the contrary, could take a direct part in the management, and with its accumulated capital make advances to the mills, or, what is more important, indorse the notes of the mills so that banks would be willing to accept them. At that time the chief credit was with the selling house.

The selling house made it possible to grant long credits to the persons who bought the cloth. Southern and western buyers could not pay for the cotton cloth, boots and shoes, and other New England products, till several months after delivery. " We sell our fabrics, which are made in the North, to the southern buyers on credit of from six to ten months," it was stated in 1849.[1] " Neither do we receive a similar credit in return, for the reason that they are not in a condition to grant it. All the great staples sent from the southern market are sold for cash, or on a credit of sixty days. It is in this way that the foreign and the home manufacturers supply themselves with cotton. Though there are many rich men in the large cotton growing states, the number of moneyed men is very small. The planters are usually in debt more or less, either from having extended their business beyond their means, or from the habit of anticipating their incomes by borrowing of their cotton factors, the banks, or by credit at the stores." In other words the capital of merchants in Boston and other northern cities aided in the development of other sections of the country, and indirectly facilitated the extension of the slave system.

[1] *Hunt's Merchants' Magazine*, vol. xxi, p. 628.

With the progress of time the services performed by the American selling houses became more diverse, both in distributing the products and in providing credit. " Some corporations," it was stated in 1852,[1] " arrange with selling agents merely to dispose of the goods, and hand over to the treasurer the obligations received therefor; while others require these agents to cash the paper and furnish the company with funds whenever required to do so. In some cases the selling agent directs in regard to qualities, patterns, and so forth, of the goods to be manufactured, while in others these duties devolve on the treasurer or general agent. This diversity of duties causes a difference in the compensation paid to selling agents; but the commission usually paid is one per cent on the gross sales of the whole production of the establishment, in addition to the commission paid upon sales elsewhere than in this city."

After the goods were received by the selling house they still had to be placed in the hands of the retailers. Up to the time of the introduction of the power loom the American people (*i. e.* those who did not make their own homespuns) depended largely upon imported cottons and woolens, and it was but natural that the same means of selling domestic cloth should be tried as were in use for the distribution of the foreign fabrics. This accounts for the sale of the first products of the Waltham factory at auction,[2] since it was then customary to sell English, French, and other foreign wares, cloth as well 'as hardware, tea, and other commodities, at public auctions.[3]

The auctions of domestic dry goods were held in Boston and Philadelphia, the former being more important. They were attended by local jobbers and also by jobbers from more or less distant cities. As business conditions became more settled and commercial reputations more firmly established, the auction gradually gave way to direct sales to the jobbers by the selling houses. During this transition both methods persisted side by side, and in 1826 a society was organized in Boston, the

[1] *Report of Sturgis Committee*, p. 3.

[2] See *ante*, page 196.

[3] Advertisements of these sales were published in the daily newspapers, the *Boston Advertiser* for example.

chief object of which seems to have been to facilitate the sale
of cotton cloth and other goods of American manufacture.

The New England Society for the Promotion of Manufactures and the Mechanic Arts was incorporated [1] in Massachusetts March 3, 1826, by Patrick T. Jackson, Jesse Putnam,
John Doggett, and Henry A. S. Dearborn. Mr. Jackson was
prominently connected with numerous cotton mills, and his
associates were men of standing in the city. The society was
authorized by its charter to hold public sales and exhibitions,
and to award premiums for inventions and discoveries. The
public sales, moreover, were exempt from the tax on auctions.
The first sale was held September 12, 1826, and thereafter semi-
annually for about five years. The history of this undertaking
is obscure, but we know that at the first five sales nearly $2,000-
000 worth of goods were disposed of, and that from time to time
premiums and medals were awarded.[2]

The object of these public sales by the New England Society
was to encourage home manufactures and at the same time to
provide an outlet for the goods, since, to judge from the advertisements,[3] anyone could send in goods and have them entered in
the catalogue from which the sales were made. The last reference to these sales was in 1832, when *Niles' Register* gave
the following account.

" The New England sales were closed on Saturday evening,
having gone off with much better spirit and prices than was
anticipated. The deductions from former prices, however,
were very considerable in the leading articles, but if the purchasers had substantial reasons for being satisfied with their
bargains the manufacturers had much less ground for complaint
than they expected to have. A great many lots, however,
were withdrawn after selling the first parcel, in consequence
of low bids. It was estimated that at least $1,500,000 worth
of goods were brought together on this occasion. The display
of calicoes and chintzes was very fine. They occupied almost

---

[1] *Massachusetts Statutes*, 1825–26, chap. 120.
[2] A. Bowen, *Picture of Boston*, pp. 60–61.
[3] *Boston Advertiser*, March 8, 1831.

entirely the centre hall under the dome (Quincy Hall). Among them the muslins from Robinson's, Fall River, printed on imported fabric, were decidedly elegant. This article sold for forty cents. The calicoes were very rich, but not in so great variety as the improved condition of that manufacture would seem to warrant." [1]

In spite of the assurance of this report that the sales were a complete success, the withdrawal of part of the cotton goods and the dearth of calicoes signify waning interest on the part of the manufacturers, who did not wish to advertise new wares in this way. A year later semi-annual sales of shoes and furniture were held in March at the same place,[2] but in the advertisements no mention of cotton goods is to be found, nor is the name of the New England Society attached to the notices. Occasional auctions were held in Boston after that date, but they were of comparatively little importance, taking place only when it was desired to unload a stock of goods quickly. The decline of auctions and public sales was due to the increased volume of output, which necessitated a more regular and a more reliable market, and to the improvements in communication which began about 1830. Continued changes in transportation facilities and credit conditions led to further alterations in the market organization.

During the first half of the nineteenth century Boston and Philadelphia were the chief centres of the trade in domestic cottons. At Boston the selling of the product of the New England mills was concentrated, while at Philadelphia was located the most important market for " blue goods," — denims, checks, stripes, and the like.[3] Meanwhile New York was becoming by far the largest market for imported cloth. Partly because of the attraction of the import trade, and more especially on account of the rise of New York as a financial and commercial centre after the opening of the Erie Canal and the establishment of rail communication with other parts of the country,

---

[1] *Niles' Register*, March 31, 1832, p. 79.
[2] *Boston Advertiser*, March, 1833.
[3] *One Hundred Years of American Commerce*, vol. ii, p. 556.

that city began to assume the leadership in the domestic dry goods trade, which had grown to such dimensions that greater centralization was inevitable.

The movement to New York, which hitherto had had almost no dry goods commission business, began in 1846, when Boston firms opened branches there,[1] A few years later nineteen branch houses were located in New York, for the sake of the facilities for shipping to the South and West, and of the advantages for credit.[2] The Boston and Philadelphia selling houses continued to stand in the same relation to the mills as formerly, and to transact a large business at their home offices. They had, however, expanded so as to secure a wider market.

Previously the domestic dry goods trade at New York had been grafted upon the import trade. The goods imported into New York early in the century were sold by means of auctions, just as they had been sold at the other ports of entry. James Flint wrote in 1822, "At present vast quantities of English goods are selling by auction in the ports of the United States. New York is the chief market in this way. Merchants from the country attend these sales, sometimes for many days and even weeks together." [3] The auctions continued to be of importance for many years. They were, however, opposed by the jobbers, who sought legislation for restraining them.[4]

To this end the state of New York in 1817 imposed a tax on auctioneers of one per cent on their total sales of goods brought from beyond the Cape of Good Hope, and one and one-half per cent on goods imported from Europe. This did not satisfy the jobbers who desired still heavier taxes, and merchants not only from New York but also from Boston, Philadelphia, and Baltimore petitioned Congress almost every year for the next fifteen years. This was the period when the importation of English goods was particularly heavy and the pressure on the prices of domestic fabrics great. Nevertheless no federal legisla-

---

[1] *Professional and Industrial History of Suffolk County*, vol. ii, p. 155.
[2] *Ibid.*, p. 155.
[3] J. Flint, *Letters from America*, p. 33.
[4] *Hunt's Merchants' Magazine*, vol. x, p. 154.

tion was enacted. The state tax on auctions and the opposition did not cause an abandonment of the practice. In 1851, for example, about $7,500,000 worth of dry goods, two-thirds foreign and one-third domestic, were disposed of at New York in this way.[1]

The introduction of more regular communication with Europe and the establishment of more definite methods of trade within the country led to a relative decline of the auctions. They came to be used more and more only as a means of getting rid of accumulated stocks. The change can be traced from the annual reports on the dry goods trade published by the New York Chamber of Commerce.

Early in the spring of 1860 the tone of the market for imported goods was dull, hence " jobbers, perceiving the fears of importers, were determined in bringing them to the auction room, which they effected without much difficulty, so that the public sales were unusually early, and large almost beyond precedent." [2] In the autumn of the same year, " the auctions commenced about a month later than usual." [3] Thus auctions were still a regular occurrence, but not for disposing of the greater portion of the goods.

In 1861, " the importers having sold what goods they could at private sale to good customers, now forced their goods in the auction room. From the auctioneers they were sure of their pay, and preferred to take low prices, with certainty of payments, to selling to purchasers as they came, and running the risks of bad debts." [4] The credit structure was not yet free from flaws.

While at the dates just referred to no mention of public sales of domestic goods is made, the markets for imported and domestic goods were so closely bound together in New York that they cannot be considered separately. And in 1877, " several important auction sales of the cotton and woolen productions of Eastern manufacturers, represented in this market (New York)

[1] *Hunt's Merchants' Magazine*, vol. xxv, p. 610.
[2] Chamber of Commerce of the State of New York, 3d *Annual Report*, p. 151.
[3] *Ibid.*, p. 151.
[4] *Ibid.*, 4th *Annual Report*, p. 233.

by prominent commission houses," were held.[1] The next year, in May, occurred an important auction sale of 12,000 packages of (domestic) cotton goods,[2] followed by other sales.

" In May, 1883, surplus stocks began to find their way to the auction room, the first sale being of 2,000 packages of a well-known brand of tickings. This was followed in July by an offering of 13,000 packages of denims, tickings, ducks, corset jeans, ginghams, and bleached goods; this again in August by the sale of some 17,000 cases of a similar character. Later in the year a sale of some 3,000 cases of cotton flannels was made, which, with some small offerings, made up a total of (domestic) cotton goods disposed of at auction of over 40,000 packages, with a value of about $3,500,000."[3] Although this amount was much smaller than the total value of cotton goods sold in the city in that year, it was by no means negligible. At this date the auctions of American cloth had become more important than those of foreign-made goods.

The sales continued more or less regularly, since in 1888 it was remarked that " cotton goods were kept so closely sold up by the commission houses during the year, that no public sales were found necessary as in former years."[4] The following year, 10,000 cases of cotton goods were sold at auction,[5] but this was the turning point, as the sales occurred less frequently in subsequent years. Two large public sales were held in 1893, that of the Amoskeag in September and that of Bliss, Fabyan in November,[6] after the crisis had caused a sharp decline in the market and the large stocks manufactured in anticipation of a heavy demand had become a burden to the selling agents. In December, 1894, 27,000 packages, largely colored cotton goods, were sold in this way.[7] In 1896 one gingham mill closed out its stocks at auction and changed to the production of other

[1] Chamber of Commerce of the State of New York, 20th *Annual Report*, p. 97.
[2] *Ibid.*, 21st *Annual Report*, p. 112.
[3] *Ibid.*, 26th *Annual Report*, p. 112.
[4] *Ibid.*, 31st *Annual Report*, p. 86.
[5] *Ibid.*, 32d *Annual Report*, p. 83.
[6] *Ibid.*, 36th *Annual Report*, p. 86.
[7] *Ibid.*, 37th *Annual Report*, p. 88.

goods,[1] and in 1897, 20,000 packages of staple cottons were sold at auction by Catlin & Co.[2] There the sales ended. Instituted in the first place in New York, as in other cities, for the purpose of selling imported goods, auctions were a ready means of getting domestic goods into the hands of the wholesalers, but as the market organization settled down to more fixed forms, the public sales were held less and less regularly, and now have ceased to be employed, even for disposing of an accumulated surplus.

But to return to the period prior to the Civil War. At first the mills had manufactured whatever goods they and their selling agents thought could be readily sold, but gradually they began to sell ahead, that is accept orders for goods before they were manufactured. However, as practically all of their products were staples, they accumulated stocks in their warehouses, if orders for future or immediate delivery were lacking.

The selling houses were accustomed to grant long credits until the outbreak of the War. The Boston Board of Trade report on the dry goods trade in 1858, for example, stated: " The experience of the past year has been productive of some good results. The rule of giving eight months' credit to southern and western buyers, and frequently extending it afterwards for two, four, and even six months, will hereafter be discontinued by the leading commission houses. Six months has been fixed as the outside limit and liberal inducements will be offered buyers to purchase for cash or on shorter time." [3] This indicates, also, that the prices charged for the cloth had been so high that the sellers were compensated for waiting and the capitalists had not suffered from having their capital tied up for a long period.

The first cloth manufactured at Waltham was sold in the gray, and in following years considerable quantities were placed in the hands of jobbers in that condition. Bleacheries were established, also, where the cloth was bleached on commission, usually

[1] Chamber of Commerce of the State of New York, 39th *Annual Report*, p. 91.
[2] *Ibid.*, 40th *Annual Report*, p. 83.
[3] Boston Board of Trade, 4th *Annual Report*, p. 132.

for the mill. Manufacturers weaving colored yarn either dyed it themselves or sent it to job dye-works, except for the small quantity purchased already dyed. Piece dyeing, likewise, seems to have been done chiefly at the plant where the cloth was manufactured, or on commission. Printed goods, however, were handled somewhat differently. Most of the Lowell and Lawrence mills introduced their own printing equipment either when first built or within a few years thereafter. But in addition to these, several independent print works were put into operation during the first half of the century. The cloth manufacturing companies with print works occasionally bought goods for printing when unable to supply enough from their own mills or when desiring goods of different construction from those which they made, and the independent companies also bought the cloth which they printed.[1] Thus the printer owned the fabrics which he converted and sold them ordinarily through a selling house.

From the first many print cloth mills which sold gray cloth for printing had no selling agents, but disposed of their goods directly to the printer, since they were manufacturing staple products which conformed to recognized standards, and, furthermore, both parties were in a position to communicate with each other and to appreciate each other's business reputation. The printer, moreover, did not keep the goods long in his hands, and could therefore pay cash or give a short term note to the cloth manufacturer. The need of credit came after the goods were converted, and there the selling house usually stepped in. Thus in 1872 the textile directories indicate that nearly all of the Fall River print cloth mills were selling direct, without a selling agent. The method of selling direct became still more important in subsequent years, and in 1890 it was said that the desire to economize had led a number of mills to dispense with agents and commission houses.[2] This was one among the many economies sought by reason of the competi-

---

[1] The first print cloths manufactured in Fall River were sold to a local printer.— H. H. Earl, *History of Fall River*, p. 28.

[2] Chamber of Commerce of the State of New York, 33d *Annual Report*, p. 81.

tion of the southern mills. Those which were not manufacturing goods which required an elaborate selling department, and which were strong enough financially, cut down their expenses by assuming the merchandizing part of the business. The same tendency is apparent today.

Another middleman, however, interposed himself as the industry expanded. This was the merchant-converter, an individual or firm having no manufacturing plant and no finishing plant. He bought cloth and had it converted, — bleached, dyed, or more commonly printed, on commission, and then resold it. Just when he entered the dry goods trade is uncertain, but the first mention of converters which I have been able to find was in 1881, when the placing of orders by converters is spoken of.[1] Three years later converters are again mentioned in the trade report, as though they were a regular institution.[2] They evidently began operations before 1880, and since then have gradually assumed a larger and larger place.

During this evolution of the market organization two attempts have been made to institute selling bureaus. The first was in 1891 when nearly all of the southern plaid mills sought to remedy unsatisfactory market conditions by establishing a joint selling agency in New York [3] with power to regulate styles and production.[4] The trouble, however, was more fundamental, and the venture was so unsuccessful that it was speedily abandoned. The other attempt was made by fifty-two Fall River print cloth mills which signed an agreement to curtail output and pool practically the entire stock of certain classes of goods, including print cloths.[5] The disposal of the goods was entrusted to a committee of five, with two trustees.[6] After three years of existence the pool was dissolved in August, 1901, when it became apparent that with the revival of trade and the restoration of

[1] Chamber of Commerce of the State of New York, 24th *Annual Report*, p. 90.
[2] *Ibid.*, 27th *Annual Report*, p. 106.
[3] *Commercial and Financial Chronicle*, vol. lii, p. 351.
[4] Chamber of Commerce of the State of New York, 34th *Annual Report*, p. 83.
[5] *Commercial and Financial Chronicle*, vol. lxix, *Cotton Crop Supplement*, p. 5.
[6] Chamber of Commerce of the State of New York, 41st *Annual Report*, p. 86.

normal conditions it was no longer necessary.[1] Perhaps the doubt concerning its legality also had some influence in bringing about its disruption. These two pools were merely temporary devices and are of little importance in the history of the market organization, except to show the diversity of the experiments out of which the present organization has developed.

The evolution of the cloth market, therefore, has been the gradual working out of forms adapted to the conditions. Just as mechanical inventions have had to stand the test of time and experience, likewise the less tangible merchandizing arrangements have been the product of necessity and experiment. The result is a complex organism at the present time which even now is undergoing change.

Present Organization

Four methods of selling cotton cloth are followed: — (1) selling direct, (2) by a selling house, (3) through a broker, and (4) to a converter.

(1) When a cotton manufacturing company sells direct, the goods are marketed either by an officer of the company or by a salesman employed solely for that purpose. The business is generally transacted by the treasurer, who accepts the orders and arranges the terms of sale. Several large companies, however, have established private selling offices under the control of the treasurers, in which the trade is attended to by salesmen. The Lorraine Manufacturing Company of Pawtucket has its treasurer's office at the mills and a selling office in New York, with branches in Chicago and other cities. The Amoskeag Manufacturing Company instituted a similar plan in 1910, and the product of the American Printing Company is now sold by M. C. D. Borden & Sons, which, in view of that firm's control in the printing company, amounts to selling direct. But as yet few manufacturers operate on a scale sufficiently large to permit the maintenance of a separate selling department. In the majority of instances where the products are sold direct, the work is personally superintended by the treasurer.

[1] Chamber of Commerce of the State of New York, 44th *Annual Report*, p. 95.

Selling direct is particularly characteristic of the New England mills which manufacture staples. Those mills are located chiefly in southern New England, in the vicinity of New Bedford and Fall River. They produce plain goods of standard styles, the selling of which is easier than the marketing of fancy goods with seasonal designs. Moreover, the standard goods are sold for cash or on short term notes, whereas longer credit must be granted on the other class. Still, not all New England mills producing staples sell direct, for reasons to be explained later. In the South many of the yarn mills, but few of the cloth mills, sell direct.

The standard goods disposed of in this way are sold in the gray, that is unfinished. The mill normally has orders about three months ahead, especially on the finer grades, but if the market prospects are good, the mill is kept running even if no orders are immediately at hand, and the cloth is warehoused till there is a demand for it. To express it in trade terms, when the manufacturer has not sold ahead, he manufactures for stock, since there are many spot sales of this class of goods.

Manufacturing for stock was formerly common for all classes of fabrics. The results were the auctions. But the auction room meant a loss to the mills, and consequently the manufacturers of finished goods have gradually given up the practice. For them there is always a danger inherent in any accumulation in their warehouses. Their market is not as flexible as that of the gray cloth manufacturers. Yet even the latter, as well as the former, generally find a policy of immediate curtailment desirable whenever a panic occurs.

The gray goods manufactured in Fall River are usually sold f.o.b. Fall River, the manufacturer ending his responsibility, except for faults in the fabric, when the cloth is delivered to the transportation company. The cloth is finished wherever the purchaser desires, and at his own responsibility.

The advantage of selling direct is that the mill is more independent. There is no conflict between the treasurer and the selling house, and no suspicion that the selling agent is not trying to serve the best interests of the mill. The treasurer may not always be as capable as the specialists of the selling house in judging the market, but the amount that would have been paid to the selling house as commission is saved.

(2) The selling house, sometimes called selling agent or commission house, is a separate firm and is in most cases the sole agent for the mill whose goods it handles. A few mills have two selling houses, each for a different kind of product. For example, a mill may have one selling agent for yarns, if it makes yarn for sale, and another for cloth. A small number of mills which employ a selling house also sell goods direct. But in the main one concern markets all the goods produced by the mill, and the mill is not at liberty to sell through any other agency. A selling house, however, is agent for several mills, and frequently markets woolen as well as cotton goods.

The selling houses have gradually expanded their business with the increase in the size of the plants of the companies for which they are agents and with the acquisition of the business of new mills. The larger houses have offices in New York, Boston, and numerous other cities. The more prominent ones have from ten to twenty mills for which they act as selling agents. In all instances they accept the orders and control the marketing of the goods, the treasurers merely collecting the bills. The selling agent has two distinct functions, — the distribution of the goods and the provision of financial assistance. As was indicated in a preceding section, both those functions were performed by the early selling houses. The two services are not of equal importance in New England at the present time, but in the South both are utilized by numerous mills.

For southern mills the difficulties of marketing the cloth give an opportunity for selling agents. The distance from the markets and the lack of intimate acquaintance with market conditions are obstacles to direct selling by southern manufacturers. Moreover the holding of stock in southern corporations by selling houses, while less common than in New England, is by no means unknown. But the dearth of capital has had fully as great influence as any other factor in causing the southern mills to rely upon selling houses. Inasmuch as their quick capital has seldom been adequate, the southern mills have borrowed money either by receiving advances on the goods or by an indorsement of their notes. Spinning mills occasionally obtain funds directly from the southern banks in exchange for a lien on their stock of cotton. But for advances on the product and the indorsement of notes or guaranteeing of accounts northern selling houses have been employed and have frequently loaned from 75 to 90 per cent on the value of the cloth.[1] In return they have received not only interest on money advanced and a higher commission for indorsement of notes or guarantee of account, but also the exclusive agency for the sale of the product.

The commission charged for the sale of southern goods is higher, because of greater risk. A southern manufacturer pays his selling agent three and one-half or four per cent, a northern manufacturer one and one-half or two per cent. The commission on southern goods includes two per cent for selling and two per cent for guaranteeing the payment of the purchasers' accounts. The majority of New England mills are so strong financially and their credit is so firmly established that the additional indorsement of their commercial paper by a selling house is seldom little more than a matter of form; hence they are relieved of the extra charge. In the case of the southern mills, which are generally smaller, less strong financially, and too remote to be easily watched, there is greater risk. Southern goods are more apt to have flaws and do not, as a rule, enjoy the reputation of northern fabrics.

The relations between the southern manufacturers and their selling agents have not always been most cordial. Not only have the manufacturers complained of the higher commission which they pay, but they have also accused the selling agents of disposing of consignments of goods at unremunerative prices. They allege that the selling agents have sold such goods at whatever prices were obtainable, even if the market were dull, instead of carrying them till trade improved. It was this dumping of

---

[1] D. A. Tompkins, *Cotton Mill-Commercial Features*, p. 33.

consigned goods that was felt most keenly by the New England manufacturers and gave rise to the complaints against southern competition in the 'nineties. The selling houses have been accused of causing severe injury and even bankruptcy of southern mills in this way, just as they have also been charged with bankrupting some New England companies. The fault, however, would seem to be ascribable to the consignment system; for it has been consigned goods which were sold at ruinous prices.

Consignment trade is nearly always unsatisfactory and nearly always gives rise to complaint. It is not peculiar to the American domestic trade in dry goods, since foreign manufacturers who send consignments to New York import houses frequently make similar accusations. A manufacturer who produces more than he has orders for, and who cannot hold the goods in his own warehouse, or send his own salesmen into the field, places himself at the mercy of sudden market changes. A selling house can seldom afford to carry a stock of goods, especially on a falling market, and has to take what it can get. The fault of the selling house in this respect does not appear to lie so much in the actual sale of the goods as in the failure to forecast the market correctly and advise its clients to curtail shipments. At all events, dissatisfaction with the selling houses has fostered the spread of the practice of selling direct.

The selling house has maintained a strong foothold in New England also, although not in New Bedford and Fall River. In some instances large holdings of stock in a mill by a selling house or some of its members has continued the connection between the two when otherwise it would have been broken. Secondly, gray cloth manufacturers situated in the more remote parts of New England would perhaps find it difficult to keep closely enough in touch with the market to sell direct. Others are so weak financially that the credit of the selling house is almost indispensable. They have not sufficient ready capital to provide for current expenses, — the payment of wages, purchase of raw material, and settlement of other charges incurred during the process of manufacture and until the goods are paid for by the purchaser. Nevertheless for a majority of the New England manufacturers, advance of money or indorsement of notes is not essential. The chief credit has come to be primarily with the mill. Consequently financial aid is no longer as influential in securing exclusive agencies for New England cotton mills by the selling houses. On the other hand, the selling houses have found an increased scope for activity in the marketing of other than staple fabrics.

The mills which manufacture fancy goods of seasonal design, such as fancy prints or ginghams, ordinarily employ a selling house. They are mills which do not sell in the gray. The selling house either selects the designs itself, or is at least asked to give its opinion on the designs before the patterns are set up. Later, samples of cloth bearing the various designs are sent to the selling house by the mill, by means of which orders are solicited from regular customers and from the trade in general. The selling of these fancy goods requires especial skill in judging the designs, in securing orders, and in estimating the probable demand. The selling of staples is much simpler; if the goods are not in immediate demand at satisfactory prices they may be stored away in the warehouse. But the fancies must be sold to meet the prevailing fashions during the season for which they are produced. Otherwise they can be disposed of only at a loss, owing to the dislike for last season's designs. It is essential that the marketing of the fancy goods should be in the hands of skilled salesmen.

Complexity of designs and necessity of securing orders before the goods are manufactured have made it necessary to send out the designs long before the season in which the goods are to be placed upon the retail market. Each mill usually has two seasons. For example, a mill may have a flannel season and a wash goods season. For the latter, designs are sent out in the autumn, the goods are made during the winter and put upon the market in the spring. For the former, the designs are issued in January, and the goods made ready to be shipped in the autumn. Likewise in ginghams and fancy prints there are spring and autumn designs. While the special seasons are well defined, designs are also sent out by the mills during the intervening periods. The designs are submitted to the trade much earlier than formerly, now usually six months ahead, whereas fifteen years ago cards were made up in January for spring delivery. The marketing of fancy goods, therefore, has become specialized along with the specialization of the industry.

The selling department must understand the market thoroughly and this can be accomplished better by a selling house than by the treasurer or his subordinates.[1] A selling house has so many agents scattered over the country that it can feel every pulse beat of the market. It can foretell more or less accurately the probable strength of the demand for the individual lines and understands the local tastes. Certain styles are better received in some localities than in others, and in general there are distinct sectional characteristics. For example, the people in the south-west prefer light gay colors and those residing in the north-west darker gray goods. These local preferences and the fluctuations of a wide market offer opportunity for specialization in selling fancy cotton fabrics.

The seasonal goods are made to fill orders which the selling house has secured before the manufacture of the cloth is begun. Of course, if the selling house thinks that the market will absorb more of the goods than it has orders for, it accordingly requests the mill to manufacture a larger quantity. As a rule no order is accepted for less than 2,000 yards by some mills, and by other mills for not less than 6,000 or 10,000 yards of a single design. In every case the order must be large enough to pay for setting up the design and adjusting the machinery, without necessitating the charging of exorbitant prices.

A practice of which the mills complain is lenience in allowing customers to cancel orders after they have been accepted by the selling house, given to the mill, and the cloth made. In the recent depression following the panic of 1907 many orders were cancelled, thus causing loss to the mills. The competition

---

[1] This statement refers to the company of average size. Only a company with a very large output can afford to maintain a selling department equal to that of a selling house.

between the mills and the desire to retain customers led to the extension of a practice which the mills would be glad to get rid of. The merchants, however, justify their action in cancelling the contracts on the grounds that the mills were tardy in filling the orders which had been accepted. "During the great rise in cloth during 1906 and the early part of 1907, the experience of the buyers was that the vast majority of the mills were behind on their promised deliveries, in some cases the mills not making any deliveries on their contracts for three or four months past the time promised. In other cases, where they began fairly promptly, their weekly deliveries were much smaller than promised. The consequence was that when the crash came in the fall of 1907, the buyers had contracts outstanding which should have been completed by the mills, and in addition to this they had finished goods on hand that had been carried over from the season before through inability to get their goods from the mills when promised. About ninety per cent of the rejections after the panic were based by the buyers on the fact that the mills were behind on delivery." [1] This statement, in the words of one of the buyers, throws light upon the other side of the controversy.

Irrespective of the extent to which the cancellations were justified in 1907, it is to the interest of both parties that a formal arrangement be instituted to prevent abuses in the future. To this end the two large cotton manufacturers' associations have undertaken to formulate a uniform cloth contract and to provide for some sort of an arbitration board to pass judgment upon cases arising from breaches of the contract. In order to protect themselves an agreement between the mills is necessary. The individual mills are not only reluctant to take the matter to court when an order is cancelled, because of the relatively small amount involved in each cancellation, and because of the disadvantage in competition to which they might be subjected, but also because of the technicalities involved and the uncertainty of securing a favorable verdict. No piece of cloth is perfect and a slight flaw may be made the basis of a refusal to

[1] *Textile World Record*, vol. xxxix, p. 63.

accept the piece at all, thereby placing the blame on the mill. The question of cancellation has assumed more importance with the increase in the length of time between the giving of the order and the delivery of the goods. It has become more difficult to foretell what business conditions will prevail at the time of delivery, and if the market suddenly collapses, there is a loss to be borne by some one. Where a mill has not been punctual in fulfilling its contracts, it has little right to seek relief, but on the other hand a uniform contract and an arbitration board would prevent the burden being unjustly thrust upon the mills which had met their obligations.

The selling house performed a valuable service in the early years of its existence as a distributing agent for the manufacturers and in giving financial aid to the mills which lacked sufficient capital. It still plays an important part in the marketing of special kinds of goods and in some cases in indorsing the notes of the mill. Another function of the selling house is the centralizing tendency which it has stimulated in the movement for integration to which reference has already been made. A few selling houses, however, are little more than parasites, holding mills tightly within their grasp as creditors.

(3) Unlike goods that are finished at the mill where woven, usually sold by a selling agent to the wholesaler or large retailer, cloth sold in the gray ordinarily passes through the hands of a broker to a converter. The broker is a middleman who brings together the buyer and the seller. In New York, Boston, Fall River, and some other cities, there are a number of these cloth brokers who buy no cloth themselves and accept no responsibility but merely act as intermediaries. In Fall River the greater part of the cloth, probably ninety per cent, is sold through brokers, and in other places where standard goods are manufactured, brokers usually aid the treasurer or the selling house in securing orders for cloth in the gray. The New York cotton goods brokers are by far the most important, however, and the number has increased from eighteen[1] in 1907 to thirty-nine[2] in 1911. If a man wishes to purchase a

---

[1] *Dockham's Textile Directory*, 1907.   [2] *Blue Book Textile Directory*, 1911–12.

certain quantity of a specified style of cloth, the broker finds a manufacturer or a manufacturer's agent who can fill the order. Thus by keeping in touch with the buyers and with the sellers, the broker is able to bring together the right parties, and with the expansion of the industry and the growing volume and diversification of products such a middleman secures an increasingly large place in the market organization. The purchaser is able to find more readily the goods which he wants, and the manufacturer economizes in time spent in seeking customers.

For his services the broker usually receives one-half of one per cent on the value of the goods which he is instrumental in selling. As the greater part of the southern goods are sold in the gray by the selling house through a broker, whereas many New England mills manufacturing this kind of goods employ only the broker, it is evident that the commission paid to the selling house is saved to the northern mills.

(4) The purchaser of the gray goods is either a printer [1] or a merchant-converter, another middleman. The term converter is used in several senses, but here is applied to the class of men who buy cloth in the gray, have it converted, and then sell it to the wholesaler or large retailer. The converter secures the order for a certain style of finished goods, or thinks that he can dispose of such goods, and then buys the cloth from a manufacturer. He gauges his purchases by market conditions, " going in " lightly or heavily according to trade prospects and the price at which he can obtain the cloth. He sends the cloth to the converting establishment which offers the best terms or has a specialty in the kind of finish which he desires. The cloth is bleached, dyed, or printed, as the case may be. For printing the converter may have his own designs; a few converters who specialize in prints and offer fancy patterns even send agents to Paris for the latest ideas.

---

[1] The printer is also a converter in the sense that he buys gray cloth and sells finished goods, but it seems advisable to limit the use of the term converter to the merchant.

The converter has become particularly prominent within the last ten years.[1] The increase in the scale of production, the specialization of the industry by the separation of cloth manufacturing and cloth finishing, and particularly the demand for greater diversification of styles and finish have caused a great increase in the converter's business. By having the cloth converted on his own responsibility, the converter relieves the manufacturer and the finisher of a certain amount of risk. This encourages an increase in the scale of production and enables the manufacturer and the finisher to give more attention to the refinement of their respective branches. The converter also brings in capital and credit, buying the goods on short terms of payment, carrying them till they are converted, and, if need be, providing credit to the purchaser. The development of the converter, therefore, signifies a diversification and specialization of the distributing functions and renders the market more plastic. An increased volume of trade can be more nicely adjusted to the varying demands.

The mercantile organization of the American cotton goods trade is undergoing a change at the present time, and the position of the merchant-converter is the key to the situation. Although several printers still convert on their own account, cloth printing tends to follow bleaching and dyeing and become a commission or jobbing trade. A few converters, it may be stated, carry on a wholesale business. On the other hand, the cutters-up, or ready-made garment manufacturers and shirt, collar, and cuff makers, occasionally invade the converter's field and buy goods in the gray to be converted on their account. One of these firms, Cluett, Peabody & Company, has recently purchased a bleaching plant to be operated in connection with its collar factory. Yet, notwithstanding these variations in practice, experience in this country and abroad indicates that the merchant-converter will probably be increasingly important in the future.[2]

[1] *Dockham's Directory* listed 108 converters in New York in 1907 and the *Blue Book Directory* enumerated 181 in the same city in 1911. These were not merely merchant-converters, however, but included manufacturing converters.

[2] It also seems probable that a cotton goods exchange will be organized in New

The cloth may go through many hands, therefore, after it is woven. If the manufacturer employs selling agents, the cloth is handled by them, at least on their books. Then a broker may aid in selling it to a converter who has it finished before passing it on to the cutter-up, the wholesaler, or the retailer. So that from the time it leaves the mill till it is placed upon the counter in the retail store, it has been the subject for possibly five or six different transactions. Not all cloth goes through so many hands. It may be sold directly by the mill to a large retailer. For example the large department stores are seeking to deal directly with the manufacturers and converters and to buy from the jobbers only when the latter are " caught long " and are willing to make concessions on prices. But a large quantity of cloth is handled by all the various agents and middlemen that have been described.

Knit goods are sold either direct or by a selling house. A broker may take part in the selling of the goods, but his place is not large, and the converter has no place at all since the goods are usually finished at the mills where they are made. Some lines are sold ahead, but the bulk of the goods are staples so that they can be carried in stock if the mill has not enough orders on hand to take all that it produces. Though some of the mills produce specialities, the greater part of the trade is in standard products which are sold as cotton cloth is sold and frequently through the same channels.

The chief market centre for all kinds of cotton goods is New York, where in Worth Street and its neighborhood the offices of selling houses, brokers, and converters, and the establishments of numerous jobbers are located. Although the volume of business transacted in Boston is still large and the western markets are constantly increasing in importance, the trade gravitates toward New York. That city is the centre of the import and export trade, and its position at the head of our financial and commercial system helps to make it the leading American dry goods market.

York. The increase in the number of brokers and converters will necessitate the establishment of some means of concentrating the market.

To summarize the present tendencies in the development of the organization of the American cloth market, merchandizing is becoming more diversified and more specialized. The selling house is apparently less important than formerly except in a few special branches. It might lose its hold there, even, since the mills manufacturing fancy seasonal goods are large and might open their own selling offices, were it not that these are the mills in which the old selling houses have the largest holdings of stock. For the sale of gray cloth the selling house seems to be losing ground. On the other hand, the broker is gaining a stronger foothold. But it is the merchant-converter who is coming most rapidly to the front.

CHAPTER XII

EXPORT TRADE

SOON after the manufacture of cotton cloth was firmly established in New England, the mills began to export part of their product, and the amount slowly increased until in 1860 the export trade in cotton goods was valued at ten million dollars. The war, however, cut off the export trade by greatly diminishing the quantity of goods manufactured and upsetting price levels, and it was not till 1877 that the figure of 1860 was again reached. From 1877 to 1896, although the exports of cotton manufactures fluctuated, the average was nearly constant, but since the latter date there has been an enlargement of the foreign market.

AVERAGE ANNUAL EXPORTS OF COTTON GOODS[1]

(In Millions)

	Total	Uncolored Cloth	Colored Cloth	Other
1856–60	$7.5	$2.4	$2.3	$2.8
1861–65	3.7	.4	.9	2.4
1866–70	4.1	.9	.3	2.8
1871–75	3.1	1.7	.6	.7
1876–80	10.0	6.1	2.6	1.2
1881–85	13.0	8.0	2.9	2.1
1886–90	12.4	7.4	3.2	1.6
1891–95	13.3	7.7	3.0	2.5
1896–1900	20.4	11.6	4.4	4.3
1901–05	31.3	17.2	7.0	7.0
1906–10	35.1	16.8	7.2	11.0

The first point in the above table to attract attention is the preponderance of uncolored cloth in the exports, and it is in the main not only uncolored but also unbleached. When the export trade revived in the latter half of the 'seventies, uncolored cloth was in the lead and ever since has continued to predominate. That indicates the general character of our exports of cotton goods.

[1] *U. S. Statistical Abstract*, 1910, p. 491.

The exports from year to year seem to conform to no well-defined tendencies, varying only in accordance with the state of the markets at home and abroad. But dividing the trade into periods we can see certain fundamental influences at work. From the close of the war in 1865 till the panic of 1873 the industry was in a state of convalescence and recuperation. The depression after the commercial disasters of 1873 caused the manufacturers to seek new markets. Later the return to sound currency and the technical progress of the industry aided them in their attempts to dispose of fabrics in foreign countries. For twenty years, however, they did not energetically push their wares in the new fields, but were content to let the foreign market serve merely as a safety valve in keeping the home market fairly stable.

The panic of 1893 again cut down the domestic trade of the cotton manufacturers, as well as of other manufacturers, and once more they began to look further afield. At that time, as during the beginning of the previous period, special influences made themselves felt. The ring spindle had been greatly improved and the Northrop loom was just coming into use, thus enabling them to meet their foreign competitors to better advantage. Moreover the pressure on the home market from the large additional output of the southern mills accentuated the desire to dispose of more goods outside of the country. Some of these southern mills gave themselves over entirely to manufacturing for export; sixty per cent of the total exports in 1899–1900 came from the South and South Carolina alone supplied nearly one-half of the entire exports of cotton cloth.[1] The export trade reached its highest point in 1906, falling off with the speculative advance in prices just before the panic of 1907, and affected during the next two years by the instability of market conditions and the unusually high prices of cotton.

Of the various fields for the further expansion of the export trade in cotton goods manufactured in the United States, Canada is, perhaps, the most promising and that trade will develop of itself, hindered only by artificial tariff barriers. Europe, on

[1] 12th *U. S. Census*, vol. ix, p. 25.

the contrary, on account of commercial restrictions and local production, offers little chance to the American cotton manufacturer. In South America, Central America, and Africa, however, as well as in China and other parts of Asia, a trade much larger than at present could probably be secured if proper methods were adopted. It is to the peculiarities of these neutral markets that special attention is to be given.

By showing the distribution of the exports of cotton manufactures since 1891 according to the larger geographical divisions we can distinguish some of the characteristics of the trade.

EXPORTS OF COTTON MANUFACTURES FROM THE UNITED STATES [1]

(*In Millions*)

	North and Central America	South America	Europe	Asia	Other
1891	$3.0	$2.2	$1.2	$5.8	$1.2
1892	3.1	2.8	.9	4.5	1.7
1893	4.1	3.1	1.0	2.0	1.3
1894	4.6	3.3	1.5	3.4	1.2
1895	4.5	3.6	1.3	2.5	1.6
1896	5.7	3.3	1.4	4.9	1.3
1897	5.7	2.8	1.7	9.1	1.4
1898	4.8	2.3	1.5	6.9	1.2
1899	6.5	2.7	1.4	11.3	1.2
1900	7.5	2.0	1.9	11.0	1.6
1901	6.6	3.3	2.7	6.3	1.2
1902	6.6	3.0	2.4	18.2	1.7
1903	7.2	4.0	2.6	16.3	1.9
1904	7.8	3.6	2.7	6.3	1.7
1905	9.1	4.1	2.4	31.3	2.5
1906	10.1	3.6	3.6	32.9	2.5
1907	10.9	3.8	4.2	9.2	4.2
1908	10.1	2.7	4.4	5.2	2.6
1909	11.5	3.0	3.7	10.6	3.0
1910	12.5	3.3	4.8	7.5	5.2

The exports to South America, Europe, Africa, and Australasia have increased somewhat in value, yet are of relatively minor importance. The course of that trade contrasts with the steady rise of exports to North and Central America, particularly to Canada. Located close at hand and forming part of the same

[1] U. S. Bureau of Statistics, *Exports of Manufactures from the U. S., 1800–1906* (1907), p. 17; and annual *U. S. Commerce and Navigation Reports.*

general market area as the United States, with similar economic conditions, it is but natural that Canada should purchase cotton goods in this country. Here is an opportunity for our cotton manufacturers which holds forth many possibilities for the future. True, Canada may develop cotton manufacturing within her borders from the nucleus already established. Yet New England with its superior climate, its shipping facilities, and the advantages accruing to the industry from long establishment should be in a superior position for many years, and the South should also be able to get a share in the trade. The obstacle in the way has been the tariff, — Canada's tariff on imports of cottons and our tariff on the various products which we might obtain from Canada. It will be a short-sighted policy for the American cotton manufacturers not to do all in their power, even to giving up some of their own cherished protection, to promote a liberal reciprocity treaty.

The countries to the south of us, Mexico, Central America, and the West Indies, fall into the same category as South America and Africa. The conditions encountered there are different and special efforts will have to be put forth if a larger trade is to be built up. That attention has not yet been bestowed, and the English, Germans, and to a less extent the other Europeans, have not only taken advantage of the allegiance of colonial subjects and former fellow-citizens to push their goods, but have also established closer commercial relations by means of steamship lines, banking houses, and other mercantile connections. They have made a vigorous and continuous effort to expand their markets.

Asia, the ancient home of the cotton manufacturing industry, with its millions of consumers, now affords the largest market for cotton cloth manufactured in the Occident. British India alone takes over a hundred million dollars worth of cotton cloth from Great Britain each year besides smaller quantities from Germany and the United States. The Asiatic markets receive, on the average, more of the cotton goods exported from America than are sent by us to any of the other grand geographical divisions, but the trade is less stable than that with Canada.

China is the chief foreign recipient of American cotton manufactures and it is to the Chinese market that the most attention has been given. A similar position was held by China prior to the American Civil War; in 1860, for instance, she took thirty-five per cent of our total exports of cotton fabrics. With the upward movement of the foreign trade in American cotton goods in the 'seventies China was in the forefront, and ever since that time the great fluctuation in those exports has been due to the varying quantities shipped to China. Her demands have been affected by internal disturbances and the changes in prices. The ebb and flow of this trade is indicated by the following statement of the values of cotton cloth exported from the United States to China: — 1874, $200,000; 1881, $4,300,000; 1890, $1,400,000; 1906, $29,800,000; and 1908, $3,400,000. The present reaction has been caused by a cessation of the speculative demand that had arisen during the Russo-Japanese War and also by the upward course of the prices of raw cotton. This trade, we may conclude, is still casual and unstable in amount.

The British exports of cotton goods to China, on the contrary, are steady in volume and average from twenty-five to thirty million dollars annually. This is due to the care exercised by the British in regulating the quality of the product so as to avoid altering the price each season. Together Great Britain and the United States supply over nine-tenths of the total cotton cloth imported into China, — one hundred and eleven million out of one hundred and seventeen million taels in 1905.[1] But each of the two countries has a special field in which its influence predominates and in which the demands are for certain special kinds of cloth. American sheetings and drills control the market in Manchuria, whereas English shirtings and light sheetings hold sway in southern China.

Of the cotton piece goods which are imported into Manchuria, it is stated that seven-eighths are from the United States.[2] These goods are used for the clothing of natives too

---

[1] H. B. Morse, *Trade and Administration of the Chinese Empire*, p. 286.
[2] *Foreign Markets for the Sale of American Cotton Products* (1907), p. 14.

impecunious to buy fabrics made of other material, and yet requiring protection against a rigorous climate. " They dress in padded clothes made of two thicknesses of cloth with cotton sewed in between. Sheeting is often used for the inside and drills for the outside thickness. Both trousers and coats are so padded, and this padded cloth has become the distinctive dress of the northern Chinamen. In winter they usually wear five or six coats, one over the other." [1] Shanghai is the port of entry whence the American cotton manufactures are distributed by Chinese importers. The cloth is usually imported in the gray, but, as white is a badge of mourning in that country, it has to be dyed.[2] The dyeing is done by commission dyers in small primitive shops, the color and shade, usually blue, being adapted to the tastes of the local merchants.

The quality of the American cloth has enabled it to extend and retain its market, since the English manufacturers have not found it possible to offer pure-sized goods at so low a price as that quoted by the American manufacturers. In this trade, as is also the case in the trade in parts of Africa and other countries, the trade mark is the standard according to which the sales are made. These trade marks, or " chops," with long established reputations, such as the " Indian Head," " Beaver," " Flying Horse," " Dog and Deer," " Buffalo," and others,[3] are a valuable asset to their owners.

In southern China the English have the upper hand, partly because the Americans have made no serious attempt to enter the field, and partly because of the trade conditions. The demand in the southern district is for light sheetings and shirtings,[4] particularly the latter. It is said that the English white shirtings have an advantage because of better finish. But of more importance is the preference of the dealers for goods which have filling stripes in the head end,[5] stripes produced by weaving in either coarser filling or tinsel. This means that each particular order has to be cared for separately, a practice not consistent

---

[1] *Foreign Markets*, etc., p. 21.

[2] *Ibid.*, p. 28.

[3] *Ibid.*, p. 36.

[4] *Ibid.*, p. 65.

[5] *Ibid.*, p. 67.

with present American methods of producing large quantities of a single pattern. The additional cost of weaving in these stripes could be overcome by developing a large trade with customers in different places, who would be willing to accept the same stripe as merchants in other towns provided each had a monopoly in his own neighborhood. Such an elaborate foreign market organization, however, has not yet been adopted by American manufacturers and exporters of cotton goods.

The reasons for the lack of a more vigorous export trade in American cotton fabrics can be classed under two heads, (1) those over which the manufacturers or merchants have no immediate control and (2) those with which they alone are concerned. The former comprises better shipping facilities and better banking accommodations. More frequent communication by water with South America would, perhaps, encourage the South American dry goods buyers to visit the American market instead of going only to Europe. Yet, on the whole, the shipping service with South America seems to be adequate for the present volume of commerce.[1] Additional steamship lines from the United States to that country and other parts of the world would doubtless be established, provided there were prospects of an adequate traffic in cotton cloth and other goods from the United States. In this way a relaxation of our prohibitive tariff policy might be expected to react upon the export trade.

For promoting commerce with foreign countries, banking and credit institutions are essential, but few American institutions have been established in those parts of the world where they could be utilized by American cotton manufacturers and merchants. Experience in this direction must be acquired and new methods adopted.[2] Nevertheless it seems highly probable that adequate banking facilities, as well as shipping, would be provided were it evident that there was sufficient trade to make it profitable.

---

[1] D. Kinley, "The Promotion of Trade with South America," *American Economic Review*, vol. i, p. 65.

[2] *Ibid.*, p. 68.

The American cotton manufacturers, in the next place, are charged with not meeting the situation, with showing a disregard for the needs of individual markets. This disregard manifests itself in various ways, but can be summed up by saying that they do not cater to the demands of the merchants in the foreign countries. For one thing, they are unwilling, the consuls state,[1] to grant as long credits as the German merchants. Yet this factor is undoubtedly over-emphasized, since the English do not, as a rule, give long credits,[2] and they are the ones whose competition is the keenest.

American goods, secondly, are not infrequently packed in such a way that they are injured by the rough usage to which the bales or boxes are subjected. Almost every consular report which mentions cotton goods has something to say concerning the lax methods of packing in this country. These complaints have such a similarity that if there were not more definite evidence than most of these reports furnish, one might suspect that they were not always based upon careful investigation, but merely included on general principles by a consul who needs must send some report and find some fault. We have, however, specific examples. In packing the cotton cloth sent to China, too narrow ties are frequently used in fastening the bales, with the result that these ties cut into the bales and injure the goods. The English carefully put in additional waterproof wrappings, and for the finer goods, which are packed in cases, use heavy boxes lined with tin, whereas the American shippers pack their goods in more fragile cases not tin-lined.[3]

The cancellation of sales by American manufacturers is not so rare as to be passed over without mention. It occasionally happens that when trade is dull at home a cotton manufacturer by solicitation secures an order in China or elsewhere, but with a revival of business in this country he finds that he can sell his goods to better account here and therefore cancels the

---

[1] See, for example, *Foreign Markets*, etc., p. 82; *U. S. Special Consular Reports*, vol. xxxvi, p. 235.

[2] *Foreign Markets*, etc., p. 99.

[3] *Ibid.*, pp. 69–70.

former contract.[1]   This involves a loss to the Chinese merchant
who is thereby disgruntled and unlikely to look with favor
upon such offers in the future.   If the sale is not actually cancelled, the delivery may be delayed, and again it is the foreign
merchant who suffers.   Suppose a consignment of cotton goods
ordered for October does not arrive in Shanghai till November.
Then cold weather may have locked up the northern harbors
so that the goods will have to be warehoused at Shanghai for
four months, the importer paying the charges.[2]   A consul in
Australia reported in 1905 that "in one instance one of the
leading importers (in Victoria) had cotton goods delivered
eighteen months after date, and in another instance had deliveries three months after due date, with the result that the
market was entirely lost."[3]   These are not regular occurrences,
to be sure, for otherwise our exporters would experience even
greater difficulty in securing orders.   They merely illustrate
the lack of seriousness with which several of our manufacturers
seek foreign outlets.

The American manufacturers, finally, have not attempted,
with a few exceptions, to meet the demands of the local trade in
the various foreign countries.   They have not sent out trained
agents equipped with a knowledge of the foreign language to
study the conditions and solicit orders, nor have they established branches in the commercial cities whereby they could
carry on transactions with the native merchants.   Every
manufacturer of finished cotton goods knows that the tastes
of the inhabitants of the different sections of the United States,
even, are not the same, and that one sort of goods is suited to
one section, another sort to a different part of the country.
How much more important are the divergences in taste between
this country and the foreign countries!   Yet it has usually
been assumed that goods for which there was a demand here
could be sold in Cuba or Venezuela, in Madagascar or British
India.   They have made goods which suited their own con-

[1] *Foreign Markets*, etc., p. 71.
[2] *Ibid.*, p. 72.
[3] *U. S. Special Consular Reports*, vol. xxxvi, p. 306.

venience, not what their prospective (foreign) customers desired. Moreover they have been unwilling to make up packages containing a variety of patterns, although such requests have been acceded to by German and English shippers, who have not tried to force the foreign buyer to accept a large quantity of a single design or quality. These are the real obstacles to the expansion of our foreign trade in cotton fabrics.

That our trade has reached its present size is not due to any special effort, therefore, on the part of our cotton manufacturers. In this connection the Census of 1905 remarked that " the export trade, — that with China as well as with other countries, — may be described as an accident rather than a business. Up to a certain point it grew rather than was created." [1] Furthermore, the character of the trade with northern China, our largest customer, does not impose the same conditions as the trade with most other foreign countries. The Manchurian market demands heavy gray goods of plain texture such as our mills can make in large quantities at a small labor cost.

For the manufacturer himself to cater to the demands of foreign merchants in other countries for a variety of designs, and to send cases of assorted patterns would not be consistent with the methods usually followed in this country. Such action would dissipate the advantages of large scale production of standardized goods by means of which our labor cost has been cut down. Nor would the American manufacturer, under present conditions, find it advantageous to try to keep his quotations in foreign markets stable by varying the quality of the product so as to offset changes in the cost of cotton or of labor. In fact, one of the most valuable assets of the American exporter is the reputation which American goods enjoy for their consistently high quality.

If a manufacturer were to undertake to develop the markets into which American cotton goods have not yet been pushed, he would have to alter his present methods of manufacture. This he will not do as long as the home market offers the same

[1] *U. S. Census of Manufactures*, 1905, *Bulletin* No. 74, p. 35.

opportunities which it has furnished in the past. It is to the needs of the domestic market that he has, properly, directed his attention, instead of entering into competition with the English and Germans who have a superior export market organization and smaller scale of production. The time will come, however, when pressure from within will spur on our cotton manufacturers to try to find some way of successfully combating the Europeans in the neutral markets. Can this be done without reorganizing our present system of production? It can, it seems to me, but not wholly by the manufacturers themselves. Their part consists in reducing the cost of production, if it is still above that in Europe, by means of new inventions and superior organization. That in itself, however, will not be sufficient, but must be supplemented by an elaborated market organization.

The spurt which our exports of cotton goods have taken during the last fifteen years has led to the establishment of new facilities for the trade. Trading companies have been formed for disposing of American cotton goods in China. These trading companies are in constant cable communication with the Chinese markets on the one hand, and on the other are immediately in touch with the brokers through whom they buy the cloth from selling agents who keep them informed as to prices.[1] The native merchant in China desiring to purchase cotton goods goes to one of the foreign importers in his locality, who procures the cloth from an exporter in New York. The combined compensation of the exporter and importer is a commission of one and one-half per cent on the total which includes f.o.b. cost, freight to destination, and marine insurance.[2] Documentary drafts form the basis for the financing of the trade. The middlemen are necessary not only for ease in obtaining the goods but particularly for maintaining the credit arrangements, since the documents must bear the name of some well known merchant before a banking house will advance cash on them.

[1] *U. S. Census of Manufactures*, 1905, *Bulletin* No. 74, p. 36.
[2] Howard Ayres, "Certain Aspects of the Export Trade," National Association of Cotton Manufacturers, *Transactions*, no. 28, p. 144.

Although this may well serve as a nucleus for the organization of a larger trade, it is insufficient even for the trade with China where the demand is for standard goods manufactured by a comparatively small number of mills. Judging from the experience of other countries, we may say that an export trade in cotton goods involves a highly developed mercantile system. It is necessary to have merchants who can study the demand,[1] accept small orders, and if necessary pack the goods in assorted lots. They would collect a number of orders for a single pattern and thus be able to take large quantities from the manufacturer. The merchant is also essential for purposes of credit, and to him should fall the duty of ascertaining the reliability of the foreign purchasers and of assuming the risk involved in foreign trade.[2] Specialization is as important in merchandizing as in manufacturing, and, in time, when capital and experience have been gained, on the basis already established a distributing organization may be effected which will be as efficient as the manufacturing organization.

[1] An effort in this direction was made in 1909, but it is too early to judge whether or not it is to be seriously continued. "An extension of international banking facilities is now under way by which domestic merchants anticipate a broadening of cotton goods trading with South America. Four of the largest New York houses have combined to send men over the territory to sell goods and to obtain first hand information of what the field offers in the way of special opportunity for fabrics that find a ready market in other countries." — Chamber of Commerce of the State of New York, 52d *Annual Report*, p. 92.

[2] See article by W. C. Downs, " Commission House in Latin American Trade," *Quarterly Journal of Economics*, vol. xxvi, pp. 118–139.

CHAPTER XIII

Cloth and Fancy Goods

THE import trade, unlike the export trade, does not lack an elaborate mercantile organization. External factors, however, particularly the tariff, have exerted more influence on the growth of the volume of imports than methods of purchasing. Inasmuch as reference to the American trade will be made in the later chapter on European market organization, the manner in which the import business is transacted will be but briefly outlined before proceeding to the history of the tariff on cotton products.

Imported goods are no longer consigned to merchants in Boston, New York, or Philadelphia to be auctioned off as in the early years of the nineteenth century. Nor are they imported by the owners of the vessels, as in the days of the old Asiatic trade. Regular ocean steamers, whose trip is measured in days instead of weeks or months, and trans-oceanic telegraph cables have brought about a more systematic method of trading. This has been followed by a diversification of the import market organization.

Foreign producers and merchants sell a small quantity of cotton goods in the United States by means of private salesmen or branch offices in New York. A somewhat larger quantity, it appears, is consigned to New York houses by the manufacturers, the consignee usually selling on commission. The consignment trade has dwindled, however, because of its unsatisfactoriness. The shipper can never be sure of what price he will receive and is occasionally disappointed. The consignment business is also said to have suffered from the imposition of specific in the place of ad valorem duties, which lessened the possibility of securing additional profit from selling the goods at a price above that stated in the invoice. Another trade which has almost disappeared is that of the commission importer, who obtains goods in Europe to fill specific orders. Finally, there is a minor trade by correspondence, the ordering of goods by letter or cable on the basis of specification or sample. The bulk of the imports, however, are bought through other channels.

The importers of cotton products who predominate in this market are American jobbers and retailers. They are nearly all large concerns; the retailers who import directly are mainly the big department stores. These importers, both jobbers and retailers, regularly send buyers to Europe to make their purchases. The number of buyers sent by a single house depends on the volume and diversity of its trade. The largest importers send fifty or seventy-five buyers to the European dry goods markets twice a year. Each buyer then confines his purchases to a single narrow line. To conduct trade on such a large scale, to attend to inter-season orders, and to superintend the financing of the business and the shipment of the goods, it is necessary for these importers to have representatives in the European markets. Some maintain their own branch offices in Manchester, Nottingham, Paris, Chemnitz, and other cities, but for others a commission agent suffices. More will be said on that point later.

The American importers can afford to send their buyers on the long journey only because they buy in large quantities. They are able, no doubt, to select the most desirable patterns and to secure the most favorable terms by transacting the business on the spot. But the volume of trade is the determining factor. The American houses pay cash immediately after delivery and thus obtain higher discounts than those who purchase on three or six months' credit.

Aside from the department stores, there are few retailers who can undertake to purchase directly in the European market. They lack credit facilities and could not ordinarily place sufficiently large orders. It is the wholesale importer who finances the trade and parcels out the goods to the ordinary retailer. The department stores have encroached upon the wholesale importer's field, but the elimination of the latter could be brought about only through the crowding out of all the smaller retailers by department stores or similarly large establishments.

Direct buying is one of the means by which the cost of importation has been reduced and the burden of the tariff lightened. Lower freight rates, more regular communication, and better banking accommodations have exerted an influence in the same direction. But the tariff itself has not been appreciably lowered since the inception of the high protectionist regime during the Civil War. It is to a history of these tariff schedules that we will now turn, after a statement of the course of the import trade.

From 1860 to 1900 the total value of the imports of cotton manufactures, — including not only cloth but yarn, embroideries, laces, and knit goods, increased but slightly, yet during the last decade there has been a marked advance as is shown by the following statistics.

COTTON MANUFACTURES IMPORTED INTO THE UNITED STATES

(Average annual value in millions)

	Total	Cloth	Laces	Yarn	Furnishings	Knit Goods	Other
1855–60	$28.1	$19.6	$ .9	$1.4	$—[1]	$3.0	$2.9
1861–65	13.9	6.3	.5	1.1	—[1]	1.1	5.5
1866–70	23.2	10.2	.9	.9	.6	4.5	5.8
1871–75	31.2	8.3	—[1]	—[1]	—[1]	5.1	17.7
1876–80	22.1	2.7	—[1]	—[1]	—[1]	5.1	14.1
1881–85	31.7	3.2	4.0	.3	.2	7.5	16.2
1886–90	28.8	3.5	10.8	.8	.3	6.7	6.4
1891–95	29.4	4.7	10.8	.6	1.7	5.9	5.4
1896–1900	33.4	6.0	13.7	1.0	1.7	4.9	5.8
1901–05	47.1	7.7	23.7	2.1	2.0	5.8	5.6
1906–10	66.7	11.3	35.7	3.5	3.5	7.6	5.0

The significance which is to be attached to each group of imports depends upon the connection in which it is considered, whether the interest is primarily in the part it plays in the total imports, or in comparison to the total home production. Both deserve attention, but especially the latter, since that involves the effect of the protective duties which have been imposed from time to time.

[1] Included in " Other."

The importation of yarn is, on the whole, the least important. The statistics in the above table do not include spool thread in the same group with yarn but class it with the miscellaneous articles. Thus the figures represent only yarn or thread which is imported to be used for further manufacture. The organization of the industry whereby spinning and weaving are united in the same plant has limited the demand for foreign yarn. The imports are chiefly the finest counts and a few specialties which are not manufactured in this country. The tariff has somewhat restricted the quantity imported, but too much influence should not be accredited to it.

The spinners, fearing foreign competition, have requested a high tariff and their wishes have been gratified. Under the tariff of 1857 [1] cotton yarn paid a duty of nineteen per cent ad valorem. In 1861 it was raised to thirty per cent. In 1862, under the pressure for revenue to carry on the war and to compensate the American manufacturers for the heavy taxes to which they were subjected, it became thirty-five per cent, and on March 3, 1865 it was made four cents per hank (840 yards) plus 30 per cent ad valorem.

During the war period, then, the duty on yarn was raised, but till 1865 it was ad valorem. In 1870 a special act was passed, affecting only the duty on cotton yarn, by which such yarn was divided into four classes, according to value, and a compound specific and ad valorem duty placed on each. These duties were equivalent to an ad valorem duty varying from forty-five per cent upwards.

This duty was not disturbed again till 1883, except for the ten per cent provisions of 1872 and 1875 which applied alike to all import duties. In the act of 1883 the number of classes into which cotton yarn was divided was increased to eight, and the duties, except on the highest class, made entirely specific. These specific duties were somewhat lower on the coarser grades than those collected under the previous law, while on the finest counts, which constituted the bulk of the imports, they were

---

[1] For the earlier history of the tariff on cotton goods, F. W. Taussig, *Tariff History*, should be consulted.

fully as high. As the results showed, the average duty was equivalent to about forty-six per cent. The treatment of this schedule was an instance of the way in which the various schedules in the tariff on cotton manufactures were handled at that time and at succeeding tariff revisions. The House bill, which proposed lower duties, was materially changed by the Finance Committee of the Senate,[1] and although minor reductions in the rates were made by compromise, the Senate Committee had substantially its own way.

The McKinley Act did not alter the cotton yarn tariff, except to raise the duties on the classes valued from 25 cents to 60 cents per pound. The result was to make the average duty on yarn the equivalent of fifty per cent.

In 1894 the House sought to reduce the duties on cotton yarn to ad valorem rates varying from twenty to forty per cent. The Finance Committee of the Senate was not to be denied, however, and when the bill emerged from their hands an entirely new scheme had been introduced by which the duties proposed by the House were raised, although somewhat lower than those of the previous act. The Senate's arrangement was incorporated in the act as it was finally passed. The schedule was complex, and its importance is not great enough to deserve an extended analysis. Suffice it to say that the ad valorem equivalent of the duties on yarn collected in the year 1895–96 was nearly thirty-eight per cent.

The duties on cotton yarn were changed in 1897 by adding a new class in bleached, colored, and doubled yarn, and enlarging one of the former classes. The provisions that the duty should not exceed certain maxima and that all yarn valued at more than forty cents per pound should pay forty-five per cent were repealed, leaving only specific duties. These alterations were unimportant.

Nor was there any material change in 1909.[2] The duty on the coarsest numbers of gray, carded yarn (not doubled), not exceed-

---

[1] *Congressional Record*, Feb. 3, 1883, p. 2022.

[2] The whole cotton schedule of the Tariff of 1909 was discussed by the author in the *Quarterly Journal of Economics*, vol. xxiv, pp. 422 ff.

ing No. 15, was cut from three to two and one-half cents per pound; on Nos. 16 to 30 from one-fifth of a cent per number per pound to one-sixth of a cent; and on all yarn over No. 30 from one-fourth to one-fifth of a cent per number per pound. But the duty on colored, combed, or doubled yarn was left practically unchanged, and a slightly higher tax imposed on yarn finer than No. 200. The duty remains fairly high on the finer and more costly yarns, and thus accounts in part for the small importations.

Cotton thread on spools is not included with the other cotton yarn, and as the importations are small the statistics are combined with those for miscellaneous itcms. A separate provision for spool cotton was not made in the tariff till 1862 when the duty was fixed at forty per cent. In 1864 thread was subjected to a tax of six cents per dozen spools of not over 100 yards each, plus thirty per cent ad valorem. For every 100 yards additional per spool an equal amount was to be paid. In 1865 a slight change was made, the duty on spools containing not over 100 yards remained the same, but for every additional 100 yards per spool the ad valorem part of the duty was to be thirty-five per cent. The Act of 1883 substituted for these duties a plain specific duty of seven cents per dozen on spools containing not over 100 yards with an equal amount for each 100 yards in excess of that quantity. The later acts similarly fixed 100 yards as the standard and made analogous provisions for all excess. The Wilson Act of 1894, the next one affecting spool cotton, reduced the rate to five and one-half cents per dozen spools, but the Dingley Act put it up again to six cents, where it still remains.

The duty on spool cotton, although now lower than the War rate, has been really protective, in fact almost prohibitive. The shelter which it has afforded has induced English thread manufacturers to establish plants in this country and to secure control of American thread mills, so that the American housewives may pay them tribute. The concerns manufacturing this product are, as we have seen, controlled in England, and their profits have not been small.

The value of the imports of laces, embroideries, and such goods, has increased at a more rapid rate than the total imports. From 1885 to 1900 this class constituted over one-third of the total value of cotton manufactures imported into the United States, and since 1900 has been just about one-half. Compared with the domestic production of these goods, the importation is very important. The foreign products, however, are mainly of the finer grades, the manufacture of which has not yet been attempted in the United States.

These fancy goods come from Switzerland, France, Germany, and England. Switzerland has always been the largest contributor and at the present time supplies about one-third of the total. France is now next in importance, although until ten years ago it was in a relatively inferior position. Comprised in this group are the braids and embroideries from Barmen, the laces from Nottingham, Gera, Plauen, Calais, St. Gall, and other centres, and miscellaneous specialties. In the manufacture of all these products the item of labor is very considerable, while for the better grades not only a large amount of labor, but highly skilled labor, is needed. The increase in the imports of these goods can be attributed largely to the accumulation of wealth in this country and is symptomatic of the increased expenditure for articles of luxury.

The tariff has stimulated the production in America of a small quantity of lace of the plainer sort which can be manufactured by machinery in large quantities. For some years Congress has given the experimenters the assistance of a protective duty. From 1857 to 1861 the duty was nineteen per cent, for the next year thirty per cent, and from 1862 till 1883, except for the horizontal reduction of 1872, thirty-five per cent. The act of 1883 left the duty on cords and braids at thirty-five per cent, and raised that on laces and embroideries to forty per cent. It was altered but little in 1890, and today the various articles, though subject to somewhat different rates of duty, in the main pay forty-five and fifty per cent, practically the same tax as imposed in 1894.

The duties on these fancy goods have virtues which few of the other duties in the cotton schedule can claim. They yield a comparatively large revenue without at the same time bolstering up a weakling in this country. Moreover they are taxes which fall most heavily upon the classes of consumers who can best afford to pay them. To be sure, they have fostered the establishment of some plants in this country which have been transferred, workmen and all, from England and the Continent. But not many laborers are supported at greater expense in order that the product may be manufactured on this side of the Atlantic.

The goods grouped under the head of " Furnishings " or, according to the *Commerce and Navigation Reports*, " Ready-made Clothing," are analogous to those in the preceding class. They comprise handkerchiefs, mufflers, waists, skirts, and other articles of clothing. While the volume of imports of this class has become greater during the last twenty-five years, part of the increase is due to changes in classification whereby goods have been taken from the " basket clause " and separately enumerated. The furnishings are brought mainly from France and Germany, the latter alone providing about one-half of the total at the present time.

The duty on this wearing apparel was thirty-five per cent, in the main, from 1864 till 1890, when it rose to fifty per cent. In 1894 it was reduced ten per cent, only to be replaced in 1897 by a more complicated schedule with duties ranging from forty-five per cent upwards.

The import trade in cloth has a more vital interest to the American cotton manufacturer, since cloth constitutes by far the largest part of the output of the cotton manufacturing industry in this country. The average imports of cloth in the quinquennium 1856–60 show the extent to which the American people relied upon foreign goods at the close of the first half of the century. The imports then were larger than ever before, although the industry in this country was in a flourishing condition. Prosperity had stimulated both. The next decade was a period of especial affliction for the cotton manufacturing industry, hence the imports have little significance. Nor can we assume that conditions became normal till about 1880. From that date onward the value of cotton cloth imported steadily increased. But the imports have not reached the level which existed prior to the war, and have not increased in anything like the same proportion as the output of cloth within the country.[1]

These imports are mostly of the fine and fancy grades, of high quality or of special design. About five-sixths of this cloth is imported from England at the present time, a little less than one-twelfth from France, and nearly all of the remainder from Germany and Switzerland in approximately equal amounts. England has been the chief source of supply through all the vicissitudes of the century, always having something finer or something more novel to offer when the American manufacturers closed what had previously been a lucrative opening. The increasing wealth of the American people has enabled them to afford more and more costly fabrics, and the distinction which attaches to imported cloth has kept up part of the trade that otherwise might have languished.

The tariff act of 1857 imposed an ad valorem duty of nineteen per cent on gray cloth and twenty-four per cent on bleached, dyed, and printed cloth. With the recrudescence of protectionism and the pressure for revenue to carry on the pending war, the duties were increased in 1861 and at the same time made specific. However the tariff could not supply raw cotton to relieve the mills from their peculiarly disadvantageous position during the subsequent years, notwithstanding the higher duties levied under the acts of 1862 and 1864. The horizontal reduction of ten per cent in 1872 and its restoration in 1875 had slight effect. The depression which followed the panic of 1873 caused much greater disturbance to the dry goods trade than could be brought about by alterations in the tariff.

The fiasco of 1883 is familiar to all students of our tariff history, and the duties on cotton cloth received treatment similar to that accorded those on other articles. The schedule for

---

[1] See *ante*, pp. 17, 22.

cotton manufactures was simplified somewhat, particularly by eliminating the separate provision for jeans, denims, drillings, ginghams, plaids, etc., which, since 1862, had been subject to a duty different from that on other cloth. This classification has been confusing for obvious reasons. Hence by abolishing it the administration of the act was facilitated. Duties on the coarser cloth were cut down, but on the higher priced fabrics they were raised. A large class of goods which had previously been allowed to come in for thirty-five per cent now had to pay forty per cent. This forty per cent duty was levied on all goods above a certain value, those below that value paying specific rates. Although the ad valorem duty might be presumed to indicate the general scale intended, we find that in actual operation the specific duties were considerably higher. Consequently, in spite of the large proportion of imports which were sufficiently high in value to come in at the forty per cent rate, the greater weight of the other duties brought up the average duty on all cotton cloth to forty-four per cent. The nominal reduction in the duties on the lower grades was offset by the fall in the price of cloth, and since they were specific they continued to be equivalent to an ad valorem duty fully as high, in most cases, as that collected under the previous act.

In the tariff of 1890 the schedule was arranged on the same plan as in 1883, but it contained five classes instead of three, according to the number of threads per square inch. These five classes were (1) not exceeding fifty threads per square inch, (2) fifty to one hundred threads, (3) one hundred to one hundred and fifty threads, (4) one hundred and fifty to two hundred threads, and (5) over two hundred threads per square inch. On the first and second classes the specific duties, which applied to cloth below a certain value in each case, were reduced; and the ad valorem duty on cloth above that limit, which, by the way, was lower than previously, was cut down from forty per cent to thirty-five per cent. The specific duties on goods in the third class were reduced, but the ad valorem rate on the more valuable grades remained the same as before. Yet these changes were less important so far as protection and importation were concerned than those on the two higher classes. For the fourth class the specific duties were raised one-half cent per yard and the ad valorem duty increased from forty to forty-five per cent. The schedule for the highest grade received similar treatment. Throughout, as in previous laws, the ad valorem duties proved to be less than the ad valorem equivalent of the specific duties levied on the cloth below the minimum values. The net result of this act was to raise the average duty from forty-four per cent to over forty-seven per cent. The forces which were behind these advances do not appear on the surface, and the complexity of the schedules frustrated the efforts of the opponents of high protection to get at the facts.

The Wilson Act of 1894 made but a slight breach in the walls of protection. It has been said that this act pleased no one, and very likely it was pleasing to few persons, either the advocates or the opponents of protection. Nevertheless it did satisfy the cotton manufacturers. The cotton cloth schedule was enlarged and made more complex. The same general classification according to number of threads per square inch was retained and special provisos were applied to all cloth over a certain value, but in addition the coarser cloth in each class was divided according to weight. Here is a sample, stripped of the legal verbiage.

Cotton cloth exceeding one hundred and not exceeding one hundred and fifty threads to the square inch, counting both warp and filling, was to pay, if in the gray and not exceeding four square yards to the pound, one and one-half cents per square yard; exceeding four and not exceeding six square yards to the pound, two cents per square yard; exceeding six and not exceeding eight square yards to the pound, two and one-half cents; exceeding eight square yards to the pound, two and three-quarters cents; if bleached, two and one-half cents, three cents, three and one-half cents, and three and three-quarters cents per square yard, respectively, for each of the above classes according to weight; if colored, three and one-half cents, three and three-quarters cents, four and one-quarter cents, and four and one-half cents respectively. But it was also provided that gray cloth valued at more than nine cents per square yard should pay thirty per cent; bleached valued at over eleven cents, thirty-five per cent; and colored valued at over twelve and one-half cents per square yard, thirty-five per cent. This is but one of five paragraphs, each of which was constructed on the same plan.

What did it all amount to ? In the first place the specific duties for the heavier fabrics were lower than before, while on the finer grades they remained practically the same. The ad valorem rates on the more valuable textures in each class were diminished by about ten per cent. Nevertheless the average duty collected in 1895 on all cotton cloth was equivalent to slightly over forty-one per cent.

This amplified plan, as stated above, met with the approval of the manufacturers, but to whom does the credit for its adoption belong, since the representatives of the cotton manufacturing districts belonged to the party which was in a minority at the time ? The Finance Committee of the Senate was responsible. By this committee amendments were proposed which materially raised the rates of the House bill, and which were incorporated in the act as finally passed. When these amendments were offered in the Senate, they were accepted with remarkable rapidity and almost no debate. The silence of the opposition, particularly of the New England senators who had piloted the cotton schedules of previous acts, led Senator Dolph to comment on the absence of debate and to ask what that signified.[1] In reply to Senator Dolph, Senator Aldrich said, " This schedule, which was prepared by a number of manufacturers of Fall River, so far as the price of cloth is concerned, is perhaps the most scientific schedule that has ever been devised upon the subject." [2] He then went on to remark that the duties were not as high as the cotton manufacturers would like, but that they and their friends recognized the futility of opposition, and were satisfied with the mode of imposing the duties.[3]

[1] *Congressional Record*, June 11, 1894, p. 6101.   [2] *Ibid.*, p. 6101.

[3] I am informed on what I believe to be credible authority that the plan was drawn up by a group of cotton manufacturers in Fall River, and that it was due to their efforts, primarily, that the scheme was adopted. The way in which it was

The arrangement of the schedule adopted in 1894 gratified all expectations, so that in 1897 it needed to be revised in only one or two respects. In the Dingley Law the duties on cloth containing less than two hundred threads were left untouched. But instead of a single class for all cloth over two hundred threads, a new division was introduced, — from two hundred to three hundred threads, and over three hundred threads. In each of these classes the specific duties on the heavier grades were made about one cent per yard higher than they had been in 1894, a little lower in some cases than in 1890, in others slightly higher. And the cloth above a certain fixed value was to pay forty per cent. This new classification and the augmentation of the duties was, again, the work of the Senate.

The schedule was once more amplified in 1909. Instead of a single ad valorem duty on all cloth above the specified value in each class, a comprehensive scheme was applied to the whole series of the " countable " paragraphs, whereby the duties on the more valuable cloth were increased. Specific duties were substituted for the ad valorem rates on the cloth which falls into the specified classes. These specific duties were ostensibly fixed at a point which would correspond to the specific duties levied on cloth below the previous minimum, and for all above the new minimum the former ad valorem rates were retained. As the specific duties had proved to be higher than the ad valorem rates, this meant an increase in duties in most instances, or at least their maintenance.

accomplished illustrates the " scientific " care with which protective tariffs are promoted. After the scheme had been arranged, those in charge of it, as I have been told, called in a local Democratic politician of Fall River.   This politician was a lawyer, whose clients were chiefly mill operatives with cases against the mill corporations for damages.   He was informed by the local tariff committee that it was absolutely essential for the prosperity of the Fall River mills that the new schedule be embodied in the tariff law.   The suggestion was made that if duties were reduced and a non-scientific schedule adopted, the closing of the mills would send away all of his supporters and destroy his law practice.   His own future well-being was dependent, so he is said to have been told, upon the welfare of the workmen in the mills, and thus upon the prosperity of the mills themselves.   Hence the Fall River politician, accompanied by a mill worker, went to Washington, it is said, and with such other aid as could be mustered, induced the Democratic leaders to adopt the new schedule of duties on cotton cloth.

A quotation from the law itself, in spite of its non-intelligibility to anyone except an expert, may, perhaps, show how the manoeuvre was effected. " 317. Cotton cloth, not bleached, dyed, colored, stained, painted, or printed, exceeding one hundred and fifty and not exceeding two hundred threads to the square inch, counting the warp and filling, and not exceeding three and one-half square yards to the pound, two cents per square yard; exceeding three and one-half and not exceeding four and one-half square yards to the pound, two and three-fourths cents per square yard; exceeding four and one-half and not exceeding six square yards to the pound, three cents per square yard; exceeding six square yards to the pound, three and one-half cents per square yard; *any of the foregoing valued at over ten and not over twelve and one-half cents per square yard, four and three-eighths cents per square yard; valued at over twelve and one-half and not over fourteen cents per square yard, five and one-half cents per square yard; valued at over fourteen and not over sixteen cents per square yard, six and one-half cents per square yard; valued at over sixteen and not over twenty cents per square yard, eight cents per square yard; valued at over twenty cents per square yard, ten cents per square yard,* but not less than thirty per cent ad valorem." This is one-third of one of the five paragraphs for cotton cloth. The italicised words indicate the new provisions.

The reasons for these changes are apparent on an examination of the importations under each sub-division and of the relative ad valorem equivalents of the duties levied. As the Dingley Act worked in practice, the specific duties on the coarser grades in each paragraph were higher (in ad valorem equivalent) than the ad valorem duty on cloth above the specified value. But by far the greater part of the cloth actually imported was above that value and therefore paid the ad valorem duty. By introducing the new specific duties graduated according to value and adjusted so as to correspond to the specific duties on the lower grades, the rate was, in most cases, increased above that actually paid from 1897 to 1909. Cloth which had been paying twenty-five, thirty, or thirty-five per cent, now has to pay the equivalent of about thirty-eight, forty, or even as much as fifty per cent.

These manipulations were the work of that bulwark of protection, the Finance Committee of the Senate. As had so frequently happened before, the manufacturers made no demands upon the House committee, except to request that the duties be undisturbed,[1] but when the bill reached the Senate they became active, and headed by certain men who were especially interested in the manufacture of the more costly goods which would benefit from the proposed increases in duties, were able to induce the Senate committee to accede to their wishes. The members of the committee were also willing to defend vigorously these duties when they were attacked in the Senate Chamber.

The object in making these changes, as stated by Mr. Aldrich and his supporters,[2] was to restore the rates which it had been intended to levy under the act of 1897. Yet it must have been a gross oversight in that act if these ad valorem rates on cloth above the specified value — twenty-five, thirty, thirty-five per cent — were made five or ten per cent lower than was intended. Ad valorem duties are the simplest of all, and most clearly tell their own tale. Certain it is that in no case were the duties on cotton cloth lowered by the act of 1909, and that on the higher priced goods there was some increase.

Another change in the act of 1909 was the introduction of a duty of one cent per square yard upon all mercerized cloth, in addition to the duty paid under the countable paragraphs. This was justified on the ground that mercerized cloth, although the process is no more expensive in the United States than in England, is lighter than unmercerized cloth, and consequently might be subject to a lower duty by virtue of having been made more valuable. This would be true, of course, for the lower grades, but since most of the mercerized cloth would be sufficiently high in price to prevent such a calamitous event, this

[1] The New England manufacturers stated that they wished the duties to be left unchanged "with the exception of some very minor points."—*Tariff Hearings,* 1908–09, p. 3067.

[2] *Congressional Record,* June, 1909, pp. 2613, 2614, 2834, etc.

practically provided additional protection to those manufacturing this product.

At least one volume might be written on the history of the tariff on cotton manufactures, the changes, the attempts, more or less successful, to introduce "jokers," the debates, and all the devious paths which each bill followed. But for the present, at least, that does not seem worth while. The length to which the discussion has drawn itself out in the preceding pages almost over-emphasizes the part that the tariff has played in the progress of the industry. The arguments employed in support of the duties on cotton manufactures differ in not the slightest detail from those commonly advanced by protectionists. The requests for assistance have been based mainly upon the handicap said to be imposed by the higher American wages.

To consider only some of the more recent statements, in 1893 one man who appeared at the tariff hearings said that "whatever of protection is abated will merely come off the present wages of our employees." [1] Another witness, who made a similar statement, admitted that the labor cost had fallen, but since wages (earnings) had not diminished he argued that the tariff should not be reduced.[2] A third manufacturer stated that "the rates imposed are not out of proportion to the differences in American and foreign wages." [3] He added, "Here the working people have been elevated and prospered as much as the mill owners, while there (England) the mill owners have been enriched rather than the working people." [4] The Industrial Commission in 1901 likewise was told that it was necessary "to do something to overcome the higher cost of labor (in cotton manufacturing) in this country as compared with the cost of foreign labor." [5]

Other arguments have sometimes been added, as, for example, greater cost of supplies, higher interest rates, higher cost of transportation, and higher taxes. Here is an instance of the last. In England, it was said in 1897, the laborer bears the

---

[1] *Tariff Hearings*, 1893, p. 697.
[2] *Ibid.*, p. 702.
[3] *Ibid.*, p. 712.
[4] *Ibid.*, p. 710.
[5] Industrial Commission, *Report*, vol. xiv, p. 476.

taxes whereas in New England the manufacturers " pay everything in taxes and whatever the laboring man gets, he gets.
He has no taxes to pay except the poll tax and most of them
manage to evade that." [1] Almost more absurd was the statement made in 1893 that the southern states would lose half
of their custom for Sea Island cotton, were the tariff on fine
yarn lowered.[2] According to this reasoning the spinning of
fine yarn in America could be displaced without an equal quantity of Sea Island cotton being spun elsewhere. Our protectionists, however, have failed to appropriate an argument suggested by a witness at the French " Enquête," [3] who remarked
that after the agricultural depression in France had caused
the import duties on grain to be raised, the Americans " faithful
to the Monroe doctrine" retaliated with a higher duty on French
textiles.

But to return to the labor argument. All cotton manufacturers are not unanimous in their tariff views, and even the
advocates of protection occasionally make conflicting statements.
For example, the superintendent of a print cloth mill in Fall
River, who was familiar with conditions in England, informed
me that the output per operative was so much greater in this
country that the English could " touch us only on the finer
grades." Later in the same day the treasurer of the same
mill stated that he would have to close his mill, if the tariff
were reduced, and gave as his reasons the (alleged) facts presented during the debate on the Dingley bill by the practical
men in Congress. Another manufacturer, after a prolonged
denunciation of all free traders, ended by saying that quality
for quality he could produce ginghams as cheaply as they were
manufactured in England, and to him the only real service of
the tariff was to prevent the dumping of English goods when
trade was bad.

Other instances more or less analogous can be given. In
the report of the Secretary of State in 1881 on the *Cotton*

---

[1] *Tariff Hearings*, 1896–97, p. 1165.

[2] *Tariff Hearings*, 1893, p. 708.

[3] *Enquête sur l'Etat de l'Industrie Textile*, vol. ii, p. 293.

Goods Trade of the World [1] it was said that "undoubtedly the inequalities in the wages of English and American operatives are more than equalized by the greater efficiency of the latter and their longer hours of labor." In 1886 the remark was made that the "labor per piece or per pound is as low, and in some localities lower, than in Lancashire." [2] Again, during the debate [3] on the Dingley bill in 1897, figures which had been privately collected were offered to prove that even in mule spinning the English had little advantage over the Americans, and the following statement by Mr. M. C. D. Borden, the president of the American Printing Company and the Fall River Iron Works (a cotton mill with 460,000 spindles), was quoted: "So far as our business is concerned it does not make much difference what Congress may do to any tariff bill. American print cloth manufacturers are now able to beat the world." More recently Mr. E. N. Vose has said, "I firmly believe that in ninety-nine instances out of one hundred the American manufacturer can beat his English competitors on prices if he sets out to do so, and that the element of labor cost will work out in his favor at least as often as it is against him." [4] My own observations in American and European mills confirm that opinion.

Whenever the labor argument is exploited in defense of the tariff or to secure an increase in duties, earnings, not labor costs, are compared. Logic is sacrificed for the sake of making the comparison appear favorable to the protectionist cause. Earnings, without reference to output, are not at all indicative of the relative costs in America and Europe. Yet the earnings, to say nothing of labor cost, are seldom forty or fifty per cent lower in England than America. [5]

Labor, moreover, is not the only item in the cost of manufacturing. It constitutes only seven per cent of the total expenses for producing a coarse cloth weighing $3\frac{1}{2}$ yards to the pound,

---

[1] Pp. 98–99.
[2] *Report on Revision of the Tariff*, 1886, p. 81.
[3] *Congressional Record*, June 17, 1897, p. 1783.
[4] National Association of Cotton Manufacturers, *Transactions*, no. 80, p. 214.
[5] See *infra*, pp. 296–305.

eleven per cent for a 6 yards-to-the-pound cloth, twenty per cent for a heavy gingham, thirty-eight per cent for a fine gingham, and forty-five per cent for a very fine fancy cloth, according to information obtained from manufacturers themselves. Therefore the total expenditure for labor would in very few cases equal the import duty imposed on the cloth. For the coarser grades the import duty far exceeds the total labor cost, and for the finer grades is at least equal to that cost. In other words, the duty covers not merely the (assumed) difference in expenses for labor, but those expenses in their entirety.[1]

Raw cotton is a considerable item in the cost of manufacturing cotton cloth. For a very fine fabric, woven with colored yarn, the cotton may constitute but thirty-five per cent of the total costs, but for a coarse plain cloth eighty to eighty-five per cent of the expense is for raw cotton. For the bulk of the cotton cloth produced in America the proportion of the total charges which is made up by raw cotton would be from sixty to eighty-five per cent. Nevertheless, raw cotton costs no more in New England than it does in England, France, and Germany.

While this labor cost " justification," therefore, fails to justify, it has been a powerful argument. Not only has it appealed to the self-interest of the operatives themselves, but as part of the whole protectionist platform has been accepted by those employed in other industries. Without doubt most of the manufacturers do take an interest in the welfare of their employees, yet one may well inquire who the American workman is for whom they so solicitously defend the tariff ? Is he the English immigrant with his troublesome labor unions ? Or the Irishman ? Or the French Canadian ? Or the Slav, the Pole, the Greek, the Italian, or the Syrian not able to speak English ? Moreover, when the question of more stringent regulation of the conditions of labor, better enforcement of existing laws, or an increase in wages arises, how often does the ardent protectionist remember his former pleadings for a meas-

---

[1] This was written several months before the Tariff Board's *Report on Cotton Manufactures* was published. The conclusions here stated, however, are entirely substantiated by that report.

ure which was supposed to safeguard the standard of living of the workers ? And how would he welcome a further restriction upon immigration, the surest means of promoting the progress of his employees ? It is far more comfortable to shift onto the tariff the responsibility for their welfare.

In giving all the credit for the progress of the industry to the tariff the American cotton manufacturers are too modest. Their own inventions and their organizing and administrative ability have played a far more important part. Internal competition, fortunately, has forced them to put forth these efforts, and the advance of the industry in the South came as a blessing, however unwelcome, to the New England manufacturers, since it compelled them to adopt more economical methods and to diversify their product. Thus the possibly benumbing effects of protection were averted. Finally, although it may enable the fine cloth manufacturers to obtain somewhat higher prices, the protective tariff has been for years and is now, for the majority of American cotton manufacturers, an empty and imaginary guardian. The prices of the grades of cloth produced in the United States in the largest quantities are practically the same as those obtaining in England.[1] Yet if the tariff does not raise the prices how can it possibly yield any benefit?

If the manufacturers were willing to give up some of this useless " protection " and seek a reduction in the duties on their supplies, they would strengthen their competitive position.[2]

---

[1] On August 17, 1910, a Burnley manufacturer stated to me that his lowest quotation on 64 x 64, 28-inch print cloth at that time was 4 cents per yard. The American quotation on the same day was 3¾ cents, according to Shepperson's *Cotton Facts*, ed. 1910, p. 27. A more extensive comparison of English and American prices has not been undertaken because of the difficulty of ascertaining the relative quality of the cloth. See my summary of the Tariff Board's report in the *American Economic Review*, Sept. 1912.

[2] Mr. Shepperson in his *Cotton Facts*, ed. 1906, p. iv, expresses the same opinion. " Our cotton mills," he writes, " are so handicapped by the high tariff duties on machinery, and also on practically everything which enters into the cost of manufacturing, that except for the plainest descriptions of goods they cannot compete with European manufacturers, even for the trade of countries so near us as Mexico, the West Indies, and South America. The permanent prosperity of our cotton mills demands the lowering of the tariff rates on everything necessary for their equipment and operation."

Machinery, which is protected by a forty-five per cent duty, costs more in America. Part of this duty on machinery in turn goes to the steel manufacturers. The duties on dye-stuffs and other minor requisites are also handicaps to the American cotton manufacturer in his competition for a foreign market.

Eventually these facts will be recognized by our cotton manufacturers. They will be better appreciated when the manufacturers begin earnestly to seek an export market. Just as the first effective instigation of the free trade movement in England came from the manufacturers themselves, we may expect a downward revision of the American tariff when the desire of our manufacturers for a larger export trade becomes stronger.

CHAPTER XIV

IMPORT TRADE (CONTINUED)

Knit Goods

THE value of knit goods imported into the United States, as was shown by the table previously given,[1] has not changed greatly since the Civil War. This has been a period of very rapid expansion of the industry within the country. From a household industry it has become a factory industry, employing highly specialized machinery for the production of large quantities of hosiery and underwear. While the value of the output has jumped from seven million dollars to two hundred million dollars, the imports have remained nearly stationary. Whereas we formerly secured half as many goods abroad as were manufactured in our own knitting mills, our domestic production is now twenty times as great as the imports.

Germany, for many years the chief source of supply, has gradually assumed a larger and larger proportion of the total trade until at the present time about eighty-seven per cent of our imports of knit goods come from that country.

IMPORTS OF COTTON KNIT GOODS [2]

(Average annual value)

	From Germany	From Great Britain	All Other	Total
1873–83	$4,116,000	$1,514,000	$1,202,000	$6,832,000
1884–90	5,331,000	907,000	533,000	6,771,000
1891–94	5,045,000	381,000	406,000	5,831,000
1895–97	5,490,000	209,000	409,000	6,108,000
1898–1905	4,623,000	128,000	532,000	5,283,000

Germany has largely ousted Great Britain and the other European knit-goods manufacturing countries from their trade with

---

[1] See *ante*, p. 234.
[2] *U. S. Commerce and Navigation Reports.*

the United States.   Great Britain's export trade in knit goods
has declined in other directions also, for the total fell off from an
average of £2,876,000 in 1875–79, and £1,112,000 in 1880–84,
to £436,000 in 1900–04.   The Saxon manufacturers, on the contrary, utilizing the machinery invented in England, have shown
special aptitude in this branch of the textile industry, and the
United States is their best market.

The history of the tariff on cotton knit goods has much resemblance to the history of the tariff on other cotton fabrics, and
has many of the same ear-marks; but starting from a slightly
lower level it has soared upward more swiftly.   The act of
1861 increased the ad valorem duty from fifteen to twenty-five
per cent, the act of 1862 to thirty per cent, and that of 1864
to thirty-five per cent.   The industry, as we have seen, was
already established, but it was not strong enough to secure
especial favors, nor was it as timid as in later years when the
(declared) fear of foreign competition increased in direct proportion to the size of the industry.

This duty was, of course, subject to the horizontal reduction
of 1872 and the restoration of 1875.   Until this period the duty
on cotton knit goods had been as much for revenue as for protection, and what protection was afforded could be largely
justified on the grounds of an infant industry.   In 1883 the
infant began to look out for itself, however, and at the instigation of the Philadelphia Association of Hosiery and Knit-
Goods Manufacturers,[1] the duty on fashioned hosiery was increased to forty per cent.   The duty on cut hosiery, which constituted only one-fifth of the imports, was left at the former
rate.   This change applied to underwear as well as to hosiery,
but did not have the same significance, since over four-fifths
of the underwear was entered at the thirty-five per cent rate.

The period from 1883 to 1890, with its improvements in technique, was a happy one for the knitting business.   The result
was that by 1890 the industry had assumed large proportions.
None the less, the previous protection was no longer sufficient,
at least it was deemed inadequate by the framers of the McKinley

---

[1] *Report of Tariff Commission*, 1882, vol. ii, p. 2271.

Act. By that act the duty on cut goods and all knit goods not otherwise provided for was not disturbed. But in place of the simple ad valorem tax of forty per cent on fashioned goods, a system of compound specific and ad valorem duties was devised and hosiery divided into four classes. The first of these classes included all fashioned hose and half-hose valued at not more than 60 cents per dozen pairs, and the duty was equivalent to fifty-four per cent ad valorem during the years that it was in force. The importations in this lowest class were by no means negligible, but they were far less than those in the second group, valued from 60 cents to $2 per dozen pairs. Three-fourths of the total imports of hosiery fell into this class, on which the duty was equivalent to seventy-two per cent.

A similar scheme was applied to the schedule for underwear, which was divided into five classes, and with the same result. Nearly sixty per cent of the imports were of the two grades, valued from $1.50 to $3.00, and from $3.00 to $5.00 per dozen pairs, on the former of which the duty proved to be equivalent to seventy-four per cent, and on the latter seventy-three per cent. The duties on the other classes of hosiery and underwear were somewhat lower.

The Wilson Act did away with the complex arrangement of the schedule for knit goods, and imposed an ad valorem duty of fifty per cent on all fashioned goods, both hosiery and underwear, and of thirty per cent on all other knit goods. The House bill had placed the duty on the former class at forty-five per cent, but the Senate pushed it up to fifty per cent, where it remained. Thus they did not go back even to the rates which prevailed prior to 1890. The use of cut goods had been declining, so that practically all of the imports paid fifty per cent. There was some justification, however, for not further reducing the duties, when we consider the precarious business conditions of that period and the injury that might have been inflicted upon those who had embarked their capital under the McKinley Act.

The law which was passed in 1897, with the avowed object of restoring the duties of the McKinley Act, in the case of the knit goods re-introduced the system of classes according to value, with compound specific and ad valorem duties. But the formulae of these compounds were new. The division into classes was also somewhat different. The first class included all hosiery valued at not more than $1, instead of not over 60 cents per dozen pairs, and the Dingley duty on this class was higher than that of the McKinley Act, being equivalent to sixty-eight per cent. On the classes of hosiery worth more than $1 the duties were lower than in 1890 and averaged about sixty per cent. Approximately three-fifths of the quantity of hosiery imported after this act went into force, however, was valued at less than a dollar per dozen pairs, and hence was hit hardest by the new tariff.

Though the Dingley law in general arranged knit underwear in just the same classes as had the McKinley Act, it added a new class by dividing all goods valued at more than $7 per dozen into two classes, (1) valued from $7 to $15, and (2) over $15. The compound specific and ad valorem duty on the lower of these two classes was equivalent to sixty-one per cent while on the higher the simple ad valorem was only fifty per cent. The duties on every class except the highest were compound and proved to be equivalent to over sixty per cent ad valorem in each case, an advance over the rates of 1894, but, with a single exception, a reduction from those of 1890. The exception was the duty on underwear valued at less than $1.50 per dozen pairs, which had paid only thirty-five per cent in 1890, and which now had to pay the equivalent of sixty-one per cent. Yet it should be said that the importations in this class were not large. Underwear, unlike hosiery, felt the foreign competition more severely in the higher priced grades.

The most recent tariff act (1909) purported to make a downward revision of the tariff. We have already seen how the revision of the cloth schedule raised the rates, on the pretext of restoring the duties which it had been intended to collect under the previous act. Those increases were not unimportant, but the additions made to the duties on hosiery were even more considerable.

On class one, valued at not over $1 per dozen pairs, the House proposed to increase the Dingley duty from 50 cents per dozen pairs plus fifteen per cent ad valorem to 70 cents plus fifteen per cent; on class two, valued from $1.00 to $1.50, from 60 cents plus fifteen per cent to 85 cents plus fifteen per cent; on class three, valued from $1.50 to $2.00, from 70 cents plus fifteen per cent to 90 cents plus fifteen per cent; and on class four, valued from $2.00 to $3.00, from $1.20 plus fifteen per cent to $1.50 plus fifteen per cent. On the highest two classes the duties were not disturbed by the House bill.

When the Payne bill was reported from the Finance Committee of the Senate, the Dingley rates on hosiery were restored, since the knit-goods manufacturers probably did not have as powerful friends at court in the Senate as in the House, and also because there had arisen a storm of protest against the tactics which were being pursued in revising the bill, especially against such obvious increases in protection as in the case of the hosiery duties. In this form the bill went to the conference committee.

The duties on hosiery were among those most hotly contested in the conference committee, owing to the criticism which had been aroused and the pressure brought to bear from both sides. The higher duties, in the end, prevailed, with the exception of that on the third class where the specific part was reduced from $1.00 to 90 cents, and the fourth class where the Dingley duty was retained. The exact reasons why the Senate yielded to the House will very likely never be known. Perhaps the plaintive petitions of the operatives who went to Washington excited the sympathy of the legislators, or at least gave them an excuse. On the other hand, it is alleged that the speaker of the House was especially interested in these duties, since he had promised to pay a political debt by granting such an increase. His influence and the pretext offered by the petitions may well have been sufficient to turn the tide and secure the assent of the Senators, who were only lukewarm advocates of the lower rates.

By this law, therefore, the duties on the lowest class of hosiery which had formerly been equivalent to sixty-eight per cent were made equivalent to at least eighty-five per cent, and this is the class in which there are the largest imports. On the second class the ad valorem equivalent became at least seventy-one per cent as compared with sixty per cent; and on the third at least sixty per cent as compared with fifty-two per cent actually collected in the preceding years. For all goods in each class valued at less than the maximum the equivalent will be higher than the minimum rate here stated and therefore the average will show a greater increase.

The object of these changes (in 1909) was to stimulate the manufacture in this country of full-fashioned goods,[1] now largely imported from Germany. This transfer is very difficult to accomplish for the reason that the greater part of the stockings made in the United States are knit upon circular automatic machines, and these are far better adapted to American industrial conditions than are the Cotton frames on which full-fashioned goods are produced. If the cheap German hose are shut out, the principal effect will probably be the stimulation of a further development of the production of seamless stockings. It is the domestic producer of seamless goods against whom the would-be manufacturer of full-fashioned hosiery must primarily contend, and against him no tariff barrier can be raised.

The duties on underwear remain where they were placed in 1897, being equivalent to over sixty per cent for all goods not exceeding seven dollars per dozen in value and from fifty to sixty per cent on those above that margin. These duties, however, are of less significance than those on stockings, since the imports are much less, between five and six hundred thousand dollars worth per year. The American, manufacturing on a large scale with the circular knitting machine and the highly specialized making-up machinery, can produce shirts and drawers about as cheaply as they are manufactured by the foreigner. At any rate the difference is not sixty per cent.

The history of the tariff on knit goods is but another illustration of the way in which our tariff was raised after the close

---

[1] The requests came from manufacturers of full-fashioned goods. — *Tariff Hearings*, 1908–09, pp. 4746, 4748.

of the Civil War. The changes have been demanded for the same reasons that alterations in the duties on other products have been sought. Differences in labor cost have been asserted as a justification of the higher rates. Before the Tariff Commission in 1882 a knit-goods manufacturer stated that " if the duties are decreased, the American manufacturer must remain out of the market until he has starved his employees into accepting wages on the European basis, which is, at best, English one-half and German one-third the American, while the consumer will continue to pay about the same price for his goods as now." [1] Curious logic, to say nothing of the disregard of the greater extent to which labor saving machinery was even then used in the United States.

The hearings in 1893 were productive of many similar remarks upon the lower labor cost in Europe. One manufacturer requested a " fair and square protective tariff for our home industries so that the manufactuiers here would be protected against the pauper labor of Europe." [2] Another said: " The whole question is one of labor as between our people who have, by their brains and perseverance, got the standard of wages where they can live comfortably and in great contrast to the half-starved laboring class of foreign countries." [3] This was after the most radical improvements in machinery had become available and the employment of immigrant labor had become common. The statements were in several instances supported by figures (not statistics) by means of which the wages in Europe and America were compared. As usual, however, it was the earnings which were used as the index to the divergence in labor cost, [4] irrespective of the differences in the machinery.

The economy of superior organization was disregarded by a witness in 1897, in comparing conditions in Germany and this country. He said: " Wages are as one to four. Besides that, they have these small machines spread all over the country

---

[1] *Report of the Tariff Commission*, 1882, p. 2273.
[2] *Tariff Hearings*, 1893, p. 737.
[3] *Ibid.*, p. 767.
[4] *Ibid.*, pp. 755, 762; *Ibid.*, 1908–09, p. 4749.

and can work night and day, if they wish to, and they work for a mere pittance." [1] As at previous hearings, conclusions were brought forth concerning the greater cost of manufacturing knit goods in this country, which were based on comparisons of earnings.[2]

These statements in regard to higher earnings of the operatives in this country undoubtedly have some truth in them, although they are to be taken with a grain of salt. Nevertheless, as has been pointed out, the circular automatic machines so generally used in this country, the larger scale of production, and the more economical factory organization counteract the disadvantage of a higher wage level. Even if it be true (as it very likely is) that there is a somewhat greater labor cost here, the difference is by no means as great as the difference in earnings, and even from a protectionist standpoint does not justify the duties now imposed.

Even if the duties at the present time are unduly protective, may it not be that the growth of the industry has been due to protection ? Is not this an illustration of an infant industry ? Perhaps. But no one can be absolutely sure of the extent to which the tariff has actually spurred on the industry. The improvements in technique, which began in the 'fifties under a low tariff, were possibly accentuated by the higher duties of the war period, but had already been brought to a high standard by 1890. On the basis of these inventions the industry has expanded rapidly during the last twenty years, and they have probably had far more influence than the high duties of 1890, 1894, and 1897. Without the inventions the tariff would have had little effect. With them, but without the tariff, the growth would very likely have been nearly as rapid. In fact, one might maintain that the higher duties have been the result of the growth of the industry rather than the cause; the increased size and stronger interests have had greater influence when the time for tariff revision came around.

[1] *Tariff Hearings*, 1896–97, p. 1180.
[2] *Ibid.*, pp. 1183, 1188.

The *post hoc propter hoc* reasoners who give the credit to the tariff rather than to inventive and organizing ability must explain why the tariff on woolen knit goods has not been as effective as that on the fabrics made of cotton. From 1883 to 1890 the ad valorem equivalents of the duties on woolen knit goods were from sixty-two to seventy-three per cent; 1890 to 1894, from eighty to three hundred and twenty-four per cent; 1894 to 1897, from thirty-five to fifty per cent; and 1897 to 1909, over ninety per cent. Yet the output of these goods has steadily declined in the United States. The truth of the matter seems to be that woolen yarn cannot be knit as cheaply as cotton yarn, and the woolen branch of the industry did not benefit as greatly from the inventions. The cheaper cotton hosiery and underwear usurped part of the share of the market previously held by woolen, and the tariff was powerless to prevent it.

But discussion as to the effects of the tariff on knit goods, or its justification, is of slight avail. The imports have not greatly declined with the higher duties, yet we cannot say assuredly that they would not have have increased without them. The machinery has been improved, and the improvements may or may not have been due to the protective tariff. Although the manufacturers are likely to demand still higher duties, perhaps even the prohibition of the importing of competitive products, none the less the industry is now established on such a firm basis that it seems nearly to have passed the stage of infancy.

CHAPTER XV

DIVIDENDS AND PRICES

Two ways in which the results of the progress in the American cotton manufacturing industry can be judged are (1) the dividends paid by the mill corporations and (2) the changes in the prices of the products. The former indicate the attractiveness of this industry as a field for investment, and the latter show the advantages which have come to the purchasers of cotton goods. Both deserve attention in judging the effects of the tariff.

When we undertake to determine the profitableness of American cotton mills we are beset with difficulties in obtaining information on which to base any conclusions. The stock of a number of mills is closely held and only meagre reports given out. And the mills, especially those in New England, are more or less undercapitalized. On this point the Census of 1900 concludes that " there must be an excess of at least twenty-five per cent of assets over the nominal value of the share capital," [1] a very conservative estimate. The degree of under-capitalization varies and few of the officials are willing to state its extent in particular instances. One treasurer has informed me that his plant is capitalized at $200,000, but insured for $750,000, and this insurance valuation does not include the value of the land nor the quick assets. Hence in this case the book value is only one-fifth of the actual value of the plant.

We have a test of the extent of undercapitalization in a comparison of the book value per spindle with the cost of construction per spindle at the present time. The actual cost of building a cotton mill in the United States under present conditions is from $15 to $20 per spindle. [2] It varies from this amount upward

---

[1] 12th *U. S. Census*, vol. ix, p. 31.

[2] *Ibid.*, vol. vii, p. cccxxvi. The cost stated there is $15 per spindle, but a manufacturer informs me that it is often $20 per spindle.

according to the equipment. In addition to the cost of construction a certain amount of ready cash is necessary for financing the operations of the mill. A considerable sum is tied up in raw material and stock in process, in finished goods in the storehouse and in goods delivered but not paid for. The amount of quick capital necessary varies according to the grade of product. A few mills could get along with only $3 or $4 per spindle, while others need at least $15. The average sum per spindle which is needed to construct and finance a cotton mill at the present time is not far from $30.

Let us see how this compares with the book value of some of the New England mills, selected at random. The book value per spindle of the Androscoggin is $13.93; American Linen, $6.65; Bates, $14.61; Cornell, $3.69; Granite, $5.36; Great Falls, $11.36; King Philip, $4.65; Laurel Lake, $5.84; Naumkeag, $14.46; Pepperell, $12.78; Pocasset, $8.09; Troy, $6.31. These are typical examples of mills in first class condition which could be replaced only at a cost from two to five times as great as their present capitalization. Moreover some of them own valuable trade marks, an asset which might well be included in capitalization.

This undercapitalization makes the dividends on the nominal capital seem low, since they are paid, in reality, on an investment larger by the amount of earnings which have been turned into improvements. But the improvements have increased the value of the property, and are reflected in the high market value of the shares. The apparently low return on the total investment is counterbalanced, since if the earnings had been paid out in the form of dividends and then re-invested, the average rate of dividend would have been higher. Numerous mills have also accumulated a big surplus.

I have attempted to estimate the average rate of dividends paid by New England cotton mills during the twenty years from 1889 to 1908. The period embraces all sorts of commercial weather, and is also the time when the competition from the newly established mills in the South was most severely felt. Hence the period itself is a fair one in which to judge the returns

on capital invested in the New England mills. It is not possible
to ascertain the amount of dividends paid by several large and
profitable concerns, among them the Fall River Iron Works,
the Durfee Mills, the Knights' mills, and a few others whose
stock is so closely held that no information as to earnings or
dividends is published. Nevertheless the number of mills
included is large enough to be fairly representative, and the
result is too low rather than too high.

The method adopted for making this estimate, which includes
returns for seventy-six mills,[1] was as follows. The total capitalization of each mill was multiplied by the number of years
it was in force, — by twenty if unchanged throughout the
period, by ten when changed at the end of ten years and in that
case the new capitalization by ten, and so on. This gave the
gross amount of capital on which dividends were paid. The
gross dividends were the sum of all dividends paid. Then by
dividing the gross dividends by the gross capitalization the
average rate was determined. Thus due weight was given to
the heavier capitalization of the large concerns, and although
open to the objections that may be raised against any average,
it seems to be a fair index to the financial prosperity of the
New England cotton mills since 1889. The result obtained
was seven and seven-tenths per cent.[2]

The estimate which I have just made does not include the
amount spent in improving the plants, or in accumulating a
surplus.[3] It is not an estimate of earnings. The only additional
index which we have to the probable earnings of those mills is
the degree of undercapitalization and the amount of surplus
which they have. Capitalization has already been discussed.
The surplus, like everything else, varies widely. The Amoskeag
Manufacturing Company with a capitalization of $5,760,000

---

[1] See table in appendix. The data for this compilation was obtained from the
annual tables of *Stock Fluctuations* issued by J. C. Martin, and the reports of
Sanford & Kelly of New Bedford, and E. J. Cole, Fall River.

[2] It has been found impossible to obtain data on which to make a similar estimate for the southern mills.

[3] Large amounts are often written off for depreciation and it is possible that
high salaries may sometimes take the place of dividends.

had a surplus of $3,720,691 in 1907. In the same year the Bates Mills had a surplus of $1,376,361, with a capitalization of $1,000,000; the Pacific Mills with a capitalization of $3,000,000, a surplus of $6,332,854. These are among the highest surpluses. From these instances, where the surplus even exceeds the capitalization, we find all gradations, down to those mills which are in debt.

Several mills (as may be seen by examining the table in the appendix) have paid very high dividends and at the same time accumulated a surplus while a few have paid very low dividends and one or two none at all during the last twenty years. The reasons for the poor showing of the latter and for the remarkable success of the former are doubtless to be found in each case in the degree of efficiency with which they have been organized and managed.

The prices of cotton manufactures have been acted upon by both external and internal forces. Of the former the most important have been the monetary conditions, such as those of the period of inflation at the time of the second war with England and during the Greenback era, or, finally, the great augmentation of the world's supply of gold within the last twenty years. These have disturbed all prices. Within a narrower sphere there are the influences which have assisted to increase the supply of raw material, the more important being the opening up of new lands, the building of railroads, and improvements in methods of cultivation. The downward tendency thus stimulated has been subjected to such temporary checks as bad weather and the war of 1861–1865, and has been constantly retarded by the steady expansion of the cotton manufacturing industry. On the other side, conditions in the cloth market have left their impression, prices falling in times of depression and rising to a high point during prosperity, as happened at the climax of 1907. The increase in the population of the country and changes in taste, likewise, have had a bearing upon the course of prices.

In addition to these factors, there has been the introduction of economies in manufacturing and merchandizing, the history of which has been outlined in the foregoing chapters. These economies have constantly acted as a weight upon prices, and have tended to narrow the margin between the cost of the raw material and the selling price of the goods. The success in this direction, moreover, and the elaboration and diversification of the product have resulted in an invasion into the fields of the other textile industries. All textile products are, to a certain extent, competitive, and the cheaper cotton goods have been substituted for some of the fabrics made of wool, silk, and flax.

The decline in the price of cotton cloth was especially rapid during the first quarter of the nineteenth century. The price of ordinary sheeting, for example, fell from 40 cents a yard in 1815 to 22 cents in 1822, 8½ cents in 1829, and 7 cents in 1850.[1] At the same time the price of raw cotton fell from 24 cents per pound in 1800 to 21 cents in 1815, 14.32 cents in 1822, and 9.88 cents in 1829, but had risen in 1850 to 12.34 cents.[2] Thus the price of sheeting declined more rapidly than the price of raw cotton during the period in which the power loom was introduced and various other labor saving devices applied.

From 1861 to 1879 the severe affliction of the cotton industry by the war and the disturbance of price levels by inflation render it impossible to make satisfactory comparisons of price changes within that period. But the result of any changes will be shown by comparing 1860 and 1880, at the beginning and the end of the Greenback period. Middling upland cotton averaged 11 cents per pound in New York in 1860,[3] and 11.51 cents in 1880. Notwithstanding the slightly higher cost of cotton the price of cloth was lower at the latter date: — standard sheeting selling for 8.51 cents per yard in 1880 as compared with 8.73 cents in 1860, standard drilling at 8.51 cents and 8.92 cents, bleached shirtings at 12.74 cents and 15.50 cents, standard prints at 7.41 cents and 9.50 cents, and regular (64 x 64) print

[1] S. Batchelder, *Early Progress of Cotton Manufacture*, p. 56.
[2] M. B. Hammond, *Cotton Industry*, appendix.
[3] The following price quotations are from the *U. S. Statistical Abstract*.

cloths at 4.51 cents and 5.44 cents respectively at the two dates.

A downward tendency in the prices of cotton goods[1] was apparent from 1880 to 1898, but at the latter date the forces which have brought about the recent rise in prices began to make themselves felt. Sheetings fell gradually, except for a slight reaction in 1887–88, to 4.20 cents per yard in 1898, rising again to 7.62 cents in 1907, and going back somewhat the year after the panic to 6.75 cents in 1908. Drillings, similarly, were sold for 4.10 cents in 1898, 7.62 cents in 1907, and 7.15 cents in 1908. Bleached shirtings, in which the proportional cost for labor is greater than in the other goods quoted, were not affected to the same extent, reaching 8 cents in 1898, 13 cents in 1907, and 11.54 cents in 1908. Regular print cloths fluctuated more in price than the goods just mentioned, but showed the same tendency; they were at their lowest level, 2.06 cents, in 1898, rose to 4.62 cents in 1907, and receded to 3.50 cents in 1908. Standard prints averaged 3.96 cents in 1898, 6 cents in 1907, and 5.37 cents in 1908. They all followed more or less closely the changes in the price of raw cotton.

The correspondence between the fluctuations in the average price of cloth and of raw cotton is apparent from the fact that the latter also reached the lowest mark in 1898, at 5.94 cents per pound, and stood at 12.1 cents in 1907 and 10.62 cents in 1908.

As the prices of both raw cotton and cotton cloth have changed at the same time, it is only by considering the relative change in each that an estimate of the effects of the economies can be made. The fairest way to do this, perhaps, will be by taking for comparison a year in which the price of cotton was about the same as in 1860. The average price of middling cotton was 11 cents per pound in 1860 and 11.18 cents in 1903, hence they may safely be compared. In the two years the prices of the various standard goods were as follows: — sheetings,

---

[1] Tables of prices and a chart are given in the appendix.

8.51 cents and 6.25 cents; drillings, 8.51 cents and 6.37 cents; bleached shirtings, 12.74 cents and 10.75 cents; standard prints, 9.50 and 5 cents; regular print cloths, 5.44 cents and 3.11 cents respectively. This was a very considerable reduction in the prices of cloth; yet raw cotton cost slightly more in the later year.

Take another set of years, — 1880 and 1906. In the former year the average price of middling cotton was 11.51 cents per pound, in the latter 11.50 cents per pound. Sheetings brought an average price in New York in the later year of 7.25 cents as compared with 8.51 in 1880; drillings 7.37 cents and 8.51 cents at the two dates; bleached shirtings 10.93 cents and 12.74 cents; regular print cloths, 3.63 cents and 4.51 cents; and standard prints 5.12 cents in 1906 as compared with 7.41 cents in 1880. These comparisons show the results of the more economical methods of manufacturing and selling.[1]

The prices of cotton goods have declined not only in the United States but in all parts of the world. This decline, which has accompanied the expansion of the cotton manufacturing industry and its constantly increasing volume of output, has favored cotton fabrics in the competition with the other textiles. Articles made of cotton are no longer luxuries, as they were when imported from India in earlier centuries, but have come to be counted amongst the necessities of life. The progress of the cotton manufacturing industry has been in contrast with that of the woolen, silk, and linen industries.

The wool manufacturing industry has advanced, but has not kept pace with the cotton industry. Demands which were formerly filled by cloth made of wool have partially shifted to cotton goods. Flannels and woolen knit goods have been especially oppressed by the competition of cotton. And where there has not been a substitution of pure cotton fabrics for pure woolen or worsted cloth, a mixture has frequently taken place. Worsted manufacturers often utilize cotton yarn for the warp in making dress goods. Other cloth, of the finest

---

[1] They also indicate how little the tariff has influenced the development of the industry.

as well as the coarsest grades, dress goods as well as shoddy, is manufactured from yarn which contains a mixture of the two fibres. The manufacture of mixed and imitation goods has reached its highest development in Germany, — the fine dress goods and shoddy from Saxony and the " buckskins " of M. Gladbach standing at the head. In the United States the quantity of raw cotton used in wool manufacturing establishments [1] (not including knit goods) was 27,869,000 pounds in 1880, 42,996,000 pounds in 1890, and 43,414,000 pounds in 1900. In addition these mills purchased in 1900, 55,217,000 pounds of cotton yarn spun from 65,000,000 pounds of cotton, and in 1890, 51,376,000 pounds of yarn made from 60,000,000 pounds of cotton. In 1900, therefore, the total quantity of raw cotton consumed by the wool manufacturing industry in the United States was over 108,000,000 pounds, or more than one-fourth of the quantity of raw wool (394,369,000 pounds) used in the same year.

Cotton has had an advantage over wool in that the raw material can be obtained more cheaply. Moreover the natural difference in price has been enhanced [2] in the United States by import duties on raw wool. These duties have had an additionally retarding effect by checking the importation of certain grades of wool that could be advantageously utilized in blending.

The cost of manufacturing cotton is also less. Cotton fibres are more uniform than wool fibres, and not as curly; hence they are more easily manufactured. It was chiefly for this reason that the inventions of textile machinery were first applied in the cotton industry and the advantages of the factory system and large scale production earlier realized. The production of cotton goods was standardized sooner, and even today cotton fabrics are less affected by the vagaries of fashion than are woolens and worsteds.

---

[1] 12th *U. S. Census*, vol. ix, p. 95.

[2] The status of wool production in America is set forth by C. W. Wright, *Wool-Growing and the Tariff*.

The silk industry [1] has been handicapped by conditions similar to those which have caused the relatively slower development of the wool manufacturing industry. Not only is the growing of silk costly, but its manufacture is more laborious because of the delicacy of the tender fibres and the state in which they are obtained. That the silk industry has not remained still further in the rear has been due in part to the invention of the Lister comb which made possible the preparation of waste silk for spinning. By that means the silk manufacturers were relieved from entire dependence upon thrown silk. Within the last twenty-five years, moreover, numerous technical inventions, many of them originating in the United States, have induced an expansion of the factory system. Yet even at the present time a large number of hand looms are at work in the Lyons, Crefeld, and Basel districts under the putting out system for the production of cloth for which fragile threads are used or which is woven in a complex design.

Standardization has been difficult in the silk industry, since silks belong more or less to the class of luxuries, and their market is not only more dependent upon general business prosperity but the demand to which they cater requires greater novelty in design.   This is especially true for pure silk goods, since the ordinary grades have encountered the competition of cloth made of cotton and of artificial silk.

Cotton manufacturers have steadily introduced finer and finer fabrics, and since the mercerizing process was perfected have been able to give their cloth a silk-like appearance. Recently the manufacture of artifical silk in France and Germany has added another competitor. Silk manufacturers, finally, have followed the practice of the wool manufacturers in substituting cotton. The American silk manufacturers in 1905 used 17,-276,690 pounds of silk materials (yarn) and 9,018,295 pounds of cotton yarns.[2] In other countries, similarly, cotton has

---

[1] A recent work on the American silk industry is by F. R. Mason, *The American Silk Industry and the Tariff.*

[2] *U. S. Census of Manufactures*, 1905, *Bulletin* No. 74, p. 177.

invaded the silk mill, and thus competes from within as well as without.

Linen is the other textile fabric that has had to struggle against the product of the rising cotton industry. Linen warps were used in the looms of the first English cotton manufacturers, but Arkwright's water frame made them unnecessary, and soon cotton cloth began to take the place of linen. In every country except Ireland the linen industry has actually declined, and the Irish industry has for some time been stationary.[1] The substitution of steamships for sailing ships caused a falling off in the demand for linen sails, but that only partially accounts for the relatively backward development of the industry. The chief factor has been the competition of cotton.

The raw material for the linen industry, as for the woolen and silk industries, has been dearer than cotton. Its cultivation is more costly and the first stages of treatment disagreeable and expensive. Again, the machinery cannot be operated at as high a rate of speed in a linen mill as in a cotton factory, and it was not till about 1850 that it became possible to use the power loom for weaving linen. On the Continent of Europe, as for example in Silesia and Saxony, cotton spinning and weaving were introduced in localities where linen was manufactured and gradually took possession of the field, although the linen industry has lingered along and is even combined with the cotton industry today in a few mills. Finally, the demand for linen goods has suffered since the cotton manufacturers began to place upon the market excellent imitations of table linen and other specialties.

In all these fields, therefore, the cheaper cotton material, aided by technical improvements and refinements of design and finish, has had an effect upon the progress of the other textile industries. To be sure, internal competition within each industry would have tended to cause reductions in the cost of manufacturing, but the prices at which cotton substitutes were offered served as an added stimulus.

[1] H. Cox, *British Industries under Free Trade*, p. 40.

The American cotton manufacturers have been progressive in the fields of invention and organization. They have had an important share in bringing about the advance of the cotton manufacturing industry. The preceding chapters have given a view of the historical development and the present status of the American cotton manufacturing industry. Its elements of strength and weakness have been set forth. That furnishes a basis for our final task, the comparison of the conditions in Europe and America.

PART II

THE RELATIVE POSITION OF THE UNITED STATES

THE RELATIVE POSITION OF THE UNITED STATES

CHAPTER XVI

GEOGRAPHICAL FACTORS

THE history of the American cotton manufacturing industry and the analysis of its organization at the present time indicate the soundness of the foundations and the strength of the structure. But to test its durability and power to maintain itself in the world-wide competition, it should be compared with the cotton manufacturing industries of other countries. This section, therefore, aims at setting forth the relative position of America in the cotton manufacturing world, from both the industrial and the commercial standpoints.

For convenience and clearness the industrial aspects are classed under four heads, geographical factors, labor conditions, technique, and combinations; the knit-goods industry is treated separately as a fifth division.

The numbers of spindles in the various countries in 1910 are given in the report of the International Federation of

SPINDLES, AUGUST 31, 1910

Great Britain	53,397,000
United States	28,349,000
Germany	10,200,000
Russia	8,234,000
France	7,100,000
India	5,657,000
Austria	4,643,000
Italy	4,200,000
Japan	1,943,000
Spain	1,853,000
Switzerland	1,496,000
Belgium	1,321,000
Other	4,982,000
World	133,384,000

Master Cotton Spinners' and Manufacturers' Associations, which furnishes the most reliable figures on this subject.

According to the table given on page 275 Great Britain has almost twice as many spindles as are in operation in the United States, and those two countries together own over one-half of the cotton spindles in the world.

Great Britain, moreover, not only has the largest number of spindles, but these are more highly concentrated in a single district than are those of any other country. About ninety per cent of all the cotton spindles and looms in Great Britain are located in the County of Lancaster,[1] which has an area only one and one-half times as large as the state of Rhode Island.

Lancashire was one of the earliest seats of the industry in Great Britain, owing to its natural advantages and the presence of textile workers in the district. In the early years of its growth the water-power furnished by its streams, the port of Liverpool through which food supplies and raw materials were imported and yarn and cloth exported, and the systems of canals and (later) railroads, favored Lancashire. Recently the transportation facilities have been augmented by the construction of the Manchester Ship Canal. In the concentration which has taken place, however, there are three factors which outweigh the others. In the first place, Lancashire is rich in coal, and since it has become necessary to employ steam for power, this supply of good coal, which can be delivered at the mills for $2.50 per ton, has aided the cotton manufacturers. Secondly, the climate of Lancashire is so even in temperature and so humid that it surpasses that of every other place in the world in its suitability for cotton manufacturing. Finally, the Lancashire operatives have so long been accustomed to following the mule-carriage or changing the shuttles of a loom that their skill is a valuable asset.

Not only is the industry concentrated within the borders of Lancashire, but, attracted by the magnetic force of the

[1] In 1911 Lancashire had 58,002,435 spindles (including doubling spindles which are not included in the above table) and 741,260 looms operated by 1,966 firms engaged in the cotton industry. — Worrall's *Directory*.

economies of localization, each branch of the industry has drifted toward a particular section of the cotton manufacturing area. Southern Lancashire, with the adjoining parts of Cheshire and Derbyshire, is the spinning and doubling district. In Oldham and its neighborhood, moreover, only coarse and medium counts are spun, whereas Bolton and Manchester are the centres for the spinning of fine yarn. Stockport is preëminently the seat of doubling mills. And in northern and eastern Lancashire weaving predominates; many of the spinning mills formerly located there have migrated southward.[1] Within the weaving district there is a similar local segregation, — the manufacture of fancy cloth in Preston and Chorley, colored fabrics in Colne and Nelson, heavily sized shirtings and dhooties in Blackburn and Bury, T-cloths and domestics in Bacup, printers (print cloth) in Blackburn, and India and China shirtings in Darwen. In fact almost every town has its specialty. Outside of the Lancashire district there are two centres of interest to the student of the British cotton manufacturing industry, — Nottingham for hosiery and lace and Paisley for sewing cotton. The chief reasons for this local specialization are the advantages derived from the employment of workmen trained in a single narrow branch of the industry.

The geographical distribution of the German cotton mills contrasts sharply with the English centralization. The former are scattered over the entire Empire with the exception of the northern and north-eastern sections.

Although the density of the spindleage is not uniform throughout any of these districts, there is little localization. Dispersion is characteristic of German cotton manufacturing, just as it is characteristic of the other textile industries and the metal, leather, and chemical manufactures in that country. One reason for the scattering which is common to all these industries is the political sub-division which prevailed in Germany prior to 1871. Local conditions have also affected the location of cotton mills, and these we will now examine in detail.

---

[1] The geographical distribution of spindles and looms is shown by the table on p. 321.

DISTRIBUTION OF GERMAN COTTON MILLS, 1909 [1]

	Spindles	Looms
Rhine Province and Westphalia	2,692,964	56,820
Bavaria	1,787,296	33,977
Alsace	1,730,264	41,957
Saxony	1,480,850	45,537
Saxony (Vigogne Yarn)	692,168	.....
Württemberg and Hohenzollern	839,125	23,610
Baden	547,280	17,429
Silesia	143,827	20,325
Rhine Palatinate	142,241	1,710
Other	333,224	18,958
Total	10,389,239	260,323

This decentralization of the cotton industry is due, in the first place, to the establishment of mills where the power offered by the streams could be utilized. Secondly, local supplies of immobile labor have had some influence. And finally, capital and enterprise have been employed in local undertakings in preference to ventures in distant fields.

The lower Rhine district is not only the one which has the largest number of spindles and looms, but it is there that the progress has been most rapid in recent years. In Westphalia alone over one million spindles, eighty per cent of its total at the present time, have been erected within twenty years. The Westphalian mills are near the richest coal fields of Germany and for their raw cotton have a short inland haul from Bremen. The mills on the opposite side of the Rhine are in a position but slightly inferior.

Whereas the Westphalian mills have cheap coal, the cotton factories in Bavaria and Württemberg have had water-power. Mills have been erected on the streams of both northern and southern Bavaria, but are more densely located in the Augsburg district than elsewhere in that kingdom. In Württemberg there is complete dispersion along the Neckar, the Danube, and the other rivers and their tributaries. Nearly every mill, however, in this south German region has to rely partially upon steam power.

[1] W. Rieger, *Verzeichnis der im Deutschen Reiche auf Baumwolle laufenden Spindeln und Webstühle*, ed. 1909.

The number of spindles in Alsace has been practically stationary during the forty years that have elapsed since it became German territory. The first spinning and weaving mills in Alsace were erected to provide cloth for the print works at Mülhausen. Later the water-power of the streams in the eastern Vosges encouraged mill building. Now the mills have to use steam during part of the year at least, and the coal must be brought, as in Bavaria and Württemberg, from northern Germany. The transfer of allegiance in 1871, moreover, involved a change in market. The demand for the relatively fine fabrics of Alsace was not as great in Germany as it had been in France, and a lower tariff at the same time permitted the English competition to be felt more severely.

The conditions in Saxony are not very different. Some small mills are operated almost entirely by water-power, but the larger factories have to use steam. The coal fields in the extreme western part of the kingdom supply the local mills, but the mills in the central section find it as cheap to import coal from England. In the eastern region German coal and lignite furnish fuel. The comparatively dense population of Saxony has offered an abundant labor supply. The number of spindles in Saxony is nearly three times greater than twenty years ago, and progress has been more rapid than in any other part of Germany except Westphalia.

The remaining districts manifest characteristics similar to the larger cotton manufacturing sections to which they are adjacent. The mills in Baden, for example, are in relatively the same position as those of Württemberg, and the spinning centre in Hannover adjoins that of Westphalia.

Each district produces goods of about the same kind and quality as are made in the other sections. In general it may be said that the finest spinning and weaving are in Alsace, the coarsest in the lower Rhine district, and the largest production of colored goods in Saxony. The specialities, however, which make up the bulk of the German export trade, are identified with certain localities. Chemnitz is the centre for the manufacture of knit goods and upholsteries, Plauen for embroideries,

Crimmitschau and Werdau for the spinning of vigogne yarn,[1] Gera for fine dress goods of mixed wool and cotton, Barmen for braids and small wares, Crefeld for velveteen, M. Gladbach for " buckskins " (cotton and half-cotton trouserings), Elberfeld for certain sorts of colored goods, and Mülhausen for prints. The only reason for supremacy in a particular line seems to be the advantage gained from long experience.

Climatic conditions are practically the same for the several states, but there are considerable variations in the important items of the cost of coal and freight charges for the transportation of cotton. The freight rate on cotton from Bremen to M. Gladbach is 10.68 cents per 100 pounds, and coal costs $3.75 per ton. The manufacturers in the Chemnitz district pay 17 cents per 100 pounds for the transportation of cotton from Bremen and $4.25 to $4.50 per ton for their coal. Part of the cotton for the Alsatian spinners is obtained from Havre but the freight charge to Mülhausen is the same as from Bremen, 22.4 cents per 100 pounds, and coal costs $5.00 per ton. The freight rate from Bremen to Stuttgart is 22.7 cents per 100 pounds of cotton and is slightly higher to Reutlingen and other points further south. The charges for the Augsburg district are still heavier, 24 cents for the freight on cotton, and the price of good quality Ruhr coal (No. 3 Nuss) is $6.40 per ton.

The industry is more localized in France than in Germany, but does not approach the English concentration. The chief cotton manufacturing sections in France are the Nord, the Vosges (Est), and Normandy. Outside of these departments there are but few cotton mills. In the Est[2] there are now 2,836,000 spindles and 64,000 looms, located in 158 mills dispersed along the valleys of the rivers and streams. The industry had spread into the western Vosges from Alsace before the latter was taken by the Germans. After the war several Alsatian manufacturers migrated across the border. This, however,

[1] Vigogne yarn is spun from low grade cotton and cotton waste, dyed in the raw state.

[2] This district comprises not only the Vosges but also the surrounding departments of Muerthe-et-Moselle and Haute Saone, the territory of Belfort and Daubs.

does not account for the greater part of the expansion, since the number of spindles in the Vosges increased only from 412,-000 in 1873 to 451,990 in 1885 and 680,980 in 1891. From 1873 to 1891, likewise, the number of looms increased from 14,475 to 21,934. But in 1896 there were 1,092,266 spindles and 30,107 looms in that section.[1] The development after 1890 seems to have been due, at least in part, to the tariff of that year, which gave preferential duties to French cloth imported into the Colonies. The gray and white goods and the products of the dye and print works of the Vosges were the ones for which there was the greatest demand in the colonial markets.

Although now partially outgrown, the water-power of the Vosges was formerly of primary importance to the manufacturers. The labor supply, though not skilled, has been sufficiently abundant to be called a factor in the development. For the rest, local entrepreneur ability must receive the credit. The Vosges district is so far from the sea and from fuel supplies that freight charges have been a serious burden. The freight rate on cotton from Havre to Epinal, the commercial centre of the Vosges, is 29 cents per 100 pounds, and coal costs $6.00 to $6.40 per ton delivered at the mills. It is in spite of these comparatively high charges that the number of spindles has shown the greatest augmentation in the " Est " during the last twenty years.

The Norman cotton industry, in contrast to the Vosgian, has for a fairly long period been practically stationary. There are now about 1,800,000 spindles in this district. Rouen is the centre for Normandy, and its proximity to Havre gives it the advantage of a low freight rate on cotton, 5.4 cents per 100 pounds. By its position on the Seine, Rouen can receive importations of coal directly from England, yet the cost of coal in this district is rather hard to estimate, since frequently English and French coal are mixed in the furnaces. Beaumont states that the price of coal at Rouen is $4.00 to $4.40 per ton.[2] The failure of the cotton industry to expand more rapidly in Normandy can hardly be attributed to lack of natural advan-

---

[1] A. Lederlin, *L'Industrie Cotonnière*, p. 23.
[2] G. Beaumont, *L'Industrie Cotonnière en Normandie*, p. 146.

tages or lack of enterprise, but rather seems to be due to the greater attractiveness, from the business standpoint, of the transhipment trade and other industries such as oil refining. At any rate, Rouen has an outward appearance of at least as great prosperity as any other provincial town in northern or eastern France.

The third large cotton manufacturing region in France is the department of the Nord, at Lille, Roubaix, Tourcoing, and Amiens. The number of spindles in the department is now about 2,000,000. The industry has long existed in the Nord, and, together with the linen and wool manufacturing industries, has an asset in the supply of labor accustomed to textile work. Local coal mines supply fuel at a cost of $3.20 to $4 per ton, delivered at the mills. The climate is fairly humid. Hence the natural conditions are favorable. The canal system and the short distance to the sea are less of an advantage to the cotton industry than to others. Egyptian cotton is generally imported through Dunkirk and Indian cotton through that port or Antwerp; [1] but most of the American cotton is obtained through Havre and pays a freight rate of 15.4 cents per 100 pounds. So far as freight on American cotton is concerned, therefore, the Nord has a rate about midway between Rouen and Epinal.

There is more or less distinction between the products of these three districts. In the Nord there are few weaving mills, and the production of yarn is of primary consideration. Lille is the seat of the finest spinning on the Continent, and a few firms rival the English spinners of fine numbers. The climate and skilled labor account for this development. The fine yarn is sold to lace manufacturers in Calais and elsewhere, and also to weavers in all parts of France. In Roubaix, Tourcoing, and the surrounding neighborhood, a number of mills spin American upland cotton, and a large proportion of that yarn is woven in the same district. Upholstery weaving mills producing cotton

---

[1] Indian cotton is so low in quality that when arriving via Antwerp it is not charged with the surtax that is imposed on goods not imported directly from the country of origin.

fabrics take a part of the yarn. But of more importance is the demand from the linen weavers, who use cotton thread in manufacturing their linen fabrics. The manufacture of ordinary cotton cloth is very small in the Nord. Although within the same district, Amiens stands quite by itself. In that town various textiles are manufactured but among those made of cotton, velveteen and corduroy predominate.

The spinners located in Normandy sell yarn to weavers in other parts of France, particularly Roanne, and to knit-goods manufacturers, but the bulk of the yarn produced in Normandy is woven in the local mills. Gray cloth for converting is not an unimportant item in the product of the mills of Normandy, but that part of France has long been known for its " rouennerie," or striped and figured cloth woven with dyed yarn. The print works of Normandy draw their supply of cloth not only from the surrounding mills but also from the Vosges.

In the Vosges the predominating product is gray and white cloth of diverse structure. There are less than 500,000 spindles in the Vosges using Egyptian cotton, so that the output of fine yarn is relatively small; 28 warp and 37 weft are the common numbers. St. Dié is the only place in the district where dyed yarn is woven on any considerable scale.

Mention should also be made of a few scattered cotton manufacturing centres. At Troyes a few spinning mills supply a fraction of the local demand from the knit-goods manufacturers. Roanne is a weaving centre where cottonades and drills are manufactured, and in St. Quentin manufacturers of piqués and other goods of high quality are located. Cotton yarn is also consumed in large quantities by the silk manufacturers of Lyons and by silk and wool manufacturers elsewhere in France. But cotton manufacturing in towns outside of the Vosges, the Nord, and Normandy is relatively unimportant. The causes for local specialization can generally be traced to the reputation established by the early entrepreneurs. Aside from the humid atmosphere for fine spinning in the Nord there are apparently no particular advantages for local specialization except those acquired from experience.

The cotton mills of Italy [1] are located mainly in the northern part of the country, — Lombardy (1,850,000 spindles), Piedmont (1,000,000 spindles), Venetia (550,000 spindles), Campania (250,000 spindles), Liguria (250,000 spindles), and Tuscany (100,000 spindles).[2] In the Milan district colored and fancy goods predominate, in the neighborhood of Turin the finest spinning, and in Venetia the coarsest spinning. The industry has developed in those localities where it was first established. Water-power and labor supply have been the chief factors determining the location of the mills.

The Swiss cotton mills are located in the eastern provinces, — Zurich (620,000 spindles), St. Gall (275,000 spindles), Glarus (255,000 spindles), and Aargau (100,000 spindles).[3] The mills are scattered among the small villages of the valleys where water-power is available, and where the climate is most humid. Switzerland is in a peculiarly disadvantageous position in regard to transportation, with the result that coal costs from $6.00 per ton upwards [4] and cotton is one-half cent dearer per pound than in England.[5]

Geographical factors have not been the only considerations in deciding the location of European cotton mills, nor is the element of distance of paramount importance. So far as freight rates are concerned, raw cotton can be delivered in some of the Continental cities as cheaply as in Lancashire. Ocean freight rates are variable, fluctuating according to the quantities of cargo to be sent and the capacity of available steamers. The following rates, for November 18, 1910, are typical of the charges paid during the season of heavy shipments: — from New Orleans to Liverpool 38 cents per 100 pounds, to Manchester 35 to 38 cents, to Bremen 33 to 36 cents, to Havre 34 to 37 cents, to Antwerp 30 to 38 cents, and to Genoa 31 to 35 cents per 100

---

[1] The following information concerning Italy and a part of that for Switzerland has been taken mainly from *The Cotton Industry in Switzerland, Vorarlberg, and Italy*, by S. L. Besso, an excellent study.

[2] S. L. Besso, *op. cit.*, p. 132.

[3] *Ibid.*, p. 6.

[4] *Ibid.*, p. 15 (note).

[5] *Ibid.*, p. 9.

pounds. In other words, the ocean rates are practically the same from New Orleans to all the chief cotton importing ports of Europe. The rates from the ports to the interior points, however, are more closely adjusted to distance. The current freight rates on cotton are as follows: —

ENGLISH INTERIOR FREIGHT RATES PER 100 POUNDS [1]

	via Manchester (Ship Canal and Railroad)	via Liverpool (all rail)
To Manchester	7.8 cents	15.8 cents
Stockport	11.	15.8
Bury	11.	17.2
Oldham	12.	18.3
Bolton	12.5	16.8
Preston	14.4	17.2
Blackburn	15.	19.3
Darwen	15.	19.3
Burnley	16.3	22.5

The rates from Bremen and Havre to the cotton manufacturing districts in Germany and France have a higher average.

FREIGHT RATES FROM BREMEN PER 100 POUNDS

To M. Gladbach	10.68 cents
Chemnitz	17.
Mülhausen	22.4
Stuttgart	22.7
Augsburg	24.

FREIGHT RATES FROM HAVRE PER 100 POUNDS

To Rouen	5.4 cents
Lille	15.4
Epinal	29.

Lancashire gains less from lower freight rates on raw cotton than from its wealth of coal and its humid climate.

The following table states the freight rates on raw cotton which were in force August 2, 1911, from three southern ports to New England.[2]

[1] These rates include dock charges. They were given in a circular issued by the Manchester Ship Canal Company, August 2, 1910.

[2] For these figures I am indebted to Mr. T. F. Leavitt, Manager of the New England Cotton Freight Claim Bureau.

FREIGHT RATE PER 100 POUNDS

	To Boston	To Fall River	To Lowell
From New Orleans ....34 cents		33 cents	38 cents
" Savannah 25		31	25½
" Galveston 36		36	40

The rate from New Orleans to New England, using that for purposes of comparison, is almost identical with that from New Orleans to European ports. By land the present rate per 100 pounds of cotton from Memphis to New England points is 57½ cents. For the crop year 1910–11, I have the record of one shipment from Memphis to Manchester (England) at the rate of 64 cents per 100 pounds, and another at 57 cents per 100 pounds. Since these were stated to be typical examples, they indicate the slight difference in freight charges on raw cotton for the American and European spinners. Except for the more remote cotton manufacturing districts on the Continent, therefore, cotton can be delivered at the European mills almost as cheaply as in New England.

Coal costs more in New England than in Lancashire, from $3.50 to $4.10 per ton in the former [1] and $2.50 per ton in the latter district. However, few of the Continental manufacturers can obtain fuel of equal quality as cheaply as it is to be purchased in New England. Water supplies a larger percentage of the power used by cotton mills in the United States than in England, and fully as much as on the Continent. The English climate surpasses the American and Continental climates in its suitability for cotton spinning and weaving, but the French and Germans have no advantage over the Americans in this respect.

The dense localization in England has of itself yielded advantages which are not realized elsewhere. The English concentration has caused the establishment of repair shops and special works of various sorts. It has fostered specialization and market centralization. Finally it has also been a cause as well as a result of the development of a supply of highly skilled operatives.

[1] National Association of Cotton Manufacturers, *Transactions*, no. 88, p. 236.

CHAPTER XVII

RELATIVE LABOR CONDITIONS

THE chief points to be considered in our comparison of labor conditions are the composition of the labor force, legal restrictions, trade unions, wages, and textile education. The labor conditions in European cotton mills contrast with those in our own factories in many respects. In the first place, the European cotton mill operatives are, for the most part, a permanent, comparatively immobile class, whereas in America the immigrants in the North and the native whites in the South occasionally move from place to place and also more frequently change their occupation.

Lancashire is especially well provided with skilled laborers who are accustomed to the mule and the loom from childhood and are brought up in the atmosphere of the cotton mill, so that for them spinning and weaving becomes almost a second nature. In the older Continental centres, likewise, the second and third generations of operatives are now at work in the cotton mills. But where the industry has expanded most rapidly, as in parts of Germany, in Italy, and in Russia, the workers have no heritage of skill. In none of these countries do the people often migrate from one cotton manufacturing district to another, and they seldom shift to other industries.

The proportion of women, in the second place, is higher in Europe than in America. In England the total number of persons employed in cotton mills in 1901 was 529,131. Of these, 173,239 or 32.7 per cent were males over fifteen years old; 296,119 or 56 per cent were women; and 59,873 or 11.3 per cent were children under fifteen years of age. Moreover the proportion of men has remained almost stationary since 1871; the decline in the percentage of children has been offset by the employment of relatively more women. In the United States, it will be remembered, the proportion of men has been increasing, and is now higher (51.3 per cent in 1910) than in England. The percentage of children is nearly equal in the two countries.[1]

The employment of proportionately more women in England cannot be accounted for on the ground of legislative restrictions, since the English regulations are no less stringent than our own. It is entirely for technical and economic reasons that the Americans employ relatively more men. The solution must be sought by analyzing the proportions in each department. In the opening, picking, and carding processes the employees are almost exclusively men in both countries. A few more men are employed as drawing frame tenders in America, and the use of longer and heavier fly-frames has caused the introduction of some men into this department in the United States, whereas the tenders of the English fly-frames are always women. However this difference would but slightly alter the percentages.

In spinning the proportions are such as to increase the divergence, inasmuch as mule spinners are always men and ring spinners generally women or girls. The number of men employed in spinning in England in 1901 was 53,975, the number of women 29,016, and of children 15,869; whereas in the United States in 1900 the corresponding numbers were 12,651 men, 19,171 women, and 16,513 children. Thus there were nearly twice as many men as women in the English spinning rooms, in contrast to fifty per cent more women than men in America. The processes intermediate between spinning and weaving, furthermore, employ about the same proportions of men and women in both countries.

Only the weaving department remains, therefore, to account for the preponderance of women in English cotton mills and to offset the higher proportion of men in spinning. The English Census of 1901 reported 154,781 women and 59,324 men as engaged in weaving cotton cloth; the United States Census of 1900 showed 47,941 women and 41,776 men in that occupation.

---

[1] The percentage of children under 16 years of age in American cotton mills was 12.9 in 1905. Making allowance for the difference of one year of age in the English statistics, the percentage for England would be no lower.

Hence among the English weavers the women outnumbered the men by nearly 100,000, as compared with an excess of only 6,000 in the American factories. Moreover the numbers were almost equal for the two sexes in America in 1905, — 48,325 women and 48,248 men. The possibility of giving a man more looms, either plain or automatic, has brought about this result in our country. The men can accomplish more and earn higher wages even with lower piece rates.

The relative numbers of each class of employees in the German cotton industry in 1907 were 96,757 men (33.4 per cent), 136,910 women (53.2 per cent) and 23,573 children (13.4 per cent) under sixteen years of age. These percentages, making allowance for the one year's age difference in classifying children, are almost identical with those for England, but the distribution throughout the separate departments is not the same. Women are occasionally employed as picker and card tenders and as mule spinners' assistants in Germany. Moreover the relatively greater use of the ring-frame gives a larger proportion of women as spinners. On the other hand there are relatively more male weavers in Germany. In passing it is worth while to remark that the total number of employees in Germany is nearly one-half of that in England although the number of spindles is only one-fifth as great; and in comparison with the United States, Germany employs 84 per cent as many employees for 33 per cent of the number of spindles and 42.7 per cent of the number of looms.

Comparative statistics are also available for Italy, and in that country in 1903, twenty-five per cent (34,335) of the total number of operatives (138,880) were males over 15 years of age, fifty-nine per cent (82,056) were women, and sixteen per cent (22,489) were children less than fifteen years old.[1] The proportions for France and Switzerland would probably approximate those of England and Germany rather than those of Italy. All, however, show a greater preponderance of women than are employed in American cotton factories. Labor laws enter to

---

[1] S. L. Besso, *op. cit.*, p. 182.

a slight extent in explaining the divergence. Social customs may also have an effect. But the primary consideration seems to be the greater capability of a man.

Does restrictive labor legislation impair competitive power ? The evidence offered by the cotton manufacturing industry is not to that effect. Great Britain has led the world in factory legislation, and since the first factory act in 1802, her restrictions upon the labor of women and children have become more and more stringent. The hours of labor have been shortened, the minimum age for the employment of children raised, and provisions for improved sanitary conditions enacted. At the present time no child under twelve years of age may be employed, and children from twelve to fourteen years old are permitted to work only half time. Moreover the hours of labor for women and persons less than eighteen years of age are limited to fifty-five and one-half per week and night work is forbidden. These restrictions are supplemented by requirements in respect to the fencing of machinery, the position of self-acting mules, the cleaning of machinery in motion, the periodic cleansing of factories, and the regulation of humidity in weaving sheds. These provisions for protecting the health and the safety of the operatives are rigidly enforced.

The German law prohibits the employment of children under thirteen years of age in factories and limits the hours for those under fourteen to six per day. Women and persons from fourteen to sixteen years old are permitted to work only ten hours per day and night work is prohibited for those classes.

In France the minimum age is thirteen years except for children twelve years old who have a certain school certificate. Minors under eighteen and women are to work not more than ten hours per day for six days in the week and may not be employed at night. The French law of 1902 put a stop to the relay system, whereby during the preceding ten years the protected classes had worked in shifts.

The Swiss government prohibits the employment of children under fourteen, and those from fourteen to sixteen years old are obliged to observe certain requirements concerning education and religious instruction.[1]

In Italy twelve years is the minimum age, and girls under twenty-one and boys under fifteen must procure a medical certificate before they become factory employees. Night work for children under fifteen and women is not allowed. The hours for the former are restricted to eleven per day and for the latter to twelve.[2]

England, therefore, has on the whole more severe restrictions than any other European country, and in general the limitations are greater in England than in America. England and Massachusetts are, in this respect, on an almost equal footing, yet they are the leaders in cotton manufacturing. The prosperity of the industry in these places cannot be attributed to factory laws, yet it seems that the English and Massachusetts employers have not been placed at the mercy of their competitors by these protective measures.

Another contrast between the labor conditions in England and America is in the progress of trade unionism. The strongest labor unions in England are in the cotton industry, whereas the unions among cotton mill operatives are conspicuously weak in America. The Lancashire cotton mill employees have been among the foremost in the union movement, and today have reached a high stage of organization. The British Board of Trade received returns in 1909 from one hundred and forty-eight unions in the cotton industry, with a membership of 271,124. The several unions are federated in the United Textile Factory Workers' Association, an organization established in 1886 for political purposes.

Among the unions which constitute this central association the largest is the Amalgamated Association of Operative Cotton Spinners. This association was organized in 1870, and has gradually expanded until it now includes ninety-six per cent of the mule spinners in Lancashire. In 1909 it had sixty branches and a membership of 22,506 spinners and 27,843 piecers. The other large unions in the English cotton industry, with their

---

[1] S. L. Besso, *op. cit.*, p. 100.　　　　[2] *Ibid.*, p. 210.

membership in 1909, are: — the Burnley and District Weavers, Winders, and Beamers, with 7,585 male and 10,915 female members; the Blackburn and District Power Loom Weavers' Association, with 4,933 male and 9,867 female members; the Oldham Provincial Card, Blowing, Ring, and Throstle Room Operatives, with 2,386 male and 13,875 female members; the Nelson and District Power Loom Weavers' Association, with 5,500 male and 5,500 female members; and the Bolton Card, Blowing, Ring, and Throstle Room Operatives, with 1,134 male and 7,366 female members. Women predominate, evidently, in the weavers' and card-room operatives' unions, which embrace, however, a smaller percentage of the total number of persons eligible [1] than is the case with the mule spinners' organization. Yet all these unions are powerful and utilize their strength in collective bargaining.

The weakness of the American cotton mill operatives' unions has been attributed primarily to the influx of the immigrants. The development of the English organizations has been facilitated by the greater stability of the conditions and the higher skill of the workmen. This is not a complete explanation, however, since only a few miles from Lancashire, across the hills in Yorkshire, the operatives in the woolen and worsted mills are not nearly as well organized as the cotton workers of Lancashire. The willingness of the Lancashire operatives to follow sagacious leadership must be given a share in the credit for the progress of trade unionism in Lancashire.

The labor unions in the German cotton industry are hardly more potent than those in America. There are two classes of labor unions in Germany, the socialist and the non-socialist (Christliche) unions, the " reds " and the " yellows," and both have a foothold in the cotton trade. In a few places the socialist unions are alone in the field, those operatives who are not socialists remaining unorganized. But in a majority of the mill towns where any textile union has been formed, there is both a socialist and a non-socialist organization. The two

---

[1] About 62 per cent of those eligible are members of the weavers' unions and 70 per cent in the card-room operatives' unions.

do not work in harmony, and if they are nearly equal in strength, the one is played off against the other so as to nullify all efforts.[1] If one is preponderatingly strong, the other becomes a nonentity. In numerous cotton mills none of the employees are members of a union, and in others they are associated in a purely local organization under the patronage of the employer.

The French labor unions are very similar to those of Germany. There are socialist and non-socialist organizations, but the former are the stronger. These unions generally include members from the different textile trades, and hence are not able to give careful consideration to the separate branches. They have, in fact, more political than economic significance.[2] The union membership of cotton mill employees is strongest in the north and is practically negligible in the east. The labor unions in the Swiss cotton industry have little influence,[3] but in Italy Besso states that they exert considerable power.[4]

For the Continent as a whole, therefore, we may say that in the cotton industry trade unionism is much weaker than in England. The socialistic and political activity of the unions has kept part of the workers outside, and the dispersion of the industry has retarded combination of the operatives.

The American operatives have made little resistance to the introduction of labor saving machinery. The English operatives have also taken a broad view on that subject during recent years, and have striven to share the benefits of greater productivity instead of hindering the employment of new machines. The mule spinners' union, for example, enforces a higher piece rate where the minders are provided with antiquated mules, thus penalizing the manufacturers who fail to keep their equipment up to a high standard. Their object is to enable all the members of the union to maintain a fairly even income. The weavers

[1] Until recently the non-socialist unions were riven by internal religious dissentions, but have now become reconciled. — O. Müller, *Die christliche Gewerkschaftsbewegung Deutschlands*.

[2] The socialists oppose trade, or craft, unions where the attention is given to the problems of individual industries rather than to the " class struggle."

[3] S. L. Besso, *op. cit.*, p. 105.

[4] *Ibid.*, p. 217.

do not look with favor upon the automatic loom, yet they are not opposing its introduction except by keeping up the piece rates.

The employees in Continental mills have a dislike for new machines that tend to replace labor, but open hostility is rare. The comparatively ill success of the Northrop loom in Europe is to be attributed in part to this dislike which has prevented the weavers from seeking to obtain the best results. Yet the weakness of the labor unions in the Continental cotton factories has prevented serious manifestations against new machines. Owing to the lower scale of wages in Europe the Continental manufacturers themselves have been less ready than the English and both less ready than the Americans to adopt labor saving machinery. The differences in wages are shown in the following paragraphs.

Wages

All international comparisons are difficult, but this is especially true in the case of wages. The conditions are so diverse that erroneous conclusions may easily be drawn. The English mills, particularly the spinning mills, are highly specialized, so that a laborer is often employed continuously on a single grade of work. In the United States the machinery is readjusted more frequently, and on the Continent changes are even more frequent than in this country. Again, in America unskilled workers are occasionally employed to assist the more highly paid operatives, whereas such assistance would not be given in European mills. The type of machine and its accessory equipment must also be taken into account.

The relative expense for labor in the cotton mills of the various countries could best be stated in terms of percentage labor cost, were it possible to secure the data. Unfortunately the unwillingness of many manufacturers to state their percentage labor cost for specified products and the lack of uniformity in methods of computation preclude such a comparison.

In the second place, it is impossible to compare piece rates. The English standard lists are for the most part terrifying in their complexity, and in America and the Continental countries

there are no standard lists. The only practicable method, consequently, is to compare earnings.

As an index to comparative cost and relative advantages
in international competition a bald statement of earnings,
however, is likely to be misleading. The relative output per
operative must also be considered, since it is the expense per unit
of product which determines the price at which the manufacturer
can afford to sell. That output can be indicated by the number
of machines per operative and the speed at which they run.
On this basis a comparison of relative labor cost is undertaken
in the following pages.[1] The results are at best but approximately correct, yet the method adopted has the virtue of using
the more easily ascertainable and therefore the more easily
verified data.[2]

In each country the elements in this comparison vary between
more or less distant extremes, and many exceptions to any gener-
alization can be found. The following averages are those which
from personal investigation [3] and inquiries seem to be typical.
They are not arithmetical averages, but representative, full-time
earnings. The amounts earned in New England are generally
higher than those in the southern United States, but the former
are given as representative of the American industry since they
are the level which is being approached. The data for England
are the most accurate inasmuch as they have been collected not
only from the manufacturers but also from the secretaries of
the trade unions which represent such a large proportion of the

---

[1] The Tariff Board, I find, has used this method for drawing conclusions in
regard to relative weaving costs in England and America. My own work was
entirely independent of that of the Tariff Board and the writing of the manuscript
completed several months before that report appeared. The conclusions, however,
are not very different.

[2] There have been two detailed studies of the history of wages in the English
cotton industry, — A. L. Bowley, *Wages in the United Kingdom in the 19th Century*,
and G. H. Wood, *History of Wages in the Cotton Trade*. The latter is the more
exhaustive.

[3] Part of the information for Switzerland and all of that for Italy has been taken
from the report of Mr. Besso. The statements of the number of machines per
operative in Switzerland are given on pages 90–92, in Italy, pages 201–205, and for
earnings on pages 69–70 and 201–205 of Mr. Besso's book.

Lancashire operatives.   The wide experience of these secretaries and the use of standard lists give particular weight to their statements.

The number of machines per operative is influenced not only by the skill of the workmen but by the size of the mill, the character of the product, and the employment of unskilled assistants to help the skilled workmen.   Yet it is almost invariably true that where there is a supply of labor to be had at comparatively low wages, more labor and less capital are employed than where labor is relatively dear.

Picker tenders are generally men, and their task does not require a great amount of skill since they only remove the laps from one machine, place them on the next, and keep the machine clean.   In America the number of machines per man is from two to six, generally four or five.   In English mills the standard is three per man, except that where the long combination machines are used the number is reduced to two.   The French or German [1] picker tender has two or three machines, averaging somewhat less than the English.   In Switzerland and Italy there are only two machines per man.   The earnings are the same in England and America, $7.00 to $8.00 per week, but lower on the Continent, $4.50 in Germany, $3.60 in Switzerland and $3.00 in Italy.

Card tenders belong to the same class as the men in the picker room.   American card tenders care for fifteen to twenty machines and receive $7.00 to $8.00 per week; the English fifteen or sixteen machines at $7.50 to $8.75 per week.   Yet the English operative in this department has to do some work that would be cared for by a few more highly paid men in an American mill.[2] The French or German operative generally has ten to twelve cards and receives $4.00 to $4.50 per week.[3]   Mr. Besso states

[1] For Germany my data were collected in Chemnitz, Mittweida, M. Gladbach, Rheydt, Köln, Kulmbach, Augsburg, the Reutlingen district, and Mülhausen: in France at Amiens, Lille, Epinal, and Rouen.

[2] The English card tender grinds the cards, supplies the laps, cleans the machine, and makes all ordinary repairs.

[3] The reports of the British Board of Trade on *Wages and the Cost of Living in Germany* and *France* furnish data on wages, which may well be used for com-

the number of cards per man to be six to eight in Switzerland and seven to nine in Italy. The wages are $3.40 to $4.20 in the former country and $2.65 to $3.60 in the latter.

Drawing frames are watched by women or boys in America and by women or girls in other countries. The standard is the number of deliveries, since each machine is composed of three, six, or eight parts (deliveries) exactly alike. The number of deliveries per operative is commonly twenty-four in America, eighteen to twenty-one on the same grade of work in England, six to twelve in Germany, twelve in France, twelve or less in Switzerland, and twelve to eighteen in Italy. The weekly wages average about $6.00 in New England, $5.85 in Lancashire ($6.25 for twenty-four deliveries), $3.75 to $4.25 in Germany [1] and France, $3.00 to $3.60 in Switzerland, and $2.00 to $2.40 in Italy.

Fly-frames are of various lengths, and wages are adjusted accordingly. The English standard is eighty-four spindles per slubber, one hundred and twenty-four spindles per intermediate, and one hundred and sixty-four spindles per roving frame. The American average would not be far different. The American operative usually attends to two sides and receives $7.00 to $9.00 per week,[2] but on fine work three sides is not uncommon. The English standard rate for an operative with two sides on the grade of work common in America is now $5.90 for slubbers, $5.75 for intermediates, and $5.25 for roving frames. In addition there is one assistant per pair of slubbers at $2.75 per week, one per pair of sides of intermediates at $2.70, and one for four sides of roving spindles at $2.60 per week.

In France a woman and girl are required for two sides, the former receiving $3.90 to $4.80 per week, the latter $1.80 to

---

parison with those given above. They give the following wages, — for picker tenders in Crefeld $5.25, in Mülhausen $3.75 to $4.50, in Belfort $3.60 to $3.89, and in Rouen $3.95 to $4.35; for carders in Mülhausen $4.10 to $5.25, in St. Quentin $3.95 to $4.35, in Belfort $5.50 to $6.25, and in Rouen $3.95 to $4.60.

[1] The wages of drawing frame tenders are no higher in South Carolina than in France and Germany. — *Cf.* A. Kohn, *Cotton Mills of South Carolina*, p. 44.

[2] When men are employed as slubber tenders in America they earn from $8.50 to $10 per week.

$2.40. The German operative may have two short sides and no assistant. Occasionally she has two sides of normal length and is assisted by a girl, the woman being paid $3.75 to $5.00 and the girl about $3.00. But a majority of the German manufacturers employ one woman per side and pay $3.40 to $4.50 per week. In Switzerland the fly-frames are generally short, and there is one slubber, one side of an intermediate frame, or two sides of a roving frame per woman. The roving frame tender has an assistant. The women in this department of a Swiss mill earn $3.60 to $4.20 per week. The Italian girl has one side and is paid $2.40 per week.

The style and speed of all the machines up to this point are, as has previously been stated, quite similar in all countries. What divergences appear are in the direction of higher speed in America than in England or on the Continent. The average output per machine is also lessened in Continental mills by the employment of more old machinery. Hence, when the output per operative is taken into account, it appears very doubtful if the American manufacturer has to pay much more relatively for labor in the preparatory processes.

Ring spinners are invariably girls or women in both America and Europe, and the work is not highly skilled. While American ring spinners are occasionally put in charge of as few as four hundred and fifty spindles, the average is from seven hundred and fifty to one thousand.[1] The earnings average $6.50 to $7.50 per week in New England and about $6.00 in the South. According to the secretary of the union, the most competent authority, the number of spindles per girl is from four hundred to eight hundred in England, and the earnings from $3.75 to $5.50. Ring spinners in northern Lancashire earn more than those in the southern districts, even for the same grade of work, a fact which can probably be accounted for by the demand for women as weavers in the former section.

[1] The spinner is generally paid so much per side but the frames are of various lengths. American frames are shorter than most of those in Europe, but that does not prevent giving the spinner more spindles. The average number of sides in America is eight per operative, varying from six to ten or even more.

To give definite examples; in one Lancashire mill spinning 30's the average number of ring spindles per girl was 510 and the wages $5.00 per week; in another, spinning 32's to 50's, 768 spindles per girl at a wage of $6.00 per week. But in many mills both averages would be lower.

A similar variation exists on the Continent. The number of spindles per ring spinner in Germany averages not over 500, and the weekly earnings from $3.75 to $4.25. Occasionally the number of spindles per spinner is greater and the earnings correspondingly higher; in one mill a girl with 800 spindles was receiving $7.00 per week. In the French mills, although there are numerous exceptions, the wages of ring spinners average about $4.20 per week and the number of spindles per spinner 500. In the Lille district it is a common practice to employ a woman and a girl to attend to 600 spindles, the former being paid $4.20 and the latter $1.80 to $2.40 per week. The Swiss ring spinner receives about $3.60 per week for taking care of 400 to 500 spindles, the Italian girl $2.10 for 400 to 600 spindles.

The speed at which the ring spindles are operated is lower in England than America, since the Lancashire average is only 9,000 revolutions per minute and the American 10,000. In Continental mills the average is at least as low as in England. Nor are the ends kept up any better by the European spinners. As a rule, the work runs fully as smoothly and with as few break-ages in American mills. Rings, moreover, are used in the United States for the production of yarn that would be spun only upon mules in England.

Mule spinning is relatively less important in America, but is nevertheless essential for the production of fine yarns. For each pair of mules one spinner (minder) and one piecer are employed in America, a minder and two piecers (big and little) in England, a minder and two or more often three, or even four, assistants in Germany, France, Switzerland, and Italy. The English mules are the longest. Although mules of less than 1,000 spindles each are in operation in Lancashire, the majority are from 1,000 to 1,450 spindles in length. When the length exceeds 1,200 spindles, however, a third piecer is employed. In Germany the mules are from 750 to 1,000 spindles in length, rarely more; in France 500 to 1,000, occasionally 1,200; in Switzerland 560 to 1,000, averaging about 700;[1] in Italy 750 to 1,000 or 1,200, but about 800 on the average.[2] The mules in use in America are of practically the same length as those in Germany, France, and Italy.

The mule spinner receives a weekly wage of $12.00 to $20.00 (average about $13.50) in America; from $8.00 to $18.00 in England, the actual average being between $11.00 and $12.00; $6.00 to $7.50 in Germany and France;[3] and $4.80 to $5.40 in Switzerland and Italy. For assistants, the American piecer is paid $8.00; the big piecer $4.75 and the little piecer $3.00 to $3.50 in England; big piecers $4.00 to $5.00[4] each and little piecers $3.00 per week in Germany; $4.20[5] and $2.40 respectively in France; all piecers $3.00 to $3.25 in Switzerland; and the first piecers $3.00 to $3.60, the second piecer $1.85, and boys $1.50 in Italy. The number of assistants of each class varies in Continental mills according to the length of the mules. But in a majority of cases there are four operatives per pair of mules, even if there are only 600 or 750 spindles per machine.

In no department, however, is the comparison of earnings more dangerous than in mule spinning, for it is there that the skill of the workman is of particular importance. To be sure, the high specialization in the English spinning mills fosters the acquirement of dexterity by the mule spinners, but for other reasons also the English operatives are particularly adept and their high earnings do not constitute a comparatively heavy burden upon the English employers. It is very doubtful if

---

[1] S. L. Besso, op. cit., pp. 22–25.

[2] Ibid., pp. 150–153.

[3] British Board of Trade Reports: — Germany, Chemnitz (p. 141), $6 to $6.25; Crefeld, $7.50 to $8.50; Mülhausen (p. 354), $6.75 to $7.50; France, St. Quentin, $6.60 to $6.85; Rouen, $5.40 to $6.10; Belfort, $6 to $6.30; Roubaix, $6 to $7.50; and France generally (p. 166), $6 to $7.80.

[4] Ibid., Germany, Mülhausen (p. 354), $4.55 to $5.

[5] Ibid., France (p. 166), piecers $4.40 to $5.40.

French or German mule spinners transferred to English mills could command appreciably higher wages than in their native land.

In making these comparisons, it is to be remembered that in England and other European countries mules are employed for spinning many counts that would be spun upon the ring-frame in America. This is true not only of coarse yarn but also of finer numbers. Not much yarn finer than 40's, and very little higher than 60's is produced upon the ring-frame in Europe, whereas practically all warp yarn, even up to 120's, is spun upon that machine in America. When the ring-frame is used for work that on the other side of the ocean would be left to the mule, it is hard to discover wherein the American spinner is at a disadvantage.

American spoolers vary from fifty to one hundred and fifty spindles in length, but relatively few exceed one hundred. A girl tends one of these machines, infrequently two, and receives from $6.00 to $7.00 per week. The English girl, when equipped with a Barber Knotter, cares for fifty to sixty-five spindles. The majority of English manufacturers, however, have not yet adopted the Barber Knotter, and in their mills the number of ends per operative is only thirty to forty on cop-winders, and forty to eighty on bobbin-winders. Many English machines require that the cops be skewered and placed upon pins, whereas in American factories the ring bobbins are merely slipped into the wire bobbin-holders. In spite of higher speed the ends are kept up better in American spooling departments, and a greater production is obtained. Although the earnings fluctuate widely owing to their dependence upon the quality of the yarn, the English operative generally receives from $4.00 to $4.50 per week on cop-winding and $4.50 to $6.00 on bobbin-spoolers.

Except for a more wide-spread employment of the Barber Knotter in Germany, the methods of spooling closely resemble those of the English manufacturers. The number of spindles per girl is approximately the same, and the wages are $4.00 to $4.50 per week. No material difference is manifest in the French factories. The Swiss spooler-tenders have twenty-five spindles each and earn $3.50 per week; the Italian twenty to forty spindles at $1.80 to $2.16 per week.

The number of warping machines which one woman ordinarily tends is four in America, but generally one, rarely two, in other countries. The American piece rates are lower [1] although the earnings are higher. The weekly wages of an American warper are $7.00 to $9.00, of an English warper tending two machines (man) $8.75, tending one machine (woman) $6.00 per week; of a German (one machine) $3.75; of a French or Swiss operative (one machine) $3.60 to $4.20; and of an Italian (one machine) $2.40 to $3.00. The American tender, however, seldom does her own creeling; an average of one creeler at a wage of about $7.00 per week is required for every three or four machines. That work is done by the warper tenders themselves in Europe. Nevertheless, the labor cost per machine is lower in America than in England, and less time is lost in creeling. When the latter factor is considered, the American cost appears to be at least as low as on the Continent.

Approximately the same quantity of labor is required for the sizing process in all the countries. The earnings, moreover, are practically the same in England and America, namely $11.00 to $12.00 per week per man. On the Continent [2] they are less, $6.00 to $8.00. However the cost of labor for sizing does not constitute a heavy charge for the cotton manufacturer.

It is in the weaving room that the expense for labor is relatively the heaviest. The finer the cloth or the more complex the pattern, the smaller the number of looms per weaver. In American mills which produce fine or fancy goods, a few weavers have only two looms, but usually, even on this class of work, they tend four or six looms. In plain cloth mills, where a less progressive management has not equipped the looms with automatic warp stop-motions, each weaver tends six to eight ma-

---

[1] Mr. Young stated that these piece rates were 50 per cent higher in England than America. — *American Cotton Industry*, p. 10.

[2] The British Board of Trade *Report* for France states the weekly earnings of sizers to have been $7 to $8 in St. Quentin (p. 332), $6.15 to $6.70 in Roanne (p. 265). Mr. Besso gives $6 to $7.20 as the wage in Switzerland (p. 92) and $4.80 to $6 in Italy (p. 205).

chines, but where the warp stop-motion has been provided, the number of looms per weaver is ten, twelve, or even fourteen. These are ordinary looms on plain work.

Few English weavers care for more than four looms, and on cloth of high quality the number is less, — two or three. English six-loom weavers, moreover, are provided with small assistants to as great an extent as any American weavers.

Considering only cloth of simple construction, for purposes of comparison, the output per loom is but slightly greater in England, although the speed of their looms is from ten to twenty per cent higher. The English weaver spends more time in bringing in his warps and in remedying bad places which could be prevented by the use of warp stop-motions. The average output per loom per week is about 250 yards of print cloth in Fall River. And Mr. Nasmith states [1] that in Lancashire " a fair output of plain cloth, 64 picks, 30 inches wide, from one loom is 250 yards in 56 hours." Probably that weekly production is more frequently exceeded in England than in America; but even in the latter country the output per loom per week occasionally amounts to 275 or 300 yards. Nevertheless, an American weaver tends twice as many looms as the English weaver.

Weaving piece rates are so complex that a comparison is out of the question. But we can contrast the weekly earnings per loom and per weaver in the two countries. In Fall River at the present rates the amount paid for weaving five and one-half cuts of regular print cloth, the weekly production per loom, would be $1.08.[2] In England the weekly earnings per loom on plain weaves are from $1.30 to 1.55. This indicates the difference in piece rates in favor of American manufacturers. The weekly earnings per weaver, however, are higher in America, $8.00 to $10.00, in comparison with $5.20 to $6.20 for an English weaver of plain fabrics. It should also be remembered that the English weaver is paid the same piece rate irrespective of the number of looms tended, whereas in America the piece rate is diminished as the number of looms per weaver is increased.

---

[1] J. and F. Nasmith, *Recent Cotton Mill Construction* (3d ed.), p. 156.
[2] The rate per cut has been 19.66 cents since May 25, 1908.

A Northrop loom weaver earns slightly more than the plain loom weaver in this country, and has charge of fourteen to thirty machines. An English Northrop loom weaver runs twelve to twenty looms, and for the latter number earns $8.50 per week. In the United States the Northrop loom piece rate is about one-half the piece rate paid on plain looms; hence when Northrops are employed in this country to weave cloth similar to that produced on plain looms in England, there is a great saving in comparative labor cost to the American manufacturer.

The Continental mills are, for the most part, equipped with English looms, and the speeds approach those attained in England. The output per loom does not fall far short of that obtained in British cotton mills. Four looms per weaver is the maximum on the Continent, however, and three the average. A German weaver earns $5.00 to $6.00 per week,[1] a French weaver $4.80 on the average,[2] a Swiss $3.60 to $5.40, and an Italian woman (two looms) $2.15 to $2.75 per week. In Continental countries, as in England, the weaving piece rates, at least for plain cloth, do not fall below American standards.

Definite conclusions as to the exact difference in labor cost between the several countries cannot be drawn. One thing is certain, however; the earnings of American cotton mill operatives more closely approximate those received in England than we have commonly been led to suppose. And when the output per operative is taken into account, it appears very doubtful if the labor cost on ordinary goods is appreciably higher in our country. The difference in the preparatory and spinning processes is slight, and in weaving the advantage is in favor of the Americans. The Germans may excel in the production of

---

[1] British Board of Trade *Report* for Germany: — Weavers' wages in Chemnitz (p. 141), $5 to $6; in Mülhausen (p. 354), $4.10 to $4.90.

[2] British Board of Trade *Report* for France: — Weavers' wages in Belfort (p. 47), $4.20 to $5.55; in Amiens (p. 36), $3.83 to $4.20; in Lille (p. 166), $4.60 to $5.39; in Rouen (p. 294), $4.20 to $4.40; in St. Quentin (p. 327), $4.50 to $5.54 (two looms); in Roanne (p. 265), $3.85 to $4.95 (two looms); and in Roubaix (p. 279), $5.20.

The maximum number of looms per weaver in the Rouen district is two. — *U. S. Daily Consular Reports*, October 27, 1911, p. 479.

the cheaper novelties and the French in certain fancy goods, but England is still the great exporter of cotton fabrics although her work people obtain higher earnings. Similarly, the high American wages do not necessarily denote a handicap. The cheapest labor may be the dearest. At all events, I have no hesitation in asserting that higher wages are one of the least of the obstacles which stand in the way of American cotton manufacturers in international competition.

Wage Agreements

Standard lists have been in vogue for many years in several branches of the English cotton industry but have not been adopted by cotton manufacturers in other countries. Each mill at first had its own scale but this condition has been gradually superseded by the development of lists applying to larger areas. The extension of these has been concomitant with the rise of the labor unions, which have sought to bring about uniform conditions in the payment of wages. As early as 1823, at least, standard lists were in use,[1] and from 1840 to 1875 were gradually extended.

None of the lists comprehend all the factories engaged in any one branch. There are two important spinning lists, the Bolton list and the Oldham list.[2] The former was adopted in 1858, but has been revised from time to time. It is based upon the principle of payment by weight. The Oldham list, which has been subjected to little change since its introduction in 1876, differs from the Bolton list in that it is worked out on the basis of the length of yarn spun. In 1894 it was stated in the Board of Trade *Report* that these two lists regulated the wages of seventy-five per cent of the mule spinners of Lancashire and Cheshire, and the proportion is over ninety per cent at the present time.

The spinners' lists were established earlier than those for operatives in other departments, as a result of the greater prog-

---

[1] S. J. Chapman, *Lancashire Cotton Industry*, p. 263.

[2] British Board of Trade, *Report on Wages and Hours of Labor*, 1894, part ii, pp. xix, 22.

ress of labor organizations among the spinners. At the present time, however, standard lists have been adopted in nearly all departments. A list for slubber, intermediate, and roving tenders was adopted in Blackburn in 1873, and later the Amalgamated Association of Card and Blowing Room Operatives established universal lists for all their members except the ring spinners. This remaining department cannot easily be brought under a universal list since there is a divergence in the rates of northern and southern Lancashire, but efforts are being constantly directed toward a solution of the problem.

The wages of operatives employed in spooling, warping, sizing, drawing in, twisting, and weaving are regulated by standard lists in so far as those employees are members of unions. But the lists are not uniform for all Lancashire. In weaving, the chief list is that for North and North-East Lancashire, prepared in 1892 by a joint committee of representatives of employers and operatives.[1]

The complexity of these lists has necessitated the employment of experts for their interpretation. The laborers, on their side, delegate the safeguarding of their interests to the secretaries of the trade unions. To insure competence, the secretary is usually chosen by means of a competitive examination, a method which was introduced in 1861.[2] The employers' associations, likewise, have engaged salaried experts who devote all their time to that service. Whenever it becomes necessary to revise the lists, representatives chosen for that purpose by the employers and by the employees confer, but the interpretation is left to the experts.

The results of this method of fixing wages have been beneficial. Webb says that "the universal satisfaction with and even preference for the piece work system among the Lancashire cotton operatives is entirely due to the existence of these definitely fixed and published statements."[3] These products of long

---

[1] British Board of Trade, *Report on Wages and Hours of Labor,* 1894, part ii, p. 27.

[2] Webb, *Industrial Democracy,* pp. 195–196.

[3] Webb, *Trade Unionism,* p. 293.

experience and special knowledge are respected alike by those who receive and by those who pay the wages. Each feels that he is receiving justice when the judgment is based on the recognized standard. Moreover, the influence of the expert secretaries, grounded upon a thorough understanding of the conditions, has been exerted for a conservative policy, has tended to eliminate many of the excesses which labor union leaders sometimes advocate, and at the same time has promoted the welfare of the workers. The demands of each party have received fair consideration, and serious friction has been minimized.

All danger of a disastrous labor dispute is not dissipated, however, by these lists and the provisions for their enforcement, as was shown by the protracted strike which began in 1892 and lasted till March, 1893. Worn out by strife, the contestants, after much parleying, agreed to a treaty of peace. This was the " Brooklands Agreement," [1] which was signed March 24, 1893, by the Federation of Master Cotton Spinners' Associations, the Amalgamated Association of Operative Cotton Spinners, the Amalgamated Association of Card and Blowing Room Operatives, and the Amalgamated Northern Counties Association of Weavers, Warpers, Reelers, and Winders. By the terms of this compact, notice of any complaint was to be given, and in the future no strike or lockout was to take place till after the dispute had been submitted to a committee of at least six members, three chosen by each side, and the two secretaries. Full evidence was to be presented, and a strike or lockout declared only after it had become evident that sufficient concessions were not forthcoming. Among other clauses, one stipulated that wages should not be changed more than five per cent in any one year, either by reduction or increase. The risk of loss was compensated by the stability which the plan promised. The Brooklands Agreement is still in force, having survived the vicissitudes of eighteen years. Disputes still occur, chiefly in respect to interpretation, but they are infrequent and both sides are in favor of tolerant arbitration.

[1] British Board of Trade, *Report on Wages and Hours of Labor*, 1894, part ii, pp. 9–10.

The English experience indicates that the employers as well as the employees benefit by having both sides organized so as to become parties to a contract for the regulation of wages. That the interests of the laborers are furthered by the elimination of the danger of exploitation, is self-evident. Similarly, the employers profit by the assurance that their competitors are paying the same rates for their labor and by the protection from strikes which the wage agreement tends to afford. One risk of loss is diminished.

The American cotton manufacturer would gain something from such agreements, but he turns instability to greater advantage. There has been a constant inflow of cheap labor which he could exploit. Although he sacrifices the advantages of uniformity and is subject to continual change, he can keep wages at a lower point and resist the demands of his workmen. Consequently American cotton manufacturers, as a rule, abhor labor unions, and even in Fall River have looked upon the wage agreement as a necessary evil.

Against this exploitation by their employers the American cotton mill operatives have protected themselves mainly by their willingness to change their place of abode. It is doubtless true that this mobility has weakened the union spirit, but it has enabled the workmen to take advantage of the competition of employers over a wide area. Yet the greater mobility of American laborers during a period of rapid industrial expansion has been at best but a poor substitute for the protection which the English operatives secure from their unions. The Continental cotton mill employees have not enjoyed equal safeguards from either of these sources; yet it is to be remembered that many of the Continental mills are situated in agricultural districts where work upon the soil offers an alternative to employment in a cotton factory.

From the laborer's point of view not only earnings but the cost of living ought to be compared; that, however, is a task that would require an investigation beyond the scope of this study.[1] The manufacturing companies in America, England, Germany, and other countries frequently own dwellings, which are rented to their employees. It is not uncommon, particularly in the southern United States and in Germany, for the rent to be placed at a nominal figure; hence the unremunerated expense of building these houses and keeping them in repair should be charged to the wage account. A few company stores are still to be found in the southern United States and in Germany, in the more isolated villages, but the abuses of the trucking system are apparently absent.

The conditions under which the operatives work are very diverse within each country. In America there are mills where the rooms are well lighted, free from dust, and with proper hygienic sanitary arrangements. The same statements hold true for England, Germany, and France. A few mills in all these countries are dirty, ill-ventilated, and without decent toilet facilities. But, although the larger mill towns are not attractive in appearance, the condition of the operatives and their habitations must be distinguished from the conditions in the mills themselves. To the observer the latter seem, for the most part, to be good.

Textile Education

In conclusion the status of textile education should be considered. As we have seen, the American textile schools are particularly useful in serving the operatives themselves. The Lancashire textile schools, similarly, lay the greater emphasis on the evening classes. The textile course at the Manchester Municipal School of Technology in 1909–10 had an enrolment of 108 day students and 426 evening students. In the other large cities in Lancashire, as in Preston, Bolton, and Burnley, there are technical schools with textile departments, but, in many of these, classes are conducted only in the evening. The students are mainly young men, — mechanics, designers, spinners, and occasionally weavers, who undertake to fit themselves for higher

[1] The recent *Reports on the Cost of Living in France* and *Germany*, issued by the British Board of Trade, contain much valuable information on this point.

positions. The overseers are recruited from this class. But the majority of the operatives do not attend the schools, and the proportion seeking such education is less than in the New England cities where textile schools are available.

German textile education is primarily for the sons of mill owners, directors, merchants, and others who can afford to devote all their time to study, and the instruction is largely confined to day courses. Although there are a few evening schools, young men of promise sometimes enter the day courses of the textile schools after having worked several years in a mill, the expenses being paid from their savings or by their employers.

The courses for the day students in Germany are generally shorter than in America or England.[1] A few specific examples will make this clear. The textile school at Reutlingen, which averages 140 to 150 students per year, has a one year course in spinning, a one year course in weaving, a two year course in designing, and other supplementary courses of one year each. The M. Gladbach institution has a spinning course and a weaving course, each of one year's duration, and a finishing course for which two years are required. The Mülhausen Spinning and Weaving Schools each offer a one year course, the number of students in both averaging sixty. In other schools the courses are from three months to two years in length.

Technical education in France bears much resemblance to that of Germany. The schools in which textile courses are given have varying standards of requirements for admission. The National Technical School at Lille, in which the courses in spinning and weaving are of three years' duration, imposes a high standard. The Municipal Spinning and Weaving School in the same city is of lower grade. The National Professional School at Armentières, which has only a weaving department, trains boys who have been apprenticed to that trade. At St. Quentin and Amiens, technical schools with textile courses are supported by the local manufacturers' associations. That at Amiens is of long standing, having been established fifty-five years. Both of these institutions, unlike the others, hold

[1] The courses in spinning and weaving at Manchester are three years each.

classes in the evening as well as in the day. But the number of students is not large; there were thirty-five evening students in weaving at Amiens in 1911. At Epinal a branch of the Industrial School is devoted to spinning and weaving, but only day sessions are held. The number of students enrolled in this school in 1910 was twenty. Except for the evening schools, we may say that the object of the various institutions is to fit the students for positions as overseers or managers.

The contribution of the Continental textile schools is not to be belittled, yet one may suspect that too much credit is occasionally given to these institutions for the part they play in the development of the industry in their respective countries. The number of students attending the day classes is comparatively small, and the number of evening students still smaller.

The New England textile schools, in addition to the advanced work of the day classes, open opportunities for instruction to the immigrants and in that way improve their efficiency as laborers, and accomplish more perhaps for the operatives themselves than for the manufacturers. The English employers, likewise, benefit from the increase in the supply of men who can take responsible positions in the mills. Yet there again, it is the social significance which attracts particular attention. The ambitious youth, although he has to work all day in the mill, may materially improve his condition, provided he has sufficient mental capacity and enough energy. The evening textile school is a valuable means of economic and social advancement. But on the Continent it is only the very exceptional boy from the operative class, who can make use of the trade school. The bulk of the operatives cannot improve their condition in that way, and social barriers are thereby kept more impregnable. In our own country the efforts of the textile schools should be heartily supported, if for no other reason than to give a better chance to those workmen who are willing to help themselves.

CHAPTER XIII

PLANT; SCALE OF PRODUCTION; SPECIALIZATION

THE equipment, arrangement, and management of plant, the scale of production, and specialization are subjects so closely allied that they have been included in a single chapter in the continuation of our comparison of the European and American cotton manufacturing industries from the industrial standpoint.

Plant

The first of these topics, plant equipment, has been partially discussed in the chapter on technical development and therefore here needs only to be supplemented and summarized. Although each important invention has been imported from the country where it was made into the other cotton manufacturing countries, technical equipment is by no means uniform. Inasmuch as the majority of Continental mills are equipped entirely or in part with English machines and the machines manufactured upon the Continent are, with few exceptions, modeled upon English types, the chief differences are between English and American machinery.

In a few mills in England and on the Continent the cotton from the bales is still loosened by hand without a bale-breaker. But except for the methods of transferring the fibre from the bale-breaker to the opener or hopper feeder[1] and the more frequent employment of one or two extra machines, the beaters, in European factories, the bale-breakers, openers, and pickers are in general much the same in Europe and America.

A few of the old roller-and-clearer and also Wellman cards are in operation in English mills for regular carding work, in addition to those employed for carding waste. The labor cost is two and one-half times as great on the old-fashioned machines, but their owners consider that this extra expense would be offset

[1] See *ante*, p. 58.

by the cost of replacement. On the Continent a few roller-and-clearer cards and also stationary-flat cards (not self-stripping) are still at work in cotton mills where the owners are especially economical in capital expenditure. But a majority of the European mills are provided with revolving-flat cards. The differences in the drawing frames and fly-frames used in America and Europe are only in minor details.

The relative position of the mule in England and the ring-frame in America has already been explained. On the Continent there is no such predominance of one type of spinning machine. The number of ring spindles is nearly equal to the number of mule spindles. In 1907 they stood as follows: —

SPINDLES, 1907 [1]

	Mule	Ring
Germany	5,740,000	3,722,000
France	4,122,000	2,481,000
Austria	2,307,000	1,277,000
Italy	1,015,000	1,852,000
Russia	1,031,000	1,320,000

The mule and ring are used to about the same extent, but the ring is gaining ground. Although in the older cotton manufacturing centres a supply of mule spinners has been available, it has not been sufficient to provide for all the new mills. And where plants have been established in fresh localities, reliance has had to be placed upon untrained labor. The improvements in the ring-frame, moreover, have overcome previous prejudices. These factors have encouraged the installation of ring-frames. As a counter-influence, fine spinning has caused the retention of part of the mules, especially in France, and the more extensive use of short staple American cotton and low grade Indian fibre has also favored that machine. The Continental spinners, notably the Germans, purchase relatively large quantities of low grade material. Finally, the life of a mule is long and the difference in the labor cost of mule spinning and ring spinning is not so great in the Continental countries; hence the mules have not been scrapped as fast as in America.

[1] From the circular issued by the International Federation of Master Cotton Spinners' and Manufacturers' Associations in 1907.

Where the ring-frame is employed in mills that have no weaving department, the English and particularly the Continental spinners frequently use pasteboard tubes instead of bobbins. In this way they get around the inconveniences of either reeling the yarn or shipping it upon the heavy wooden bobbins. The tubes, however, do not give as good results as the bobbins.

The speed of the ring-frame, lastly, is lower on the average in Europe. Although some spinners drive their spindles at a speed of 9,500 and 10,000 revolutions per minute, the majority do not exceed 9,000. The cotton which they use is shorter and not as capable of withstanding the more severe strain of the highest speeds.

Spoolers of the English type, without the wire bobbin-holder, are employed in Continental factories. The Barber Knotter is more prevalent on the Continent than in England, although not as universal as in America. English warpers are commonly used in Continental mills, but machines of the American type are more numerous than in England. The American warp-tying machine, moreover, has found a more ready acceptance in Germany than in England, in spite of the fact that the conditions for its use are no more favorable.

The under-pick loom, which is exclusively used in America, is employed in Europe only for special types of heavy loom. Over-pick looms of English design prevail. The European looms, except the automatics, are rarely, if ever, provided with warp stop-motions. As has been stated, the speed of the looms is higher in England than America. The Continental manufacturers approach the English standard, but seldom reach it. Most of the mills on the Continent are equipped with humidifiers, but these devices are not required by many of the English mills, although a few have them ready for use on the dry days so rare in Lancashire.

The finishing machines in Europe are as diverse as in America, and of similar type. In converting establishments, also, the technical appliances resemble those in this country. But the American manufacturers convert larger quantities at a single operation. English printing machines are at work both in

America and on the Continent, but aside from better construction they are not different from those of domestic manufacture. The output per machine, however, is not the same. The average weekly production per printing machine is about 75,000 yards in America, 20,000 in England,[1] and from 15,000 to 20,000 in Germany. This contrast is accounted for by the smaller orders accepted in the European countries, which necessitate more frequent changes of the rollers and thus incur loss of time. In English bleacheries cylinders or stenters are ordinarily employed for drying the cloth, but the use of sheds has not been entirely given up, and in Germany large quantities of cloth are dried by being hung from the top of big rooms filled with hot air. This shed, or stove, drying not only takes more time, but is far more laborious. For the American the slight superiority in the appearance of cloth dried in that way would not counterbalance the extra expense for labor that would be involved.

In conclusion, it may be stated that cotton manufacturers, whatever their nationality, have in the main adjusted their machines to the economic conditions under which they work. The best in one place may be inferior when transplanted.

While English textile machinery is exported to other countries in large quantities, the boilers and engines made in England are no better and perhaps inferior to Continental machines. Several English mills, in fact, have installed Belgian engines which have proved very satisfactory. The German mills all have German engines, but the Babcock and Willcox self-stoking boiler is widely used. For transferring the power the rope-drive is almost universally employed in Europe, whereas the American mills ordinarily have belts. Until 1876 nearly all of the Lancashire mills had toothed gearing,[2] but that is still retained by only a few of the older mills. The electrical drive has made less headway in England than in America or Germany, but its progress is slow in these latter countries. Nasmith

---

[1] T. M. Young, *American Cotton Industry*, p. 119; also S. H. Higgins, *Dyeing in Germany and America*, p. 49.

[2] J. and F. Nasmith, *Recent Cotton Mill Construction* (3d ed.), p. 12.

summarizes the advantages of the electric drive thus:[1] — "The prime mover and the machinery may be placed in any relative position; each machine can be driven independently, without reference to the others, or where grouping is necessary, greater simplicity is possible with less cost in regard to shafting; greater steadiness of driving, and consequently greater output per machine; greater immunity from break-down; less cost in running on light loads; and continued check on power consumed." The elimination of shafting and belting also gives better light.

Another method of eliminating the darkness and shadows from the interior of the cotton mill is by means of the saw-tooth roof. In Europe as well as the United States weaving sheds of recent construction, and occasionally other mill buildings, are very often lighted from the roof in this way. Everywhere the advantages of superior lighting have been recognized.

Cotton mill buildings have much the same appearance in Europe and America, although the factories in the latter country are more frequently of greater height than in Europe. The internal arrangement is so heterogeneous in European factories that it is very difficult to fix any standard for comparison. We may say, however, that the most modern European structures are generally well-planned. A good example is the new mill of the Mechanische Spinnerei und Weberei in Augsburg.[2] Among the unique features of that plant is the basement in which are located water pumps, oil pumps, machines for recovering and purifying oil, and an elaborate system for compressing, heating, humidifying, and distributing fresh air to all parts of the mill. The windows of the mill are of special glass, designed by Director Fessman, which is grooved at angles which diffuse more light than is admitted by ordinary glass. The overseer's office in each department is built in the wall at the end and raised above the level of the machinery, so that the overseer can observe everything that goes on in the room, even while he is engaged in making his tests or preparing his reports. Finally,

---

[1] J. and F. Nasmith, *op. cit.*, p. 275.

[2] The director and one of the overseers of this mill are the inventors of the Fessman-Hammerle creel and warper.

convenient cloak-rooms with lavatory facilities are provided for the operatives, one for the men and another for the women.

The cost of constructing a new mill is lower in England than elsewhere. A spinning mill equipped with mules costs from $7.00 to $7.50 per spindle; a ring spinning mill, which requires more preparatory machinery for the same number of spindles, $10.00 per spindle.[1] The cost of a weaving mill is entirely dependent on the style and width of loom installed and auxiliary machinery required. One authority places the cost for a plain goods mill at $126 per loom.[2] This may be considered as the minimum. The estimates for the cost of a mill in the United States ($15.00 to $20.00 per spindle) were for the typical establishments that have both spindles and looms. In England a ring spinning mill with full complement of looms would cost from $13.00 to $16.00 per spindle.[3] One reason for the higher cost in America is the duty of forty-five per cent on imported machinery, in addition to the natural protection of about twenty-five per cent that the American machinery manufacturers enjoy because of the extra cost of shipping from England.

In Germany, to give a typical example for the Continent, a spinning mill costs from $10.00 to $17.00 per spindle, averaging about $15.00 for coarse and medium counts, and a weaving mill from $200 to $300 per loom.[4] Thus a combined spinning and weaving mill would cost from $15.00 to $25.00 per spindle. The average for the coarse and medium counts would be very nearly the same as in America. The price of textile machinery in Germany is likewise affected by the tariff.

There has been speculative promotion of mills in the southern United States, but little in New England. In Lancashire, during the recent mania for erecting cotton mills, the speculative element was prominent. A few men joined hands to start an

---

[1] When business is unusually slack, the cost may fall slightly below these figures.

[2] A. F. Barker, *Textiles*, p. 333.

[3] The cost of an English spinning mill without looms has occasionally been compared with the cost of an American mill that embodied both departments. Mr. Young (*American Cotton Industry*, pp. 8–9) states that the cost for similar mills is but slightly higher in America.

[4] *Jahrbuch für die gesamte Baumwoll-Industrie*, 1911, p. 328.

enterprise and then solicited subscriptions to the stock. A Liverpool broker was given the exclusive privilege of buying the cotton provided he took a block of shares. Machinery manufacturers exchanged machinery for stock, and other supply dealers, such as oil merchants and belt merchants, accepted stock in return for which they were granted compensating privileges. Finally, a yarn merchant would purchase a small amount of stock for the sake of the agency for the product. Thus the mill started out, bound hand and foot, subject to competition in the disposal of its output, but enjoying few of the advantages of competition in procuring its supplies.

Management

There is greater heterogeneity in the distribution of the responsibility for mill management and direction in England than in America. It varies with the size of plant, specialization, and form of ownership. First in order is the large joint-stock company, carrying on both spinning and weaving, and perhaps finishing. In this case one director assumes responsibility for one department, another for another, and under each is a works manager. The selling of the goods, also, may be in the hands of a single director, and the relations of these managing directors to each other regulated by the whole board. In the next place, a joint-stock company which only spins or weaves will have a managing director, corresponding to the American treasurer, who assumes the whole responsibility. But he will very likely have a works manager to superintend the mill. This approaches most nearly to the American practice.

In addition to the joint-stock companies there are the private concerns, with and without limited liability. In these the ownership is generally in the hands of one man or, at most, one family. The owner attends to the merchandizing and may also take an active part in superintending the mill, although he frequently leaves that almost entirely to a manager. A small manufacturer (weaver) or even spinner may manage his plant personally and also sell the goods. For the latter purpose he may secure assistance from an agent, although it is by no means uncommon for him to undertake the sale of the yarn or cloth himself on the Manchester Exchange.

The superintendent, or works manager, in an English mill has not, as a rule, had so much experience as an American cotton mill agent or superintendent. Nor does he receive nearly as high a salary. A majority of English mills confine their operations not only to either spinning or weaving, but to a limited range of work within one field. Hence the management is not as difficult as the superintendence of an American cotton mill in which all the processes from the opening of the bales of raw cotton to the weaving and perhaps the finishing of the cloth are united in a single plant.

The Continental mills are superintended on the same system as the English, but the private, unincorporated concern is more common than in England, and in general we may say that the proprietors exercise a closer oversight over their establishments. While this is possible where small mills are the rule, the scale of production in America necessitates a division of the labor of management.

An elaborate system of reports has been adopted by very few English cotton mills. Each mill has some means of identifying every lot of material, to ascertain to which workmen it has been entrusted. A record of output is also kept, since most of the operatives are paid piece rates and reports are essential for making up the pay-roll. There the report system stops. A spinning mill usually limits itself to the production of a few numbers, hence each machine regularly performs a certain share in the work. The power cost and machinery charges, therefore, are well known to the spinner. The wages, furthermore, are fixed by the union list, and the charge for each number and kind of yarn specified. The amount allowed for raw material depends on the current market quotations. Finally, the remaining element, the charges for superintendence, insurance, etc., do not have to be distributed over a great number of different products, and from past experience it is possible to determine with sufficient exactness how much should be ascribed to each lot of yarn.

Many English weaving mills, likewise, although they manufacture a wide variety of goods, seldom take up new lines, and therefore consider that their rough-and-ready methods of costing the goods are sufficient for their needs. The following is the formula used by many Lancashire manufacturers for deciding what quotations to offer. They ascertain the cost of the yarn required, add the labor charge for weaving as fixed by the union list, and then for general expenses add an amount equal to the weaving price. If business is dull, they seek only three-fourths or one-half of the weaving price, while in times of unusual prosperity twice the weaving price is charged for general expenses. This method may be adequate for plain goods, but where a mill is manufacturing goods of fancy design, a formula of this sort will hardly suffice. There a more scientific method of cost determination would be advantageous.

Scale of Production

Although the cotton manufacturing industry was one of the first in England to be brought under the factory system, the domestic system was not at once entirely superseded, as is shown by the prolonged struggles of the hand loom weavers. The practice of spinning on commission, also, was continued well into the second quarter of the nineteenth century.[1] These spinners rented room and power in a mill building where they could operate a few machines. Those favored by prosperity gradually expanded their business and some eventually became prominent. By 1860, however, the factory system predominated and since then the size of the mills has steadily increased.

At the present time a typical Lancashire spinning mill of recent construction has about 80,000 spindles. The older mills are somewhat smaller. The following data have been compiled from Worrall's *Directory* for 1911.

---

[1] S. J. Chapman, *Lancashire Cotton Industry*, pp. 60–64. A similar method was tried in Fall River early in the nineteenth century but continued only a short time. — H. H. Earl, *History of Fall River*, p. 23.

LANCASHIRE COTTON MILLS, 1911[1]

District	Spinning		Spinning-Weaving			Weaving	
	Estab.	Spindles	Estab.	Spindles	Looms	Estab.	Looms
Oldham	198	15,115,131	14	940,202	13,234	5	3,144
Manchester	85	8,156,434	16	768,367	16,740	95	33,603
Bolton	69	7,501,793	13	681,232	13,504	42	20,191
Rochdale	48	2,899,540	16	583,590	10,155	23	8,832
Ashton u. L.	34	2,377,514	6	412,714	8,625	4	2,741
Stockport	21	1,837,364	9	386,272	8,112	4	1,589
Preston	14	851,030	20	1,333,218	30,801	46	34,312
Bury	5	334,702	23	620,704	11,499	16	10,356
Chorley	5	339,360	11	609,952	15,103	19	12,911
Blackburn	7	295,946	17	971,884	23,946	86	64,299
Burnley	4	124,328	14	457,098	14,202	110	85,740
Accrington	6	459,656	8	172,800	4,477	40	29,925
Darwen	3	127,784	5	148,710	2,731	43	31,841
Bacup	1	70,000	11	279,072	7,743	6	1,902
Nelson	1	23,200	..	....	......	118	52,709
Colne	..	....	2	147,500	3,876	77	21,232
Other	94	4,366,884	51	3,020,932	61,268	125	68,867
Total	595	44,880,666	236	11,634,247	246,016	859	484,194
Per cent of total	35.2	79.5	14	20.5	33.7	50.8	66.3
Aver. per establishment		75,430		49,300	1,042		564

For these mills, therefore, the averages are: — 75,430 spindles per spinning mill; 49,300 spindles and 1,042 looms per spinning and weaving mill; 68,000 spindles per mill for all mills which spin (including both of the former); 564 looms per establishment for mills devoted only to weaving; and 667 looms for all mills which weave. Thus the average size of the spinning mills in Lancashire is approximately the same as in New England, but a much larger proportion of the American mills have looms as well as spindles.

Classifying all the mills in which cotton yarn is spun in Lancashire,[2] we obtain the following results. 675 have less than 100,000 spindles, 103 from 100,000 to 149,000 spindles, 26 from 150,000 to 199,000 spindles, 17 from 200,000 to 249,000 spindles, 6 from 250,000 to 299,000 spindles, and 4 over 300,000 spindles.

[1] Doubling spindles, and spindles in mills spinning waste are not included. The districts do not correspond exactly to Worrall's divisions in a few instances, and the returns are not entirely complete.

[2] Compiled from Worrall's *Directory*.

The largest spinning concern, excluding the combinations, is the Musgrave Spinning Company of Bolton, with 460,000 spindles. This is larger than any concern in the United States except the Amoskeag Mills and the Fall River Iron Works.

In weaving, five manufacturers operate over 3,000 looms each, and seventeen have 2,000 to 2,999 looms. At the other end of the scale, fifty-six each have only 100 looms or less. The largest weaving company is Horrockses, Crewdson & Co., with 9,530 looms in two plants. The same company also has 250,000 spindles in its mills, thus making it the largest independent enterprise in the English cotton industry.

The number of small weaving concerns has been mentioned. Many of these are in Colne and Nelson, where the so-called "room and power system" is predominant. A group of capitalists build a weaving shed, with all the equipment necessary for preparing and weaving the yarn, and then lease the plant in whole or in part. Sections, partitioned off so as to hold from fifty to two thousand looms each, are leased to different parties, the power being supplied by the syndicate. To quote from Mr. Whittam, there are three different plans on which leases are made.[1] "First. The tenant rents room and power only, installing his own looms. For this he will pay from $9.15 to $10.80 per loom per year. Second. Renting room and loom only will cost from $8.40 to $10.80 a year per loom.[2] Third. Renting room, loom, and power involves a rental ranging between $13.20 and $16.80 per loom a year." The persons leasing these establishments are weavers who begin on a small scale and gradually expand their business. They fill small orders for fancy goods, and in this way the workmen with skill and managerial ability have an opportunity to utilize both.

In 1911 only four of the one hundred and nine manufacturers in Nelson[3] were established in buildings not shared by others. In several instances only two weavers were located in a single factory, but other factories contained a larger number. A few

---

[1] W. Whittam, Jr., *Report on England's Cotton Industry*, p. 14.
[2] This form is not common.
[3] Worrall's *Directory*.

manufacturers had looms in two or more sheds. In Colne forty-two manufacturers each used part of a building, and fourteen had entire factories. This system has assisted the expansion of the industry in that corner of Lancashire.

The factory system developed more slowly in Germany than in England or the United States. Spinning, in part at least, had been brought under the factory system before 1860, but the mills were small; the average size of spinning mills in Saxony in 1861, according to Martin,[1] was only 4,263 spindles. During the rapid industrial expansion which has taken place since the close of the Franco-Prussian War, the cotton manufacturing industry has been in the front rank, and with this progress the size of the mills has increased. In 1892 Martin stated the average size of the spinning mills in the Empire to be 25,000 spindles, although there were several larger factories.[2]

At the end of 1908, by Rieger's list,[3] there were 396 mills in Germany which were spinning cotton yarn, and the average number of spindles per mill was 26,235. Separating the mills into groups classified according to size, two had more than 200,000 spindles; two 150,000 to 200,000; seven 100,000 to 150,000; forty-three 50,000 to 100,000; two hundred and twelve 1,000 to 10,000; and nineteen less than 1,000 spindles each. The number of large mills has increased since 1898, when there were only seven with more than 100,000 spindles and twenty-three with from 50,000 to 100,000 spindles;[4] but the survival of so many small mills is significant.

In the weaving branch of the German cotton industry, the domestic system, which was extensive in 1860, did not disappear until the end of the nineteenth century, and small mills are still numerous. Although in 1908 seven mills had more than 2,000 looms[5] and thirty-eight 1,000 to 2,000 looms each, two hundred

---

[1] R. Martin, "Der wirtschaftliche Aufschwung der Baumwollspinnerei im Koenigreiche Sachsen," *Jahrbuch für Gesetzgebung*, 1893, p. 650.

[2] *Ibid.*, p. 672.

[3] Wm. Rieger, *Verzeichnis der im Deutschen Reiche auf Baumwolle laufenden Spindeln und Webstühle*, ed. 1909.

[4] A. Oppel, *Die Baumwolle*, p. 666.

[5] Wm. Rieger, *Verzeichnis*.

and nineteen had each only 100 looms or less, and the average for the 811 weaving mills for which Rieger gives details was 321 looms per mill.[1]

The small cotton mills persist because of the lower scale of remuneration to labor and because of their adaptability to the production of special kinds of goods. It is a characteristic which is manifested by nearly all the German industries. Small cotton mills have been located in country villages to utilize the labor there available, and in rural spots where water-power was to be had. But even in the larger cities there are small concerns which have to rely upon steam power.

In spinning it is solely the low wages and salaries that make possible the continuation of small scale production. But in weaving, although the labor factor is of fundamental importance, the small weaver has an advantage in that he can execute little orders for fabrics of unique design. In a large weaving mill, even in Germany, there must be more or less standardization, but by the production of novelties and the acceptance of small orders the little mill is able to maintain itself.

For France no satisfactory statistics as to the size of the mills are available. The Census does not supply them and there is no textile directory which gives the desired details. At the present time, I am informed by the Secretary of the Spinners' Association, there are about 2,500,000 spindles in the 60 spinning mills of the "Department du Nord." The average for that section, therefore, where the largest mills are located, is about 41,700 spindles per mill. All these factories are exclusively for spinning.

In the "Region de l'Est" in 1903 the average number of spindles per factory in all mills where cotton was spun was 32,400.[2] They were distributed as follows: — fourteen mills with less than 10,000 spindles each; twenty-eight 10,000 to 30,000 spindles each; sixteen 30,000 to 50,000 spindles each; seven 50,000 to 90,000 spindles each; and three over 90,000

---

[1] The room and power system appears in several districts at the present time.

[2] *Enquête sur L'Etat de l'Industrie Textile*, vol. iv, p. 270.

spindles each.   In the Rouen district there are seventy spinning mills and the average size is 20,000 spindles each.[1]

The factory system did not predominate in the French weaving industry till after 1880, and the domestic system is hardly extinct at the present time.   In the district around Amiens about two thousand hand loom weavers are still employed in their homes for weaving Utrecht velvet, a fabric containing both cotton and wool.   In the Vosges there are about twenty commission weavers,[2] with little mills where they fill orders received from the larger manufacturers.   The cutting of velveteen is another important domestic industry at Amiens.   About thirty merchants in that city purchase velveteen and corduroy and put it out to be cut.

The size of the weaving mills in France is probably not much greater than in Germany.   In the " Region de l'Est " in 1903 [3] fourteen cotton mills had not over 100 looms each; forty-seven 100 to 300 looms each; thirty-six 300 to 600 looms each; eleven 600 to 900 looms each; and twelve over 900 looms each.   Since that date the average size has become somewhat greater.   The largest factory in that section, it may be added, has at the present time 155,600 spindles and 2,838 looms.   In the Rouen district there are sixty weaving mills, which average 400 looms per establishment.[4]

The sixty-eight spinning companies in Switzerland average 22,000 spindles each; the fifty-three gray cloth weaving companies 320 looms each; and the thirty colored cloth weaving companies 200 looms each.[5]   The typical Swiss mill has 30,000 spindles, the smallest 6,000, the largest 100,000 spindles.[6]   Hand loom weaving in the homes is still important in Switzerland.[7]   Small establishments are not uncommon, finally, in Italy and

[1] *U. S. Daily Consular Reports*, October 27, 1911, p. 478.

[2] A very small number of commission weavers are to be found in England.

[3] P. Mairet, *La Crise de l'Industrie Cotonnière*, p. 33.

[4] *U. S. Daily Consular Reports*, October 27, 1911, p. 479.

[5] S. L. Besso, *Cotton Industry in Switzerland and Italy*, p. 4.   This is not the average per factory, since several companies own two or more mills.

[6] *Ibid.*, p. 13.

[7] *Ibid.*, p. 40.

Bohemia,[1] and in Belgium in 1905 over one-fourth of the persons employed in the weaving of cotton cloth worked at home.[2]

In all the branches of cotton manufacturing the United States stands in the forefront so far as large scale production is concerned. The pressure to reduce the labor cost, the stimulus which has resulted from a high wage level, has necessitated these improvements in organization. This difference in the size of the establishments is of significance in determining the relative strength of the industry in the various countries and the ability to meet foreign competition. There may be more chance for the countries now backward to improve their organization and thus use their other resources to greater advantage. But at the present time the country which has the more highly developed organization realizes economies that appreciably affect the comparative costs of manufacturing cotton.

Specialization

Specialization in the manufacture of cotton has made greater progress in England than in any other country. The first striking contrast is the separation of spinning and weaving. In the table previously given [3] it is shown that, in 1911, 595 Lancashire [4] mills were engaged in spinning only and contained 79.5 per cent of the spindles; 859 mills, secondly, were for weaving only and in them were located 66.3 per cent of all the looms. Thus only 20.5 per cent of the spindles and 33.7 per cent of the looms were located in mills where cotton was both spun and woven.

The separation of spinning and weaving facilitates a narrower specialization in the former branch. Scores of factories have only mule spindles and at least forty spin only ring yarn. Numerous English mills spin as many counts as the average American mill. Others confine themselves to a narrow range,

---

[1] W. A. G. Clark, *Cotton Fabrics in Middle Europe*, p. 125.

[2] *La Belgique, 1830–1905*, pp. 600–601.

[3] See *ante*, p. 321.

[4] Lancashire is here used in the sense of the Lancashire district, including the adjoining parts of Cheshire and Derbyshire.

such as 30's to 42's, or 50's to 70's. A smaller number have a still more limited scope, producing only 36's, 42's weft, or some other single number. In all the English spinning mills the machines are changed from one count to another less frequently than in the factories of other countries. An English weaving mill, on the contrary, produces as great a variety of fabrics as are turned out by any of the American mills.[1] In fact it is doubtful if any of the former are so highly specialized as some of the Fall River print cloth mills or southern mills which manufacture goods for the export trade.

The separation of spinning and weaving in Lancashire is made possible by the dense localization of the industry and encouraged by the economies of management which can be realized. The nature of the market, however, is the fundamental factor, since the economies in manufacturing are at least partially counterbalanced by the costs of selling the yarn. England exports large quantities of yarn; hence the spinner sells indifferently to domestic or foreign customers and therefore has more freedom than if dependent on the former alone. The broad market for standard products steadies the demand, and thereby enables a spinner to restrict his production to a few counts. The English cloth manufacturers rely upon the foreign outlet to an even greater extent. But the multiplicity of finishes and designs renders the cloth market less uniform, less standardized, and to a certain degree less stable than the yarn market. The demand for cloth is so varied, and the English manufacturers cater to orders from so many diverse sources that the majority use a larger number of counts of yarn than could economically be spun in a single mill.

The combined spinning and weaving companies operate both spindles and looms either because of their organization prior to the opening of the period of high specialization or because of the nature of their product. The producers of goods which bear renowned trade marks, such as Dacca calicoes or Horrockses' sheetings, and several firms which are interested pri-

---

[1] A Burnley mill of 2,300 looms, for example, had in its storehouse in 1910 about 20,000 harnesses for a great variety of patterns.

marily in the home trade insure the maintenance of quality by spinning the yarn which they weave.

Doubling is another process which is more or less specialized in England. As far as could be ascertained from the 1911 textile directory for the Lancashire district, doubling spindles were located in sixty-nine spinning mills, twenty-three spinning-weaving mills, a half dozen weaving mills, and in ninety-two independent doubling mills. The demand for doubled yarn requires many counts, and shifts from one to another. The doubler who purchases yarn or doubles on commission can accept any order, but the spinner-doubler ordinarily accepts orders only for those counts which he spins. The volume of trade is sufficiently great to warrant the establishment of the independent doubling plants, which are more easily adjusted to fluctuating requirements. In addition to these mills, there were also five sizers, and fourteen beamers, reelers, or winders, who were independent of other establishments.

In England printing, dyeing, and bleaching are seldom united with spinning or weaving. A few manufacturers bleach, dye, or print their cloth, and some of the colored goods makers dye the yarn which they use. But the bulk of the converting is in the hands of specialists, working on commission. There are also special finishing plants, where the cloth is given its final touches.

Many of the new designs are brought from Paris, but there are special designers in Manchester, and firms whose sole business is the engraving of copper rollers for printing. Some calico printers rely entirely upon the outside engravers, and all employ them for part of their work since the trade is so fluctuating in volume that it does not pay a printer to maintain a force of engravers large enough to meet the needs of the most pressing moments. Jacquard cards are sometimes prepared in the Jacquard weaving mills, but other weavers of Jacquard fabrics employ the job card-punching firms in Manchester and Maccles-field. The cutting of the pile of corduroys and velvets is still another special branch,[1] although of minor importance. Finally,

---

[1] This is likewise done on commission for the most part. — *Census of Production*, 1907, part iii, p. 20.

the packing of the goods is partly in the hands of professional packers in Manchester. This dense network of specialists in the Lancashire trade is a development which can hardly be matched elsewhere in the industrial world.

In no respect is the difference between England and Germany more marked than in specialization. In 1908, Rieger's list showed that 23.7 per cent of the cotton manufacturing firms, operating 59.6 per cent of the spindles, were spinners only; 14.6 per cent, operating 40.4 per cent of the spindles and 39.5 per cent of the looms, were both spinners and weavers; and 61.7 per cent, operating 60.5 per cent of the looms were weavers only.[1] The combination of spinning and weaving was most common in Alsace, where 62.5 per cent of the spindles and 68 per cent of the looms were in " Spinn-Webereien," in contrast to 46.5 per cent of the spindles and 47.5 per cent of the looms in Bavaria, 31 per cent of the spindles and 38.3 per cent of the looms in the Rhein Province and Westphalia, and 9.3 per cent of the spindles and 13.5 per cent of the looms in the " Spinn-Webereien " of Saxony. Separate spinning mills are supported in Saxony by the market for yarn afforded by the knitting industry. And the great diversity in the product of the weavers is not favorable to a combination of processes. The small colored goods mills (Buntwebereien), so numerous in Saxony, use many kinds of yarn and consequently it is more economical for them not to undertake spinning.

None of the mills in Germany restrict themselves to a narrow field. One Alsatian mill, for example, spins from 8's to 200's; another mill, in a different section, from 20's to 200's; and the majority from 6's to 32's, 4's to 44's, 8's to 38's, or a similar range.[2] The weaving mills operate between limits equally broad.

[1] This proportion of combined spinning and weaving mills has increased since 1875, when 98 per cent of the spindles and looms were in establishments in which only a single branch was carried on.—K. Kuntze, "Die Baumwollindustrie," *Handbuch der Wirtschaftskunde Deutschlands*, vol. iii, pp. 583, 585.

[2] W. Rieger, *Verzeichnis*. 6's to 32's, for example, is a wide range in comparison with the English practice although at first thought it seems narrow. It includes both coarse and medium counts.

Doubling is more rarely separated from spinning in Germany than in England. In 1909 seventy-nine per cent of the doubling spindles were in spinning mills.[1] A few weaving mills have their own doubling equipment, but their spindles constitute only a small percentage of the total.

Converting is principally in the hands of independent works in Germany. There is one mill in M. Gladbach which spins, weaves, and prints, another in Reutlingen, three in Mülhausen, and a few elsewhere. In a small number weaving and converting are united. The large colored goods mills (Buntwebereien), as in America, ordinarily have their own dye-houses. But the greater part of the yarn and cloth is dyed, printed, or bleached in separate establishments.

There are specialists for the minor details in Germany, also, but they are relatively less numerous than in England. Four engraving firms in Mülhausen prepare all of the rollers for the Alsatian print works. Elsewhere in Germany there are occasional engraving firms, but the printers generally have their own engraving department. Other specialists are comparatively unimportant.

In the north of France spinning and weaving are completely divorced, since the district is primarily a spinning centre. In the Vosges nearly one hundred small weaving mills are to be found, and about twenty mills which are confined to spinning. Yet combined spinning and weaving mills are twice as numerous as the " pure " spinning mills. In Normandy, although the combined concerns are the largest, a majority of the spindles are in " pure " spinning mills.

The range of counts is as wide in a French factory as in a German mill. The bulk of the doubling spindles are in spinning mills, and there are probably not more than a dozen independent doublers in France. Little French cloth, finally, is converted in the mill where woven.

/Designing, identified with Paris, is a French specialty of great renown. Artist designers are numerous in Paris, and with them

---

[1] *Verzeichnis der Baumwoll-Spinnereien in Deutschland*, etc., Bremer Baumwoll-Börse, 1909.

originate the greater part of the new designs employed by cotton manufacturers in Europe and America. Their preëminence, of long duration, is to be attributed to the artistic nature of the French [1] and the environment in which the designers work. In other countries schools of design have been established; yet none of their products rival the Parisian. French designers have been transplanted, to Manchester for example, but their creative aptitude languished in the foreign environment. The foreigners are still tributary to the Parisian designers.

The statements of the conditions in Germany and France indicate, in a general way, the contrast between the English and Continental organization.

European mills accept smaller orders than our American manufacturers. The contrast in this respect is greatest in the orders for converted fabrics and goods of complex design. In England a manufacturer seldom accepts an order for fancy striped goods of less than 4,000 yards, but an order for 500 yards is occasionally placed. The rate charged for dyeing and printing diminishes as the size of the order increases, but lots of 110 and 150 yards are frequently dyed. The printers will accept orders for 300 yards or less if the customer is willing to pay the extra cost, but 10,000 yards is generally the minimum.

The German weaver of fancy colored goods will accept an order of 200 yards, and some printers will set up their machines for an order of 40 yards if a profitable customer requests it. For such tiny orders, however, an extra charge is levied, and the minimum order is generally 400 to 600 yards. Here are some orders, for illustration, taken from the books of a company which specializes in fancy prints. One order was for 1,200 yards of a six-color design printed with six variations of color effects; another for 1,000 yards of an eight-color design with five variations; and a third for 28,000 yards of a two-color design with two different color effects. The more elaborate patterns are usually printed in smaller lots, on fine cloth. They can bear

---

[1] This artistic nature must be considered a national characteristic, and as such could be accounted for only by a prolonged study of the history of the French people.

a higher charge, but under American conditions the extra cost would be prohibitive. American manufacturers economize in large scale production by distributing their indirect costs over a big product. The greater standardization of product and the larger orders involve less frequent changes of gearing and fewer readjustments of the machines.

The English are supreme in two lines, the coarsest goods and the finest. As competition has become more severe, the English cotton manufacturers have proceeded to produce finer and finer yarns and cloth. In that way they have utilized their advantages in climate and skilled labor. They have also built up a large export trade in heavily sized goods, which find a market in Asia and, to a less extent, in Africa and South America, where there is a demand for cheap cloth of low quality. They have sought to satisfy the tastes of the wealthy Europeans and Americans by improving the quality of their product, and to meet the demands of the Asiatic of small means by lowering the quality. At the same time their trade in the goods of ordinary grade has not declined. The German manufacturers produce goods which are, for the most part, of coarse and medium grade. Their lower wages and small mills have given them an advantage in novelties and imitation fabrics. The French manufacturers turn out more fine goods than are produced in any other Continental country, yet coarse and medium grades are predominant. Elsewhere on the Continent the product consists mainly of coarse fabrics. In brief, the English are the leaders of the cotton manufacturing world in specialization, particularly in spinning, but the American manufacturers excel in large scale production and standardization.

Specialization has been made possible in England by the very growth of the industry and its concentration. Nevertheless specialization reacts and fosters further expansion. Although an acquired and not a natural characteristic, it is none the less potent in strengthening the English manufacturers' hold upon foreign markets.

CHAPTER XIX

COMBINATIONS

JUST as there are associations and combinations of various sorts in the American cotton manufacturing industry, similarly in Europe the manufacturers have found it expedient to harmonize their efforts for certain purposes. With the rise of labor unions among the English cotton mill operatives in the 'fifties and subsequent years, there was a corresponding development of masters' associations. At first these associations were local in scope, but they were eventually united to form large federations.

One of the earliest federations was the United Cotton Spinners' Association, which in 1892 became the Federation of Master Cotton Spinners' Associations.[1] At that date its membership included firms in seven districts, owning 16,896,486 spindles, while sixteen years later, in 1907, its members owned 33,000,000 spindles in twelve districts and in 1910 controlled 40,000,000 spindles. The old association was one of individual members, its successor a federation of local associations. The function of this association is to promote the interests of the trade in general and to secure united action in labor disputes. Unlike its predecessor, the federation takes cognizance of labor troubles, and is a party to the Brooklands Agreement. It is also active in other directions, such as the leading of the short time movement during the speculations of 1904, and again in 1910.

The North and North-East Lancashire Cotton Spinners' and Manufacturers' Association, formed in 1872, is a federation of the local associations of employers in Blackburn, Preston, and Burnley.[2] In 1894 about two-thirds of the employers in

[1] *Report of 4th International Congress of Master Cotton Spinners' and Manufacturers' Associations*, held at Vienna, 1907, pp. 190–192. This report is referred to in the following pages as the *Report of Vienna Congress*, and the report of the meeting at Milan in 1909 as the *Report of Milan Congress*.

[2] British *Parliamentary Papers*, Drage Labor Commission, Final Report, 1894, p. 251.

those districts were affiliated, and the proportion has since then been increased. Its prime object is to counterbalance the power of the labor unions. The spinners' and the manufacturers' (weavers') associations do not coöperate, but act independently.[1]

In England there are no associations which correspond to the National Association of Cotton Manufacturers in the United States. But the English employers necessarily have stronger organizations for negotiating with the powerful labor unions, the thorough-going organization of both sides insuring the maintenance of wage agreements and lists. The Arkwright Club has no counterpart in England, although some of its functions are performed by the various organizations in that country.

A unique but important society in England is the British Cotton Growing Association, which was organized in 1902 for the purpose of promoting the cultivation of cotton in the British colonies wherever suitable conditions could be found. The undertaking was initiated mainly because of the rising prices of cotton, and by this means the English cotton manufacturers hoped to relieve themselves from almost absolute dependency upon the supply of raw cotton from the United States. The sufferings of the cotton famine during the American Civil War have been recalled to emphasize the dangers of dependence upon a single source of supply. Another stimulus has been the spirit of imperial federation, the desire to bring into closer touch with each other the different parts of the British Empire. The greater significance of the cotton growing association, however, lies in the diversity of the sources whence support has been given. It is a united attempt by all interested parties, the spinners, weavers, and finishers, the laborers, and the merchants, to safeguard the welfare of the industry, thus recognizing the interdependence of the various interests.

In Germany, also, we find a series of associations. The Verein Süddeutscher Baumwoll-Industrieller was formed in 1867. " Its sphere covers the whole of South Germany, with the exception of Alsace Lorraine; it includes Bavaria, with the Rhine Palatine, Württemberg, Baden, and Hohenzollern.

---

[1] *Report of Vienna Congress*, p. 194.

Ninety-four firms are members of the association (1907), of which forty-one belong to Bavaria, thirty-eight to Württemberg, and nineteen to Baden."[1] Of these ninety-four firms, thirty-one were spinning mills, thirty-three spinning and weaving mills, twenty-one weaving mills, four doubling and sewing cotton establishments, three bleacheries and print works, one wadding manufacturing establishment, and one establishment making paper tubes. In 1906 the members operated 2,644,562 spindles and 45,595 looms, and employed 50,000 persons. " The object of the association," to quote once more from the report of the Fourth International Congress of Master Cotton Spinners' and Weavers' Associations, "is the safeguarding of the economic interests of the cotton industry of South Germany. The principal activity of the Association extends to the German tariff and commercial policies in general. The Association acts both independently and conjointly with other associations, such as the German Master Cotton Spinners' Association, and the Central Federation of German Industries."[2]

A similar organization is Die Vereinigung Sächischer Spinnerei-Besitzer of Chemnitz.[3] This association was formed in 1836 and incorporated in 1896. Its fifty-five members in 1907 controlled 1,582,200 spindles including doubling spindles. Until 1899, membership was confined to firms which carried on both spinning and weaving, but at that date membership was opened to cotton spinners and doublers in Saxony. Two years later, two spinning mills in Saxony, two in Silesia, one in Austria, and the Association of Union Spinners in Crimmitschau were affiliated. Its purpose is similar to that of the South German Association. In addition, for the information of its members, it compiles monthly statistics of stocks on hand, orders, and production, and by an arrangement with the spinners' association of Rhineland and Westphalia, the two associations exchange reports. A uniform set of instructions for mill workers has been introduced, uniform conditions of payment established, and united action in labor disputes secured.

[1] *Report of Vienna Congress*, p. 195.   [2] *Ibid.*, p. 196.
[3] *Ibid.*, p. 200.

Another of these organizations is the Verband Rheinisch-Westfälischer Baumwollspinner,[1] which was founded in 1887. In 1909 it had sixty-eight members controlling 1,980,910 spindles and 10,032 looms. Seventy-one of the one hundred and fifty-two members of the Elsass-Lothringisches Industrielles Syndicat in 1909 were engaged in the manufacture of cotton goods.[2]

The objects of all of these German associations are very similar. At first they were especially interested in influencing tariff legislation. More recently they have undertaken to promote their common interests by securing greater uniformity of contracts, by collecting trade statistics, and by acting together in dealing with their employees. Lochmüller summarises the significance of these associations when he says[3] that, "The fundamental principle of all these combinations has been united action in respect to market conditions, the recognition of the solidarity of interests."

In France there are two federations and nine local associations. The local associations are Le Syndicat Cotonnier de l'Est, Le Syndicat Normand de la Filature de Coton, Le Syndicat Normand de la Tissage de Coton, Le Groupe Cotonnier du Nord, Le Syndicat Patronal des Industries Textiles de Mont-beliard, Le Union de l'Industrie Cotonnière de Roanne, Le Syndicat des Industries Textiles de Laval du Départment de La Mayenne, Le Syndicat des Filateurs et Rétordeurs de Coton de Lille, and Le Syndicat Picard des Industries Textiles. The purposes of these local associations correspond to the objects for which the two federations strive.

L'Union des Syndicats Patronaux des Industries Textiles follows labor legislation,[4] but its membership is not confined to cotton manufacturers. It is a federation of fifty-six textile "Syndicats," comprising (in 1904) 2,224 of the most important textile manufacturing establishments in France.[5]

---

[1] *Report of Milan Congress*, p. 267.
[2] *Ibid.*, p. 263.
[3] W. Lochmüller, *Die Baumwoll-industrie in Deutschland*, p. 66.
[4] *Report of Vienna Congress*, p. 212.
[5] *Enquête sur l'Etat de l'Industrie Textile*, vol. i, p. 12.

The other federation is Le Syndicat General de l'Industrie Cotonnière Française. It was formed in 1901 at a time of depression, and in 1907 included all of the local associations except the Syndicat de Roanne.[1] It attempts to promote the general interests of the cotton manufacturers, as is shown by the following quotation from its report to the Vienna Congress. " Its principal departments are statistics of purchases, sales, and production, and it proposes the bringing about of an understanding between the different united groups on the subject of the claims which the French cotton industry believes itself legitimately entitled to put forward to the public authorities, especially with respect to custom-house tariffs, commercial agreements, and so forth. It is even its duty to invite such demands on the part of the affiliated associations or syndicates, and to centralize them, in order to succeed in bringing about for the benefit of its members a movement which would be all the more efficacious through not being scattered."

In the other European countries in which cotton is manufactured similar associations exist. In Austria there is the Association of the Cotton Industry of Austria, the Association of Master Cotton Spinners of Austria, the Association of Master Cotton Manufacturers of Austria, and the Association of Master Calico Printers of Austria.[2] In Italy the Cotton Manufacturers' Association, founded in 1894, now includes practically all of the cotton manufacturers in the kingdom.[3] In Switzerland the Master Cotton Spinners', Doublers', and Weavers' Association had in 1906 one hundred and nineteen members, who employed 1,467,752 spindles and 18,259 looms.[4] In Belgium there is the Belgian Master Cotton Spinners' Association.[5] Throughout these associations a similarity of purpose is found.

Not only have local associations and national federations arisen in all the cotton manufacturing countries of the western world, but in 1904 an international association was formed.[6] The immediate cause of its formation was the depression result-

[1] *Report of Vienna Congress*, p. 241.
[2] *Ibid.*, p. 216.
[3] *Ibid.*, p. 221.
[4] *Ibid.*, p. 222.
[5] *Ibid.*, p. 222.
[6] *Ibid.*, p. 193.

ing from the speculative dealings and the attempted corner of the cotton market in that year. Looked at from a broader point of view, it was a recognition of the interdependence of cotton manufacturing interests in all parts of the world. Meetings have been held annually, and the association has steadily increased in strength. Among other things, it has sought to encourage the widening of the cotton producing area in countries other than the United States.[1] It has discussed uniform cotton, yarn, and cloth contracts, has undertaken to bring about improvements in the baling and shipping of American cotton, and, perhaps most important of all, has compiled statistics of the quantity of cotton in the hands of spinners, the annual consumption of cotton, and the increase in the number of spindles. These statistics have been based upon returns from the members of the association in the different countries, and have been confidential. From them the spinners could judge to better advantage the probable demand and supply when the crop reports of the United States Census and of the financial papers were issued. They could thus to some extent guard against speculative manipulations of the price of their raw material.

The International Federation has been active in the promotion of an international " short-time " policy. Because of the rapid augmentation of the world's spindleage, particularly in England, from 1900 to 1907, the manufacturing capacity temporarily outstripped the supply of raw material. To the depressing influence of this maladjustment were added the effects of general business inactivity and two successive short crops of cotton. It was this last factor which most affected the cotton manufacturing industry. The recent improvements in technique would very likely have permitted a sufficient reduction in the price of cloth to enable the manufacturers to find an ade-

---

[1] For decades efforts have been exerted in this direction. At the present time there are many optimists in Europe who believe that they are about to realize their hopes. Mention should also be made of the experiments with other fibres which might be substituted for cotton. The most promising of these is kapok, a fibre growing wild in Africa and South America. Herr Stark of Chemnitz, Germany, has recently patented a process for manufacturing cloth from kapok. The fabric is somewhat harder than cotton and takes a brilliant shade when dyed.

quate market for their product, had the raw cotton supply been larger. The problem which has arisen from this source has been one of excess capacity rather than overproduction. Nevertheless it had to be met in the same way, by operating the mills at less than full speed, and the International Federation has encouraged that policy.

Suggestions concerning the restriction in output may be observed in years of crop shortage, but when it comes to a restriction of mill building, the root of the difficulty, it is doubtful if the Federation has great influence. Under present conditions an agreement to be truly effective over a period of years seems to be impossible of realization. The Federation, by means of an educative policy, can merely indicate the danger involved in reckless mill building. Nevertheless this international association, although it has not gained wide support in the United States, is a beginning of united action among the cotton manufacturers in different countries.

Amalgamations

The amalgamations which have been formed in the English cotton manufacturing industry are, — J. & P. Coats, the English Sewing Cotton Company, the Fine Cotton Spinners' and Doublers' Association, the Bleachers' Association, the Calico Printers' Association, and the British Cotton and Wool Dyers' Association.[1]

The Coats firm was founded early in the nineteenth century.[2] From small beginnings its business steadily expanded, and in 1890 the company of J. & P. Coats was incorporated. In 1895 the firm of Kerr & Co., of Paisley, was bought up, and in 1896, its chief rivals, Clarke & Co., of Paisley, James Chadwick & Co., of Bolton, and Jonas Brook & Co., of Meltham, amalgamated with the Coats company. These four firms had previously acted together through a central agency which marketed all their

---

[1] The amalgamations in the English cotton industry have been described at length by H. W. Macrosty in his *Trust Movement in British Industry.* On that authority many of the following statements are based.

[2] H. W. Macrosty, *Trust Movement in British Industry*, pp. 126, 127.

products, but a closer organization was desired; hence the amalgamation.   At the time of combination the properties owned by the constituent members included sixteen factories and six branches.   Among the factories were mills in the United States, Canada, and Russia.   Since that time mills have also been built in other European countries,[1] a coal mine purchased, and large blocks of stock in other companies acquired.   Their holdings of stock are especially large in the Fine Cotton Spinners' and Doublers' Association, and in the English Sewing Cotton Company.   Their interest in the former gave them control over their yarn supply, and their interest in the latter secured the coöperation of a competitor.

The Coats company was conservatively capitalized, and has been carefully organized and well managed.   The Central Thread Agency, which had existed before the amalgamation, continued to sell the products, and thus effect economies in marketing.   The investments in other concerns have paid well.   In fact a member of the firm stated in 1899 that " by far the larger part of the company's profits was derived from shares in foreign manufacturing companies, and not from mills in the United Kingdom." [2]   Thus they had taken advantage of the protective tariffs in foreign countries.   The company has accumulated a large reserve, improved its equipment, and in the twelve years ending in 1908, had averaged an annual dividend on its ordinary shares of twenty-seven per cent.   The London *Economist* said of this company in 1907, "As it is the foremost of industrial companies in the country, so it is one of the best managed.   The policy of the directors has always been conservative in the extreme, in the way of building up large reserves against all possible contingencies, and in keeping machinery and so forth thoroughly efficient and well up to modern requirements." [3]

Closely connected with the Coats combination and a direct result of its successful formation is the English Sewing Cotton

---

[1] *Economist*, November, 1908, p. 926.
[2] Quoted by Macrosty, *op. cit.*, p. 128.
[3] *Economist*, November 2, 1907, p. 1865.

Company.[1]   After the largest firms in the cotton thread industry
had been amalgamated by Coats, about twenty concerns were
left in the field.   In 1897 fourteen of these combined to form the
English Sewing Cotton Company.   Later two more firms were
added.   The combination was not a complete amalgamation
as each of the constituents retained part of its independence,
the management not being entirely concentrated in the central
company.   The company was badly organized, poorly managed,
and heavily overcapitalized.   In order to secure better results
the management was reorganized in 1902, with more centralized
authority, and in 1904 three of the constituent firms were sold.
The English Sewing Cotton Company has never paid nearly
as high dividends as the Coats Company, although it has received
large returns on its investment in the American Thread Company.

From the first the Coats company took an interest in the
English Sewing Cotton Company and held 200,000 of the ordinary shares.   After the formation of the American Thread
Company in 1898, under the auspices of the English Sewing
Cotton Company, the three combinations with allied interests
dominated the world's market for sewing cotton.   Friction
arose, however, between the two English combinations over
their respective rights, and for the sake of harmony the English
Sewing Cotton Company converted a mill which it owned in
Spain into a plant to spin yarn for piece goods, and in 1900 transferred its foreign sales business to the Central Thread Agency,
which, it will be recalled, is a Coats subsidiary company.   Later
the English Sewing Cotton Company turned over the selling
of its domestic product to the Central Thread Agency.   Thus,
through inter-holdings of stock, agreements, and this central
selling office, the English sewing cotton business is monopolized,
and the world's trade in this product controlled.

The success of the Coats amalgamation also encouraged the
formation of the Fine Cotton Spinners' and Doublers' Association.   This was a combination, formed in 1898, of thirty-one
firms [2] engaged in spinning Sea Island Cotton and producing the

---

[1] H. W. Macrosty, *op. cit.*, pp. 129–133.
[2] *Ibid.*, pp. 137–140.

finest yarn in England. Within the next three years ten more British firms were absorbed, and a controlling interest was secured in their chief French competitor. A colliery also was purchased in 1900, and in 1911 an American plantation, where they could grow extra stapled cotton, was acquired.[1] Although the combination has a monopoly in the spinning of Sea Island cotton, it has to meet the competition of the spinners of Egyptian cotton. Its chief advantage lies in the ownership of certain brands or trade marks of fine cotton yarns, with long established reputation, a very important factor in the fine yarn market. The association was well organized and has been well managed. Consequently it has paid good dividends.

Previous to 1900 voluntary associations had existed among the bleachers for the regulation of prices. But with hopes of securing a monopoly, fifty-three firms engaged in this business were combined to form the Bleachers' Association.[2] Five more firms were later added. In 1910 about sixty-five per cent of the Lancashire bleaching trade, measured both by number of firms and by quantity of output, was in the hands of the association. Each member continued to manage his own business, but subject to the central office in the regulation of charges and expenditures. The combination has had an advantage in that it controlled a large part of the available water supply, an asset so important in bleaching. But too much water was put into the stock; the association was overcapitalized.

Of all the amalgamations in the English cotton industry, the Calico Printers' Association, organized in 1899,[3] has been the least successful. The participants were influenced more by the mania for combination than by a careful consideration of the obstacles to be encountered. At the outset it was made up of forty-six print works and thirteen merchant firms, to which were later added five printing plants, a merchant house, a finishing plant, a colliery, and a large establishment in France. Fif-

---

[1] This extreme integration is warranted only by the recurring difficulties in securing the requisite supplies of long stapled cotton for spinning super-fine yarns.

[2] H. W. Macrosty, *op. cit.*, pp. 141–144.

[3] *Ibid.*, pp. 144–153.

teen small plants have been closed. The system of organization was very inadequate. At first the plants were not specialized and continued to compete with each other. Lack of centralized authority was also displayed in such matters as the duplication of purchasing departments. These faults were partially remedied by the reorganizations of 1902 and 1907, but it is said that the various departments are not yet sufficiently in touch with each other. Another drawback has been the combination of commission and independent printing, *i. e.* the printing of cloth for others and at the same time for themselves. Merchants have naturally preferred to have their cloth printed, as far as possible, by concerns which did only a commission business, rather than by the combination which was also a competitor in the market for prints. The combination in 1907 even extended its business to weaving,[1] to supply its own gray cloth, but the financial depression gave at least a temporary check to this venture.

While at the time of its formation the Printers' Association controlled eighty-five per cent of the printing trade, now, as a result of the closing of some of its works, its price policy, and the preference shown to independents by the merchants, its proportionate share is only about fifty per cent. Finally, in addition to the other difficulties, the capitalization was excessive, several plants having been purchased at valuations far above their market rate. As might have been expected, the financial results have not been satisfactory.

The last combination of this type is the British Cotton and Wool Dyers' Association,[2] which represents the amalgamation of forty-six firms. Since its formation in 1900, six more firms have been absorbed, and thirteen of its small plants closed. This association coöperates with the Bradford Dyers' Association (wool), and together they control eighty-five per cent of the trade in the two branches of the industry. The British Cotton and Wool Dyers' Association is overcapitalized and has not been successful financially. Its members are widely scattered

---

[1] *Economist*, Sept. 21, 1907, p. 1582.
[2] H. W. Macrosty, *op. cit.*, pp. 163–168.

and from the outset many of them have been weak. The combination has practically a monopoly of mercerizing, and has an agreement with the Fine Spinners' Association whereby it does all their mercerizing work. But as with several of the other combinations, little benefit has accrued from what amounts to an increase in the scale of production.

In Great Britain, as in the United States, the amalgamations in the cotton manufacturing industry have been confined to special branches, and have not affected the ordinary spinning and weaving trade. As Macrosty has said, " It is in the derivative and not in the primary industries that we find combination attempted." [1] These English combinations were formed at about the same time as those in the American cotton manufacturing industry. With the exception of the Coats concern and the Fine Cotton Spinners' and Doublers' Association, there have been occasional reorganizations. As a rule, neither appreciable economies nor effective monopoly have been realized. This is similar to the experience of the duck and yarn combinations in the United States. The small units were fairly well managed, and in the case of the English combinations in the finishing processes it was found difficult to organize them effectively on the large scale demanded by their extent. A loose association of separate concerns secured as good results and avoided many of the difficulties. The necessity of including weak firms in a merger of these extensive trades impaired the efficiency of the combinations, and the overcapitalization is a burden which may yet prove too heavy. These experiences emphasize the difficulties which would attend any attempt at wholesale amalgamation of the spinning or weaving business in the English or American cotton manufacturing industry.

There have been sporadic instances of integration in the English cotton industry, but chiefly in connection with amalgamations. The most prominent are the Central Thread Agency of the thread combination, the inclusion of merchants in the Calico Printers' Association, and the acquisition of collieries by Coats, the Fine Cotton Spinners, and the Calico

---

[1] H. W. Macrosty, *op. cit.*, p. 121.

Printers. Rylands & Sons combine spinning, weaving, bleaching, dyeing, and finishing with the manufacture of clothing, corsets, oil cloth, etc., and carry on a large foreign and domestic wholesale trade. But that is a unique concern, and, taking the English industry as a whole, the movement has, up to the present time, been toward specialization rather than integration.

In the Continental countries, where a relatively smaller scale of production predominates, the associations meet all the needs of the situation. Through them the manufacturers can secure whatever harmony of action is necessary. When the units are comparatively small and widely scattered, competition does not reach the combining stage.

CHAPTER XX

KNIT GOODS

General Comparison

ALTHOUGH England is the original home of machine knitting, the English knit-goods industry is of smaller dimensions than the American. About one-half as many persons are employed in this industry in England and the value of the product, so far as census figures can be trusted, is much less than half. The value of the knit goods manufactured in the United Kingdom was stated at the Census of 1907 as follows: —

KNIT GOODS MANUFACTURED IN UNITED KINGDOM

Hose and half-hose	£4,326,000
Underwear	2,672,000
Sweaters, shawls, &c.	869,000
Gloves	256,000
Other	250,000
Total	£8,373,000 ($40,776,000)

The product of the American knitting mills in 1905, it will be remembered, was valued at $136,500,000, or over three times as high as that of England. One would naturally expect English prices to be lower and the product more nearly equal to the American output in quantity than value, yet our only test of the quantity relation does not support such a view. 14,167,000 dozen pairs of hose and half-hose, valued at approximately $21,000,000, were manufactured in the United Kingdom, and 44,144,000 dozen pairs, valued at $43,591,000, in the United States. Hence the average value per pair was actually fifty per cent less in America. Allowing for all discrepancies and inaccuracies, it seems indisputable that the American industry is much the larger. The German knitting industry is probably of greater magnitude [1] than the English, but, so far as one can

[1] Until the complete report of the German industrial census of 1907 is published it is not possible to secure data more recent than the antiquated statistics of 1895.

346

judge, does not surpass the American in volume. France [1] and the other continental countries are secondary to Germany in knit-goods production.

The knitting industry is less localized in America than in England. Nearly all of the English knitting mills are in the neighborhood of Nottingham and Leicester, cotton predominating in the former and woolen in the latter. Lee, the inventor of the knitting frame dwelt in this district, and here the industry has been concentrated from the outset.

Knit goods are manufactured in many parts of Germany, but Chemnitz, in Saxony, over-shadows all the other centres. Chemnitz owes its preëminence to events similar to those which brought about the growth of the industry in Philadelphia and the Mohawk Valley, and at Nottingham. From the twelfth to the eighteenth century Chemnitz [2] was a prosperous textile town as the result of market privileges, the bleaching monopoly, and the introduction of weaving. The production of knit goods in Chemnitz began with the arrival of French Protestant refugees in the eighteenth century, but it was not till after Cotton frames were brought thither from England about 1870 that Chemnitz really commenced to outstrip the other German districts. In the successful advance of Chemnitz, entrepreneur ability has been a factor of no mean importance.

The " Department de l'Aube," around Troyes, has the densest concentration of the hosiery manufacturing industry in France; yet knitting mills are located in numerous other departments. In the Vosges at St. Dié, for example, knitted underwear is produced. The reasons for the geographical distribution are acquired advantages and local enterprise, not the favors of nature. In general, we may conclude that American knit-goods manufacturers have as great advantage in location as any of their European competitors.

---

[1] It is stated that the value of the knit goods manufactured in France is $40,000,000 per year — cotton, $25,000,000; woolen, $12,500,000; silk, $2,000,000; linen, $500,000. — *U. S. Daily Consular Reports*, July 25, 1911, p. 371.

[2] *Festschrift zur 39 Hauptversammlung des Vereines Deutscher Ingenieurer*, 1898, pp. 23–28.

Although in England a few American circular automatic machines have been installed for manufacturing stockings, the Cotton (flat-bed) machine predominates.   But circular frames are more numerous than Cotton frames in the English underwear factories.   For making up, German, American, and English machines are employed.

In Saxony all types of knitting machines are in operation, including the Cotton, Paget, Terrot, and a few American seamless machines.   In the production of stockings the Cotton frame predominates, as in England; but in spite of the adaptability of that machine, it is not suited to the manufacturing of the finest and most elaborate articles.   For that purpose the Paget machine or a hand-frame is employed.   More underwear is knit upon circular frames than upon those of the other types; and the fabric for gloves is knit upon machines of special design.   The making-up machines, finally, are, for the most part, of German manufacture but copied from the American inventions.   The French knitting factories closely resemble the German mills in technical equipment and have more or less German and English machinery.

The methods employed in the European knitting industry are those requiring relatively more labor.   The American machines are more automatic and for their operation labor less in quantity and of little skill is employed.   The American technical equipment, however, is not inferior.

Scale of Production

It was not till after the middle of the nineteenth century that the factory system began to be applied in the English knit-goods industry.   In 1845 it was stated that knitting was "for the most part a domestic branch of industry" having "no connection with the factory system."[1]   Again, in 1882, Mr. Smith, United States Consul at Nottingham, reported in regard to the business of I. & R. Morley, the largest hosiery concern in the United Kingdom, that the "greater part of their hosiery was made by hand power.   Hand workers were employed

---

[1] *Journal of Franklin Institute*, 1845, p. 359.

by them in villages for twenty miles around Nottingham. Many of the hand machines were owned by the workers. Those machines were often worked on premises which did not belong to the parties employing them, largely in private houses occupied by the workers. This system prevailed to a large extent throughout the hosiery business in Great Britain." [1] Thus in 1882 the domestic system seems to have been predominant in the manufacture of knit goods in the British Isles. Twelve years later, in 1894, the Drage Labor Commission in its final report stated that the knit-goods trade was " unfortunately in the hands of middlemen, who brought out the work from the warehouses, giving the same out to the workmen." [2] Later in the same report the statement was made that " the introduction of machinery worked by steam power had almost entirely transformed the hosiery trade from a domestic to a factory industry." [3] These apparently conflicting statements, however, can be reconciled. The former refers to the finishing of the goods, the latter to knitting. This is shown by the Census of 1901 which commented on the replacement of the old hand-frames by power machines for knitting, but added that most of the goods were still finished by hand. [4]

According to the Census of 1907, 44,724 persons were employed in English knitting mills, and in addition 4,950 out-workers were reported. Of the latter, 543 were men, who were employed by the Nottingham manufacturers to knit cotton and lisle hose on hand-frames in their homes; there continues to be a demand for the elastic product of the hand-frames. The female out-workers were engaged in making up the knitted garments.

The number of knitting establishments (Haupt-Betriebe) in Saxony in 1907 was 16,531, employing 59,040 persons. [5] Of these establishments, 13,326 were " Allein-Betriebe," in which no assistants or wage workers were employed; 2,146 each had

---

[1] *U. S. Consular Reports*, 1882, no. 23, p. 77.
[2] Drage Labor Commission, *Final Report*, 1894, p. 239.
[3] *Ibid.*, p. 243.
[4] British *Parliamentary Papers*, 1904 (cd. 2174), p. 121.
[5] *Statistik des Deutschen Reiches*.

from two to five employees; 386 six to ten employees; 472 eleven to fifty employees; 167 fifty-one to two hundred employees; and only 34 employed more than two hundred persons. Exclusive of the " Allein-Betriebe," the average number of employees per establishment was fifteen.

In the promotion of new factory undertakings in Saxony, the machinery manufacturers have been active. Selecting a small manufacturer or a workman of promise, the machine-builder has often erected and equipped a factory for him, to be paid for in easy instalments. The room and power system, where several small entrepreneurs share a single building and rent space and power from the owners, is also prevalent in the Chemnitz district. The small scale manufacturers often accept orders from those who have larger factories for small quantities of goods of novel design which the latter cannot conveniently produce in their own works.

The putting out, or domestic, system persists in the Saxon knit-goods industry, but not to the same extent nor under the same form in all branches of the trade. Hose and half-hose are ordinarily manufactured in factories, because of the size and cost of the Cotton machines. What home work remains is almost entirely for making up. In the country villages the stockings are frequently given out by the manufacturers to be made up, although the entire process is more commonly completed in the factory. Some home work has continued, because in this way women who would not enter the factories could be employed. A single machine suffices for seaming an entire stocking, and no elaborate equipment is required by the home workers. The sewing machines, it may be added, are usually owned by the manufacturer who gives out the goods.

There are several large underwear factories in the Chemnitz district, but every manufacturer employs home workers, some having as many employees outside the factory as within. Several thousand machines are at work in the homes knitting the web for cut underwear. The yarn is supplied by the manufacturer, and when the web is finished it is returned to the factory to be made up. Many an old woman may be seen in the streets of

Chemnitz trudging along to a factory with a heavily laden basket of underwear upon her back. The knitting of these fabrics can be done at home, for the machines are neither complex nor expensive and do not require as much power as the Cotton frame. The making up, on the other hand, has been taken to the factories where a series of specialized machines are used and the labor sub-divided.

The system under which fabric gloves are produced is just the reverse of that for underwear. Fashioned gloves are knit at home on machines that require a large amount of hand labor, but the bulk of the gloves are made from cut fabric. The machines for knitting this fabric are heavy and costly, so that they are installed in small factories,[1] and the fabric is cut there after it has been dyed and finished. Then it is given out by the manufacturer to be sewn and decorated. Some of these home workers own their sewing machines, but in the majority of cases the machines are the property of manufacturers. The making up requires but a single machine and the decorating is mainly hand work; hence the home industry has continued. A larger proportion of the output of gloves than of hosiery is made up by home workers, and women living in Leipsic, Dresden, and even in Silesia, are engaged in sewing gloves for the Chemnitz trade.

In this Saxon industry the putting out system has become subsidiary to the factory. There are a few merchants who give out yarn to be knit and who have no workshop of their own, but they employ a very small proportion of the home workers. The remainder are employed by factory owners. In all branches of the knitting industry, to sum up, small establishments and the putting out system enable the German manufacturers to accept small orders for special styles and designs, whereas the American manufacturers produce large quantities of a few patterns.

Several large knit-goods manufacturers in England produce both stockings and underwear, but ordinarily only one or the

---

[1] Although a few factories employ 200 persons, the normal size is 6 to 20 employees. — W. Greif, *Die Limbacher Wirkwaren-Industrie*, p. 43.

other is manufactured by a single concern. In each factory,
however, cotton, wool, and, perhaps, silk are used. In Saxony,
hosiery, underwear, and glove manufacturing are separate
industries; they are seldom united. Cotton, cashmere, lisle,
and silk goods are made in almost every Saxon factory,
but each manufacturer ordinarily confines himself to the production of one grade of goods, — coarse, medium, or fine. He
does not restrict his operations to the knitting of a single kind
of yarn (cotton, wool, or silk) because of the seasonal character
of the trade. The same machines can be used for the yarns of
different fibres, and when the orders for one season have been
filled, those for the next are taken up. In England and in
Germany the knit goods are dyed for the manufacturers at
independent works, not at the mills where they are manufactured.

Few power machines for knitting were adopted in France
till after 1871.[1] And, although the factory system has developed,
home work has not entirely vanished. The British Board of
Trade *Report* (1909) gives the following data for the French
knitting industry.[2] In the " Department de l'Aube " 12,630
persons were employed in 680 mills, an average of 19 persons
per factory. In Troyes 47 establishments employed less than
100 persons each, 11 from 100 to 150 persons each, 8 from 150
to 500 persons, 3 from 500 to 1,000 persons, and one over 1,000
persons. And it was estimated that one-fifth of the knit goods
produced in France were made in the homes.

Although some manufacturers employ knitting frames in the
workers' homes and merchants who have only finishing establishments put out yarn to be knit,[3] the home work in France
is mainly for making up. Hose are made up under the domestic
system, and in Troyes one sees women carrying home wheel-
barrow loads of unseamed goods. Some underwear is also
hand finished by domestic workers, although for that the factory
is gradually supplanting the putting out system.

---

[1] *Enquête sur l'Etat de l'Industrie Textile*, vol. v, p. 74; also Amé, *Les Tarifs de Douanes*, vol. i, p. 409.

[2] British Board of Trade, *Report on Wages and Cost of Living in France*, pp. 355–356.

[3] *Ibid.*, p. 356.

While the scale of production has been growing larger in France, recently there has been a revival of small shops, " ateliers de famille." These small undertakings are located in the country and employ petroleum as the motive power to drive their modern machinery. The reason for their development is said to be the freedom from factory regulations. Since the factory laws do not apply to them, they can run longer hours and thus compete with the larger factories. At the same time the workmen enjoy a certain amount of independence and freedom from factory discipline.

The equipment of the European factories is generally on a par with that of American knitting mills. But the larger size of the mills, the operation of machinery at a higher speed, and the concentration upon the production of a relatively small number of standardized patterns favors the American manufacturers.

CHAPTER XXI

RAW COTTON MARKETS

OUR viewpoint changes. Up to this point we have been comparing the industrial aspects of the cotton manufacturing industries of Europe and America. We shall now consider the commercial methods, and commence with the raw cotton market.

The English spinners procure their cotton through channels similar to those by which the raw fibre makes its way into the hands of American mill owners. Cotton is shipped to Great Britain by three classes of dealers; (1) by American shippers, who consign it to Liverpool merchants; (2) by buyers sent out from Liverpool and Manchester houses; or (3) by American firms which have a branch office in England.

The importing merchant does not always deal directly with the spinner. In Liverpool, with some exceptions, the importer entrusts the disposal of his cotton to a selling broker, and the spinner employs a buying broker who assembles samples of the required grade to be inspected on the occasion of the weekly visit of the spinner to Liverpool. The spinner who purchases in this way has one or, at most, two buying brokers with whom he regularly deals. The buying broker and the selling broker each receive a commission of one-half of one per cent on the value of the cotton. In Manchester the importers deal directly with the spinners, not as brokers but as merchants. This does not apply, of course, to the cotton sold by the agents of Liverpool brokers who are present at the Manchester Exchange on market days, but only to those firms which have their head offices in Manchester. While some of these merchants sell several kinds of cotton, others handle only a single quality, such as long staple cotton, Memphis cotton, or some other special grade.

Egyptian cotton is sold in England by the agents of the large Alexandria houses. The agents, who sell on commission, are located in Manchester and Liverpool and deal directly with the mills. There are also Egyptian cotton merchants in Liverpool who are independent of the Alexandria companies, but a large proportion of the business is handled by the agents.

At the time of the opening of the Manchester Ship Canal it was freely anticipated that Manchester would supersede Liverpool as the chief raw cotton market in Great Britain. For several years the imports did increase, but during the last ten years they have remained practically stationary, averaging about 300 million pounds or one-fifth of the total quantity entering the country each year. Liverpool has retained its position as the chief port of entry in spite of extra freight expense [1] and higher selling charges. Some Lancashire spinners have preferred to continue their dealings in Liverpool because of their respect for the practice of their ancestors and the pleasure of making a weekly visit to that city; at least this is a common opinion in Lancashire. Another reason, and a far more substantial one, has been that the spinner could exercise a wide choice in selecting his cotton from the numerous samples collected by the broker. Finally, the brokers themselves have taken a precautionary step in order to avoid being stranded without customers. During the mania for mill building which culminated in 1907, Liverpool brokers subscribed to stock in new companies on condition that they be granted the exclusive privilege of buying the cotton for a period of at least ten years. These influences have checked the diversion of the raw cotton trade to Manchester.

The English spinner buys spot cotton, *i. e.* for immediate delivery, and also makes contracts for future deliveries of so much per month. These contracts for future delivery extend over three, six, or even twelve months. The price for spot cotton is fixed by current market quotations. But for future deliveries it is often arranged that the spinner shall pay a certain number of points " on " or " off " the Liverpool quotation at the time he receives the cotton or at whatever time he designates. The points on or off depend upon the quality of cotton purchased. Thus the spinner is sure of obtaining the desired grade of cotton, but the price which he is to pay will be determined by the

[1] See *ante*, p. 285.

course of the market.   The actual payment for the cotton may
not be made till sixty days after delivery, but at the present
time ten days is the more common term.[1]   If a spinner asks for
more than sixty days' credit, he is subject to suspicion.

Unlike the American manufacturer, the English spinner
rarely accumulates a stock of cotton early in the season.   Unless the market be exceptionally favorable, he buys only when
he has sold the yarn, and few mills have warehouse accommodations for more than one or two months' consumption.   Commodious warehouses are available in Liverpool and Manchester,
where the cotton may be held pending delivery.   Moreover
the shipments for future delivery are arranged by the merchant
so as to arrive at about the date they are to be handed over to
the spinner.

The Liverpool Exchange, therefore, is not used by the English
spinner for the purchase of the actual cotton which he is to use.
He cannot rely upon " contract " cotton any more than the
New England spinner can supply his needs by means of the contracts of the New York Exchange.   The rules of both exchanges
permit the delivery on the contracts of cotton of several grades
(with corresponding adjustment of price), whereas the spinners
in both countries require even-running lots of a single quality.

The Liverpool Cotton Exchange was organized after the
"cotton famine" of the 'sixties,[2] at about the same time as the
New York Exchange.   There had previously been sales for
future delivery, but not speculation in " futures."   The uncertainty as to the obtaining of supplies of cotton during the American Civil War and the period immediately following encouraged
a specialization of risk taking.   And the extension of the telegraph system, the laying of the Atlantic Cable, and the improvements in ocean transportation culminating in the 'seventies
provided the means of communication so essential to a well-
organized speculative market.

---

[1] This refers only to American cotton.   The terms for Egyptian cotton are
usually c. i. f., 3 months.

[2] T. Ellison, in his *Cotton Trade of Great Britain* and in his *Gleanings and
Reminiscences*, presents the details of the development of the Liverpool cotton
trade and the history of the Exchange.

The rules of the Liverpool Exchange [1] are quite similar to those in New York, but more perfectly adapted to securing a harmonious movement of spot and future quotations. The presence of a larger supply of cotton in Liverpool, because of the transhipment trade, also steadies the market and renders it more suitable for hedging.

The contracts of the Liverpool Exchange are extensively utilized as a means of insurance against loss in the raw cotton trade of Great Britain. Practically all of the cotton imported into that country is hedged on either the New York or Liverpool Exchange and the banks generally refuse to advance money on cotton that is not thus protected. Merchants who accept orders before they have secured the cotton cover their obligations with Liverpool contracts, which are liquidated as soon as the cotton is purchased. The spinners ordinarily place an order for cotton at the same time that they accept a contract for yarn, and as both prices are fixed they have no occasion to hedge. A spinner who buys cotton ahead of yarn orders, a rare procedure in England, hedges in Liverpool, but it is the importers and merchants who make the greatest use of the Liverpool Exchange for hedging.

Continental spinners formerly obtained large quantities of cotton through Liverpool, but the amount has declined. Bremen has taken control of the German trade and is the largest raw cotton market on the Continent. Some American cotton is imported at Hamburg, and a large proportion of the Indian cotton arrives at that port. In Eastern and Southern Germany small purchases are made from Havre, and in Alsace about one-half of the cotton consumed is bought in Havre. But the Bremen trade predominates. A cotton exchange, the "Bremer-Baumwollbörse," has been organized in that city. Nevertheless it is only an association for adjusting contracts and regulating transactions, not for organized speculation.

A few spinners buy part of their material directly in America, and the largest spinning company in Germany has its own plantation in Africa. Some cotton is consigned to Bremen

---

[1] C. P. Brooks, *Cotton*, p. 275, and W. J. Ashley, *British Industries*, p. 76.

agents by American shippers and sold by them for a commission of three-fourths of one per cent. But the bulk of the cotton is handled by Bremen importers and merchants who dispose of it through agents located in the manufacturing centres.

The trade in Indian cotton is in the hands of European merchants who purchase it from the peasants and factors in India and import it into Europe. Three firms ship sixty-six per cent of the total quantity exported from India, the remainder being divided among a number of smaller shippers. While *en route* or, more often, after the arrival of the cotton in Hamburg or Antwerp, notices are sent out by the importers to their agents in the manufacturing districts, stating the details and the conditions under which orders are to be solicited.

American, Indian, and also Egyptian cotton is disposed of by agents at the interior points in Germany. Each agent represents more than one firm. He generally sells for one Egyptian cotton dealer (if Egyptian cotton is used in his district), one Indian cotton dealer, and several American cotton merchants. As far as possible he limits himself to the representation of non-competing houses; in the trade in American cotton he may sell for one merchant who handles only " Franko-Waggon " [1] cotton, and another who always sells " c.i.f." cotton.[2] By acting as the agent of several houses he is able to offer cotton at all times, even if one of his correspondents temporarily withdraws from the market. In this way he avoids the loss of customers. The importers do not employ exclusive agents since the business of a single importing house is not great enough in any one locality to enable the employment of a salesman of the desired ability and social standing. The agents receive a commission of one per cent on the value of the cotton, and accept no responsibility.

The German spinner, like his competitors in England and America, buys cotton for immediate delivery and for forward

---

[1] " Franko-Waggon " signifies free on board or delivery of cotton at transportation office in Bremen.

[2] " C. I. F." Price quoted includes cost, insurance, freight, delivered at the mill.

delivery in monthly instalments. The warehouses of the German mills are generally larger than those in England, and if the prospects are favorable at the opening of a new crop year, the German purchases two or three months' consumption for immediate delivery. The average quantity carried by a German mill is larger than in England, where the spinners profit from their proximity to Liverpool. At the commencement of the season the cotton arriving at Bremen is shipped inland at once, but beginning in November more and more is stored in the commodious warehouses at the Bremen docks. When American cotton is sold on future delivery contracts, each instalment is paid for as soon as received, but the terms of payment for spot deliveries are usually sixty days. The purchaser of Indian cotton ordinarily receives a credit of ninety days.

While there is some speculation in cotton " futures " in Hamburg, the dealings are insignificant and the Liverpool or New York market is used for hedging. The importers safeguard their cotton or their contracts in just the same manner as the English importers. But the German spinners, although they carry more cotton not covered by yarn orders, hedge less frequently than the English spinners. They are so far from the speculative markets that they cannot act with sufficient promptness, and the decentralized German yarn and cloth market is not as responsive to changes in the price of cotton as the English market.

Spinners of Sea Island or other long staple American cotton whether located in America, England, Germany, or France, buy their supply very early. They may even place orders with merchants for two or three years ahead. The supply of this high quality fibre is so limited that such action is warranted. The difficulties of obtaining that grade of material have even induced the English Fine Cotton Spinners' Association to purchase a plantation in America. When the cotton is sold so far in advance, the merchant, of course, takes the earliest opportunity to hedge his order.

Havre is the principal cotton market in France. The French spinners formerly bought part of their supply directly from

American shippers, but the difficulties of adjusting the claims for tare and the recent bill of lading frauds have discouraged that method. The spinners now buy their American cotton from Havre merchants through agents residing in the mill districts. The agents are paid a commission of one-half of one per cent or one per cent, and resemble the German agents in all respects.

The Havre merchants buy the cotton from importers and American shippers, generally through the medium of brokers. Sworn brokers (*courtiers assermentés*) record the sales and fix the official quotations, receiving one-fourth of one per cent as their remuneration but they do not take part in business transactions on their own account. The buying and selling is done by the common brokers, who likewise receive a commission of one-fourth per cent.

The Havre Cotton Exchange is very similar to the Liverpool institution, and is an important speculative market. Future contracts are used by the Havre merchants for hedging, and the spinners also frequently hedge when they have bought cotton ahead of yarn orders. The dealings at Havre, however, are confined to American cotton. The Egyptian cotton used in Lille is bought from the agents of Egyptian firms and imported at Dunkirk.

For raw cotton buying the English spinners are more advantageously situated than the other Europeans. The raw cotton market organization in England works more quickly, more smoothly, and more surely than any on the Continent, and is fully as efficient as the American.

CHAPTER XXII

ENGLISH MARKETS

Manchester Yarn and Cloth Market

THE commercial centre of the English cotton industry, so highly concentrated in Lancashire, is Manchester. To explain how Manchester attained its position of preëminence would be a long story, involving its early history as a market town and the consequent freedom from restrictive regulations;[1] the development of fustian dyeing and finishing on the banks of the Irwell; the change in the practice of the chapmen (fustian dyers) whereby they began to put out cotton to be spun and yarn to be woven, delivering the material to persons who came to Manchester instead of themselves journeying to Bolton to buy cloth in the gray;[2] and, finally, the business experience and financial strength of the merchants, which developed along with the rise of cotton factories in the surrounding district. The result is that Manchester at the present time is by far the largest primary market in the world for cotton yarn and cloth.

The pivot on which the Manchester trade turns is the Manchester Royal Exchange. Unlike the Liverpool Exchange the Manchester institution is a traders' exchange, and the contracts made there are fulfilled by actual delivery. 'Change is held every day, but the meetings on Tuesday and Friday afternoons witness the greatest activity. On these market days the floor of the Exchange is thronged with spinners, manufacturers, salesmen, agents, merchants, finishers, machinery and supply dealers of all sorts, a gathering which is representative of all parties interested in the Lancashire cotton industry. The number of members of the Exchange in 1910 was 9,600. Not all of the business of Manchester is transacted on the floor of this indispensable institution, but the volume of sales consummated there is im-

[1] James Ogden, *Manchester 100 Years Ago* (Axon reprint), p. 93.
[2] *Ibid.*, p. 74.

mense. It is the point at which the multiplicity of factors affecting the trade are concentrated. Further references to the place held by this exchange will be made in the following analysis of the diverse forces culminating there.

If the organization of the American cloth market is complex, that of the English yarn and cloth trade is even more intricate. Salesmen, agents, and several types of merchants participate in the disposal of the product of the Lancashire mills.

Both yarn and cloth are sold direct in England, and in an increasing proportion. Direct sales, it may be remarked, are understood to be those in which no broker or agent takes part. Many of the limited spinning companies employ salesmen who are present on the Exchange each day. The directors of other limited companies and the owners or managers of many private concerns attend the meetings at the Exchange on market days and there secure orders for yarn directly from weavers or merchants. In the cloth trade, similarly, the weaver may sell directly to a merchant on 'Change, and during the intervals between those gatherings he may accept orders which come to him directly. The merchant who desires a cloth of particular quality or design generally goes directly to the manufacturer who is identified with that product. Finally, there are several large houses in Manchester which have their own spinning and weaving mills, and which sell to wholesalers and even retailers. It is estimated that about one-half of the yarn and cloth is disposed of by direct sales, the remainder by agents.

Two types of agents can be distinguished in the Lancashire trade. Those of the first type are practically brokers. They are not identified with particular mills, and the yarn which they sell does not pass through their hands although they collect the bills. They operate on a small scale and are confined almost entirely to the yarn trade. A spinning company which has its own salesman in Manchester may also place orders through these brokers, and others accept their services. The place which they hold, however, is comparatively unimportant.

Agents of the second type regularly dispose of the product of particular mills. Some of these agents have the exclusive right to sell the entire product of the mills which they represent. Others control only a part of the output, the remainder being sold directly or through other agents. The agents which have the exclusive privileges are for the most part old houses and their clients long-established spinners and manufacturers. One agent rarely deals in both yarn and cloth, and some handle only a limited range of products in one branch. The larger houses sell all sorts of yarn or cloth indiscriminately, but they then have separate departments for the special lines. The agents secure orders from Manchester merchants, and in the yarn trade a few have their own representatives in foreign countries.

The English agents of the second type perform services similar to those of the American selling houses. They secure orders and give financial assistance. In numerous respects, however, there is a contrast. Unlike the American selling agents, they do not announce the identity of the mills which they represent. In Manchester the orders are placed with the agent and transferred by him to the spinner or weaver, but he cannot fix the price. The yarn or cloth may be shipped directly by the manufacturer to the merchant, but it is more commonly sent to the agent's warehouse to be parcelled out to the customers. The bills are always paid through the agent, not directly to the producer. When trade is dull, goods may be consigned to agents to be disposed of as occasion arises, or, if the agent anticipates a rise in prices, he sometimes orders cloth from the weavers, has it finished on his own account, and thus plays the part of a merchant.

In England it is the smaller firms and the private concerns which employ agents most extensively. The volume of the trade of such manufacturers is not large enough to warrant the maintenance of a salesman, and where one man superintends both the manufacturing and the selling, the agent is of great assistance.

The bulk of the goods sold through agents are the plain, standard products. Competitors are numerous, and the merchant can place his orders more easily when he does not have to consult all the mills engaged in the manufacture of the yarn or cloth which he seeks. In this respect the English agents resemble the brokers in the American trade. The agent, moreover, has an established reputation and there is less risk in dealing with him.

The agent gives financial aid to the mills which he represents. He may do this indirectly by guaranteeing the accounts and thus assuming the risk of loss; but he more commonly pays for the goods as soon as they are delivered to him although he does not receive his pay till a later date. Thus he provides credit which the spinner or weaver cannot conveniently give. In former years it was common for the agent to act as banker for the manufacturer. He received the money paid for goods delivered, held it till the manufacturer directed payment, and paid interest when a surplus was in his possession. If the manufacturer required an advance of funds beyond the amount held by the agent, then the latter received interest. This practice has been continued by the older houses in the case of clients of long standing. These services of the agent are valuable, but he has also maintained his business by other means. An agent has oftentimes made loans to manufacturers and in that way kept them in his grip. They could not free themselves from an agent to whom they were in debt. The promoters of new mills during the last decade have frequently tied themselves to agents in return for subscriptions to capital stock. The agents have invested in the undertaking for the sake of securing sole selling rights.

The commission which the agent receives is determined by the services which he performs. In the yarn trade a general agent, who does not guarantee the account, receives one-half of one per cent on the value of the sales. When he does guarantee the account, his remuneration is one and one-half per cent. A cloth agent who sells the entire product of a mill receives one per cent when he does not guarantee the account, and one and one-half or two per cent with guarantee. If he has only a partial agency, he receives two per cent without guarantee and four per cent with guarantee. These rates are not absolutely fixed, however, and special considerations cause variations.

The position held by the agents in the Manchester trade seems to be rather precarious. The proportion of the yarn and cloth sold by agents has declined during the last two decades. The number of joint-stock companies has increased, particularly in spinning, and the scale of production has become larger. When the output per mill is voluminous, a single director can assume the selling function or a private salesman can be employed. Moreover the larger concerns generally have sufficient capital at their disposal, so that they can dispense with the financial assistance of agents. The establishment of foreign departments has somewhat counterbalanced the pressure bearing down upon the agents, and long-established reputations and trade connections are not easily overcome. Except for brokers, however, who may be indispensable to the Manchester trade, the old type of agency, with exclusive privileges, appears to have passed its zenith.

Although yarn and cloth are sometimes bought and sold by an agent on his own responsibility, he is then outside of his proper sphere and has become a merchant. The term merchant is applied indiscriminately in Manchester to all who deal in yarn and cloth, except the spinners, weavers, and finishers. The merchants may be roughly divided into three classes, converters,[1] home trade houses, and foreign trade merchants. They overlap each other, since nearly all the merchants are converters and most converters invade the field of the home and foreign trade merchants. The line of demarcation between the home and foreign traders is also occasionally obliterated.

Those merchants who are primarily converters buy yarn or cloth in the gray and have it dyed, bleached, or printed. The largest firm of yarn converters in Manchester, for example, buys gray yarn, and sells it in the gray, or dyed, bleached, mercerized, or doubled, and wound in any form desired. They have their own doubling plant, but the other processes are performed for them by job dyers or bleachers. They have their own agencies in London, New York, and Continental cities,

---

[1] The term " converter " is never used in Manchester, but is employed here in the sense in which it has been used in describing the American market.

but they sell large quantities in Manchester.   They carry a stock of yarn in the forms for which there is a regular demand.   Other yarn converters have no works of their own and sell only in the Manchester market.

A cloth converter, similarly, buys gray cloth and sells it in a finished state.   Bleaching and dyeing are always done on commission for a merchant, and, as has been pointed out,[1] job printing predominates.   For prints the converter not only makes use of the designs prepared by the printer but also has his own designs.   By guaranteeing to order a large quantity of a certain design submitted by the printer, he may obtain a monopoly of that design.   He also purchases designs from Paris designers and employs a printer to have them engraved and printed. Unless the order submitted is large, the converter pays the cost of engraving.   Converters sometimes have their own rollers and send them already engraved to the printer, but the inconveniences to the converter of attending to the engraving and the impossibility of using the same roller in all printing machines have caused this practice to undergo a great decline.

While a converter may deal only in staple goods, the bulk of the converters' business is in seasonal fabrics.   Although buyers visit his warehouse, the converter obtains the larger part of his orders from samples which are sent to his customers.   A wholesaler will order goods for two or three months only, but after the samples have been submitted he expects the converter to retain them for a year and to be ready to deliver repeat orders on ten days' notice.   It is therefore necessary for the converter to carry a stock of gray cloth of the sort for which he anticipates fresh orders.   The prices quoted by the converter do not hold for a period longer than that for which an order is given, *i. e.* two or three months as a rule.   If the customer orders more cloth of the same design or finish at the end of that time, the price may be readjusted since the initial costs have already been covered.   These price changes, however, are only fractional, inasmuch as the wholesaler will continue to charge the same

---

[1] See *ante,* p. 328.

price to the retailer. The retail price has been fixed and the further away from the initial processes the less the price is influenced by cost and the more by public fancy or demand.

The customers of converters include local home trade and foreign merchants,[1] wholesale houses in London, Glasgow, and Manchester, clothiers in Leeds, Glasgow, and elsewhere, shirt manufacturers and other cutters-up, and correspondents in foreign countries.

The home trade houses of Manchester are not so numerous as the export firms, but several of them have a very large business. While cotton cloth makes up the bulk of their trade, a number of the home trade merchants also deal in ribbons, laces, furs, feathers, hosiery, gloves, and other goods. The most unique of these undertakings is that of Rylands & Sons, who operate spinning, weaving, and converting works, a factory for manufacturing articles of clothing, and an oil-cloth mill. They also buy cloth, house furnishings, and a variety of other products, such as cricket bats and novelties. A majority of the other large home traders, — Horrockses, Crewdson & Co., Henry Bannerman & Sons, Barlow & Jones, Haslams', and Tootal, Broadhurst & Lee, spin and weave part of the cloth which they sell. They are large enough to combine manufacturing and merchandizing, and have a fairly steady demand for high quality goods in a market where tastes are easily ascertained.

The home trade houses sell to makers up, wholesalers, and retailers. The practice of selling to retailers is a recent development and is viewed by the wholesalers with hostility. Only the largest concerns can sell directly to the retailers since a large force of salesmen is necessary to place the orders and to keep track of the credit of customers. The increased scale of business of these home trade houses and the presence of a larger number of good sized retail establishments have encouraged sales direct to retailers. Yet the multitude of small shops in England, to which goods must be parcelled out in small quantities, prevents the extinction of the wholesaler.

---

[1] These home trade and foreign merchants take relatively less than the other customers.

The home trade merchant maintains his position by reason of two services. First, in addition to taking the part of a converter, he buys cloth in large quantities and distributes it in smaller lots. He carries a large stock from which the wholesalers and retailers can replenish their supplies on short notice. In the second place, he provides credit. He pays the manufacturer within seven days, as a rule, after the cloth is delivered, but he, in turn, is not reimbursed by his customers till several months later. In other words his capital enables the wholesaler and retailer to carry a stock of goods on their shelves to be gradually placed in the hands of the ultimate consumers. Although no fixed percentage is added to the price of the goods by him, his remuneration is said to average from ten to fifteen per cent on the value of the cloth which passes through his hands.

The converter and the agent, as has been stated, may sell to foreigners. Several of the large companies (manufacturing merchants) which have an extensive home trade also sell abroad. Rylands, for instance, employ salesmen in the Continental countries, and in North and South America. Barlow & Jones is another house with a similarly extensive field of operations. But the bulk of the foreign trade flows through channels that have no direct alliance with the home trade.

There are two classes of foreign trade merchants in Manchester, the exporters and the shippers. The exporter has branch offices or agents in the foreign countries to which goods are consigned. The foreign branches keep the home office informed of trade conditions, and may order goods to be sent, but the business is primarily one of consignment without specific order. The volume of trade carried on by this means is small.

The shipper, or shipping merchant, on the contrary, dispatches yarn or cloth only after an order has been given to him. The orders are made by means of samples previously submitted to the foreign correspondents or samples which the foreign house sends to Manchester to be matched. Standard qualities of yarn and cloth can be ordered without samples of any sort. When prices have not already been quoted, the merchant, immediately upon receipt of an inquiry, ascertains the price at which he can offer to ship the yarn or cloth, and if his terms are accepted, he at once proceeds to fill the order. The merchant generally carries a stock of cloth to facilitate delivery and also because orders are received for smaller quantities than he can purchase at one time from the manufacturer. He buys in larger lots than he sells.

The foreign trade merchant ships yarn and cloth in the gray and in the finished state. He has his own designs and perhaps his own rollers for printing gray cloth. He not only buys gray yarn and cloth to be converted according to the orders on his books or anticipated demands, but also purchases finished goods from the merchant-converter, the printer, and the manufacturer of fancy fabrics. Each merchant has his own trade marks which he places upon the goods he sells. The remuneration of the merchant varies according to the length of time for which he has to await payment and the amount of risk involved. He pays the spinner or manufacturer within ten days after receipt of the goods, but is not reimbursed by the foreign purchaser till a later date, perhaps six months after shipment. The banks advance money to the merchants on the bills for the goods, but it is the merchant who assumes the risk of loss.

Some merchants have large warehouses and their own equipment for packing. But there are also job packers[1] in Manchester. Firms having no office, or at least no warehouse in Manchester, direct the manufacturers to whom they give orders to send the goods to a specified packer. There the several consignments are assembled, inspected, and prepared for shipment. There are numerous buildings in Manchester owned by packers who have their packing rooms on the ground floor or in the basement and lease the office rooms above to merchants for a nominal rent, or rent free, on condition that all the goods handled by the merchant be packed by the owner of the building.

---

[1] The 1911 *Manchester Directory* names 49 packers. The largest was Lloyd Packing Warehouses, Ltd., with 11 branches in Manchester, 1 in Blackburn, 1 in Bradford, and a case making works. Delaney had 3 branches in Manchester, 1 in Bradford, and a tin and wood case works. The Manchester Central Packing Warehouses had 7 branches and J. Stevenson & Sons, 3.

The packer receives about six shillings ($1.46) per bale for packing, and provides the canvas, tarpaulin, and other materials. Except for the largest merchants, this method is economical, since the packer can buy his supplies cheaply in large quantities and is able to keep his plant constantly at work.

While the larger part of the exported product of the Lancashire mills is sold by the Manchester exporters or shippers, it may pass through other hands. In foreign countries, especially those of Continental Europe, there are merchants and agents who purchase directly from the English spinners and manufacturers, sending their orders by mail or telegraph. A few foreign houses have their own office in Manchester, as, for example, Marshall Field & Co. of Chicago, and Arnold, Constable & Co. of New York. Finally, in the trade with North and South America, buyers visit England.

An institution which is intimately connected with the trade in yarn and cloth is the Manchester Testing House. All kinds of textile materials and other supplies are there submitted to chemical and mechanical tests. Some of the tests are purely experimental, but the greater part are to determine the quality of some article of trade. Manufacturers send samples of materials for analysis. Sizing ingredients are tested to ascertain whether or not they contain anything injurious to the cloth, especially if the latter is to have a peculiar finish. Cloth which has proved to be inferior in quality is tested for the purpose of fixing the responsibility. The conclusions of the Testing House are not binding in the case of a dispute, but they are generally respected. It provides a recognized means of arbitration.

Let us now summarize the characteristics of the Lancashire trade. Yarn is sold directly by the spinners to manufacturers and merchants, and also through agents. The amount which is sold direct has increased with the larger number of joint-stock companies and other big firms. The spinner seldom spins for stock, and he may have orders for six months ahead when trade is brisk. Normally he receives orders in September, October, and November which will keep his mill employed till March.

It is at that time that the new cotton crop is being placed upon the market and the prospects for the next year become apparent. The orders may be placed at any time, but even when the buyer and seller have previously corresponded, the business is, as a rule, actually concluded upon the Manchester Exchange.

Cloth, similarly, may be disposed of with the assistance of an agent, but large quantities are sold directly by the manufacturers to the printers and merchants. More cloth than yarn is manufactured ahead of orders, but the proportion which is not made to fill a specific order is very small. The sales of cloth of special quality or fancy design are not so closely confined to the Exchange as the trade in standard plain goods, in the production of which numerous mills compete. For the latter class of goods the Exchange serves as a focus in fixing the current price.

A pound of cotton arriving in Liverpool, therefore, may pass through many hands. It may happen that the importer sells it himself to a manufacturer who operates spinning, weaving, and finishing mills, and who sells the cloth to retailers in England or other countries. But more frequently the pound of cotton will pay tribute to two Liverpool brokers, to a yarn agent and merchant, to a cloth agent, converter, and merchant, and finally to a wholesaler and retailer. During its course it may also have been the property of a spinner, a doubler, a weaver, and a printer.

The advantage accruing from this multiplicity of middlemen is not inexpensiveness but flexibility. The tentacles of the Manchester trade reach out to all corners of the world, and whatever form of manufactured cotton is sought, whatever accommodation is desired, some one can be found in Manchester ready to accept the commission. Of all the assets which make it possible for the cotton industry to attain its largest dimensions in a country which does not produce the raw material, and which consumes only ten or twenty per cent of the yarn and cloth manufactured in its mills, none is more significant than the adaptability of the commercial organization.

If America is to become a large exporter of cotton fabrics, we may expect a similar diversification and specialization of the merchandizing functions. Methods which serve admirably for the domestic market do not suffice to meet the varying exigencies of a trade with countries where local conditions and local customs are very diverse. It is idle to call upon American manufacturers to study foreign markets. Their part is to stand ready to execute orders presented by merchants who understand the requirements of the customers, provide credit, and assume the risks inevitably involved in foreign trade.

Nottingham Market

Two trades are centred in Nottingham, the knit-goods trade and the lace trade. The yarn which is used in these industries is purchased from local agents, each of whom represents several non-competing spinners and doublers. They sell one sort of yarn for one spinner, another sort for another spinner. The largest manufacturers of knit goods employ salesmen in England and foreign countries, but the majority secure their orders through agents in London and Manchester. The agents sell, on commission, to home trade houses and foreign shippers.

The organization of the net and curtain trade is also simple. Curtains are sold by the manufacturer to merchants or wholesalers. Net is sometimes sold by the maker directly to the embroiderer but the greater part goes to merchants who dispose of it to English and Continental embroidery makers. The market for small laces is more complex. Brown lace, *i. e.* unfinished, is sold by the makers to finishers and to merchants. If it is purchased by a finisher, he sells it in the finished form to a merchant. If the merchant buys in the brown, he employs a job finisher. The maker frequently has an agreement with a merchant to sell only to him. The designs for the lace are bought from Paris designers by lace makers and by merchants. When a merchant purchases designs, he engages a manufacturer to set them up and manufacture the lace for him. In the home trade the merchant sells to wholesalers and large retailers, in the foreign trade to correspondents and to buyers who visit

Nottingham. The foreign buyers who go to England are mainly
the representatives of houses in the United States and Canada,
although a few South American importers follow the same
practice. The American firms purchase in such large quantities
that the travelling expenses of the buyer are offset by the
advantages in selecting goods and in meeting the producer on
his own ground. The functions of the middleman are the same
in Nottingham as in Manchester.

CHAPTER XXIII

THE analysis of the English market organization is particularly interesting on account of the volume of the trade and the variety of needs to which it has adapted itself. The conditions on the Continent are different, and the type of organization is not the same as in England or America. Nevertheless, something is to be learned from a study of the methods by which the products are sold in Germany, France, and Switzerland.

Germany

The German yarn market includes the trade in both domestic and foreign yarn. On the domestic side there are direct sales from spinners to weavers or other manufacturers, and also to agents and merchants. The larger knitting and weaving mills in Saxony generally buy domestic yarn directly from the spinner, and in the other sections direct sales are more or less common for large orders or when the weaver is desirous of obtaining the yarn of a particular spinner.

In Saxony large quantities of yarn are sold by the spinners to merchants, who accept all the risk. There are also agents in the Saxon market. And elsewhere the agent greatly overshadows the merchant. Each agent represents from one to five or six spinners, whose mills may or may not be located in the immediate neighborhood. The agent ordinarily has the sole agency in his district for each of those mills, but he avoids accepting the representation of competing spinners. Except in Mülhausen, where the agent is little more than a broker, he is identified with the mills for which he sells. An agent may deal only in yarn, or he may also sell raw cotton, cloth, and even non-textile products.

The German yarn agent accepts no risk, does not actually handle the yarn, and does not collect the bill. He merely passes on the order from manufacturer to spinner, and receives in return a commission of one-half of one per cent or one per cent on the amount of the sale.

Yarn is imported into Germany by merchants and agents. Chemnitz is a market into which much foreign yarn finds its way, so that it can serve as an example. The merchant buys yarn directly from English spinners, occasionally merchants, and carries a stock in his Chemnitz warehouse. In this way he is able to deliver to the knitters or weavers much more quickly than if he had to obtain the yarn in England after he received an order. The agent sells on commission and carries no stock, although he frequently agrees to dispose of a fixed quantity of yarn for an English spinner in a year. He is a typical German agent and has several strings to his bow. One agent will represent not only an English cotton spinner, but, perhaps, a German spinner of coarse counts, a cashmere spinner, an Italian silk firm, and even other manufacturers.

A few German manufacturers who finish their own cloth sell directly to retailers, but the volume of this trade is relatively insignificant. A few also sell directly to wholesalers and exporters. And a somewhat larger number sell gray cloth to converters without any intermediary assistance, a converter sometimes contracting to take the entire output of a mill.

In Saxony the little colored goods mills in some instances sell to a single merchant or exporter, who may have given financial assistance and taken a mortgage on the property. In Glauchau, for example, one exporter is said to control the output of several small mills producing fancy goods. But for Germany as a whole such exclusive arrangements are rare. A very large proportion of the German cloth is sold by agents.

The German cloth agent resembles the raw cotton agent and the yarn agent. There are agents with businesses of all sizes, from those who sell for only one mill to the large firms representing several mills and having offices in various cities. One of the largest is the firm of Wilhelm Rieger, which represents German and Swiss spinners and weavers, and in addition to the head office in Stuttgart has branches in Berlin, Elberfeld, and Leipsic.

The agents who represent manufacturers of finished cloth sell to wholesalers, exporters, merchants, and sometimes to large retailers such as the department stores. The gray cloth agents sell to printers and merchant-converters. In Mülhausen there are agents who sell for any mill, but as a rule the German cloth agent is identified with specified manufacturers. No responsibility, however, is accepted by the agent and the cloth is not shipped to him. Moreover he does not collect the bill. His remuneration is a commission of one per cent on small orders and one-half of one per cent on large orders.

Gray cloth for converting is purchased by the printer and the merchant-converter. Aside from Turkey-red dyeing, all the bleaching and dyeing is done on the account of merchants. While numerous printers own all or part of the cloth which they convert, the greater proportion of the work is done for merchant-converters,[1] and the latter system is gaining ground. The printer who works for others does not have any of his capital tied up in the form of cloth, and the risk is shifted to the merchant.

Although he may also purchase small quantities of finished goods from the Buntwebereien (colored goods manufacturers), the converter buys principally gray cloth. The largest firm of converters in Germany is that of Gebrüder Simon in Berlin, their business being as great as that of all the other Berlin converters taken together. As in England, the converter prepares designs for his own use and also makes use of the designs issued by the printers. But by whomever the designs are issued, they originate in Paris. When the converter does not own the designs, he may obtain a monopoly, at least for the domestic trade, by contracting to order a sufficiently large quantity. Other designs on the printer's books are open to all.

The terms on which the converter buys are net thirty days, two per cent off for cash. If more than thirty days' credit is sought from the manufacturer, interest must be paid. A converter with sufficient capital pays cash for the cloth which he

[1] S. Tschierschky, Die Zollpolitischen Interressen der Deutschen Textil-veredlungs-industrie, p. 10.

buys. But he does not receive reimbursement immediately. He has to carry the goods while they are being converted, and he grants credit to the customer. He sells the cloth to jobbers, large retailers, and exporters, the sales to the jobbers predominating.

The German exporters do not act as converters, but buy only finished cloth. This is due in part to the dispersion of the markets in Germany, but more particularly to the predominance in the exports of fabrics made from dyed yarn, such as upholsteries, " buckskins," and the like. The leading houses exporting German goods are located in Hamburg, Antwerp, Paris, and Berlin. They order the cloth from the manufacturers through agents. They pay the manufacturer soon after delivery, but grant, perhaps, unduly long credits. In fact, the credit accommodations to foreign purchasers, of which our consuls speak so frequently, originate not with the German manufacturers but with these wealthy export houses. Moreover, since they sell not only cloth manufactured in their own country, but cloth from other European countries, particularly England, as well, these export houses are somewhat international in character.

Germany is not without a cotton manufacturers' exchange; there is a " Börse " in Stuttgart and another in Mülhausen. But they are not at all like the Manchester Exchange. They are merely meetings of manufacturers for an exchange of opinions on market conditions. The Stuttgart Börse was started forty years ago. The meetings of the members of that Exchange are held every two weeks, and are attended by spinners and manufacturers from Württemberg and the neighboring parts of southern Germany. The Mülhausen Exchange meets weekly, and the gatherings are for the same object as those in Stuttgart. No trading takes place at these meetings, but the current prices are fixed by mutual opinion. Yet the prices published are in no way binding and are always " bullish," since they represent, not what the manufacturers are actually receiving but what they think they ought to receive. To the participants themselves they are of value in enabling them to feel the pulse beats of the larger market.

The export trade of Germany in cotton products other than cloth is particularly important, and the Chemnitz knit-goods trade holds the first place. Chemnitz is primarily an export market but contrasts with the English textile commercial centres in having few local merchants. The knit-goods merchants of Chemnitz are neither numerous nor important, since they conduct but a very small share of the business.

About forty per cent of the knit goods produced in Chemnitz, it is estimated, is sent to the United States, and by peculiar routes. They are bought by resident agents and by buyers who are sent out from America. In 1910 about one hundred and fifty American firms had resident agents in Chemnitz. The agent in some cases represents only a single firm, in others a number of smaller houses, occasionally as many as twenty-five. The agent may purchase goods, but the representatives of the larger firms attend only to the placing of " repeat orders," and to the payment for the goods and the adjustment of claims. Their sphere of action generally includes not only the Chemnitz district but several or all of the German markets in which their house purchases goods. The buyers visit Chemnitz once or twice a year, the large firms sending a buyer for each special line.

The buyers and agents deal directly with the manufacturers, no middleman intervening. The finished goods are packed by the manufacturer or finisher and shipped by him, although the agent generally gives directions as to time of shipment in order to have several consignments dispatched together from the port. While credit of thirty days or longer is granted at times, the goods are generally paid for within ten days after the receipt of the bill of lading at the office of the Chemnitz agent. The business with America, therefore, is done on practically a cash basis.

In addition to the trade controlled by the American agents and buyers, both cloth and knitted fabrics are shipped by Saxon manufacturers to New York importers, who receive all the product of such mills, or at least all that goes to America. The manufacturers refuse to sell to others, or accept orders from buyers only on condition that the goods be shipped through the New York importing house. The importer finances the business by paying the manufacturer and advancing the amount of the import duty, and attends to the customs inspection. He receives a commission for his services.

When the goods are thus consigned before sale, some importers may occasionally reap an extra profit from evasion of the import duty by undervaluation. If the consignment includes fancy gloves of novel design, for example, which have not previously been placed upon the market, no one can decide just how much they are worth. In that case the importer may fix a valuation considerably below the price at which he ultimately sells. The amount of duty that he has evaded then goes into his pocket. In addition to the business of their regular clients the import houses will perform the same financial and port services for others. But their business is relatively small, since the sales to buyers and resident agents in Chemnitz predominate.

The exports from Chemnitz to England are second in amount, but no English houses have agents or buyers in Chemnitz. The Chemnitz manufacturers send salesmen to England twice a year with new samples, and in the intervening periods a London agent attends to the business. These agents represent one or more houses according to the volume of their trade. The English purchasers place small orders at frequent intervals, the Americans large orders at one or two seasons of the year. It is for this reason that the Americans can afford to send buyers across the ocean. In the Chemnitz trade with England the accounts are constantly open and monthly payments made.

A few Chemnitz manufacturers have their own organization for selling in other parts of the world, one manufacturer of high grade hosiery, for instance, who employs three hundred workmen, has an office force of thirty attending to the orders which are placed by mail with foreign correspondents. But the trade with countries other than the United States and England goes largely through the export houses in Hamburg and Paris. They are the same firms which were met with in the cloth trade. These large export houses grant the credit to the foreign purchaser and accept the risk of loss.

Middlemen are conspicuously absent from the Chemnitz market since their assistance is unnecessary. In the first place the Saxon manufacturers accept small orders, so that there is no need of a distributor. In the second place, the financial function of the middleman has been superseded in the American and English trade, where the manufacturers receive payment immediately or after a short period of credit, and in the other foreign trade, where the Hamburg and Paris houses carry the burden of credit.

The Barmen trade in braids, trimmings, and other small wares also has unique characteristics. A few large manufacturers, perhaps half a dozen, send representatives to New York, but most of the American business is done by American buyers who visit Barmen, and by Barmen export commission houses. The buyers place orders with the large manufacturers and also through the commission houses. It is estimated that seventy-five per cent of the trade in Barmen wares with America is participated in by the commission houses. There are three large commission exporters and several small firms. They differ from the majority of the Chemnitz agents in that they are not identified with any foreign firms. Neither are they identified with particular manufacturers. They do not restrict their business to cotton fabrics, but handle other articles such as appear on the counters of American department stores. They send samples to American correspondents, and, as has been stated, also secure orders from the buyers visiting Barmen. For the latter they collect samples from many small manufacturers so that the buyer is able to exercise a wide choice in a short time.

The orders secured by the commission houses are transferred to the manufacturers, who pack and ship the goods when finished. The commission merchant does not himself actually touch the goods, but he gives directions as to time of shipment so as to have several consignments arrive simultaneously at the same port. In this way he is able to collect several invoices and save in consular fees and other shipping charges. He accepts responsibility for the quality of the goods, and pays the manufacturer as soon as he receives the invoice and the notice from the forwarding agent that the goods have been delivered for shipment. Moreover, he grants credit to the American purchaser, thirty days after shipment being the usual terms. In this instance we have a middleman collecting goods for large purchasers from small manufacturers, and also utilizing his capital in granting credit.

The Plauen trade [1] has certain features of both the Chemnitz and the Barmen markets. In the domestic trade the manufacturers for the most part sell directly to retailers or wholesalers in the larger cities; salesmen are sent out and buyers visit Plauen. The large export trade in Plauen laces and embroideries is more complicated. It can be divided into two fairly distinct sections, the sales to the United States and the sales to other countries. For handling the latter branch, there are about fifty Plauen export houses, and in addition the Hamburg and Paris merchants place orders with the Plauen manufacturers, Hamburg for staple goods and Paris for fancy novelties.

In the American trade, although there is a small consignment business, the greater part of the purchases are made by resident agents and travelling buyers. There were in 1905 twenty to forty American import houses and ten to fifteen American department stores sending buyers to Plauen. The latter are the largest purchasers. A dozen of the American houses have exclusive agents in Plauen; the others ordinarily employ a commission house. The agents, as at Chemnitz, assemble samples for the buyers, watch the market, place repeat orders, and attend to shipment and payment. The commission house is employed for the buyers by those firms which have no agent at Plauen. There are five large commission houses, and each serves two to ten American firms, in addition to its other business. The " commissionaire " collects samples, accepts the orders, ships the goods, and pays the manufacturer. His remuneration is three to five per cent. With his assistance a buyer can economize in time and yet obtain a wide view of the market in which

---

[1] Max G. von Loeben, *Der Absatz der Plauener Spitzen nach den Vereinigten Staaten*, p. 42. The following description is based on that monograph.

he is interested. As elsewhere, the American purchasers buy in large quantities and pay cash or receive, at most, a short term credit.

France and Switzerland

The French trade in cotton products can be separated into three parts, the yarn trade, the cloth trade, and the export trade. In the yarn trade the Lille market is the most important, since in that district spinning is completely independent of weaving. A small quantity of the Lille yarn is sold directly to the manufacturers either by correspondence or by the spinners' salesmen. There are also yarn merchants in Lille and Calais who transact business on their own account. But the greater proportion of the yarn is sold by agents located in the manufacturing districts. An agent may represent a single mill or several mills, and receives a commission of one per cent, infrequently two per cent, on the amount of his sales. The usual terms of payment in the " Nord " are net, thirty days after the end of the current month, or one per cent off for cash. In the hosiery trade the terms are two per cent, thirty days, and in other places a higher discount and longer credit, sixty or ninety days, are frequently granted. Yet the prices are always quoted at a higher figure under such conditions.

In the Vosges four or five large spinning mills have an old clientele to which they sell all their product directly. For the remaining spinners, agents frequently intervene, receiving one-half of one per cent. In Normandy several of the old spinning concerns sell through regular selling houses, which control the entire output, guarantee accounts, and are paid two per cent commission. Other spinners ordinarily sell by means of agents who accept no responsibility and obtain only one-half of one per cent commission.

In neither the yarn nor the cloth trade of France is there an exchange like that at Manchester. In Lille the cotton spinners' " Bourse " meets every week, but for intercourse, not trading. Similarly at Amiens, a weekly meeting of cloth manufacturers is held to talk over conditions and prices. Taking France as a whole, the mills are too broadly dispersed for market concentration.

In the cloth market there are both direct sales and the employment of agents. A small number of the Vosgian manufacturers sell directly to printers and merchants, a few even having their own office in Paris. But the majority are represented in Paris, Lyons, and other cloth markets by agents who are remunerated with a commission of one-half of one per cent or one per cent. The agents merely place the orders.

The Norman cloth manufacturers entrust the selling of their product to exclusive selling houses less frequently than the spinners, although the quantities of cloth disposed of by that method are by no means small. Some of the other manufacturers sell through the ordinary agent. But a larger number are represented in the cloth markets by private salesmen. In Normandy more finished cloth, stripes and fancies, is produced, whereas the Vosgian product is predominantly gray goods. The finished goods require more attention in merchandizing and this seems to be obtained most assuredly by private salesmen.

Aside from the cloth woven from converted yarn, practically the entire output of the French cotton mills is sold in the gray. A part of this goes at once into the hands of merchants, who give it out to be bleached, dyed, or printed on their account. A larger portion of the cloth which is printed, however, is bought by the printers. In the print trade the merchant-converter has a far smaller share in France than in England or Germany. On the other hand, the wholesaler has been crowded out to a greater extent in France. The manufacturer of striped and fancy cloth, the printer, and the merchant-converter sell large quantities direct to the big retail stores.

The colonies are the largest export market for French cotton goods. In the colonies near at hand, such as Algeria, colonial merchants carry on the trade by sending buyers to France. The more remote colonies, such as Madagascar, are supplied by French export houses.

The exports of cotton manufactures from France to the United States are novelty dress goods and laces. A part of this trade is in the hands of French exporters, the lace trade in particular being controlled by a few large exporters who have made a specialty of it.   But purchases by American buyers are important.   The firms which send buyers to France are either represented by agents in Paris or employ " commissionaires." The conditions and methods are much the same as in Germany. The agents are, for the most part, sole representatives, although there are three or four each of whom is employed jointly by several American houses.   The " commissionaires " are utilized by those buyers who have no agent in Paris.   They differ from the agents in that they are not identified with any firms, are paid a commission (five per cent), and have, as a rule, about twenty clients.   The buyers visit the agents or " commissionaires " to receive instructions and market information, and then place orders with the " commissionaires," merchants, or manufacturers. The ordinary term of credit granted is thirty days.

The Swiss cotton cloth trade centres in Zurich.   Yarn, it may be stated, is ordinarily sold direct by the spinner to the weaver in Switzerland, although yarn agents occasionally intervene.   There are also cloth agents, so-called, but they are comparatively insignificant.   They are said to obtain their commission by the difference in discount allowed, which nets them one per cent.   A small number of manufacturers have their cloth converted and sell directly to small jobbers or retailers.   The others sell in the gray to printers and merchant-converters.

Forms of market organization, we may conclude, are adjusted to the geographical distribution of the mills, the scale of production, and the nature of the trade.

The English industry is so highly concentrated that the business can be centralized in Manchester.   Paris is so preëminently the financial and commercial as well as the political and social centre of France that it dominates the French trade in cotton goods.   Yet there are outside local markets in France of a magnitude unknown in Lancashire.   Berlin does not hold the same place in the German commercial world that Paris has in France, and it is so far from the chief cotton manufacturing districts that it is a secondary market for cotton fabrics.   The

German primary markets are numerous and scattered. The dispersion of the industry in the Continental countries and social customs account for the peculiar forms of agency which have arisen in the domestic trade.

The influence of the scale of production is seen particularly in the trade in lace and novelties, where the middleman is a collector rather than a distributor. The nature of the market is the reason for the methods employed in selling to American purchasers, by means of buyers and resident agents.

The position of the merchant-converter in Germany is worthy of attention as it emphasizes the tendency shown in America and England for a merchant to assume the risk involved in the selection of design and finish.

Finally, in any comparison of the relative cost of selling, attention must be paid to the method of distributing risk. So far as the manufacturer and primary merchant are concerned, that risk in domestic trade in both Europe and America is evidently from one to two per cent. When the manufacturer assumes that risk it is fair to conclude that a compensating amount is added to his selling price. In each country the remunerations of the middlemen are adjusted to their services in accepting risk, in providing credit, and in distributing or collecting the goods. Although the market organizations in both America and Europe seem to be fairly well adapted to the prevailing conditions, that of Manchester is by far the most efficient for handling a trade large in volume and diverse in character.

CHAPTER XXIV

CONCLUSIONS

THE advance of the cotton manufacturing industry in the United States, as well as in European countries, has been rapid during the last half century. The period has been one of great industrial and commercial expansion under the influence of world-wide forces. In spite of numerous years of depression, it has been a period of great prosperity. Notwithstanding high protective tariffs, it has been an era of voluminous international trade. Improvements in means of transportation and communication have fostered commerce and widened markets. Yet within each country peculiar economic conditions have been encountered, and to these the cotton manufacturing industry had to be adapted. Consequently the history of that industry is primarily a study of adaptation.

In the United States the economic conditions have been continually changing; hence the industry has been almost constantly in a state of transition. This has been manifested most clearly, perhaps, in the progress of the industry in the southern states, and the reaction upon the older manufacturing sections. But taking the country as a whole, the problem to which the manufacturers have had to devote the greatest attention has been the reduction of labor cost. Face to face with a high wage level in all industries, the owners of cotton mills have been forced to find means whereby they could employ as little labor and as cheap labor as possible, and yet assure the workmen of an income sufficiently high to induce them to accept the employment. To economize in quantity of labor the manufacturers have adopted new types of machinery and automatic devices of various sorts which necessitated the minimum of attention from the operatives. To utilize the cheapest labor, the immigrants, those mechanical appliances which required the least skill on the part of the workmen were introduced.

The relatively high cost for labor has been partially counterbalanced and the burden of the overhead expense lightened by the enlargement of the scale of production and the standardization of product. The limits to which the former can profitably be carried at the present time are indicated by the poor success of the combinations of competing firms. The integration of coördinate branches, except spinning and weaving, has as yet not progressed far.

The success of the industry as a whole has also been dependent upon the entrepreneur ability of the men who have been responsible for its direction. The influence of efficiency in plant organization and factory management is most plainly shown in the relative prosperity of the individual companies. Practically every type of machine that has been invented is available to each manufacturer, since the acceptance of new inventions depends upon the appreciation of the benefits to be derived therefrom. But systems of organization are less tangible, more personal, and therefore more heterogeneous. Although no less fundamental than proper technical equipment, particularly in large scale enterprises, first class managing ability is less easily obtained.

The cotton goods manufactured in the United States up to the present time have been destined principally for the domestic market. That market has been constantly expanding, yet it has been fairly homogeneous. The methods of selling have been adjusted to the amount of financial assistance needed by the manufacturers, the length of credit required by the customers, and the difficulties in securing the orders for the cloth. As the market has become more diversified, a new middleman, the merchant-converter, who assumes the risk in the selection of finish and design, has arisen. The export trade, in the meanwhile, has not received consistent attention and the special arrangements necessary for carrying on such business have not been fully developed.

The growth of the export trade depends upon the power of the American industry to meet its European competitors in neutral markets. The American manufacturers are not especially favored by geographical conditions. Although the relatively long inland haul somewhat handicaps the French and Germans in procuring raw cotton, the Lancashire manufacturers do not pay a freight rate appreciably higher than the rate to New England. In purchasing the fibre in the southern United States, moreover, merchants of all nationalities are on an equal footing. That market is open to the world and the highest bidder secures the cotton which he desires.

Climatic conditions are the most favorable in Lancashire, and that natural advantage has not been completely overcome elsewhere by means of artifical humidifiers. In Lancashire, also, good coal can be obtained at a lower cost than in the other cotton manufacturing districts of Europe and the United States. Yet the American manufacturers obtain their fuel cheaper than the French and the Germans.

The Lancashire operatives are the most skilled cotton mill workers in the world, and their skill has been a powerful factor in the advance of the cotton industry in that country. This is in marked contrast with the labor situation in the United States, where in New England many untrained immigrants have invaded the mills, and in the South equally untrained persons of native birth have been employed. The Continental manufacturers, however, are not provided with a relatively greater supply of skilled workmen than is available in America. Earnings are somewhat higher in America than in England, and in the latter country than on the Continent. Yet the output per laborer varies in approximately the same ratio as earnings. Hence for the manufacture of coarse or medium plain cloth, the labor cost is probably no higher in America, and the difference for any but the finest and most fancy goods is not great.

The contrasts in technical equipment are due to differences in labor conditions, industrial organization, and market demands. In the American mills the equipment has been adapted to the needs of the manufacturers, and is in no wise inferior to the European.

Specialization has been carried farther in Lancashire than in other countries, as a result of local concentration and market opportunities. Yet the scale of production, particularly by the combination of spinning and weaving, is as large in America, and in the production of large quantities of standardized goods America is rivalled only by the spinning mills of Lancashire. The smaller Continental mills accept little orders for diverse fabrics, a practice that would be very unprofitable on this side of the Atlantic.

The domestic trade in America, England, Germany, France, and Switzerland conforms to the local conditions in each case. But for exporting cotton yarn and cloth the Manchester system excels all others. The large German export houses, allied with banking interests, can promote German trade, and the German manufacturers of specialties which are sold to American merchants are met upon their own ground by agents and buyers seeking to purchase their wares. Yet, as previously stated, no other country has a cotton goods export trade organized on as broad and as efficient lines as the English.

The building up of an export trade system is probably the greatest problem to be encountered in the attempt to expand the sales of American cotton goods in other parts of the world. An export market of large dimensions is not to be sought in the countries provided with numerous factories, but in neutral territories. The competition which American exporters will find most severe is the English. Yet there seems to be no reason why the American producers should not successfully meet that rivalry in various grades of goods. Nevertheless an actual decline or even cessation of expansion of the cotton manufacturing industry in any of the countries here considered is not to be expected. The question is, in which will it advance most rapidly? The answer, indicated by the converging lines of this study, is that unless thwarted by now unforeseen obstacles England and the United States have the fairest promise for the future.

APPENDIX

APPENDIX

PRICES

	Middling Cotton (cents lb.)	Regular Print Cloth (cents yard)	Standard Prints (cents yard)	Sheetings (cents yard)	Drillings (cents yard)	Bleached Shirtings (cents yard)
1880	11.51	4.51	7.41	8.51	8.51	12.74
1881	12.03	3.95	7.	8.51	8.06	12.74
1882	11.56	3.76	6.5	8.45	8.25	12.95
1883	11.88	3.60	6.	8.32	7.11	12.93
1884	10.88	3.36	6.	7.28	6.86	10.46
1885	10.45	3.12	6.	6.75	6.36	10.37
1886	9.28	3.31	6.	6.75	6.25	10.65
1887	10.21	3.33	6.	7.15	6.58	10.88
1888	10.03	3.81	6.5	7.25	6.75	10.94
1889	10.65	3.81	6.5	7.	6.75	10.50
1890	11.07	3.34	6.	7.	6.75	10.90
1891	8.60	2.95	6.	6.83	6.41	10.64
1892	7.71	3.39	6.25	6.50	5.60	10.25
1893	8.56	3.30	5.25	5.90	5.72	9.75
1894	6.94	2.75	4.9	5.11	5.07	9.50
1895	7.44	2.86	5.25	5.74	5.69	9.85
1896	7.93	2.60	4.66	5.45	5.48	9.50
1897	7.	2.48	4.7	4.73	4.75	9.25
1898	5.94	2.06	3.96	4.20	4.10	8.
1899	6.88	2.69	4.25	5.28	5.13	9.50
1900	9.25	3.21	5.	6.05	5.95	10.75
1901	8.75	2.84	4.62	5.54	5.48	10.25
1902	9.	3.11	5.	5.48	5.52	10.50
1903	11.18	3.25	5.	6.25	6.37	10.75
1904	11.75	3.44	5.	7.13	7.31	10.50
1905	9.80	3.13	4.75	7.	7.	9.
1906	11.50	3.63	5.12	7.25	7.37	10.93
1907	12.10	4.62	6.	7.62	7.62	13.
1908	10.62	3.50	5.37	6.75	7.15	11.54
1909	12.68	3.67	5.06	7.37	7.50	11.45
1910	15.11	3.87	5.62	7.87	8.	12.

Margin

(between the price of 8 lbs. of middling cotton and the price of the corresponding quantity of print cloth)

1881	108.52	1891	96.90	1901	70.38
1882	99.73	1892	118.10	1902	80.75
1883	85.79	1893	92.69	1903	66.46
1884	87.89	1894	102.47	1904	66.18
1885	85.93	1895	96.74	1905	70.66
1886	97.57	1896	74.21	1906	74.44
1887	92.58	1897	77.61	1907	106.48
1888	113.09	1898	64.90	1908	82.69
1889	108.14	1899	70.84	1909	64.90
1890	85.92	1900	81.	1910	59.24

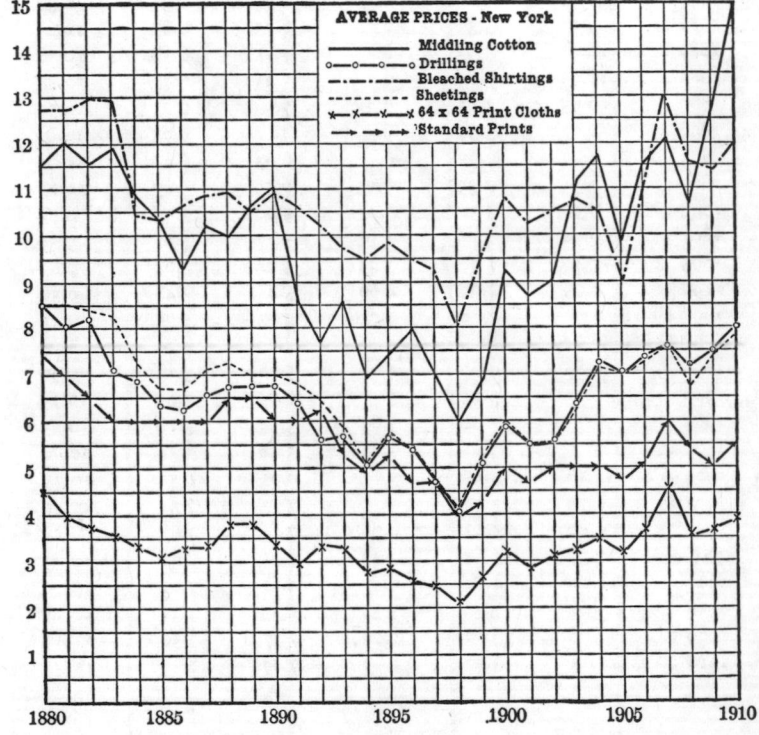

AVERAGE PRICES - New York
- Middling Cotton
- Drillings
- Bleached Shirtings
- Sheetings
- 64 x 64 Print Cloths
- Standard Prints

DIVIDEND RECORD

Company	Capital	Average Dividend				Surplus
American Linen	$800,000	6.6%	for	20	yrs.	$191,792 (1908)
Amory	1,350,000	7.9	"	12	"	
	900,000	6.	"	5	"	
Amoskeag	4,000,000	11.5	"	18	"	
•	5,760,000	16.	"	2	"	3,720,691 (1907)
Androscoggin	1,000,000	8.6	"	20	"	1,123,863 "
Appleton	600,000	1.9	"	10	"	
	450,000	8.2	"	10	"	
Atlantic	1,000,000	3.3	"	20	"	
Barnard	330,000	6.8	"	6	"	
	495,000	5.3	"	14	"	
Bates	1,000,000	9.	"	4	"	
	1,200,000	11.3	"	16	"	1,376,361 (1907)
Boott	1,200,000	4.	"	17	"	
	1,000,000	4.7	"	3	"	
Border City	1,000,000	10.8	"	20	"	107,266 (1908)
Boston	800,000	2.6	"	14	"	
	400,000	0.	"	6	"	
Boston Duck	350,000	13.	"	20	"	
Bourne	400,000	15.8	"	15	"	
	1,000,000	4.	"	5	"	
Cabot	600,000	6.	"	5	"	
	800,000	3.1	"	15	"	
Chace	500,000	11.1	"	10	"	
	750,000	6.1	"	7	"	
	900,000	7.1	"	3	"	
Chicopee	1,000,000	3.7	"	16	"	
	500,000	4.4	"	4	"	
Cocheco	1,500,000	1.	"	20	"	
Conanicut	120,000	5.8	"	15	"	
	300,000	4.4	"	5	"	
Continental	1,500,000	0.5	"	20	"	
Cornell	400,000	7.2	"	18	"	233,578 (1908)
Dartmouth	600,000	30.7	"	11	"	902,105 (1907)
Davol	300,000	8.	"	2	"	
	400,000	7.1	"	17	"	
	500,000	6.	"	1	"	105,042 (1908)
Dwight	1,200,000	12.	"	20	"	
Edwards	750,000	7.2	"	5	"	
	1,100,000	7.	"	15	"	
Flint	580,000	7.4	"	20	"	139,804 (1908)
Granite	400,000	15.3	"	4	"	
	800,000	9.	"	1	"	
	1,000,000	6.4	"	15	"	361,857 (1908)
Great Falls	1,500,000	9.5	"	20	"	960,000 "

DIVIDEND RECORD (*continued*)

Company	Capital	Average Dividend			Surplus
Hamilton	$1,800,000	4.5% for 20 yrs.			
Hargraves	400,000	0.	" 1	"	
	800,000	5.4	" 19	"	
Hill	1,000,000	3.2	" 20	"	
Jackson	600,000	6.1	" 20	"	
King Philip	1,000,000	9.4	" 20	"	$871,083 (1908)
Laconia	1,000,000	8.2	" 10	"	
Lancaster	1,200,000	4.3	" 20	"	
Laurel Lake	400,000	6.3	" 9	"	
	200,000	1.9	" 2	"	
	300,000	9.7	" 9	"	
Lawrence	1,500,000	8.	" 8	"	
	750,000	19.	" 5	"	
	1,250,000	6.7	" 7	"	787,000 (1907)
Lockwood	1,800,000	5.2	" 20	"	
Lyman	1,470,000	3.9	" 20	"	
Manchester	2,000,000	5.	" 17	"	
Massachusetts	1,800,000	5.7	" 20	"	1,431,690 (1908)
Mechanics	750,000	4.6	" 20	"	288,967 "
Merchants	800,000	5.2	" 20	"	111,305 "
Merrimack	2,500,000	5.7	" 12	"	
	2,750,000	2.9	" 8	"	
Narragansett	400,000	6.2	" 20	"	142,220 (1908)
Nashua	1,000,000	8.2	" 20	"	
Naumkeag	1,500,000	3.8	" 20	"	943,522 (1907)
Osborn	600,000	7.7	" 13	"	
	750,000	4.1	" 7	"	218,939 (1908)
Otis	800,000	10.	" 20	"	
Pacific	2,500,000	12.4	" 12	"	
	3,000,000	14.5	" 8	"	6,332,854 (1907)
Pepperell	1,200,000	18.	" 11	"	
	2,556,000	25.	" 9	"	1,628,427 (1907)
Pocasset	800,000	13.3	" 6	"	
	600,000	5.3	" 14	"	188,716 (1908)
Richard Borden	800,000	7.1	" 20	"	468,024 "
Sagamore	900,000	9.1	" 20	"	348,763 "
Salmon Falls	600,000	3.3	" 20	"	
Seaconnett	400,000	8.6	" 6	"	
	600,000	4.	" 14	"	
Shove	550,000	5.8	" 20	"	
Stafford	800,000	7.8	" 8	"	
	1,000,000	5.	" 12	"	
Tecumseh	500,000	7.	" 20	"	
Thorndike	450,000	9.	" 13	"	
	675,000	8.7	" 7	"	

Dividend Record (*continued*)

Company	Capital	Average Dividend			Surplus
Tremont and Suffolk $1,200,000		12.5% for	4	yrs.	
	1,500,000	12.1 "	7	"	
	2,000,000	3. "	9	"	
Troy	300,000	24.3 "	20	"	$366,529 (1908)
Union	750,000	15.5 "	11	"	
	1,200,000	11. "	9	"	572,544 (1908)
Wampanoag	750,000	4.9 "	20	"	
Wamsutta	3,000,000	6.2 "	20	"	
Weetamoe	550,000	3.3 "	20	"	
York	900,000	5.8 "	20	"	

In computing the average dividend the records of New Bedford mills were utilized, but they were furnished privately without permission to publish.

BIBLIOGRAPHY

The books listed below are those to which reference is made in the text. Many others have been consulted and suggestions obtained therefrom, but inasmuch as a comprehensive bibliography of publications relating to the cotton industry was recently published by Mr. C. J. H. Woodbury, it has been deemed unnecessary to give an extensive list here.

I GENERAL WORKS

A UNITED STATES

Arkwright Club. *By-Laws*. Boston, 1884.

Bagnall, W. R. *Textile Industries of the United States*. Cambridge, 1893. Only volume I, covering the period from 1639–1810, was issued. It is a compilation of facts in chronological order rather than a scientific treatise.

Batchelder, S. *Early Progress of the Cotton Manufacture*. Boston, 1863. A brief, suggestive survey of the history of the American cotton manufacturing industry during the first half of the nineteenth century, written by a man who was long engaged in managing cotton mills.

Bishop, J. L. *History of American Manufactures*. Philadelphia, 1868. Another compilation of facts, put together so as to form a connected account but without critical analysis.

Blue Book Textile Directory. New York, 1911.

Commercial and Financial Chronicle. New York. Weekly.

Cowley, R. *History of Lowell*. Lowell, 1868.

Dockham's Textile Directory. Boston. Biennial.

Earl, H. H. *History of Fall River*. New York, 1877.

Earle, A. M. *Home Life in Colonial Days*. New York, 1898.

Hammond, M. B. *The Cotton Industry. Publications of the American Economic Association*. New York, 1897. Concerned primarily with the history of cotton growing and marketing.

Helm, E. *An International Survey of the Cotton Industry. Quarterly Journal of Economics*, vol. xvii. Boston, 1903.

International Federation of Master Cotton Spinners' and Manufacturers' Associations. *Reports* of annual congresses. Manchester. In these reports various topics are discussed, such as the means of increasing the production of cotton in parts of the world outside of the United States, the progress of manufacturers' associations, insurance, methods of baling and selling raw cotton, etc. Technical methods of manufacturing are not mentioned.

Kettle, T., Editor. *Eighty Years' Progress*. New York, 1864.

Kohn, A. *Cotton Mills of South Carolina*. Columbia, 1907.

Manufacturers' Record. Baltimore. Weekly.

Mason, F. R. *American Silk Industry and the Tariff. Publications of the American Economic Association.* Cambridge, 1910.

Miles, H. A. *Lowell as it was and as it is.* Lowell, 1847.

Montgomery, J. *Cotton Manufacture.* Glasgow, 1840. A discriminating report on the status of American cotton manufacturing at that date, with comparisons between British and American practices and conditions. Mr. Montgomery had managed mills in both countries.

Murphy, E. G. *The Present South.* New York, 1904.

New England Cotton Manufacturers' Association, *Transactions.*

National Association of Cotton Manufacturers, *Transactions.* Boston. Semi-annual. 1865–1911. The second of these associations is a continuation of the first. The reports of the meetings have steadily increased in volume, and contain much valuable data, particularly on the technical development and mill management.

Professional and Industrial History of Suffolk County (Mass.). Boston, 1894.

Taussig, F. W. *Tariff History of the United States.* 6th ed., New York, 1905. One chapter is devoted entirely to the early history of American cotton manufacturing, and the history of the duties on cotton products in all the tariff acts is traced.

Textile World Record. Boston. Monthly.

Textile World Record, *Directory of the American Knitting Trade.* Boston, 1907.

Textile World Record, *Textile Directory.* Boston. Annual.

Thompson, H. *From Cotton Field to Cotton Mill.* New York, 1906. An unbiassed study of the cotton manufacturing industry in the southern states.

United States Census. In 1860 and 1870 fairly reliable statistics on manufacturing were collected for the Census, and since 1880 a special report on the cotton industry has been included in each decennial Census and in the quinquennial Census of 1905. In no other country have such thorough and comprehensive industrial Censuses been made or such complete reports prepared.

United States Congressional Documents.

United States Congressional Record.

United States Industrial Commission. Report. 19 vols., 1901.

United States Monthly Summary of Commerce and Finance. March, 1900. In addition to the regular compilation of statistics, this number contained a special report on the cotton trade.

United States Statistical Abstract.

Uttley, T. A. *Cotton Spinning.* Manchester, 1905. Mr. Uttley, an English student, visited several mills in the northern and southern states and in this book presents the facts which he ascertained. Its value lies in its collection of first hand information.

Weeden, W. B. *Economic and Social History of New England.* 2 vols., Boston, 1890. The fruits of a diligent search amongst colonial records of all sorts. Arrangement at times faulty and statements occasionally conflicting.

White, G. S. *Memoir of Samuel Slater.* Philadelphia, 1836.
Wright, C. W. *Wool Growing and the Tariff. Harvard Economic Studies.* Boston, 1910.
Young, T. M. *American Cotton Industry.* London, 1902. The author is an Englishman who here presents the results of observations made during a tour of the cotton manufacturing districts of the United States. The comparisons of British and American methods, conditions, and wages are numerous and valuable.

B GREAT BRITAIN

Ashley, W. J., Editor. *British Industries.* London, 1903. A collection of articles on various industries. The subject of the cotton industry is handled by Mr. E. Helm.
British *Census of Production, 1907.* Preliminary Tables. London, 1910. The first industrial Census undertaken in Great Britain. The replies to some of the questions were optional with the manufacturers, and the scheme not as far reaching as that of the United States Census.
British *Parliamentary Papers.*
Chapman, S. J. *The Lancashire Cotton Industry.* Manchester, 1904. A history of cotton manufacturing in Lancashire.
Cox, H., Editor. *British Industries under Free Trade.* London, 1904. A series of articles on the history and present position of the chief British industries, each written by a person intimately connected with the trade.
Economist. London. Weekly.
Levi, L. *History of British Commerce.* London, 1880.
Macrosty, H. W. *Trust Movement in British Industry.* London, 1907. A broad survey worked up with careful attention to detail.
Ogden, J. *Manchester One Hundred Years Ago.* Reprint edited by W. E. Axon. Manchester, 1887.
Whittam, W., Jr. *Report on England's Cotton Industry.* Washington, 1907. The report of one of the special agents employed by the United States Department of Commerce and Labor to study foreign industries. Largely original, but does not cover the subject thoroughly.
Worrall, J. *The Cotton Spinners' and Manufacturers' Directory for Lancashire.* Annual. Oldham, 1911.

C GERMANY

Bremen Baumwoll-Börse. *Verzeichnis der Baumwoll-Spinnereien in Deutschland, Oesterreich, Schweitz,* u.s.w. Bremen, 1909.
Clark, W. A. G. *Cotton Fabrics in Middle Europe.* Washington, 1908. The report of another special agent of the United States Department of Commerce and Labor.
Festschrift zur 39 Hauptversammlung des Vereines Deutscher Ingenieurer. Chemnitz, 1898.
Greif, W. *Die geschichtliche Entwicklung der Limbacher Wirkwaren-Industrie.* Karlsruhe, 1907. Limbach is located in the Chemnitz district. This book not only traces the historical development of the knitting

industry in Limbach, but describes the present organization, the prevalent methods, and the domestic system.

Kuntze, K. *Die Baumwoll-industrie, in Band III of Handbuch der Wirtschafts-kunde Deutschlands.* Leipzig, 1904.

L'Industrie de Mulhouse au XIXieme Siècle. Mulhouse, 1902. A compendious record of the industrial development of Mulhouse (or Mülhausen). Amongst other things it contains statistics of wages in the cotton industry.

Lochmüller, W. *Zur Entwicklung der Baumwoll-industrie in Deutschland.* Jena, 1906. A brief history of the German cotton industry.

Martin, R. *Der wirtschaftliche Aufschwung der Baumwollspinnereien im Königreiche Sachsen.* *Jahrbuch für Gesetzgebung*, 1893.

Oppel, A. *Die Baumwolle.* Leipzig, 1902. Voluminous. By undertaking to cover the whole field of cotton growing and manufacturing in all parts of the world, the author has had to rely on secondary sources and is rather superficial throughout.

Rieger, W. *Verzeichnis der auf Baumwolle laufenden Spindeln und Webstühle Deutschlands.* Edition 1909. Stuttgart. Gives the number of spindles and looms and the nature of the product of each cotton mill in Germany.

Statistik des Deutschen Reichs. Berlin, 1875, 1882, 1895, 1907. An official periodical publication in which the results of the German Censuses are published. Although an industrial Census was taken in 1907 the complete tables had not been issued in November, 1910. The terms employed in this Census are sometimes used in a special sense, as for example " Betriebe," which is used for " department " rather than " establishment."

Tschierschky, S. *Die Zollpolitischen Interessen der Deutschen Textilveredlungsindustrie.* Berlin, 1902.

D OTHER COUNTRIES

Amé, L. *Les Tarifs de Douanes.* 2 vols. Paris, 1876. The writer was in sympathy with the movement for the liberation of commerce culminating in the Cobden Treaty of 1860, and one of his aims was to show that French industry benefited rather than suffered from the lowering of the tariff wall.

Beaumont, G. *L' Industrie Cotonnière en Normandie.* Paris, 1901.

Enquête sur l'Etat de l'Industrie Textile. 5 vols., Paris, 1905. The report of an official investigation of labor conditions in the French textile industries.

Lecomte, H. *Le Coton.* Paris, 1900.

Lederlin, A. *L'Industrie Cotonnière.* Epinal, 1905. A brief monograph on the cotton industry in the Vosges.

Mairet, P. *La Crise de l'Industrie Cotonnière* (1901–05). Dijon, 1906. His conclusions in regard to the tariff and the services of the middlemen are open to criticism.

Annuario Statistico Italiano. Annual.

La Belgique, 1830–1905. Brussels, 1905. A government publication, elaborate in style, tracing the development of Belgium since 1830.

Besso, S. L. *The Cotton Industry in Switzerland, Vorarlberg, and Italy.* Manchester, 1910. The writer, an English student, made an exhaustive personal investigation of numerous cotton mills in these countries. The book is noteworthy for method of treatment and attention to detail.

II TECHNIQUE

Allen, A. H. *Commercial Organic Analysis,* vol. iii. Philadelphia, 1900.

Appleton, N. *Introduction of the Power Loom.* Lowell, 1858.

Baird, R. H. *American Cotton Spinner.* Philadelphia, 1851.

Barker, A. F. *Textiles.* London, 1910. A good summary of the technical processes employed in each textile industry.

Bean, P., & Scarisbrick, F. *The Chemistry and Practice of Sizing.* Manchester, 1906. A standard technical work.

Centennial Exhibition, 1876. *Reports and Awards,* vol. iii. Philadelphia.

Cyclopedia of Textile Work. American Technical Society. Chicago, 1907. Complete technical description of all branches of the textile industry.

Die Fachschulen für die Textil-industrie Deutschlands. 3d ed., Berlin, 1904. A list of the German textile schools with a statement of their courses.

Draper, G. O. *Textile Texts.* 2d ed., Hopedale, Massachusetts, 1903.

Felkin, W. *History of Machine-Wrought Hosiery and Lace Manufactures.* London, 1867. A history of inventions and processes with some information concerning industrial organization. The only complete work on the subject, but now out of date.

Heylin, H. B. *Cotton Weaver's Handbook.* London, 1908.

Higgins, S. H. *Dyeing in Germany and America.* Manchester, 1907. The report of an English student on American and German dye-works.

International Library of Technology. *Cotton Pickers, Cotton Cards,* etc. Scranton, 1906.

Journal of Franklin Institute, 1845. Philadelphia.

Lehmann, M. *Jahrbuch und Kalendar für die gesamte Baumwoll-Industrie,* vol. xxxii. Leipzig, 1911. Annual.

Marsden, R. *Cotton Weaving.* London, 1895.

Martin, J. G. *Stock Fluctuations.* Boston. Annual.

Mortier, A. *Le Tricot et l'Industrie de la Bonneterie.* Troyes, 1891.

Nasmith, J. *Recent Cotton Mill Construction.* Manchester, 1894.

Nasmith, J. & F. *Recent Cotton Mill Construction.* 3d ed., Manchester, 1909. An excellent text-book on cotton mill engineering.

Sansone, A. *Recent Progress in Dyeing and Calico Printing.* 3 vols., Manchester, 1895.

Scott, R. W. *Evolution of the Knit-Goods Industry.* Reprint of an article in the *Textile Manufacturer's Journal,* December 28, 1907.

Textile Manufacturer's Journal. New York. Weekly.

Textile World Record. Boston. Monthly.

Webber, S. *Manual of Power.* New York, 1879. The second part contains a history of the technical development of the American cotton industry up to that time.

Zipser, J. *Textile Raw Materials and their Conversion into Yarn.* Translated by C. Slater. London, 1901.

III LABOR

Abbott, E. *A Study of the Early History of Child Labor in America.* *American Journal of Sociology*, vol. xiv. 1908.

Bowley, A. L. *Wages in the United Kingdom in the Nineteenth Century.* Cambridge, England, 1900. One chapter is devoted to the cotton industry.

British Board of Trade, Labor Department, *Report on Wages and Hours of Labor.* 1894.

British Board of Trade, *Report on Wages and the Cost of Living in Germany.* London, 1908.

British Board of Trade, *Report on Wages and the Cost of Living in France.* London, 1909. These two reports cover numerous employments in various cities in each of the countries. The data were collected from the employers and the workmen, and the statements of earnings and budgets are fully representative.

Lincoln, J. T. *Fall River Sliding Scale.* *Quarterly Journal of Economics*, vol. xxiii. Boston, 1909.

Martineau, H. *Society in America.* 3 vols., New York, 1837.

Massachusetts Bureau of the Statistics of Labor. *Annual Reports.*

Massachusetts Bureau of the Statistics of Labor. *Bulletins.* These reports and bulletins contain information on labor conditions and laws, trade unions, and wages. The wages stated are not always representative, since the number of operatives included is not always given and several of the most important occupations are frequently omitted.

Müller, O. *Die christliche Gewerkschafts-bewegung Deutschlands.* Karlsruhe, 1905.

Persons, C. E., Parton, M., and Moses, M. *Labor Laws and their Enforcement.* *Studies in the Economic Relations of Women*, vol. ii. Boston, 1911.

Robinson, H. H. *Loom and Spindle.* New York, 1898. An account of factory life in Lowell during the first half of the nineteenth century.

Towles, J. K. *Factory Legislation of Rhode Island.* *Publications of the American Economic Association*, 1908.

United States Commissioner of Labor. *Annual Reports.* Washington. Special mention may be made of the 17th annual report, the subject of which is *Technical Education,* and the *Report on the Conditions of Woman and Child Labor*, vol. i. 1910.

United States Department of Labor. *Bulletins.*

Webb, Sidney and Beatrice. *Industrial Democracy.* London, 1897.

Webb, Sidney and Beatrice. *Trade Unionism.* London, 1894.

Wood, G. H. *History of Wages in the Cotton Trade.* London, 1910. A reprint from the *Journal of the Royal Statistical Society.* This study is somewhat more exhaustive than Bowley's and might well serve as a model for an investigation of the history of wages in the American industry.

IV MARKETS

A RAW COTTON

Boston Board of Trade. *Annual Reports.*

Brooks, C. P. *Cotton.* London, 1898.

Ellison, T. *Cotton Trade of Great Britain.* London, 1886.

Ellison, T. *Gleanings and Reminiscences.* Liverpool, 1905. These two books are concerned chiefly with the history and organization of the Liverpool Cotton Exchange.

Homans, J. S. *Cyclopedia of Commerce.* New York, 1859.

Shepperson, A. B. *Cotton Facts.* New York. Annual. A reliable collection of statistics regarding the cotton crop and the cotton market.

United States Commissioner of Corporations. *Report on Cotton Exchanges.* 3 vols., Washington, 1908–09. The report of an investigation of the methods of carrying on business on the cotton exchanges in the United States, and a criticism of certain features of the New York Exchange.

United States Senate, *Report of Committee on Cotton Growers.* 1895.

B CLOTH MARKET AND FOREIGN TRADE

Appleton, N. *Memoir of Abbott Lawrence.* Boston, 1856.

Boston Advertiser. Daily.

Bowen, A. *Picture of Boston.* Boston, 1829.

Depew, C. M., Editor. *One Hundred Years of American Commerce.* 2 vols. New York, 1895. Volume ii has an article by J. N. Beach on the dry goods trade.

Flint, J. *Letters from America.* Edinburgh, 1822.

Hill, H. A. *Memoir of Abbott Lawrence.* Boston, 1883.

Hunt, F. *Lives of American Merchants.* 2 vols., New York, 1858.

Hunt's Merchants' Magazine. New York.

Lawrence, W. *Life of Amos Lawrence.* Boston, 1888.

Loeben, M. G. von. *Der Absatz der Plauener Spitzen nach den Vereinigten Staaten.* Dresden, 1905.

Chamber of Commerce of the State of New York. *Annual Reports.*

Niles' Weekly Register. Baltimore.

Report of Mr. Sturgis's Committee to twenty-eight Manufacturing Companies. Boston, 1852. The report of a committee appointed to investigate the conditions in the cloth market.

Tompkins, D. A. *Cotton Mill — Commercial Features.* Charlotte, N. C., 1899.

Morse, H. B. *Trade and Administration of the Chinese Empire.* London, 1908.

United States Department of Commerce and Labor, Bureau of Manufacturers, *Foreign Markets for American Cotton Manufactures.* Washington, 1907.

United States Consular Reports.

Kinley, D. *Promotion of Trade with South America. American Economic Review.* Boston, 1911.

V TARIFF

Report of Tariff Commission, 1882.
Report on Revision of the Tariff, 1886.
Tariff Hearings, 1893.
Tariff Hearings, 1896–97.
Tariff Hearings, 1908–09.

INDEX

INDEX

Africa, as market, 222.
Agents:
American in Germany, 378; in Paris, 384.
Raw cotton, in Germany, 358; in France, 360.
Yarn and cloth, in England, 362–365, 370–372; in France 382–383; in Germany, 374–376; in Switzerland, 384. (*See also* Commission agents, and Selling house.)
Almy and Brown, 194, 195.
American Cotton Manufacturers' Association, 156.
American Thread Company, 169–170, 341.
Arkwright Club, 157–159, 171.
Asia, as market, 222, 223.
Auctions, Boston, 198–200; New York, 201–204; disadvantage of, 208.
Austria, employers' associations, 337.
Automatic feeder, 57, 58.
Automatic loom, 84–89. (*See also* Northrop loom.)

Bale breaker, 56, 312.
Barber knotter, 75, 301, 314.
Barber warp-tying machine, 81.
Barmen, trade, 380–381.
Batchelder, Samuel, statement of relative costs in 1860, 11.
Beaming, 76–77, 314.
Belgium, small mills, 326; employers' association, 337.
Bleachers' Association, 342.
Bleaching, 94, 152, 204, 328.
Blower, 56, 57.
Bobbins, freight on, 69, 72.
Bohemia, small mills, 325–326.
Boston, auctions in, 198–200; early

market, 196–197, 200; offices of treasurers in, 177.
Bremen cotton market, 357–359.
British Cotton Growing Association, 334.
British Cotton and Wool Dyers' Association, 343–344.
Brokers, cloth, 215–216, 364; English, take stock, 317–318, 355; Havre, 360; Liverpool, 354.
Brooklands agreement, 307.
Buyers, American, in Europe, 370, 373, 378–381, 384.

Calenders, 98.
Calico Printers' Association, 342–343.
Canada, as market, 221–223.
Cancellations, 213–215; of foreign orders, 227.
Capital, dearth at outset, 3; greater supply in North, 182; for southern mills, 49–50; supplied by merchants, 4–5, 196; worthlessness of Census statistics for, 17–18.
Capitalization, 262–264.
Card, 59–61, 99, 313.
Card tender, wages, 296–297.
Cartwright loom, 83.
Chemnitz, 279, 280, 347, 350–351; knitting machinery, 108; market, 378–380.
Child labor, 113; before 1860, 12; in ring spinning, 70; in South, 42–45. (*See also* Labor.)
China, as market, 224–226, 229, 230.
Circular knitting machines, 103, 104, 108; in Europe, 348.
Climatic conditions, 285; in France, 282, 283; in Germany, 280; in Lancashire, 93, 276; in New Bedford, 30, 149.